Table of Contents

Sources in
Patterns of World History

Volume 1: To 1600

Edited by

Candace R. Gregory
Sacramento State University

Carey Roberts
Arkansas Tech University

H. Micheal Tarver
Arkansas Tech University

New York   Oxford
OXFORD UNIVERSITY PRESS

Oxford University Press, Inc., publishes works that further Oxford University's
objective of excellence in research, scholarship, and education.

Oxford   New York
Auckland   Cape Town   Dares Salaam   Hong Kong   Karachi
Kuala Lumpur   Madrid   Melbourne   Mexico City   Nairobi
New Delhi   Shanghai   Taipei   Toronto

With offices in
Argentina Austria Brazil Chile Czech Republic France Greece
Guatemala Hungary Italy Japan Poland Portugal Singapore
South Korea Switzerland Thailand Turkey Ukraine Vietnam

For titles covered by Section 112 of the US Higher Education Opportunity Act,
please visit www.oup.com/us/he for the latest information about
pricing and alternate formats.

Published by Oxford University Press, Inc.
198 Madison Avenue, New York, New York, 10016
http://www.oup.com

ISBN 978-0-19-984617-7

Printing number: 9 8 7 6 5 4 3 2 1

Printed in the United States of America
on acid-free paper

Sources in
Patterns of World History

Primary Sources
Why Read Them and How to Use Them in World History

Candace R. Gregory, Sacramento State University

Humans are first and foremost social animals. We have an intense need not only to be around our fellow humans, and to communicate our stories to others. In fact, it is our ability to communicate in a variety of complex and simple ways that most distinguishes us from other species. Although it is widely recognized by scientists and the general populace that many animals communicate basic information, and that scientists continue to discover that animal communication is more complex than we often assume, it is still true that no animal speaks about itself, and the world around it, more often and in more diverse ways than humans. Furthermore, no animal has created communicating technology as sophisticated as human beings have. From the first gestures and oral utterances, to the simple artistic efforts of the Paleolithic era (such as carved figures, rock paintings, and the use of abstract symbols), to the more advanced technology of writing, humans have always found ways to speak to one another. The age of digital communication illustrates this point well: our very culture is defined by ever evolving communication technology. Some may argue that in this current age we adaptto technology, where once we adapted technology to fit our needs. Whichever the case, the fact remains that we find more and more ways to communicate with one another.

Communication is thus the definitive pattern of human history, for people also communicate across time. The past speaks to the present through these communication technologies. Being able to listen to the past is the most important skill a historian must develop. History is not "what" happened in the past; rather, it is our interpretation of the "what" based on the sources of the past, including textual sources. Interpreting the sources is in essence the present speaking to the past; reading and interpreting sources is a conversation across time.

How to Use This Book

The sources in this reader were selected to work closely with the Patterns of *World History* by Peter von Sivers, Charles A. Desnoyers, and George B. Stow. They have been chosen to illustrate the patterns and innovations that are explored in the textbook; however, the sourcebook can also be used on its own, for each document in it was also chosen to exemplify a key aspect of cultures and civilizations throughout world history.

There are no footnotes to distract the student from the text itself. Any names or terms not defined or explained in the text are explicated in the introduction or questions for each source. It is hoped that this will allow students to read the texts without feeling overly directed through them by cumbersome notes. Furthermore, limiting notes allows students to come to the sources as unfiltered as possible; the brief introductions that proceed each source are there to provide only the most necessary information to understand the origin of the source, and to suggest why that particular source is important for studying world history.

There are certain techniques that students should use when approaching primary sources that will help them navigate the source, and discern for themselves why that source is important to the study of history. Essentially, these are questions that need to be asked of every source, as if one were interviewing the source. However, it is important to note that reading the text in translation might mask information that could answer the questions differently or more accurately, and students must be aware that there are complications in reading sources in translation.

Question 1: What does the source say and what genre is the source?

The first task of the reader of any text, but particularly of sources written in the past, is to figure out what is going on. Because the majority of sources in this collection are excerpts, that is, brief selections from longer works, they are essentially taken out of context. Thus determining the actual story the document is trying to tell. Even though these excerpts are short, completing this task might require re-reading the document several times. Some of the documents are more philosophical in nature, and thus will not necessarily have a narrative plot of driven by characters or actions. Using primary sources in the classroom should always being with first ascertaining how the students understood the sources. Part of understanding the source is also figuring out what genre the text is written in. If it is a speech, there may not be actions within the text, or even characters.

Question 2: Who wrote the text?

Unfortunately, many sources from the past are anonymous. Yet, although the specific name of the author may not be known, a careful reader will often still be able to determine the kind of person who wrote it. Occupation, class, gender are possible characteristics of authorship that can be determined from within the source. Readers can often go past that, however, and determine more specific details about the identity of the author, such as religious or political beliefs, ethnic and linguistic background, and education. The most important aspect of the question of authorship is that of authorial bias. Readers must ask what are the deliberate or unintentional biases in the text?

Question 3: Where does the source come from?

There are several different meanings to this question. "Where" can refer to the geographic origin of a source, and it can also refer to the culture that produced the source. It could also mean from what class produced the source.

Question 4: When was the document or source created, and when was it written down?

These are two related question; sometimes the answer is the same (the source is created and written at the same time and by the same person, sometimes these two things happened at different times. Sometimes the distance between when the source was created and when it was written down is a crucial part of the story of how the document came to be. Because so many of the sources in this anthology come from the earliest days of culture and civilization, when orality was more common than writing, most sources were created long before they were written. This question is very important to answer, however, because to answer this question requires the reader to determine the full context of the document.

Question 5: Why was the source created and why was it finally written down?

Of all the questions to ask of the source, this is often the most difficult to answer. To answer this requires that the reader move beyond reading the source to empathizing with it, relating to it, and putting oneself into the mind of the creator and author. Finally, one must be aware that there is often more than one answer to the why of a source.

Let us walk through an example of how a historian approaches a source, ask the questions and determine the answers. Consider the following excerpt from Ezana, "The Destruction of Kush," which recounts the attack on Meröe by Aksum in 350 C.E.

> Ezana, the son of Ella Amtda, a native of Halen, king of Aksum and of
> Hemer (Himyar), and of Raydan, and of Saba, and of Salhen, and of
> Seyamo, and of Bega, and of Kasu (the Meroites), King of Kings, the son
> of Ella Amida, who is invincible to the enemy. By the might of the Lord
> of Heaven, Who hath made me Lord, Who to all eternity, the Perfect One,
> reigns, Who is invincible to the enemy, no enemy shall stand before me,
> and after me no enemy shall follow. By the might of the Lord of all, I made
> war upon Noba, for the peoples had rebelled and had made a boast of it.
> And "they (the Axumites) will not cross the river Takkaze (Atbara)," said
> the peoples of Noba. And they were in the habit of attacking the peoples
> of Mangurto, and Khasa, and Barya, and the blacks, and of making war
> upon the Red peoples. And twice and thrice had they broken their solemn
> oaths, and had killed their neighbours mercilessly, and they had stripped
> bare and stolen the properties of our deputies and messengers which I had
> sent to them to inquire into their thefts. and had stolen from them their
> weapons of defence. And as I had sent warnings to them and they would

not harken to me, and they refused to cease from their evil deeds, and then
betook themselves to flight, I made war upon them. And I rose in the might
of the Lord of the Land.

Question 6: What does the source say and what genre is the source?

The source is written as a kind of declaration by King Ezana of Aksum, justifying his attack on the city of Meroe. There are no events in the document, as it is a kind of speech (which is one of the genres of the text), although the text does list a series of events that has led to the current events, the war between Aksum and Meroe. But this text is more than just a declaration and a speech; notice that it often invokes the name of a deity: "By the might of the Lord of Heaven," "the Perfect One," and "By the might of the Lord of All." Thus the document is also a prayer who invoked the god of Ezana. Although the text does not specify what the religious system of Aksum is, or the specific identity of the god Ezana worships, the phrasing suggests Christianity and the Christian God. This interpretation is supported by knowledge external to the text itself; the fact that the kingdom of Aksum converted to Christianity in the fourth century.

Question 7: Who wrote the text?

The beginning of the excerpt indentifies Ezana, King of Aksum, and throughout the document the pronoun "me" is used. The implication is that Ezana is the author of the document. It is certainly possible that Ezana literally wrote the text, and it is reasonable for a student without much knowledge about that time period to read more from the document. However, if a reader is familiar with royal culture of fourth century East Africa, he or she might also consider that a Ezana dictated the text as is, or the gist of the text, to a professional writer (a scribe). The mere act of writing the text means that the scribe might have in some way "authored" the text. He (and it was most likely a he), certainly influenced the final form of the text.

Because the text was either written for or literally by Ezana, the King of Aksum, one of the biases at work in the source is that of Ezana. As the text concerns a war between Aksum and Meroe, the bias favors Aksum, and Ezana in particular.

Question 8: Where does the source come from?

In regard to this particular text, this question is easy to answer, as it is identified in the very beginning of the text: Aksum. It is also possible that it was written by a state or culture favorable to Aksum.

Question 9: When was the document or source created, and when was it written down?

There is no explicit statement of date in the source. To answer this question, a reader would have to turn to external knowledge of Aksum. The most important clue in the story is the figure of Ezana. Knowing his dates, and the dates of the conquest of Meroe by Aksum, helps to date the document to after 350 C.E. Reading the text in the original could help to date the written version, as the original language provided invaluable evidence of dating. Languages evolve, and change over time, and thus can be used to date texts.

Question 10: Why was the source created and why was it finally written down?

As suggested earlier, this is a more difficult question to answer. Ezana does not explicitly state why he has written, or caused to be written, this document. Because it is a declaration, and a prayer, something of the purpose might be discerned from the genre. Ezana lists many deeds, or rather, misdeeds, committed by the people of Meroe: "the peoples had rebelled and had made a boast of it," "they were in the habit of attacking the peoples," "twice and thrice had they broken their solemn oaths," and "they refused to cease from their evil deeds." Inevitably, the reader is led to think that the people of Meroe deserved to be conquered; they had earned their defeat. In addition, in the prayer aspects of the text, "By the might of the Lord of Heaven . . . no enemy shall stand before me," Ezana is using this text as an opportunity to acknowledge the power of his god, declare his own power as one chosen by his god.

Thus original texts have many layers of meaning. Beyond the questions, and method of reading, suggested here, readers must also consider that every primary source can be mined for factual details. Some of the details in this source are: Aksum had kings, those kings (or at least Ezana) controlled other lands than Aksum (Hemer, Raydan, Saba, Salhen, Seyamo, Bega, and Kasu are mentioned), and the people of Aksum believed their king to be an all-powerful creator. All primary sources should be read in various ways.

Chapter 1 The African Origins of Humanity

Prehistory to 10,000 BCE

The story of human evolution begins in Africa, and therefore so does the story of world history. Long before humans evolved into their present physiological form, and before we developed the ability to write our languages, we left traces of ourselves on the landscape around us, some deliberate and some unintentional. These traces are the first elements of those stories. As humans spread into different landscapes and climates, differentiation in culture and physical form appeared. This first chapter will explore the evidence we have of human evolution and some of the questions that scientists and historians have about it, of our earliest interactions with the environment around us, and of our first attempts at expressions of thought, memory, and art.

The first element of the human story is the evolution of our basic physiology. Each stage on that evolutionary path, and the final physical form that we have evolved, influenced the culture that we developed and eventually the civilizations we built. Each stage of evolution was also in a moment of interaction with the surrounding landscape, whether it was sweeping grasslands in Africa, temporary ice bridges linking Siberia to North America, or rocky deserts of Australia.

Once hominins achieve their modern evolutionary form (Homo sapiens), the historical record reveals the earliest innovations of tools and culture, of how humans viewed themselves and the world around them. Art, artifact, anthropology, and archaeology are all the information we have about this part in our past. This presents a wonderful opportunity for the student to learn something about the diverse disciplines from which all historians draw information, ideas, theories, and collaborate with.

The sources in this chapter also explore how we perceive the Paleolithic period, and the common misconceptions that we hold about it. We are naturally fascinated by our far distant past, and the scanty nature of the evidence only heightens our interest. The limited amount of material remains (which are in fact surprisingly diverse, scattered as they are over many tens of thousands of years and in many different places) has also provoked numerous debates among scientists and lay people alike. Some of the sources here offer speculative theories about the meaning of Paleolithic art, habits, and spiritual beliefs.

Anthropologists and historians have only been studying the evolution and the Paleolithic era for the last two centuries, yet there have already been many wild theories and mistaken assumptions. Much of recent writing on evolution and the Paleolithic period deal with correcting popular misconceptions about what hominins looked like, what early humans ate, who first discovered agriculture, and what were divisions existed between the genders. Selections in this chapter were chosen to address these corrections, although it would be impossible to cover all sides of every argument in this very contentious period of study. Other selections were chosen to illustrate the many different questions and debates that paleoanthropologists and historians engage in over the origins of early humans, and of early innovations such as agriculture.

In addition to providing a glimpse into the diversity of experiences found by early humans, these sources also serve to introduce the diversity of disciplines with which history and historians work. From anthropological studies on the origins and meaning of culture, and of economics and trade, to the biological development of the human form as it interacts with different environments, and to the contemporary need to personalize the earliest humans through whimsy and fiction, these sources reveal that history is not just what happened in the past; it is what many different sciences, arts, and theorists understand about the past.

1.1   Bad Hair Days in the Paleolithic

In this somewhat lighthearted essay, anthropologist Judith Berman takes on the stereotype of the wild looking, unkempt "cave man" popularized in cartoons, movies, television shows, etc. Berman argues that the typical appearance of the cave man (and woman), with uncombed and unstyled hair, is used to either convey the innate savagery of early humans, or to convey their "natural" uncorrupted state. In contrast, Berman find evidence in Paleolithic art that early humans and Neanderthals carefully tended and styled their hair, and tended to grooming in general.

Source: *American Anthropologist*, New Series, Vol. 101, No. 2 (June 1999), pp. 291-292

Bad Hair Days in the Paleolithic: Modern (Re)Constructions of the Cave Man
Judith C. Berman

How did Cave Men actually look? The answer to this question first requires some unbundling, as the historical convention often conflates Middle Paleolithic hominids (the European variety of which are familiarly called Neanderthals) with those of the Upper Paleolithic (early modern humans, some of whom were formerly termed Cro-Magnon) into one great "Stone Age." In the past century and a half, we have had at our disposal three sources of data on Middle and Upper Paleolithic humans: (1) the skeletal remains, (2) the material artifacts, and, (3) for the Upper Paleolithic, images of humans produced by Upper Paleolithic humans.

There are no extant images of Neanderthals produced by the Neanderthals themselves. The skeletal remains yield a great deal of information about appearance in terms of stature, muscle mass, sex, diet, age, and health, but do not in any way indicate how an individual wore his or her hair, or dressed, or wore tattoos, nor do these data have anything to add about skin or hair color. So the first category allows us to construct skeletons, to pose them in groups, to show young and old, male and female; it does not provide us with skin or hair. The original Neanderthal discovery, in 1856, consisted of a partial skull with thick browridges, thighbones, part of a pelvis, ribs, and arm and shoulder bones (Trinkaus and Shipman 1994:4). By 1873, only four more bones had been added to the Neanderthal corpus: the Gibraltar skull (with a face) from 1848, recognized as Neanderthal in 1864 (Trinkaus and Shipman 1994:89); and a group from La Naulette, Belgium, found in 1866, which consisted of a lower jaw, ulna, and metacarpal (Trinkaus and Shipman 1994:102-3).

The second category of data, material remains, enriches our view of the past. We can say much more about life- ways: dwellings, tools, settlement patterns, diet, activities. We may infer social behavior from these data, and we can add to our knowledge of physical appearance through the documentation of items of personal adornment, such as accessories, fastenings, combs, needles, and paints. However, we do not have direct evidence of hairdos, skin, or clothing. We might surmise that the Neanderthals, living as they did in a severe glacial period, had little opportunity or motivation to groom their hair, but this is conjecture not specifically grounded in the data.

The third category of data, visual representation, is most useful here. There are several hundred extant figural representations from Upper Paleolithic contexts, mostly of women. We have absolutely no way of judging what the creators of these images intended; for example, we cannot even say if these representations are naturalistic portrayals of contemporary humans, or if they were recorded because the subjects were typical or because they were exceptional. However, we do know that the images of animals produced by Upper Paleolithic humans are realistic representations, and we might infer that at least some of the representations of humans are also naturalistic. If we look specifically at head hair, we can see that it is styled. The images most familiar to us are the so-called "Venus figurines." While these small statues of women depict parts of bodies in some detail, they often do not apply the same amount of attention to extremities, including the hands, feet, and head. However, when there is some detail in the heads we often see hairdos. The most famous Venus figurine, the Venus of Willendorf seems to be wearing a hairnet or some kind of elaborate hairdo, and the Venus of Brassempouy has a clearly defined shoulder-length hairstyle. Other Venus figurines have dressed, or at least tamed, hair. Archaeologists have argued that there are local "styles" of Venus figurines; these local styles reflect both differences in local artistic traditions and may also reflect differences in local hairdos and other aspects of personal adornment (Gvozdover 1989a, 1989b). However, body hair (excluding that from the pubic area) is not represented on female figures (Duhard 1993:16S167). There are fewer representations of men in which hair styles can be observed. Their hairstyles are less elaborate than those of the women. Very few have facial hair, and none are represented with body hair (Duhard 1993:167).

If we can make the not unreasonable leap from Upper Paleolithic art to Upper Paleolithic behavior, the data strongly suggest that Upper Paleolithic humans were attentive to hair and that they styled it. It is difficult to make any case for the meaning of hairstyles as a personal statement, as a reflection of group membership, etc.; for my purposes here, it is enough to say that hair was attended to by Upper Paleolithic humans.

Reading and Discussion Questions

1. What physical evidence is Berman using to answer her basic question of how Paleolithic people might have looked? How is Berman using that evidence?
2. What do you think is the significance of Berman's claim that "hair was attended to by Upper Paleolithic humans"?
3. What does Berman use to defend her claim that Paleolithic depictions of humans were realistic depictions? What counterarguments could you make to that claim?

1.2   Of Lice and Men

William J. Burroughs, a scientist who specializes in physics and climate, ponders the unwelcome relationship between people and lice, and what that reveals about evolution and migration of early humans. In this excerpt, Burroughs uses the designation"kya"for dates; it refers to "1000 years ago."

Source: William J. Burroughs, *Climate Change in Prehistory: The End of the Reign of Chaos,* (Cambridge University Press, 2005), pp. 133-134

If the lengthy connection between dogs and humans seems a little far-fetched, recent work on body lice is even more extraordinary. A study by molecular anthropologist Mark Stoneking, who worked with Rebecca Cann and Allan Wilson on the original 'mitochondrial Eve' study, and colleagues at the Max Planck Institute for Evolutionary Anthropology in Leipzig, Germany, into the mtDNA of the body louse, has identified when this species evolved (Kittler, Kayser & Stoneking, 2003). Only humans carry this particular species of louse, which lays its eggs in clothing. Experts agree that body lice are a subspecieso{ head lice and that body lice probably evolved when people started to wear clothing. The results of the study suggest that the evolution of body louse occurred around 70kya. The inference from this result is that around this time humans first started wearing clothes. Yet again, we have another intriguing example of apparently important changes in the human condition taking place around 70kya.It is argued that only when humans moved out of Africa and experienced colder climates did they start to wear clothes. Although it would be unwise to attach too much importance to this specific date, it could also be argued that the dramatic cooling that took place because of the supervolcano Toba might have stimulated the wearing of clothes wherever people were living. Whatever the real explanation, the climatic upheavals that occurred at this time could well have led to radical changes in how modern humans lived.

Equally remarkable is recent work (Reed et al., 2004) that shows that there are two distinct genetic lineages of head lice. Despite looking virtually identical, these two forms of louse appear to have separated around 1.2 million years ago. This coincides roughly with the time when the archaic humans Homo erectus first ventured out of Africa. These humans lived in East Asia until about 50 kya, and the only way modern humans could have picked up their form of louse is by some social contact. This raises fascinating questions about the nature and timing of the interaction.

The geographical distribution of the two forms of louse is also interesting. One is found on people all over the world. The other is almost exclusive to the Americas. This suggests that the modern humans that crossed Beringia into the Americas carried the form of the louse that had survived for so long on our human cousins Homo erectus. What is more, the genetic patterns of the worldwide form of the louse show evidence of a bottleneck in their population around 100 kya, apparently in harmony with the tribulations of their human hosts.

All of this confirms the extraordinary range of sources being used to tell us more andmore about ourpast. This progress is summed up by the delightful connection made by *Current Biology*, when it published Stoneking and colleagues' paper: the cover carried the banner, "Of Lice and Men". What better point to bring this discussion of life in the Ice Age to a close?

Reading and Discussion Questions

1. What evidence about social customs and interactions between peoples do the recent studies on body and head lice imply?
2. What are the possible implications about the form of lice found only early humans in the Americas?

1.3   Shamans and Cave Painting

Jean Clottes and David Lewis-Williams theorize that the painted caves (such as those of Lascaux and Niaux in France) of Paleolithic people were used as a sacred space, in which rituals and ceremonies took place. The art on these cave walls, Clottes and Lewis-Williams argue, was part of a Shamanistic ritual. The creation of this art manipulated Paleolithic men and women's understanding of physical and metaphysical space. For instance, the authors suggest that the different chambers within the caves were used by different groups within a particular Paleolithic society, at different times, and for different purposes, most of them ritual or ceremonial. Clottes and Lewis-William also believe that the paintings were group undertakings, indicating a level of community organization and sophistication hitherto not associated with Paleolithic groupings. Ultimately, they believe that the Paleolithic aesthetic was sophisticated, as was the Paleolithic conceptualization of the physical world and spiritual experience.

Source: Jean Clottes and David Lewis-Williams, *The Shamans of Prehistory: Trance Magic in the Painted Caves* (Harry N. Abrams, Inc., 1998, pp. 103-104)

Whenever and wherever people used caves in addition to or in place of exterior sites, a highly significant development took place. The different degrees and modes of involvement in shamanic activity were probably separated out and allocated to different areas. What we call "embellished chambers" were a component of this ensemble.

Some sites have comparatively spacious chambers in which there are many images and in which numbers of people could have gathered. At Lascaux, the comparatively large Hall of the Bulls is near what we take to have been the prehistoric entrance. The Black Salon at Niaux is fartherunderground than the Hall of the Bulls, but it still presents an expanse of impressive imagery as well as space to accommodate alarge number of people. It also seems that a number of people must have participated in the making of these richly embellished chambers. People were needed to collect and process substances for the making of large quantities of paint; in the Hall of the Bulls, moreover, people collaborated to build scaffolds.

Yet these chambers are underground and therefore hidden. Their separation from the outside world suggests a degree of social separation as well as physical isolation. It seems likely that these chambers were important staging posts on the shamanic journey through the underworld. They point to a type of shamanic experience somewhat different from those experienced later on that spiritual and physical journey and which we discuss below. In the vestibules, people constructed a rich underworld:The images they made probably told of what lay behind the rock and, importantly, what lurked farther down the dark passages that led off the chambers. The dancing, chanting, and other activities that probably took place in the presence of these images prepared people's minds in a number of ways.

First, people were presentedwith a powerful impression of what the underworld was like, an impression with which it was difficult, but not impossible, to argue: They were, after all, already in the entrails of the dark underworld. The people who directed the proceedings and those who actually made the images were probably an elite who, by the presentation of their particular version of the underworld in such highly charged emotional circumstances, tried to enhance and reinforce their own social positions. The periodic addition of images to these panels was probably part of this process of social differentiation.

Then there was probably a wider significance. Some of these richly embellished chambers may have been the ritual centers of social groups, or bands, and the elaboration of the chambers may have been part of the negotiation of power relations between neighboring communities. The importance of decorated caves as social centers would explain the occurrence of very similar motifs in caves in the same region. Grid, or checker, motifs, for instance, are found in Lascaux and in Gabillou.The chambers were-paradoxically-conspicuous yet hidden displays of religious, and no doubt associated economic, power and influence. These unequal power relations between geographically distinct communities were probably underwritten by different degrees of exploitation of the shamanic cosmos. The most highly decorated caves proclaimed the owning group's privileged access to and knowledge of the underworld.

Thirdly, that access was used differentially within the community that owned the cave. It seems likely that embellished chambers were vestibules that prepared the minds of vision-questers for whatthey would experience in the solitude of the smaller, deeper areas. As we pointed out, in Stage Three trance people tend to hallucinate what they expect to hallucinate: The embellished vestibules stocked their minds. But the negotiation of power relations was not absent; these vestibules were away of channeling the questers' visions, of cutting down the element of idiosyncrasy, or novelty, that is present in all hallucinatory experiences. The embellished vestibules tried (but did not always succeed)to discredit any originality and individuality that may have challenged the religious and politicalstatus quo. In short, the embellished vestibules worked toward conformity of visions and so the consolidation of power.

Reading and Discussion Questions

1. Clottes and Lewis-Williams believe that each cave painting was the result of a "large number of people." Describe the evidence they offer to support that theory of artistic method.
2. How did the Paleolithic artists incorporate the geologic shape of the caves, into both content and presentation of the art?
3. According to the excerpt, in what ways were the caves used by Paleolithic peoples? What kinds of activities may have taken place there, and what meaning did those activities derive from the art?
4. In the shamanistic practice of hallucination, as it might have been practiced by Paleolithic peoples, what purpose could the cave paintings have served?
5. The authors describe the painted caves in terms that are normally used to refer to man-made structures. For instance, they refer to one area as a "vestibule," to another as a "chamber." Is there any physical evidence within the cave paintings that indicates that the Paleolithic peoples also differentiated space by specific use and purpose in that manner?

1.4   Not All Hominids Are Human Beings

In 1973, in Ethiopia, paleoanthropologist Donald Johanson stumbled across the skeleton of a hominin (or as he refers to it, a hominid) nearly 3.5 million years old. Nicknamed Lucy, it was acknowledge as the oldest known complete fossilized remains of a hominin, until a more the discovery of Ardipithecus in 1994. Although Lucy is no longer the oldest hominin remains she is still one of the most famous, in part because of Johanson's success in personalizing the skeleton. Lucy is also very controversial, from her age to her gender (a determination Johanson based on her pelvic bones but other paleoanthropologists dispute), historians and paleoanthropologists continue to interpret what the skeleton reveals about our earliest ancestors and about ourselves. The following excerpt is Johanson's description of how he Lucy differs from modern humans.

Source: "Not All Hominids are Human Beings," David Johanson and Maitland Edey, *Lucy: The Beginnings of Humankind* (Simon and Schuster, 1981, pp. 18-24).

We can picture human evolution as starting with a primitive apelike type that gradually, over a long period of time, began to be less and less apelike and more manlike. There was no abrupt crossover from ape to human, but probably a rather fizzy time of in-between types that would be difficult to classify either way. We have no fossils yet that tell us what went on during that in-between time. Therefore, the handiest way of separating the newer types from their ape ancestors is to lump together all those that stood up on their hind legs. That group of men and near-men is called "hominids". I am a hominid. I am a human being. I belong to the genus Homo and to the species sapiens: "thinking man". Perhaps I should say wise or knowing man–a man who is smart enough to recognize that he is a man. There have been other species of Homo who were not so smart, ancestors now extinct. Homo sapiens began to emerge a hundred thousand-perhaps two or three hundred thousand-years ago, depending on how one regards Neanderthal Man. He was another Homo. Some think he was the same species as ourselves. Others think he was an ancestor. There are a few who consider him a kind of cousin. That matter is unsettled because many of the best Neanderthal fossils were collected in Europe before anybody knew how to excavate sites properly or get good dates. Consequently, we do not have exact ages for most of the Neanderthal fossils in collections. I consider Neanderthal conspecific with sapiens, with myself. One hears talk about putting him in a business suit and turning him loose in the subway. It is true; one could do it and he would never be noticed. He was just a little heavier-boned than people of today, more primitive in a few facial features. But he was a man. His brain was as big as a modern man's, but shaped in a slightly different way. Could he make change at the subway booth and recognize a token? He certainly could. He could do many things more complicated than that. He was doing them over much of Europe, Africa and Asia as long as sixty or a hundred thousand years ago.

Neanderthal Man had ancestors, human ones. Before him in time was a less advanced type: *Homo erectus*. Put him on the subway and people would probably take a suspicious look at him. Before *Homo erectus* was a really primitive type, *Homo habilis*; put him on the subway and people would probably move to the other end of the car. Before *Homo habilis* the human line may run out entirely. The next stop in the past, back of *Homo habilis*, might be something like Lucy. All of the above are hominids. They are all erect walkers. Some were human, even though they were of exceedingly primitive types. Others were not human. Lucy was not. No matter what kind of clothes were put on Lucy, she would not look like a human being.

She was too far back, out of the human range entirely. That is what happens going back along an evolutionary line. If one goes back far enough, one finds oneself dealing with a different kind of creature. On the hominid line the earliest ones are too primitive to be called humans. They must be given another name. Lucy is in that category.

Reading and Discussion Questions
1. What does Johanson identify as the factors that make Lucy important to historians?
2. Johanson states that "All human beings are hominids, but not all hominids are human beings." Explain the difference. Which is Lucy?

1.5   Theories of Race and the History of Africa

One of the more tragic legacies of how evolutionary theories can be manipulated is how these theories were used to justify the suppression of one group (defined as a race) by another. Biologists, geneticists, historians, anthropologists, in fact, all contemporary people define race differently. P. Diagne discusses these often conflicting concepts of what is race in this brief excerpt. He identifies some of the problems with any one definition of race. Furthermore, he also suggests that physical differentiation between the races may have once had an evolutionary purpose, but that this is becoming less and less a necessity: distinct racial identity may be on the wane. In fact, genetic differentiation suggests a more complex understanding of race, and that genetic merging has already mixed the races.

Source: "Theories on 'race' and the history of Africa," P. Diagne, *General History of Africa*, Vol. I *Methodology and Africa Prehistory* (James Currey Ltd., 1990, pp. 100-103)

The Definition of Race

This way of differentiating between peoples also comes up against very considerable difficulties, in the first place because there are an increasingly large number of factors of differentiation and these tend to give results that are sometimes aberrant. 'Race' as determined by genetic factors and 'race' as characterized by external features do not coincide. For instance, the Pygmies and San of Africa, who are very close to the blacks of New Guinea and Australia in terms of phenotypes, are closer to the Europeans in blood structure and genes, whereas the Australian aborigines are closer to the Japanese and Chinese in terms of blood structure and genes. Hence, external appearances seems to be much more closely related to climate.

Furthermore, the work done by R. C. Lewontin on blood markers has shown that, for the world as a whole, 85 percent of the variations occur within nations. There is only a 7 percent variation between nations belonging to the same 'race' and only 7 percent between 'races'. In short, there is more difference between individuals in the same 'racial' group than there is between 'races'.

This is why more and more scholars are coming to deny the very existence of races. According to J. Ruffié, Man first emerged in the tropics and evolved for a long time in a hot climate. 'It was only during the second ice age, thanks to his efficient control of fire, that Homo erectus opted to live in a cold climate.' The human race, then, became more polytypic as it diversified and adapted to differing environments. Little by little, however, Man learned to defend himself against all the specific environments he encountered by developing culture, in the form of clothing, housing, food, and so on, to such a degree that the human species is tending to become monotypic again. Having severed its dependence on the ambient conditions, and as a result of the close contact between peoples, mankind is now virtually a single pool of intercommunicating genes.

In 1952, Livingstone published his celebrated paper on 'The non-existence of human races'. The fact is that, depending on the criteria selected, whether it be skin color, the shape of the skull or the nose, the nature of the hair, genetic features, etc., the resulting map of the races differs every time. 'In the light of the most recent advances in human genetics, no biologist nowadays any longer admits the existence of races within the human species.' Bentley Glass considers that the white race differs from the black by no more than six pairs of genes. In terms of numbers of genes, there are often greater variations than this both among whites and among blacks. This was one of the reasons for the UNESCO declaration that 'Race is not so much a biological phenomenon as a social myth.' What better illustration could there be of this claim than the fact that in South Africa a Japanese is regarded as an 'honorary white' and a Chinese as 'colored', whereas a man who is considered to be white in Brazil is considered black in the United States. The truth is that all the peoples of the world are of mixed blood, and are likely to become increasingly mixed….

The historical primacy of culture over biology has been plain ever since the offspring of the same primordial couple have roamed over planet earth, having probably set out from the African continent. When will people come to realize that it is culture, and not the nuts and bolts of biology, that makes them what they are and that can develop their humanity?

Reading and Discussion Questions

1. Diagne cites a Unesco declaration that "race is not so much a biological phenomenon as a social myth." What are the evolutionary implications about both biological and social definitions of race?
2. Diagne theorizes that genetic differences are more pronounced with one "racial" group (as defined by traditional external characteristics, such as skin color), rather than within one "racial" group. What are the implications of this for evolutionary co-mingling of these racial groups?
3. What are the markers traditionally used to define race, and what evolutionary purpose might they have once had?
4. In considering race and evolution, discuss some of your own assumptions about what defines race, and of how one race differs from another; how does this excerpt challenge or reinforce those assumptions?

1.6   Deep History and Convergent Evolution

In *On Deep History and the Brain*, historian Daniel Lord Smail postulates that "it is the similarities [between civilizations] that are the most startling," more so than the differences. In this excerpt, he also draws our attention to the continuities between the Paleolithic era and the agricultural civilizations. To this end, he uses the term "Postlithic" to refer to this latter period, rather than the traditional term "Neolithic" which would imply a more explicit break between the two. Although Smail acknowledges the fundamental changes brought by agriculture, he does so by emphasizing the patterns of conceptual and material interconnectivity between the Paleo- and Postlithic worlds.

Source: "Agriculture and Emerging Societies," Daniel Lord Smail, *On Deep History and the Brain* (University of California Press, 2008, pp. 197-200)

The shift to agriculture and sedentism had enormous if entirely unplanned implications for human societies. Of these, some of the most significant involve patterns of reproduction' Clay and, later, metal pots suitable for cooking gruel allowed women to wean their babies at a younger age. Sedentism limited women's exercise. Both factors conspired to increase fertility, creating the conditions for rapid population growth. Shorter birth-spacing intervals contributed to the creation or intensification of sibling rivalry. Shifting patterns in the sexual division of labor meant that women, major producers of calories in the Paleolithic economy, lost much of their productive capacity and invested increasing amounts of their own energy instead in reproduction.

The reemergence of political dominance hierarchies meant that, in early Postlithic societies, marriage patterns could shift away from partial Paleolithic monogamy to Postlithic polygyny and hypergamy. Women came to serve as markers of men's status, and-depending on the society we are speaking of-their clothing, jewelry, and education served to reflect male status. Even their bodies were marked and bound and sometimes even burned as a reflection of the role that women came to play in the making of male dominance hierarchies.

Some of the eeriest features of Postlithic human society are the products of convergent evolution. Within biology, convergent evolution is a process whereby wholly distinct speciesindependently arrive at the same morphological or physiological solution to a problem or an opportunity presented by their environment. The process can also operate in human culture. Agriculture was Independently invented in different continents, as were writing, pottery, royal cults, priestly castes, embalming, astronomy, earrings, coinage, and holy virginity. This list could go on for pages. Diffusion cannot explain these convergences. Watching pyramids sprout up in Egypt and Mesoamerica is like contemplating the emergence of a saber-toothed cat in both marsupial and placental lineages, separated though they were by large oceans and hundreds of millions of years of biological evolution. We celebrate the diversity of human civilizations, but it is the similarities that are the most startling, the thing that continually reminds us of our common humanity.

Reading and Discussion Questions

1. What connections does Smail find between the development of agriculture and women's status within their community?
2. Smail considers how agriculture in the Paleolithic societies altered the biology and status of women; how do you think it also altered the biology and status of men?
3. Do you agree with Smail's argument that the similarities between civilizations are more startling than the differences?

Agrarian-Urban Centers of the Middle East and Eastern Mediterranean

Chapter 2

11,500 – 600 B.C.E.

The first agrarian-based states of Mesopotamia and Egypt developed many of the firsts in human history: first agriculture, first cities, first states, first empires, the first writing systems, to name just a few. Mesopotamia, one of several regions in the larger area known as the Middle East, was until the fifth millennium, blessed with a monsoon weather pattern of rainy summers. It was a lush landscape and full of wild grains. Foraging was easy, and game plentiful. Beginning c. 11,500 B.C.E. people began to settle in villages, taking advantage of the bounty. When the monsoon rains moved west, and the rains decreased, Mesopotamia remained ideally suited for agriculture. The land was still well served by the Tigris and Euphrates Rivers, and in addition to the natural flooding of these rivers, the land was fairly easy to irrigate with canals. Settlements grew into towns, towns into cities, cities grew into city-states. The basic pattern of foragers settling down to farming had begun, as had the basic pattern of growth of urban centers. This was repeated in Egypt, which took advantage of the reliability of the Nile flooding to develop its own agrarian culture.

The societies that developed in Mesopotamia and Egypt were complex and so are the historical records they left behind. In addition to the material remains of their cities, they have left a plethora of written material to the benefit of historians. The sources in this chapter present just a small sample of the great variety of texts, and they present just a glimpse of the great variety of Mesopotamian and Egyptian societies, as well as one from Greece, a third agrarian society in the Eastern Mediterranean.

Every culture has its own theory of creation, and there are several creation stories from both societies here, as well as a third interpretation of beginnings from Greece. It is appropriate to focus on creation myths, as the beginning of things was of paramount importance to these early societies. Understanding where they came from was a method of understanding what they were as a people, and reflects a self-conscious awareness of themselves as a people. In this sense, these early creation myths are as much self-histories of the cultures that created them, as they were religious speculation. In addition to creation texts, these sources illustrate the delicate relationship between humanity and the gods, who representeda nature that was not as tamed as agriculture might suggest. Dependence upon the good will of natural elements led to rules of behavior for humans and gods, to rituals of worship and reverence. As with human laws that governed the relations between people, breaking the rules of behavior between the human and divine had consequences. Hammurabi's law code makes it clear that urban societies succeeded by constantly reinforcing that order, in this case through law.

———————————————

2.1   An Egyptian Creation Myth

Re (also spelled Ra) was one of several creator gods in Egyptian tradition; in fact, this excerpt features references to two creators: Nun and Re. Dating from the Middle Kingdom, c. 2000 B.C.E., it is a conflation of competing creation myths. The use of "Who is he?" as a refrain suggests this might have been recited or performed, and it was recorded in the Book of the Dead, a ritual text. The brief selection includes a dramatic shift; in the beginning Re was alone, and by the end he is surrounded by other deities and has become a king.

Source: "Another Version of the Creation by Atum," from *Ancient Near Eastern Texts,* James B. Pritchard, ed. New Jersey: Princeton University Press, 1969; pp. 3-4.

ANOTHER VERSION OF THE CREATION BY ATUM

The beginning of exaltations and beatifications; going up and down in the necropolis; being an effective spirit in the beautiful west; being in the retinue of Osiris; being satisfied with the food of Wen-nofer. The spell for coming forth by day, assuming any forms that he may wish to assume, playing at the draughtboard, sitting in the arbor, and coming forth as a living soul, by X, after he moors. It is of benefit to him who may do it on earth: when the speech of the Lord of All takes place:

Speech of the Creator, with Glosses

"I am Atum when I was alone in Nun; I am Re in its (first) appearances, when he began to rule that which he had made."

Who is he? This "Re, when he began to rule that which he had made" means that Re began to appear as a king, as one who was before the liftings of Shu had taken place," when he was on the hill which is in Hermopolis. ...

'"I am the great god who came into being by himself."

Who is he? "The great god who came into being by himself" is water; he is Nun, the father of the gods. *Another version: He is Re.*

"He who created his names, the Lord of the Ennead."

Who is he? He is Re, who created the names of the parts of his body. That is how these gods who follow him came into being.

"I am he among the gods who cannot be repulsed."

Who is he? He is Atum, who is in his sun disc. Another version: He is Re, when he arises on the eastern horizon of heaven."

"I am yesterday, while I know tomorrow."

Who is he? As for "yesterday," that is Osiris. As for "tomorrow," that is Re on that day on which the enemies of the All-Lord are annihilated and his son Horus is made ruler. ...

Reading and Discussion

1. How does this creation myth compare with the *Enuma Elish* from Mesopotamia?
2. Most early creation myths feature a creation of or by natural powers; where in this poem is there a connection to nature? How is does the story move beyond a direct connection to nature to something more abstract?
3. Nun is the god of water, while Re was a solar deity. How does the conflation of their two creation stories represent an fuller understanding of agriculture than relying on one aspect of nature alone?

2.2   A Mesopotamian Creation Myth

The *Enuma Elish* is one of the earliest recorded cosmogonies, or myths of creation; it probably dated from the third millennium B.C.E., although the oldest extant written version dates from the first millennium B.C.E. The *Enuma Elish* was one of many creation stories in circulation in ancient Mesopotamia (it may also have influenced the Greek poet Hesiod – see the excerpt from his *Theogony*). This particular cosmogony was connected with the city of Babylon and recited at the New Year Festival at that city in the month of April. The poem narrates the succession and struggles of the first gods and the rise of Marduk (Ashur in the Assyrian version) as the champion who defeated the primeval goddess Tiamat and her allies, who represented the forces of chaos. Marduk is exalted as the new king of the gods and creator of the world as we know it, to whom all absolute obedience. The poem ends with the recitation of Marduk's fifty names. In the recitation at the New Year festival, the poem invoked the renewal of order in the universe and of the king's sovereignty mirroring the absolute power of Marduk over his allies.

Source: from *Myths of Mesopotamia*, Stephanie Dalley, ed. New York: Oxford University Press, 1989. Tablet I; pp. 233-238; Tablet IV; pp. 249-255.

TABLET I

When skies above were not yet named,nor earth below pronounced by name, Apsu, the first one, their begetterand maker Tiamat, who bore them all,had mixed their waters together,but had not formed pastures, nor discoveredreed-beds; when yet no gods were manifest,nor names pronounced, nor destinies decreed, then gods were born within them. Lahmu (and) Lahamu emerged, their names pronounced.[1]

As soon as they matured, were fully formed, Anshar (and) Kishar were born, surpassing them. They passed the days at length, they added to the years. Anu their first-born son rivalled his forefathers: Anshar made his son Anu like himself,[2] and Anu begot Nudimmud in his likeness. He, Nudimmud, was superior to his forefathers: Profound of understanding, he was wise, was very strong at arms.

Mightier by far than Anshar his father's begetter, he had no rival among the gods his peers. The gods of that generation would meet together and disturb Tiamat, and their clamour reverberated. They stirred up Tiamat'sbelly, they were annoying her by playing inside Anduruna. Apsu could not quell their noise and Tiamat became mute before them; however grievous their behaviour to her, However bad their ways, she would indulge them. Finally Apsu, begetter of the great gods, called out and addressed his vizier Mummu, 'O Mummu, vizier who pleases me! Come, let us go to Tiamat!' They went and sat in front of Tiamat, and discussed affairs concerning the gods their sons. Apsu made his voice heard and spoke to Tiamat in a loud voice, 'Their ways have become very grievousto me, by day I cannot rest, by night I cannot sleep. I shall abolish their ways and disperse them! Let peace prevail, so that we can sleep.'

When Tiamat heard this, she was furious and shouted at her lover; she shouted dreadfully and was beside herself with rage, but then suppressed the evil in her belly.

'How could we allow what we ourselves created to perish? Even though their ways are so grievous, we should bear it patiently.'

(Vizier) Mummu replied and counseled Apsu; the vizier did not agree with the counsel of his earth mother.

---

[1] Ea and Damkina in the Assyrian version

[2] Assur (head of the Assyrian pantheon) was assimilated with Anshar from the eighth century onwards.

'O father, put an end to (their) troublesome ways, so that she may be allowed to rest by day and sleep at night.'

Apsu was pleased with him, his face lit up at the evil he was planning for the gods his sons. (Vizier) Mummu hugged him, sat on his lap and kissed him rapturously.

But everything they plotted between them was relayed to the gods their sons. The gods listened and wandered about restlessly; they fell silent, they sat mute. Superior in understanding, wise and capable, Ea who knows everything found out their plot, made for himself a design of everything, and laid it out correctly, made it cleverly, his pure spell was superb. He recited it and it stilled the waters. He poured sleep upon him so that he was sleeping soundly, put Apsu to sleep, drenched with sleep. Vizier Mummu the counselor (was in) a sleepless daze. He (Ea) unfastened his belt, took off his crown, took away his mantle of radiance and put it on himself. He held Apsu down and slew him; tied up Mummu and laid him across him. He set up his dwelling on top of Apsu, and grasped Mummu, held him by a nose-rope.

When he had overcome and slain his enemies, Ea set up his triumphal cry over his foes. Then he rested very quietly inside his private quarters and named them Apsu and assigned chapels, founded his own residence there, and Ea and Damkina his lover dwelt in splendour. In the chamber of destinies, the hall of designs, Bel, cleverest of the clever, sage of the gods, was begotten. And inside Apsu, Marduk was created; inside pure Apsu, Marduk was born. Ea his father created him, Damkina his mother bore him.

He suckled the teats of goddesses; the nurse who reared him filled him with awesomeness. Proud was his form, piercing his stare, mature his emergence, he was powerful from the start. Anu his father's begetter beheld him, and rejoiced, beamed; his heart was filled with joy. He made him so perfect that his godhead was doubled. Elevated far above them, he was superior in every way. His limbs were ingeniously made beyond comprehension, impossible to understand, too difficult to perceive. Four were his eyes, four were his ears; when his lips moved, fire blazed forth. The four ears were enormous and likewise the eyes; they perceived everything. Highest among the gods, his form was outstanding. His limbs were very long, his height (?) outstanding.

(Anu cried out)

'Mariutu, Mariutu, son, majesty, majesty of the gods!'

Clothed in the radiant mantle of ten gods, worn high above his head five fearsome rays were clustered above him. Anu created the four winds and gave them birth, put them in his (Marduk's) hand, 'My son, let them play!'

He fashioned dust and made the whirlwind carry it; he made the flood-wave and stirred up Tiamat. Tiamat was stirred up, and heaved restlessly day and night. The gods, unable to rest, had to suffer . . . They plotted evil in their hearts, and they addressed Tiamat their mother, saying, 'Because they slew Apsu your lover and you did not go to his side but sat mute, he has created the four, fearful winds to stir up your belly on purpose, and we simply cannot sleep! Was your lover Apsu not in your heart? And (vizier) Mummu who was captured? No wonder you sit alone! Are you not a mother? You heave restlessly but what about us, who cannot rest? Don't you love us? Our grip(?) [is slack], (and) our eyes are sunken. Remove the yoke of us restless ones, and let us sleep! Set up a [battle cry] and avenge them! Con[quer the enemy] and reduce them to nought!'

Tiamat listened, and the speech pleased her.

'Let us act now, (?) as you were advising! The gods inside him (Apsu) will be disturbed, because they adopted evil for the gods who begot them.'

They crowded round and rallied beside Tiamat. They were fierce, scheming restlessly night and day. They were working up to war, growling and raging. They convened a council and created conflict. Mother Hubur, who fashions all things, contributed an unfaceable weapon: she bore giant snakes, sharp of tooth and unsparing of fang (?). She filled their bodies with venom instead of blood. She cloaked ferocious dragons with fearsome rays and made them bear mantles of radiance, made them godlike,

(chanting this imprecation)

'Whoever looks upon them shall collapse in utter terror! Their bodies shall rear up continually and never turn away!'

She stationed a horned serpent, a *mušhuššu*-dragon, and a *lahmu*-hero, an *ugallu*-demon, a rabid dog, and a scorpion-man, aggressive *ūmu*-demons, a fish-man, and a bull-manbearing merciless weapons, fearless in battle.Her orders were so powerful, they could not bedisobeyed.In addition she created eleven more likewise. Over the gods her offspring who had convened acouncil for hershe promoted Qingu and made him greatest amongthem, conferred upon him leadership of the army, command of the assembly,raising the weapon to signal engagement, mustering combat-troops, overall command of the whole battle force. And she set him upon a throne.

'I have cast the spell for you and made you greatest in the gods' assembly! I have put into your power rule over all the gods! You shall be the greatest, for you are my only lover! Your commands shall always prevail over all the Anukki!'

Then she gave him the Tablet of Destinies and made him clasp it to his breast.

'Your utterance shall never be altered! Your word shall be law!'

When Qingu was promoted and had received the Anu-power and had decreed destinies for the gods his sons, (he said),

'What issues forth from your mouths shall quench Fire! Your accumulated venom (?) shall paralyse the powerful!'

(Catchline)

Tiamat assembled his creatures

(Colophon)

First tablet, 'When skies above'. [Written] like [its] original [and inspected].

Tablet of Nabû-balatsu-iqbison of Na'id-Marduk.

Hand of Nabû-balatsu-iqbison of Na'id-Marduk [   ].

TABLET IV

They founded a princely shrine for him, and he took up residence as ruler before his fathers, *(who proclaimed)*

'You are honoured among the great gods. Your destiny is unequalled, your word (has the power of) Anu! O Marduk, you are honoured among the great gods. Your destiny is unequalled, your word (has the power of) Anu! From this day onwards your command shall not be altered. Yours is the power to exalt and abase. May your utterance be law, your word never be falsified. None of the gods shall transgress your limits. May endowment, required for the gods' shrines wherever they have temples, be established for your place.

O Marduk, you are our champion! we hereby give you sovereignty over all of the whole universe. Sit in the assembly and your word shall be pre-eminent! May your weapons never miss (the mark), may they smash your enemies! O lord,[3] spare the life of him who trusts in you,but drain the life of the god who has espoused evil!'

---

[3] Bel (Cf. Hebrew Baal) "Lord" was one of Marduk's titles.

They set up in their midst one constellation,[4] and then they addressed Marduk their son, 'May your decree, O lord, impress the gods' command to destroy and to recreate, and let it be so! Speak and let the constellation vanish! Speak to it again and let the constellation reappear.'

He spoke, and at his word the constellation vanished. He spoke to it again and the constellation was recreated. When the gods his fathers saw how effective his utterance was, they rejoiced, they proclaimed: 'Marduk is King!' They invested him with scepter, throne, and staff-of-office. They gave him an unfaceable weapon to crush the foe.

'Go, and cut off the life of Tiamat! Let the winds bear her blood to us as good news!'

The gods his fathers thus decreed the destiny of the lord and set him on the path of peace and obedience. He fashioned a bow, designated it as his weapon, feathered the arrow, set it in the string. He lifted up a mace and carried it in his right hand, slung the bow and quiver at his side, put lightning in front of him, his body was filled with an ever-blazing flame. He made a net to encircle Tiamat within it, marshalled the four winds so that no part of her could escape: South Wind, North Wind, East Wind, West Wind, the gift of his father Anu, he kept them close to the net at his side. He created the *imhullu*-wind (evil wind), the tempest, the whirlwind, the Four Winds, the Seven Winds, the tornado, the unfaceable facing wind. He released the winds which he had created, seven of them. They advanced behind him to make turmoil inside Tiamat.

The lord raised the flood-weapon, his great weapon, and mounted the frightful, unfaceable storm -chariot. He had yoked to it a team of four and had harnessed to its side 'Slayer', 'Pitiless', 'Racer', and 'Flyer; their lips were drawn back their teeth carried poison. They know not exhaustion, they can only devastate. He stationed on his right Fiercesome Fight and Conflict, on the left Battle to knock down every contender (?). Clothed in a cloak of awesome armour, his head was crowned with a terrible radiance.

The Lord set out and took the road, and set his face towards Tiamat who raged out of control. In his lips he gripped a spell, in his hand he grasped a herb to counter poison. Then they thronged about him, the gods thronged about him; the gods his fathers thronged about him, the gods thronged about him. The Lord drew near and looked into the middle of Tiamat: he was trying to find out the strategy of Qingu her lover. As he looked, his mind became confused, his will crumbled and his actions were muddled. As for the gods his helpers, who march(ed) at his side,[5] when they saw the warrior, the leader, their looks were strained. Tiamat cast her spell. She did not even turn her neck. In her lips she was holding falsehood, lies, (wheedling),

'[How powerful is] your attacking force, O lord of the gods! The whole assembly of them has gathered to your place!'

(But he ignored her blandishments)

The Lord lifted up the flood-weapon, his great weapon and sent a message to Tiamat who feigned goodwill, saying:

'Why are you so friendly on the surface when your depths conspire to muster a battle force? Just because the sons were noisy (and) disrespectful to their fathers, should you, who gave them birth, reject compassion? You named Qingu as your lover, you appointed him to rites of Anu-power, wrongfully his. You sought out evil for Anshar, king of the gods, so you have compounded your wickedness against the gods my fathers! Let your host prepare! Let them gird themselves with your weapons! Stand forth, and you and I shall do single combat'

When Tiamat heard this, she went wild, she lost her temper. Tiamat screamed aloud in a passion, her lower parts shook together from the depths. She recited the incantation and kept casting her spell. Meanwhile the

---

[4] In other interpretations "one garment."
[5] The battle scene of the chief god entering battle (in the Assyrian version Assur) accompanied by the gods was depicted on the doors of Senacherib's New Year Temple, which is described in an inscription.

gods of battle were sharpening their weapons.

Face to face they came, Tiamat and Marduk, sage of the gods. They engaged in combat, they closed for battle. The Lord spread his net and made it encircle her, to her face he dispatched the *imhullu*-wind, which had been behind: Tiamat opened her mouth to swallow it, and he forced in the *imhullu*-wind so that she could not close her lips. Fierce winds distended her belly; her insides were constipated and she stretched her mouth wide. He shot an arrow, which pierced her belly, split her down the middle and slit her heart, vanquished her and extinguished her life. He threw down her corpse and stood on top of her.

When he had slain Tiamat, the leader, he broke up her regiments; her assembly was scattered. Then the gods her helpers, who had marched at her side, Began to tremble, panicked, and turned tail. Although he allowed them to come out and spared their lives, they were surrounded, they could not flee. Then he tied them up and smashed their weapons. They were thrown into the net and sat there ensnared. They cowered back, filled with woe. They had to bear his punishment, confined to prison.

And as for the dozens of creatures, covered in fearsome rays, the gang of demons who all marched on her right, he fixed them with nose-ropes and tied their arms. He trampled their battle-filth (?) beneath him. As for Qingu, who had once been the greatest among them, he defeated him and counted him among the dead gods, wrested from him the Tablet of Destinies, wrongfully his, sealed it with (his own) seal and pressed it to his breast.

Reading and Discussion Questions

1. Literary historians call Eluma Elish an epic poem; if so, how is Marduk a hero of the epic?
2. The epic opens with the line "when skies above were not yet named" and makes several other references to naming. What power does naming hold for the Babylonians?
3. One of the most obvious motifs in the poem is that of water, which is clearly an allusion to the centrality of the Tigris and the Euphrates Rivers in Mesopotamian cultures. Does the epic present water as a creative or a destructive force?

2.3   Law Codes of Hammurabi

One of the most famous texts from Mesopotamia is the law code of Hammurabi, king of the Amorites (Old Babylon) from 1792 – 1750 B.C.E. Carved into a stele for public display, the code governs nearly every aspect of city life imaginable. It is often compared to the law code of the Hebrew Bible, and is a kind of *lextalionis*, or "law of retribution." Punishments are designed to match the crime, in either a literal sense or in some kind of equitable exchange of corporal or economic penalty.

The excerpts below concern a variety of legal situations, and present a fairly sophisticated legal culture. In addition to the obvious problems of urban life, such as building codes, marital disputes, and the treatment of slaves, it also deals with the more subtle issues of reputation and judicial corruption.

Source: *The Code of Hammurabi, King of Babylon* trans. Robert Francis Harper (Chicago: University of Chicago Press, 1904)

1. If a man of rank accused another man of rank and brought a charge of murder against him, but has not proven it, his accuser shall be executed.
3. If a man of rank came forward with false testimony in a case, and has not proven the word he spoke, if that case was a death-penalty case, that man shall be put to death.
4. If he came forward with false testimony concerning grain or money, he shall bear the punishment in that case.

14. If a man of rank has kidnapped the young son of another man of rank, he shall be executed.
15. If a man of rank has helped either a male slave owned by the government or a male slave of a private citizen or a female slave of a private citizen to escape the city, he shall be executed.
16. If a man of rank has harbored in his house either a fugitive male or female slave belonging to the government or to a private citizen and has not brought him forth at the summons of the police, that homeowner shall be executed.
17. If a man of rank caught a runaway slave in the open and has taken him to his owner, the slave's owner shall pay him two shekels of silver.
19. If he has kept the slave in his house and later the slave has been found in his possession, that man of rank shall be executed.
22. If a man of rank is caught committing robbery, he shall be executed.
25. If a fire broke out in a man of rank's home and another man of rank, who went to help put out the fire, steals the goods of the home's owner, that man of rank shall be thrown into that fire.
98. If a man of rank gave money to another man of rank for a partnership, they shall divide equally in the presence of god the profit or loss which was incurred.
104. If a merchant lent grain, wool, oil, or any goods at all to a trader to retail, the trader shall write down the value and pay it back to the merchant, with the trader obtaining a sealed receipt for the money that he pays to the merchant.
106. If a trader borrowed money from a merchant and has then disputed the fact with his merchant, that merchant in the presence of god and witnesses shall prove that the trader borrowed the money and the trader shall pay three times the amount of the original loan.
128. If a man of rank marries a woman but did not draw up the marriage contracts for her, she is not his wife.
129. If the wife of a man of rank has been caught while sleeping with another man, they shall tie them both up and throw them into the water. If the husband of the woman wishes to spare his wife, then the king may in turn order his subject spared.
131. If a man of rank's wife was accused by her husband of adultery, but was not caught while sleeping with another man, she shall swear she is innocent before god and return home.
134. If a man of rank was kidnapped and there was not enough money and food in his home for his wife to survive, she may enter the home of another, with no blame incurred by the wife.
136. If, when a man of rank ran away from his town, his wife went to live in another house after he left, if that man of rank returned and wishes to take back his wife, the wife of the runaway man shall not return to him because he had abandoned his city and ran away.
142. If a woman hates her husband so much that she says "You may not have me", her case may be investigated by the city council, and if she is careful and innocent, even though her husband has been going out and treating her poorly, that woman, without incurring any blame at all, may take her dowry and return to her father.
143. If she was not careful, however, but was too busy socializing and neglected her household duties and humiliated her husband, that woman shall be thrown into the water.
148. When a man of rank has a wife who then gets seriously ill, if he has made up his mind to marry another woman, he may marry her without divorcing his wife. The wife shall live in his home and he shall continue to support her as long as she lives.
149. If that woman has refused to live in her husband's home, he shall return her dowry to her and she may leave.
153. If a man of rank's wife has caused her husband's death because of another man, the woman shall be impaled on stakes.

154. If a man of rank sleeps with his daughter, he shall be forced to leave the city.
155. If a man of rank chose a bride for his son and his son has slept with her, but later the man is caught sleeping with her, that man of rank shall be tied up and thrown into the water.
157. If a man of rank sleeps with his mother after his father dies, both mother and son shall be burned to death.
162. If, when a man of rank gets married, and his wife bears him children and later dies, the dowry belongs to her children and her father cannot claim it.
163. If a man of rank's wife dies but had not had children, if his father-in-law returns the marriage-price that the man of rank paid, her husband must return the dowry to the father-in-law.
164. If his father-in-law has not returned the marriage-price to him, he shall subtract the full amount of her marriage-price from her dowry and return the rest of her dowry to his father-in-law.
170. When a man of rank's first wife bore him children and his female slave also bore him children, if that father during his lifetime claims the children of his slave as his own, thus having counted them with his children of his first wife, after he dies the children of both his first wife and his slave shall receive equal portions of his estate, with the first-born, the son of the first wife, receiving a better share.
171. However, if the father during his life did not claim the children of his slave as his own, after he dies the children of the slave may not share in the estate along with the children of the first wife.
189. If he has not taught him his trade or craft, that child may return to his father's home.
195. If a son hits his father, the son's hand shall be cut off.
196. If a man of rank destroyed the eye of another noble, his eye shall also be destroyed.
197. If he has broken another noble's bone, his bone shall also be broken.
198. If he destroyed the eye or broken the bone of a commoner, he shall pay one mina of silver.
199. If he has destroyed the eye or broken a bone of a man of rank's slave, he shall pay half the slave's value.
202. If a man of rank slaps the face of a man of rank who is superior to him, he shall be whipped sixty times with an oxtail whip in public.
203. If a noble slaps another noble's face who is of the same rank, he shall pay one mina of silver.
204. If a commoner slaps the face of another commoner, he shall pay ten shekels of silver.
205. If a man of rank's slave has slapped the face of a noble, his ear shall be cut off.

Reading and Discussion Questions

1. How does the law code reinforce divisions of class and power?
2. How is the law code favorable to women? Is this expected of the patriarchical society that created it?
3. The law code specifies detailed provisions for the division of property after someone dies. Why are laws of inheritance so important in an agrarian-urban society like ancient Babylon?

2.4 The Descent of Ishtar To the Underworld

Ishtar is the Assyrian and Babylonian goddess of sex, fertility, and war. In this famous myth, she goes to the underworld to rescue her lover Dumuzi. Because Ishtar was a goddess of sex, when she is in the underworld, all sexual activity on the earth ceases. This presents a dilemma for the god Ea, who must convince Ereshkigal, queen of the underworld, to release Ishtar.

In a longer, Sumerian version of this story the voyage to the underworld by Dumuzi is a cyclical event, mimicking the seasonal fertility of agriculture.

Source: from *Myths of Mesopotamia*, Stephanie Dalley, ed. (New York: Oxford University Press, 1989), 155-160.

THE DESCENT OF ISHTAR TO THE UNDERWORLD

To Kurnugi, land of [no return],
Ishtar daughter of Sin was [determined] to go;
The daughter of Sin was determined to go
To the dark house, dwelling of Erkalla's god,
To the house which those who enter cannot leave,
On the road where travelling is one-way only,
To the house where those who enter are deprived of light,
Where dust is their food, clay their bread.
They see no light, they dwell in darkness,
They are clothed like birds, with feathers.
Over the door and the bolt, dust has settled.
Ishtar, when she arrived at the gate of Kurnugi,
Addressed her words to the keeper of the gate,
'Here gatekeeper, open your gate for me,
Open your gate for me to come in!
If you do not open the gate for me to come in,
I shall smash the door and shatter the bolt,
I shall smash the doorpost and overturn the doors,
I shall raise up the dead and they shall eat the living:
The dead shall outnumber the living!'
The gatekeeper made his voice heard and spoke,
He said to great Ishtar,
'Stop, lady, do not break it down!
Let me go and report your words to queen Ereshkigal.'
The gatekeeper went in and spoke to [Ereshkigal],
'Here she is, your sister Ishtar [...]
Who holds the great *keppū*-toy,
Stirs up the Apsu in Ea's presence [...]?'
When Ereshkigal heard this,
Her face grew livid as cut tamarisk,
Her lips grew dark as the rim of a *kuninu-vessel*.
'What brings her to me? What has incited her against me?
Surely not because I drink water with the Anunnaki,
I eat clay for bread, I drink muddy water for beer?
I have to weep for young men forced to abandon sweethearts.
I have to weep for girls wrenched from their lovers' laps.
For the infant child I have to weep, expelled before its time.
Go, gatekeeper, open your gate to her.
Treat her according to the ancient rites.'
The gatekeeper went. He opened the gate to her.
'Enter, my lady: may Kutha give you joy,
May the palace of Kurnugi be glad to see you.'
He let her in through the first door, but stripped off
(and) took away the great crown on her head.
'Gatekeeper, why have you taken away the great crown on my head?'
'Go in, my lady. Such are the rites of the Mistress of Earth.'

He let her in through the second door, but stripped
off (and) took away the rings in her ears.
'Gatekeeper, why have you taken away the rings in my ears?'
'Go in, my lady. Such are the rites of the Mistress of Earth.'
He let her in through the third door, but stripped
off (and) took away the beads around her neck.
'Gatekeeper, why have you taken away the beads around my neck?'
'Go in, my lady. Such are the rites of the Mistress of Earth.'
He let her in through the fourth door, but stripped
off (and) took away the toggle-pins at her breast.
'Gatekeeper, why have you taken away the
toggle-pins at my breast?'
'Go in, my lady. Such are the rites of the Mistress of Earth.'
He let her in through the fifth door, but stripped off
(and) took away the girdle of birth-stones around her waist.
'Gatekeeper, why have you taken away the girdle
of birthstones around my waist?'
'Go in, my lady. Such are the rites of the Mistress of Earth.'
He let her in through the sixth door, but stripped
off (and) took away the bangles on her wrists and ankles.
'Gatekeeper, why have you taken away the
bangles from my wrists and ankles?'
'Go in, my lady. Such are the rites of the Mistress of Earth.'
He let her in through the seventh door, but stripped
off (and) took away the proud garment of her body.
'Gatekeeper, why have you taken away the proud
garment of my body?'
'Go in, my lady. Such are the rites of the Mistress of Earth.'
As soon as Ishtar went down to Kurnugi,
Ereshkigal looked at her and trembled before her.
Ishtar did not deliberate (?), but Jeant over (?) her.
EreshkigaJ made her voice heard and spoke,
Addressed her words to Namtar her vizier,
'Go, Namtar [   ] of my [ ]
Send out against her sixty diseases
[   ] Ishtar:
Disease of the eyes to her [eyes],
Disease of the arms to her [arms],
Disease of the feet to her [feet],
Disease of the heart to her [heart],
Disease of the head [to her head],
To every part of her and to [   ].'
After Ishtar the mistress of (?) [had gone
down to Kurnugi],
No bull mounted a cow, [no donkey impregnated a jenny],
No young man impregnated a girl in [the street (?)],
The young man slept in his private room,
The girl slept in the company of her friends.

Then Papsukkal, vizier of the great gods, hung his
head, his face [became gloomy];
He wore mourning clothes, his hair was unkempt.
Dejected (?), he went and wept before Sin his father,
His tears flowed freely before king Ea.
'Ishtar has gone down to the Earth and has not
come up again.
As soon as Ishtar went down to Kurnugi
No bull mounted a cow, no donkey impregnated a jenny,
No young man impregnated a girl in the street,
The young man slept in his private room,
The girl slept in the company of her friends.'
Ea, in the wisdom of his heart, created a person.
He created Good-looks the playboy.
'Come, Good-looks, set your face towards the gate of Kurnugi.
The seven gates of Kurnugi shall be opened before you.
Ereshkigal shall look at you and be glad to see you.
When she is relaxed, her mood will lighten.
Get her to swear the oath by the great gods.
Raise your head, pay attention to the waterskin,
Saying, "Hey, my lady, let them give me the
waterskin, that I may drink water from it.",
(And so it happened. But)
When Ereshkigal heard this,
She struck her thigh and bit her finger.
'You have made a request of me that should not'
have been made!
Come, Good-looks, I shall curse you with a great curse.
I shall decree for you a fate that shall never be forgotten.
Bread (gleaned (?)) from the city's ploughs shall be your food,
The city drains shall be your only drinking place,
The shade of a city wall your only standing place,
Threshold steps your only sitting place,
The drunkard and the thirsty shall slap your cheek.'
Ereshkigal made her voice heard and spoke;
She addressed her words to Namtar her vizier,
'Go, Namtar, knock (?) at Egalgina,
Decorate the threshold steps with coral,
Bring the Anunnaki out and seat (them) on golden thrones,
Sprinkle Ishtar with the waters of life and conduct
her into my presence.'
Namtar went, knocked at Egalgina,
Decorated the threshold steps with coral,
Brought out the Anunnaki, seated (them) on golden thrones,
Sprinkled Ishtar with the waters of life and brought
her to her (sister).
He let her out through the first door, and gave back
to her the proud garment of her body

He let her out through the second door, and gave
back to her the bangles for her wrists and ankles.
He let her out through the third door, and gave
back to her the girdle of birth stones around her waist.
He let her out through the fourth door, and gave
back to her the toggle pins at her breast.
He let her out through the fifth door, and gave back
to her the beads around her neck.
He let her out through the sixth door, and gave
back to her the rings for her ears.
He let her out through the seventh door, and gave
back to her the great crown for her head
'Swear that (?) she has paid you her ransom, and
give her back (in exchange) for him,
For Dumuzi, the lover of her youth.
Wash (him) with pure water, anoint him with sweet oil,
Clothe him in a red robe, let the lapis lazuli pipe play (?).
Let party-girls raise a loud lament (?)'
Then Belili tore off (?) her jewellery,
Her lap was filled with eyestones.
Belili heard the lament for her brother, she struck
thejewellery [from her body],
The eyestones with which the front of the wild cow was filled.
'You shall not rob me (forever) of my only brother!
On the day when Dumuzi comes back up, (and)
the lapis lazuli pipe and the carnelian ring come up with him.
(When) male and female mourners come up with him,
The dead shall come up and smell the smoke offering.'

Reading and Discussion Questions

1. Ishtar is a goddess of fertility; what connections is the poem making between death and sex?
2. As Ishtar enters through the gates of the underworld, she is stripped of her clothing; when she exits the underworld, she is re-clothed in those garments. Discuss how this might suggest a ritual use for the poem.
3. Ea is referred to as a king in this story; what are his kingly powers? What might he tell us about kingship in Mesopotamia?
4. What are the textual clues in the story that the by underworld we are meant to understand the land of the dead?

2.5   Hesiod's *Theogony*

Hesiod's *Theogony* (or "birth of the gods") was composed probably towards the end of the eighth or the beginning of the seventh centuries BCE. Together with Homer, Hesiod is the first Greek author whose works are preserved. The *Theogony* is a hexametric narrative poem (in the same type of verses as the *Iliad* and *Odyssey*) about the origins of the universe and the gods and the struggle among the gods to hold power. The poem revolves around the succession of three fathers and sons, Ouranos (Sky), Kronos, and Zeus, climaxing with the figure of Zeus as the young victorious god who establishes a new order in the world. In contrast, mankind appears only marginally in the story about Prometheus. The *Theogony* collects and structures information until then circulated only through oral tradition in songs and stories, thus also functioning as a catalogue of super natural beings (e.g., gods, nymphs, monsters) and their genealogies. We know very little about the author, besides the (probably) biographical details he offers in his other poem, the *Works and Days*, where he claims to lived in Boiotia (west of Attica), where his father settled after coming from Kyme in Asia Minor.

Source: translated by C. López-Ruiz; used by permission

Invocation to the Muses

(1) Let us begin to sing of the Helikonian Muses,
      who hold high and sacred Helikon;
      around a dark-violet spring, with tender feet,
      they dance, and around the altar of the very powerful son of Kronos;
(5) after washing their delicate skin in the spring of Parmessos
      or of the Horse or of sacred Olmeios,
      at the highest point of Helikon they performed choral dances,
      beautiful, lovely ones, and they rolled down with their feet.
      Starting to move from there, covered in much mist,
(10) at night they moved uttering a very beautiful voice,
      celebrating Zeus, aegis-bearing, and Lady Hera
      of Argos, who wears golden sandals,
      and the daughter of aegis-bearing Zeus, brilliant-eyed Athena,
      and Phoibos Apollo and Artemis, fond of arrows,
(15) and Poseidon, who holds the earth, the earth-shaker,
      and revered Themis and Aphrodite of vivid glance,
      and golden-crowned Hebe and fine Dione
      and Leto and Iapetos and crooked-minded Kronos
      and Dawn (Eos) and great Sun (Helios) and shining Moon (Selene)
(20) and Earth (Gaia) and great Ocean (Okeanos) and black Night (Nyx)
      and the holy family of the other ever-existing immortals.

How the Muses gave Hesiod his song

      The ones who once taught Hesiod beautiful song
      as he was tending his sheep at the foot of sacred Helikon.
      This speech the goddesses addressed to me first,
(25) the Olympian Muses, daughters of aegis-bearing Zeus:
      Rustic shepherds, base dishonor, stomachs alone,
      we know how to tell many false things that are like truths,
      and we know, whenever we want, how to sing out truths.
      So they said, the accurate-speaking daughters of mighty Zeus,
(30) and they gave me a branch of flourishing laurel for a scepter
      after plucking it, an admirable one; then they inspired in me divine
      voice, so that I could celebrate the things to come and those past,
      and they ordered me to sing hymns to the family of the happy ever-existing ones,
      but to sing to them always first and last.

Second invocation to the Muses; how the Muses are the poets of Olympus

(35) But what do I care about these things concerning a tree or a stone?
      Hey, you! Let us begin with the Muses, who singing hymns

to father Zeus cheer up his great heart inside Olympus,
recounting the present, the things to come, and those past,
coming together with their sound, and their tireless voice flows
(40)   pleasant from their mouths; and the halls of their father,
loud-sounding Zeus, rejoices at the flowery voice of the goddesses
as it spreads out, and the peak of snowy Olympus resounds,
and the house of the immortals. Sending forth their immortal voice,
first they praise in their song the venerable race of the gods
(45)   from the beginning, whom Earth and broad Sky begat,
and those who were born from them, gods providers of goods.
Then, secondly, they celebrate Zeus, father of gods and men,
as they, the goddesses, start and end their song,
how he excels among the gods and is the greatest in power.
(50)   And then, singing of the race of humans and mighty Giants,
they please the mind of Zeus inside Olympus,
the Olympian Muses, daughters of Zeus who holds the aegis.

The Muses' birth place in Olympus, and names

Mnemosyne (Memory) bore them in Pieria, sleeping
with the father, son of Kronos – she, the guard of the hills of Eleuther –
(55)   as forgetfulness of evils and relief from troubles.
For nine nights wise Zeus slept with her,
climbing up into the sacred bed, away from mortals.
But when a year had passed and the seasons turned around
as the months wasted away, and many days were completed,
(60)   she bore nine girls, all of the same mind, with a spirit
free of sorrow, in whose heart the song dwells,
– at a small distance from the highest peak of snowy Olympus.
There they have their radiant choruses and beautiful mansions,
and by them the Graces and Desire have their houses
(65)   in the midst of feasts; and they sing emitting from their mouths
a lovely voice, and they celebrate the allotments and noble customs
of all immortals, emitting their very lovely voice.
They then went to Olympus, rejoicing in their beautiful voice,
with a divine song; and around them the black earth resounded
(70)   as they sang, and a lovely sound rose from under their feet
as they returned to their father. He is king in the sky,
holding himself the thunder and kindled lightning,
after defeating by force his father Kronos. Fairly in each detail,
he distributed to the immortals their portions and declared their privileges.
(75)   These things, then, the Muses sang, they who hold Olympian mansions,
the nine daughters begotten by great Zeus:
Clio, Euterpe, Thalia, Melpomene,
Terpsichore, Erato, Polymnia, Ourania,
and Kalliope[7] – she is the principal among them all,

---

[7] Their names mean: she who glorifies (Clio), she who delights well (Euterpe), the blooming one (Thalia), she who sings (Melpomene), she who delights in dance (Terpsichore), the lovely one (Erato), she of many hymns (Polymnia), the heavenly one (Ourania), and she of the noble voice (Kalliope).

(80)   for she accompanies revered kings as well.

The Muses give kings the gift of soothing and persuasive speech

Whomever they honor, the daughters of great Zeus,
and they behold at the moment he is born among Zeus-bred kings,
they pour a sweet dew upon his tongue,
and gentle words flow from his mouth; and from that moment
(85)   all the people look up to him as he resolves disputes
with right judgment; and speaking confidently
quickly puts an end even to a great quarrel. For this is why
sensible men are kings,[8] because, when people
are being wronged in the assembly, they manage to restitute things
(90)   easily, exhorting with smooth words.
And as he goes up to the gathering, they appease him as a god,
with gentle reverence, and he stands out among the gathered ones.
Such is the sacred gift of the Muses to men.

The Muses inspire poets, who soothe the afflictions of men

For it is surely from the Muses and far-shooting Apollo
(95)   that men who sing and play the lyre are at ease upon the earth,
but kings owe it to Zeus; and fortunate is *that* man, whomever
the Muses love; the voice flows sweet from his mouth.
For if someone, even with a sorrow in his just-battered spirit,
dries up of affliction in his heart, yet when a poet,
(100) servant of the Muses, sings of the famous deeds of men of old
and of the blessed gods who hold Olympus,
right away he forgets his troubles and does not remember
his sorrows at all; for the gifts of the goddesses quickly turned them away.

Third invocation to the Muses

Rejoice, daughters of Zeus, and give me a lovely song;
(105) celebrate the holy family of the ever-existing immortals,
who were born of Earth and starry Sky,
and of dark Night, those whom salty Pontos nourished.
Tell how at first the gods and the earth came into being,
and the rivers and infinite sea, raging with waves,
(110) and the shining stars and wide sky up there,
and those who were generated from them, the gods who provide,
and how they divided their resources and how they distributed their honors,
and also how in the beginning they got hold of Olympus of many folds.
Tell me these things, Muses who have Olympian dwellings,
(115) from the beginning, and say what came first of these things.

First elements and first gods

Surely first of all Chaos (Chasm, Void) came into being, and then
Earth (Gaia) of wide bosom, the always-safe sitting place of all
the immortals who hold the peak of snowy Olympus,
and steamy Underworld (Tartaros), at the bottom of the earth of wide path

---

[8] The phrase is ambiguous, and could be understood also as "this is why kings are sensible (wise, reasonable) men," or "this is why there are sensible kings."

(120) and Love (Eros), who is the fairest among the immortal gods,
   the limb-looser, and of all the gods and men
   he dominates the mind and the thoughtful counsel in their breasts.
   From Chaos Darkness (Erebos) and black Night were generated,
   and from Night in turn Aither and Day came forth,
(125) whom she bore becoming pregnant from her intimate union with Darkness.
   Earth engendered first starry Sky (Ouranos),
   equal to herself, to cover her from all sides,
   so as to be the ever immovable seat of the blessed gods,
   and she bore the high mountains, graceful shelters of the goddesses,
(130) the Nymphs, who live on top of mountains of many glens.
   And she also bore Pontos, the barren sea, raging with swell,
   without desirable love-making.

Birth of the Titans, Cyclopes, and hundred-handed Giants

   But after that,
   lying in bed with Sky she bore Ocean of deep whirls
   andKoios and Kreios and Hyperion and Iapetos
(135) and Theia and Rhea and Themis and Mnemosyne
   and Phoebe of the golden wreath and lovely Tethys.
   And after these crooked-minded Kronos was born, the youngest,
   most terrible of the children, and he hated his vigorous begetter.
   And then she bore the Cyclopes, who have violent hearts,
(140) Thunder and Lightning and tough-hearted Brightness,
   who gave Zeus thunder and contrived the thunderbolt.
   These were really similar to the gods in every other respect
   but a single eye was set in the middle of their forehead;
   "Cyclopes" was their assigned name, because
(145) one circled-shaped eye was set in their foreheads;
   strength and violence and contrivances accompanied their actions.
   Earth and Sky engendered yet another
   three sons, great and mighty, not to be named,
   Kottos and Briareus and Gyges, pretentious children.
(150) One hundred arms sprang from their shoulders,
   indescribable, and fifty heads for each one
   grew from their shoulders upon their study limbs;
   and the mighty strength in their great form was unfathomable.

Kronos castrates Sky (Ouranos)

   And so, these were all those born from Earth and Sky,
(155) most frightful of children, and they were hated by their begetter
   from the start; and as soon as one of them was born,
   he would keep secluding them in Earth's hiding place,
   and would not let them come up, and Sky took pleasure
   in this evil deed; but she kept groaning inside, the tremendous Earth,
(160) feeling bloated, and so she thought of a deceitful, evil trick.
   At once fabricating a type of grey adamant
   she fashioned a sickle and showed it to her dear children.
   And she said, giving them courage, afflicted though she was in own heart:

"Children of mine and of a reckless father, if you would be willing

(165) to obey me, we would avenge your father's evil

outrage; for he was the first to conceive unseemly actions."

So she said, and, as it turned out, fear got hold of them all, and not one of them

made a sound. But great crooked-minded Kronos, taking courage,

addressed with responding words his noble mother:

(170) "Mother, I might be able to accomplish this task,

if I undertake it, since I do not care for our abominable

father; for he was the first to conceive unseemly actions."

So he said, and tremendous Earth rejoiced in her great chest.

She made him sit and hid him in an ambush, and placed in his hands

(175) the sharp-toothed sickle, and she presented the whole trick to him.

And great Sky came, bringing night along, and extended himself

up against and around Earth, with desire for love-making, and stretched out

in every direction; but his son reached out with his left

hand, while he grasped in his right one the tremendous sickle,

(180) long and sharp-toothed, and with vehemence

he reaped the genitals away from his own father, and threw them back

to be dispersed behind him. And these did not escape his hand in vain:

Creatures born from the Sky's severed genitals, including Aphrodite

for as many drops of blood as shot forth from them,

Earth received them all; and as the years sailed around

(185) she bore the mighty Erinyes and the great Giants,

dazzling in their armor, holding long spears in their hands,

and the Nymphs which they call Melian[9] upon the infinite earth.

As for the genitals, as soon as he had cut them off with the adamant

and had thrown them down to the agitated sea, far from dry land,

(190) the waters carried them for a long time, and around them

a white foam rose up from the immortal flesh; and inside this

grew a girl. First she approached divine Kythera,

and from there she arrived later to Cyprus, surrounded by currents.

And out came the beautiful revered goddess, and all around grass

(195) grew from under her delicate feet. Gods and men call her

Aphrodite, the "foam-born"[10] goddess, and well-garlanded

Cytherea; (Aphrodite) because she grew in the foam;

and then Cytherea, because she reached Cythera;

andCyprogenea, because she was born in Cyprus, of many waves.

(200) and also "congenial," because she appeared from genitalia.[11]

Eros (Love) accompanied her, and beautiful Desire,

from the moment she was born and went into the tribe of the gods;

and so from the start she had an honor and received as her lot

a fate among humans and immortal gods:

(205) virginal secrets, smiles and deceits,

sweet pleasure, love-making, and kindness.

---

[9] These seem to be the ash-tree Nymphs, from whom humankind was born according to some traditions (cf. *Theogony* 563, *Works and Days* 145).

[10] The pun is with the Greek word for foam, *aphros*.

[11] The pun is between *philo-meidea*, literally "lover of smiles," and *mêdea*, "genitals." We follow G. Most (Loeb edition, 2006) in his rendering her epithet as "genial" (my "congenial") to reflect a similar pun with genitals.

And their father, great Sky, started calling them Titans
as a nickname, thus insulting his sons, whom he had begotten;
and he would say that they had "attempted"[12] to perform a great deed
(210) with recklessness, and that there would be a punishment for it later on.

Night and her offspring

Night bore frightful Doom and black Fate
and Death, and bore Sleep, and brought forth the tribe of Dreams.
Second, she bore Blame and painful Lament,
– gloomy Night, without sleeping with any of the gods;
(215) and the Hesperides, who, beyond the glorious Ocean, take care
of the beautiful golden apples and the trees that bear this fruit.
And the Moirai (Destinies) and the ruthlessly avenging Fates:
Clotho, Lachesis, and Atropo, who give mortals
good and evil to have, just as they are born,
(220) and who follow closely the transgressions of men and gods,
and the goddesses do not cease of their terrible anger
until they exact a harsh punishment on whoever acts wrongly.
Deadly Night also gave birth to Nemesis (Retribution),
a pain for mortal men; and after she bore Deceit and Intimacy
(225) and wretched Old Age, and she bore stubborn-hearted Strife.
And then abominable Strife bore painful Toil
and Forgetfulness and Famine and tearful Sorrows,
and Fights and Battles and Murders and Manslaughters
and Quarrels and Lies and Stories and Polemics,
(230) and Lawlessness and Ruin, similar to each another,
and Oath, who surely troubles earthly men the most,
when someone deliberately swears a false oath.

Offspring of Pontos (Sea)

*233-269: Account of the offspring of Pontos [Sea]: Nereus, Thaumas, Phorkys and Keto. Nereus, also
called the "Old Man," is the father, with Doris, of the fifty sea nymphs called Nereids, whose names are
given here; account of the offspring of Thaumas.*

Offspring of Phorkys and Keto

(270) To PhorkysKeto bore old women of beautiful cheeks
gray-haired from their birth, the ones whom immortal
gods and men who walk on earth call Graias,
andPemphredo of the noble robe and Enyo with the saffron robe,
and the Gorgons, who live beyond famous Ocean
(275) at the limit, towards the night, where the Hesperides of acute voice are:
Sthenno and Euryale and Medusa, who suffered sorrows.
She was mortal, while the other two are immortal and age-less;
only by her side lay down the dark-haired one (Poseidon)
in the midst of a soft meadow and spring flowers.
(280) When Perseus cut her head off from her neck,
greatChrisaor and the horse Pegasos sprang forth from it.

---

[12] The word-play is between *Titênas* (Titans) and *titainontas* "attempting" (from the verb *teinô*, "stretch by force; aim at"), and resonating even with *tisin* "punishment" in line 210.

The one had this given name because he was born besides the springs (*pêgai*)
of Ocean, and the other one for holding a golden sword (*chyseonaor*) in his hands.
And the one (Pegasos) flew away, leaving behind the earth, mother of flocks,
(285) and reached the immortals; and he dwells in Zeus' house,
bringing thunder and lightning to wise Zeus.
And Chysaor bore three-headed Geryon
Mingling in love with Kallirhoe, the daughter of famous Ocean.
This one, in turn, was slain by the force of Herakles
(290) by his rolling-footed cattle in Erytheia, surrounded by currents,
on that very day, when he drove the cattle, of broad foraheads,
to sacred Tiryns, after crossing the strait of Ocean
and killing Orthos and the cowherd Eurytion
in the steamy stable beyond the famous Ocean.
(295) And she (Medusa) gave birth to another indescribably monster,
in no way similar to mortal men or immortal gods,
inside a hallow cave: Echidna, divine and strong-hearted,
half a nymph of vivacious eyes and beautiful cheeks,
but half a monstrous serpent, terrible, huge,
(300) specked, bloodthirsty, under the hidden places of the blessed earth.
Down there she has a cave, under a hallow rock,
Far from the immortal gods and from mortal men,
for that is where the gods assigned her famous mansions to live in.
And she keeps watch amidst the Arimoi, under the ground,
(305) baneful Echidna, undying nymph and unaging for all her days.
And they say that Typhon mingled in love with her,
he who is terrible, arrogant, and lawless, with the maiden of vivacious eyes;
and once impregnated she bore children of strong hearts:
First she engendered the dog Orthos to serve Geryon,
(310) and yet second she bore something indescribable, not to be mentioned,
blood-thirsty Cerberus, the bronze-sounding dog of Hades,
with fifty heads, shameless and powerful;
and still third she engendered the Hydra of Lerna,
of perverse mind, whom Hera, the goddess of white arms, raised,
(315) immensely irritated at Herakles' strength.
Even this one the son of Zeus, scion of Amphytrion, wiped out
with pitiless bronze, together with bellicose Iolaos;
Herakles did, by the counsel of Athena, leader of hosts.
But she had also given birth to Chimaera, who breathes invincible fire,
(320) terrible and huge, swift-footed and powerful.
Three were her heads: one of a lion of flashing eyes,
another of a she-goat (*chimaera*), and another of a snake, a mighty dragon.
[a lion in front, a dragon behind, and a she-goat in the middle,
snorting a terrible force of burning fire.][13]
(325) Pegasos and excellent Bellerophon took the life of this one.
But, overpowered by Orthos, she in turn had given birth to the lethal Sphinx,

---

[13] These lines probably did not belong in the original text but were added (interpolated) later, and are identical with those in *Iliad* 6.181-82.

ruin for the Kadmeians,[14] and to the lion of Nemea,
whom Hera then raised, the illustrious spouse of Zeus,
settling it in the hills of Nemea, a suffering for human beings.
(330) While living there it went about snaring the tribes of men,
and ruled over Tretos of Nemea and over Apesas;
but the vigor of the Heraklean force overpowered him.
And lastly Keto, mingling in love with Phorkys
bore a terrible serpent, which guards the all-golden apples
(335) at the great limits in the caverns of the dark earth.
This is the offspring of Ketos and Phorkys.

Descendants of the Titans (who were children of Earth and Sky)
- Offspring of Ocean, Theia, Kreios

337-382: Children of Ocean: Catalogue of rivers and spring nymphs, known as Oceanids, who protect youths; only a small portion of the thousands of rivers and Oceanids are provided, for "the name of all of them is difficult for a mortal man to pronounce, but each of those who live around one of them knows them" (369-370). Children of Theia with Hyperion: Helios (Sun), Selene (Moon) and Eos (Dawn); children of Eurybe and Kreios; children of Eos (Dawn) and Astraios: the winds (Zephyros, Boreas and Notos) and the stars.

- Styx and her offspring, her connection with Zeus

And Styx, daughter of Ocean, mingling with Pallas, gave birth in her mansions
to Rivalry (Zelos) and Victory (Nike) of beautiful ankles,
(385) and she engendered also Power (Kratos) and Force (Bia), remarkable children.
Their house is not apart from Zeus, and there is no residence
nor path but that through which Zeus leads them,
but they always sit by Zeus, the loud-thunderer.
For this is how Styx planned it, the eternal daughter of Ocean,
(390) on that day, when the Olympian lightener (Zeus)
summoned the immortal gods to high Olympus,
and said that, whoever of the gods would fight with him against the Titans,
he would not deprive him from his privileges, but each one
would keep what he had before among the immortal gods.
(395) and he added this, that whoever had been without honor and privilege under Kronos, would have honor
as well as privilege, as it is right.
So eternal Styx came first to Olympus
with her children , by the counsel of her dear father;
and Zeus honored her and gave her abundant gifts.
(400) For he established her as the great oath of the gods,
and for her children to live with him for all days.
And so he fulfilled from start to end for everyone, just as he had promised;
for he is greatly powerful and rules.

- Offspring of Phoebe and Koios

And Phoebe in turn went to the very desirable bed of Koios;
(405) and thereafter, a goddess pregnant from the love of a god,

---

[14] The descendants of Kadmos, founder of Thebes, whom the Sphinx besieged until it was defeated by Oedipus.

gave birth to Leto of the dark robe, always soothing,
kind to both humans and immortal gods,
soothing from the beginning, the nicest inside Olympus.
And she gave birth to renowned Asteria, whom Perses
(410) once led to his great house to be called his dear wife.

- Hecate and her powers

And she (Asteria) became pregnant and bore Hecate, whom Zeus, son of Kronos,
Honored above all; for he procured her magnificent gifts:
to hold a share of the earth and of the barren sea.
And she also received her share in honor from the starry sky,
(415) and she is most honored among the immortal gods.
For even now, whenever one of the terrestrial men
propitiates her performing good sacrifices according to tradition,
he invokes Hecate; and great honor follows easily
that man, whose prayers the goddess accepts with benevolence,
(420) and she also concedes him fortune, since she surely has this power.
For as many as were born from Earth and Sky
and obtained an honor, among them all she has a part,
and not even the son of Kronos violated or took away
all that she obtained among the Titans, the former gods,
(425) but she holds it, just as the partition was first made at the beginning.
Neither did she, on account of being a single child, partake less in honor
and privileges in the earth and the sky and the sea,
but rather even more, since Zeus honors her.
By whomever she wishes, she stands grandly and helps him.
(430) In the assembly, whoever she wishes excels among the people,
and when men march armed into man-killing war,
there the goddess is present, and to those she wishes
she concedes victory, in her benevolence, and offers glory.
In a trial she sits next to revered kings.
(435) She is good, besides, when men compete in an athletic match;
there the goddess also stands by their side and helps them;
and the one winning by force and strength easily carries
a handsome price and rejoices, and gives his parents glory.
And she is good at assisting horsemen, whomever she wishes.
(440) And to those who work the gray turbulent sea
and who pray to Hecate and the loud Earth-Shaker (Poseidon),
she would easily grant abundant fish, the glorious goddess,
but she easily would take it away just as it appeared, if so she fancied.
And she is good at augmenting the livestock in the stables, together with Hermes.
(445) The cattle of caws and the broad flocks of goats,
and the herds of wooly sheep, if she so wishes in her heart,
from few she multiplies them, and from many she makes them fewer.
So is she honored, despite being the only child of her mother,
with prerogatives among all the immortals.
(450) And the son of Kronos established her as nurse of children.
of all those who after her saw with their eyes the light of Dawn of many gleams.

So was she a children nurse from the start, and these were her prerogatives.

- Children of Rhea and Kronos (Olympian gods); Kronos is deposed by Zeus

Rhea, conquered by Kronos, bore illustrious children:
Hestia, Demeter, and Hera of the golden sandals,
(455) and powerful Hades, who inhabits his residence under the earth
and has a ruthless heart, and the resounding Earth-Shaker (Poseidon),
and wise Zeus, father of both gods and men,
due to whose thunder trembles the wide earth.
But great Kronos started gulping them down, as each of them reached
(460) their mother's knees coming out of her holy womb,
with the following reasoning, that no other of the brilliant descendants
of Ouranos (Sky) might hold the royal honor among the immortals.
For he had learned from Earth and starry Sky
that he was bound to be overpowered by his own child,
(465) through the plans of great Zeus, no matter how mighty he was.
And at least about this he was not neglectful, but keeping a close watch
he kept swallowing his children; and Rhea felt horrible sorrow.
But when she was about to give birth to Zeus, father of both gods and men,
at that moment she begged her own dear parents,
(470) Earth and starry Sky, to think of a plan,
so that she could go unnoticed as she gave birth
to her dear son, and also avenge the vengeful spirits of her father
and her children, whom great crooked-minded Kronos had gulped down.
And they paid much heed to their dear daughter and obeyed her,
(475) and they both related to her everything that was bound to happen
with king Kronos and his strong-hearted son.
And they sent her to Lyktos, to the rich land of Crete,
Just as she was about to give birth to the youngest of her children,
great Zeus. Tremendous Earth received him
(480) in broad Crete, to rise him and take care of him.
Carrying him through the swift black night, she arrived there,
first to Lyktos; taking him in her arms she hid him
in a deep cave, under the deep hiding places of divine earth
in the Aigaian mountain, dense in woods.
(485) And, wrapping a great stone in swaddling-clothes, she delivered it to him,
to the great lord son of Ouranos, king of the early gods;
which then he took with his hands and put down into his belly,
the wretched, without even suspecting that behind him,
in place of the stone, undefeated and untroubled, his own son remained,
(490) who soon was going to take away his privilege, conquering him
with force and his hands, and then rule among the immortals.
And quickly thereafter the strength and splendid limbs
of the lord grew; and, after a year had passed,
fooled by the loquacious suggestions of Earth,
(495) great crooked-minded Kronos brought up again his offspring,
defeated by his son's tricks and force.
But first he vomited the stone, which he had swallowed last;
this Zeus fixed on the earth of wide paths

in sacred Pytho, in the valleys under mount Parnassos,
(500) to be a memorial in the future, a wonder for mortal humans.
      And he freed his fathers' brothers[15] from their horrible bonds,
      the sons of Ouranos (Sky), whom his father had bound foolishly.
      And they repaid him in gratitude for his kind deeds,
      And gave him thunder and smoky thunderbolt
(505) and lightning, which huge Earth had concealed before.
      Relying upon these he rules over mortals and immortals.

- Children of the Iapetos
      Iapetos married Clymene, beautiful-ankled daughter
      of Ocean, and climbed up into the same bed with her.
      And she bore him Atlas, a child of strong spirit,
(510) and gave birth to the very famous Menoitios and to Prometheus ("Forethought"),
      versatile, of sharp mind, and to clumsy Epimetheus ("Afterthought"),
      who became a disgrace from the beginning for men who survive on bread.
      For he was the first to accept a woman designed by Zeus,
      a maiden. Far-sounding Zeus threw arrogant Menoitios
(515) down into the dark, smiting him with burning thunderbolt
      on account of his recklessness and his excessive prowess.
      Atlas, in turn, holds the broad sky by hard obligation,
      at the limits of the earth in front of the acute-sounding Hesperides,
      making it stand with his head and his tireless arms.
(520) For this is the portion that wise Zeus gave him.
      And he bound Prometheus with painful fetters, the resourceful plotter,
      with hard bonds which he dragged through the middle of a pillar.
      And he set on him a long-winged eagle: she would eat his immortal
      liver, but it would grow the same all through the night,
(525) as much as the long-winged bird had eaten the whole day.
      This one Herakles killed, the mighty son of Aklmene
      of beautiful ankles, who defended the son of Iapetos
      from the evil plague and liberated him from his afflictions;
      not without the consent of Olympian Zeus, who rules on high,
(530) so that the fame of Theban-born Herakles would be
      even greater than before on the fertile earth.
      So in respect for this, he honored his celebrated son.
      Angry though he was, he ceased the rage he used to have before,
      as Prometheus would challenge the counsels of the powerful son of Kronos.
- Prometheus' tricks
(535) For when the gods and mortal men were splitting up at Mekone,
      then he (Prometheus) presented a great ox, after dividing it
      with great anticipation, trying to trick Zeus' mind.
      For first he set down for him the meat and the entrails,
      rich in fat, placed inside skin, hiding them in the ox' stomach.
(540) And then, in turn, he set down for him the white bones of the ox,
      in a deceitful trick, well arranged, hiding them in gleaming fat.

---

[15] Referring to the Cyclopes.

And surely then the father of men and gods addressed him:
"Son of lapetos, eminent among all lords,
oh pal, how unfairly have you divided up the portions."
(545) So he said teasing him, Zeus who knows eternal plans,
To which in turn responded crooked-minded Prometheus,
with a half smile, for he had not forgotten the deceitful trick:
"Zeus, most glorious, greatest among the eternal-born gods,
among these choose whichever your heart inside your chest bids you."
(550) So he said as he plotted deception; but Zeus, who knows eternal plans,
realized it and did not fail to recognize the deceit. And he was contemplating
in his spirit evils for mortal men, ones that he surely was going to accomplish.
And finally with both hands he lifted the white fat,
and became furious in his chest, and rage reached his spirit,
(555) when he saw the white bones of the ox, as part of the deceitful trick.
And since this moment the tribes of men upon the earth
burn white bones for the immortals on top of smoky altars.
And cloud-gatherer Zeus addressed him, greatly enraged:
"Son of lapetos, who knows counsels better than anyone,
(560) oh pal, it seems you did not forget your deceitful tricks yet."
So said in anger Zeus who knows eternal plans.
And from then onwards, always mindful of his rage,
he did not give the Meliai[16] the force of relentless fire
for mortal men who dwell upon the earth.
(565) But the noble son of lapetos fooled him completely
by hiding the far-seen flame of relentless fire
in a big empty cane; this in turn bit deeply the spirit
of high-thundering Zeus, and he was furious in his heart,
when he saw among men the far-seen flame of fire.
- Creation of the first woman
(570) But at once he prepared an evil for humans, in exchange for the fire;
For the very renowned Lame one (Hephaistos) fashioned from earth
the likeness of a maiden, by the plans of the son of Kronos;
and the goddess of bright eyes, Athena, girded her and adorned her,
with a silvery dress; and with her own hands she hung down
(575) from her head an embroidered veil, a marvel to see.
And around her temples Pallas Athena placed lovely
flourishing garlands, flowers from the meadow.
And around her head she placed a golden headband,
one that the very renowned Lame one had made
(580) with his own hands, to please the father Zeus.
In it he had fashioned many designs, a marvel to see,
all the terrible beasts that the main-land and the sea nourish;
many of these he put in it, and beauty breathed upon them all,
marvelous, looking like living creatures with voice.
(585) But once he made a beautiful evil thing to pay for the good one,[17]
he took her where the other gods and humans were,

---

[16] This refers to the Ash-Tree Nymphs.
[17] That is, to pay for the stolen fire.

embellished with the adornment of the bright-eyed one, fathered by a mighty one;[18]
and wonder possessed both immortal gods and mortal men,
when they saw the thorny deception, irresistible for men.
(590) For the race of female women springs from this one,
[for from her is the destructive race and tribe of women,][19]
a great pain for mortals, dwelling together with men,
no companions in destructive Poverty but only in Wealth.
Just as when the bees inside vaulted beehives
(595) maintain the drones, who only partake in base deeds,
and while the ones strive all day until the sun goes down,
every day, and set up the white honey-combs,
the others, remaining inside, sheltered by the hives,
reap the labor of others into their own stomachs;
(600) Just in such way high-thundering Zeus set up women
as an evil for mortal men, partakers in troublesome actions.
But another disgrace he provided in exchange for the good:
whoever does not want to marry, escaping marriage
and the mischievous works of women, arrives at deadly old age
(605) without an attendant; and he who did not lack sustenance
while he was alive, now that he is dead his relatives share out
his livelihood. But the one in whose destiny is marriage,
and acquires a decent wife, suited with intelligence,
for this one, with the passing of time, the evil is balanced out with the good,
(610) in a stead-fast manner; and yet he who obtains shameless progeny
lives with constant anguish in his mind,
in his spirit, and in his heart, also an evil that has no relief.
Thus it is not possible to cheat or elude the mind of Zeus.
For not even son of Iapetos, Prometheus, the savior,
(615) escaped his heavy anger, but by necessity,
astute though he was, a great chain held him down.

Zeus' war with the Titans (Titanomachy)

When their father[20] first became irritated with Obriareus,
and with Kottos and Gyges,[21] he bound them with strong bonds,
envious of their excessive prowess and also of their appearance
(620) and their size; he made them dwell under the broad-pathed earth.
There they were, withstanding pain, inhabiting under the earth
at the edge, at the limits of great earth, suffering
much and for long, holding great grief in their heart.
But the son of Kronos, together with the other immortal gods
(625) whom beautiful-haired Rhea bore in love with Kronos,
brought them up to the light again, following the advice of Gaia.
For she had explained to them everything in detail,
that it was with these that they would attain victory and splendid boast.
For they had been fighting for long, enduring distressful pain,

---

[18] Athena.
[19] This (or the previous) line probably does not belong in the text.
[20] Sky.
[21] These are the Hundred-Handers, cf. 147 ff.

(630) the Titan gods and all those who were born from Kronos,
        confronting one another in mighty clashes;
        some, the illustrious Titans, from high Othrys,
        and the others from Olympus, the gods who give boons,
        whom beautiful-haired Rhea bore sleeping with Kronos.
(635) By then, they had been fighting for ten full years,
        constantly enduring distressful battle against each other.
        Neither was there a solution for their difficult strife nor
        an end for either side, but the outcome of the war had been strained even.
        However, when he offered them[22] supplies,
(640) nectar and ambrosia, which the gods themselves eat,
        and the vigorous spirit had been restored the chests of them all,
        [as they received the nectar and desirable ambrosia]
        then the father of men and gods addressed them:
        "Listen to me, splendid sons of Earth and Sky,
(645) so I can say what my spirit in my chest tells me to.
        For a very long time already we have been fighting
        against each other, over victory and power, every day,
        the Titan gods and all of us descended from Kronos.
        But now show me your great strength and your invincible arms
(650) in deadly combat against the Titans, remembering
        our kind friendship, and how you reached again the light
        after suffering so many things under an insufferable bond,
        thanks to our counsel, from under a murky fog.
        So he said, and in turn blameless Kottos responded to him at once:
(655) "Sir, it is not an ignored thing that you are talking about, but we also
        know that you excel in thoughts and excel in intelligence,
        and that you emerged as the defender of the immortals against cold ruin.
        And through your careful plans that we were released
        back again from under a murky fog, from under unpleasant bonds,
(660) oh son of the lord Kronos, after suffering hopeless pains.
        So also now, with determined mind and well-disposed spirit
        we will defend your power in dreadful battle,
        storming the Titans in mighty clashes.
        "so he said; and the gods, givers of boons, approved
(665) after hearing their speech; for their spirit was craving war
        even more than before; and they provoked undesirable war,
        all of them, female and make alike, on that very day,
        the Titan gods and all those descendant from Kronos,
        and those whom Zeus brought to the light from the darkness under the earth,
(670) terrible and powerful, who possessed a superb strength.
        One hundred arms sprang from their shoulders,
        equal for all of them, and fifty heads for each one
        grew from their shoulders upon their sturdy limbs.
        Then they took position against the Titans in miserable combat,
(675) holding enormous rocks in their sturdy hands.
        And the Titans reinforced their ranks with determination;

---

[22] Zeus to Obriareus, Kottos and Gyges.

and both sides showed the work of their arms and their force,
and the boundless sea resounded terribly,
and the earth roared greatly, and the broad sky moaned
(680) as it trembled, and high Olympus shook from the ground
under the rush of the immortals, and the deep quake reached
from their feet to steamy Tartaros, and the loud sound
of the unspeakable clashes and of the powerful blows.
In such way they shot resounding missiles at each other.
(685) And the voice of both sides reached the starry sky
as they called on each other; for they clashed in a loud war-cry.
But Zeus could not contain his strength anymore; instead, his heart
filled with strength at once and showed his full force;
and he advanced at the same time from the sky and from Olympus
(690) continuously shooting lightning, and the thunderbolts
flew packed together out of his sturdy hand,
with thunder and lightning, whirling about a sacred and
intense flame. And all around the life-giving earth roared
as it burned, and all around the immense woods crackled loudly.
(695) The whole earth boiled, and the streams of Ocean
and the barren sea; and a hot breath surrounded
the earthly Titans, and an unspeakable flame reached
the divine aether, and the luminescent shine of the thunder bolt
and lightning blinded their eyes, powerful though they were,
(700) and an astonishing heat invaded the chasm, and to look
directly at it with your eyes and to hear its sound with your ears
seemed just like when earth and broad sky from above
approached;[23] for this kind of great roar would arise from below
as she was crushed down and he rushed down from above.
(705) Such noise produced the gods as they merged in strife.
At the same time, the winds spread the commotion and the dust
and the thunder and the lightning and the lazing thunderbolt,
the shafts of great Zeus, and brought the cry and the screaming
to the middle of both sides. An unspeakable din of deadly strife
(710) rose, and it became clear where the dominating action was.
The battle declined; for before, charging against each other
they had fought incessantly in mighty combats.
But then Kottos, Briareus, and Gyges, insatiable of war,
were among the first ones to provoke a violent battle;
(715) then they threw three hundred stones from their sturdy
arms, one after the other, and they covered the Titans
with their darts. Indeed they sent them under
the earth of wide paths and they bound them with hard bonds,
after defeating them with their hands, high-spirited though they were,
(720) so far below the earth as the sky is from the earth.

Description of the Underworld (Tartaros) and Styx

For such is the distance to the steamy underworld (Tartaros) from the earth:

---

[23] Probably referring when they mated in primordial times.

for a bronze anvil, falling from the sky for nine nights
and days, would reach the earth on the tenth;
(723a)   [so in turn is the distance from the earth to the steamy underworld;]
so in turn a bronze anvil, falling from the earth for nine nights
(725) and days, would reach the underworld on the tenth.
Around it a bronze fence stretches out, and on both sides of it
a three-layered night wraps it around its neck; what is more,
above it grow the roots of the earth and the barren sea.
There is where the Titans are hidden, under a dark
(730) fog, by the designs of Zeus the cloud-gatherer,
in a dank region, at the limits of the tremendous earth.
And they have no way out, for Poseidon installed bronze
gates, and a wall extends from both sides.
[734-745: probably interpolated lines, which add no significant information from what comes before and after]
(746) In front of these the son of Iapetos[24] holds the wide sky,
making it stand on his head and his tireless arms,
immovable, just where Night and Day passing very close
exchange greetings as they pass through the great
(750) bronze threshold; the one is going to step inside, and the other
is going out the doors, and never does the house hold them both inside,
but always one of them, going out of the house
turns over the earth, while the other, going inside the house,
awaits the time of her trip, until it arrives;
(755) The one holds for those on earth much-seeing light,
while the other holds Sleep (Hypnos) in her arms, brother of Death (Thanatos),
lethal Night, totally covered in murky fog.
And inside the children of Night have their homes,
Sleep and Death, terrible gods. Never does
(760) the bright Sun look upon them with his rays
when he goes up to the sky or down from the sky.
While one of them goes around gently over the earth
and the broad back of the sea, and is soothing for men,
the other has an iron core, a bronze heart
(765) in his ruthless chest: he keeps whomever among mortals
he gets hold of, and he is hateful even for the immortal gods.
There stand, in front, the resounding houses of the earthly god,
[powerful Hades and awesome Persephone,]
and a fearful god guards them in the front,
(770) ruthless, and he has an evil trick: upon those going in,
he fawns in the same way with his tail and with both ears,
but he does not let them go out again; instead he is vigilant
and bites whomever he catches going outside the gates
[of Powerful Hades and awesome Persephone].
(775) There dwells a goddess hateful to the immortals,
terrible Styx,[25] the oldest daughter of Ocean, of circular flow.

---

[24] Atlas.
[25] Hesiod makes a pun between the name Styx and the adjective *stygeros* "hateful, abominable" (as if we had used "stigmatized," for instance).

Far from the gods, she dwells in a famous mansion
vaulted with tall rocks; and from all sides around
it leans on silver columns, approaching the sky.
(780) And rarely swift-footed Iris, the daughter of Thaumas (Wonder),
travels there with a message over the broad back of the sea.
Whenever strife and quarrel arises among the immortals
and then one of those who have Olympian mansions lies,
Zeus would send Iris to bring a great oath
(785) from afar, the renowned water in a golden receptacle,
cold, which flows from the high steep rock;
and under the broad-pathed earth it flows abundant
from the sacred river through the dark night.
A branch of Ocean, a tenth part, she had been apportioned.
(790) Nine times around the earth and the broad back of the sea,
spinning in silver whirls he falls into the sea,
and she, as one of them, flows forth from the rock, a great pain for the gods:
Whoever among the immortals who hold the summit
of snowy Olympus swears a false oath as he pours it,
(795) lies without breath for the duration of a full year,
and he cannot go near the nourishment of ambrosia
and nectar, but lies down without air and without voice
in a covered bed, and an evil deep sleep covers him.
And yet, when he has completed this malady at the end of the year,
(800) a new trial replaces the other, a more difficult one:
for nine years he stays apart from the gods, who live forever,
and he never partakes in their council or in their banquets,
for all of nine years; but on the tenth he participates again
in the assemblies of the gods, who hold Olympian mansions.
(805) As such an oath the gods established the imperishable water of Styx,
the one of old, which flows forth through a coarse region.
That is where the sources and the ends of the dark earth
and the steamy underworld and the barren sea
and the starry sky all lay in succession,
(810) disturbing, dank, which even the gods hate.
And that is where the marble gates and the bronze threshold are,
unshakable, well fitted with unending roots,
self-generated; and beyond, apart from all the gods,
live the Titans, at the other side of the gloomy chasm.
(815) But the famous helpers of loud-crashing Zeus
inhabit houses in the foundations of the Ocean,
Kottos and Gyges; as for Briareos, since he was noble,
the deep-sounding Earth-shaker made him his son-in-law,
and he gave him to marry Kymopoleia (Wave-walker), his daughter.

War with Typhon (Typhonomachia)

(820) Yet after Zeus had driven the Titans away from the sky
tremendous Gaia bore her youngest child, Typhoeus,
in love with Tartaros, thanks to golden Aphrodite.

His hands are of the kind that attain deeds by strength,[26]
and his feet tireless, of this powerful god; and off his shoulders
(825) he has one hundred heads of a snake, a terrible serpent,
licking with dark tongues; and on these awful heads
two eyes glittered under his eyebrows like fire;
and from each of his heads fire burned as he stared;
and the voices in all of the terrible heads uttered
(830) an indescribable sound of different kinds: for some times
they would sound as if for the gods to understand,[27]
but other times the sound of a proud, loud-bellowing bull, wild
in his strength, and yet other times that of a lion who has pitiless spirit,
and another in turn one similar to cubs, a marvel to hear,
(835) and another in turn he whistled, and the high mountains echoed from below.
And an incredible deed would have been accomplished on that day,
and he would have ruled over mortals and immortals,
if at that point the father of men and gods had not acutely realized it.
He thundered hardly and loudly, and all around the earth
(840) resounded in a terrifying way, and also the wide sky above
and the sea and the streams of Ocean, and the underworld of the earth.
And Olympus shook greatly under the immortal feet
as the lord launched himself forward, and the earth groaned in response.
And a fire took hold of the dark-blue sea under both
(845) the thunder and lightening and the fire from such a monstrosity
of hurricanes and winds and flaming thunderbolt.
The whole earth boiled, and also the sky and the sea;
and then tall waves swelled on both sides of the coast, around and about,
under the impetus of the gods, and a ceaseless commotion arose.
(850) Hades trembled, he who rules over the deceased under the earth,
and so did the underworld Titans, who live around Kronos,
because of the ceaseless din and the terrifying fight.
But when Zeus indeed gathered his strength and took his weapons,
thunder, lightning and flaming thunderbolt,
(855) he struck him jumping from Olympus; and so he wrapped in flames
all the awful heads of the terrible monster.
And when he had overpowered, slashing him with blows,
he collapsed with lame limbs, and tremendous earth groaned.
A flame then emerged from the thundering lord
(860) in the creeks of the rugged dark mountain,
as it was hit, and the tremendous earth was much burned
by the awful smoke, and it melted like tin
heated with skill by vigorous men in well-perforated
melting pots, or like iron, which, even being the hardest,
(865) overpowered by scolding fire in mountainous creeks,
melts down on the divine earth by the works of Hephaistos.
So now melted the earth with the spark of flaming fire.
Then, aggravated in his spirit, Zeus hurled him into the broad underworld.

---

[26] The Greek text of this line is corrupt and the meaning not clear, so any translation is a mere guess.
[27] That is, like human speech.

It is from Typhoeus that the humid force of blowing winds comes,
(870) except that of Notus and Boreas and clearing Zephiros;
for these are from the gods by lineage, a great benefit for mortals.
but the other breezes blow randomly over the sea;
these are the ones that, falling onto the murky sea,
as a great sorrow for mortals, rush in an dangerous hurricane;
(875) and they all blow from here and there, scatter ships
and destroy sailors; and there is no escape from the disaster
for men who stumble upon them in the sea.
And these, in turn, also upon the boundless, flower-bearing earth destroy
the cherished works of dirt-born men,
(880) filling them with dust and troubling confusion.

Zeus secures his power

Next, after the blessed gods had completed their toil
and by force had assigned the prerogatives for the Titans,
then surely they encouraged Zeus, the far-sounding Olympian,
by the advice of Earth, to be king and rule over the gods;
(885) And he made a fair distribution of prerogatives for them.
Zeus marries Metis and gives birth to Athena
Then Zeus, as king of the gods, took for as first wife Metis (Wisdom),
who knows the most among both gods and mortal men.
But just when she was about to give birth to the bright-eyed goddess Athena,
he completely tricked her mind with deceit
(890) and with wily words and then he gulped her down into his belly,
by the advice of Earth and starry Sky:
for they had so advised him, lest another of the eternal-born gods
hold the royal honor instead of Zeus.
For it was decreed that children of superior mind would be born from her:
(895) first the bright-eyed girl, Tritogeneia,[28]
possessing strength equal to her father and intelligent counsel,
but after she was going to give birth to a son, a king
of gods and men, who would have an arrogant heart.
But before that Zeus gulped her down into his belly,
(900) and so the goddess would advise him on both good and evil.
(901-924 is a list of the wives that Zeus takes after Metis and the children they bore to Zeus. These wives are Themis, Eurynome, Demeter, Mnemosyne, Leto, and Hera.)
But he himself, from his head, gave birth to bright-eyed Athena,
(925) the terrible mistress, bellicose, army-leader, invincible,
for whom din and wars and battles are pleasing.
But Hera was both furious and aggravated with her husband,
and without mingling in love, gave birth to famous Hephaistos,
who excels among all in Olympus with his skills

Reading and Discussion Questions

1. How do the divinities presented in the *Theogony* think and act exactly like humans? How are they set apart from humans?

---
[28] Athena.

2. How do the gods and other divinities in the *Theogony* offer the Greeks a satisfactory way of explaining and ordering the complexity of human experience?
3. What are the similarities and differences between the *Theogony* and the Egyptian and Mesopotamian creation myths included in this chapter?

2.6   Cuneiform Tablet from Mesopotamia, ca. 2000 BCE

The earliest evidence of writing is from Mesopotamia and dates to about 5000 years ago, when clay tablets were first inscribed with wedge-shaped styluses to record financial transactions, such as bills of sale, disbursement of wages, receipts for purchases of metals, such as silver, or agricultural products such as barley, wool, or in the example shown below, she-goats and lambs. The clay tablet measures 5 centimeters wide and a little over 9 centimeters high.

Reading and Discussion Questions
1. Why would the earliest written records produced by humans be concerned with business dealings and not philosophy or poetry?
2. Thousands of similar clay tablets have been excavated throughout Mesopotamia and beyond. What evidence do they provide of the extent of regional trade networks in this period?

Source: Library of Congress

Chapter 3 Shifting Agrarian Centers in India

3000 B.C.E. – 600 B.C.E.

Indian history begins with a question. How is that a civilization that spanned a larger area than Pharaonic Egypt, was highly advanced technologically, was culturally and materially wealthy, and had large urban centers, so completely forgotten? Such is the question posed by the first urbanized culture of India, the Indus Valley, or Harappa, Civilization. First noted by the British army in the 1820s, and first excavated in 1856 by General Alexander Cunningham of the British Archaeological Survey of India, the city of Harappa revealed a truly lost civilization. Long abandoned (as early as 1500 B.C.E.), what had once been a thriving culture had been reduced to mounds of bricks that were used to construct the modern city and to line a railway bed. The Indus Valley culture is a sobering reminder of the possible fate of once successful urban societies, although the cause of its demise is still a matter of debate.

Another source of debate amongst historians is how the next period of Indian history came to be: did the Aryan peoples of the *Vedas* invade India as part of a larger migration of Indo-European speaking peoples, or did the culture evolve out of indigenous cultural traditions? Perhaps the Aryans are the result of a co-mingling of the foreign and the native. Wherever they originated from, once in India the Aryans created a rich culture of highly evolved religious beliefs and an elaborate mythology. The *Rig Veda*, and its three companion *Vedas*, are the oldest pieces of Indo-European literature, and are the starting point for some of the most extraordinary systems of religious thought (Buddhism, Jainism, and Hinduism). Although the Harappa culture may have had a lingering influence on later Indian culture, it is with the *Rig Veda* that India begins. The *Rig Veda* describes the creation of the world, the order of the universe, the gods that maintain that order, and begin to hint at the variety of solutions India's religious and philosophical traditions will offer.

The influence of the *Vedas*, and the society they created, is illustrated in the remaining texts of this chapter. Each text was chosen to illustrate an aspect of life governed by Vedic principles, or which continues the search for understanding first begun in the *Vedas*. The *Code of Manu* is a law code written approximately one thousand years after the *Vedas* were first written down, and reflects centuries of evolving thoughts on the Vedic principles of order, known as *dharma*. *Dharma* dictates how one should act according to one's *varna*, to one's social and spiritual status. The *Code of Manu* first establishes how the *varna* system originated, and then proscribes appropriate behavior accordingly. Finally, the *Bhagavad-gita* shows that *dharma* is sometimes poignant, and hints at one of the major dilemmas that will have to be dealt with by later Indian religious systems: reincarnation.

3.1 The Mystery of the Harappan Seals

Few things are more tantalizing to historians than an undeciphered script. Hundreds of broken and intact Harappan seals have been discovered in numerous sites throughout the Indus Valley, many that combine a line of symbols assumed to be text with an image of an animal. Denoting them seals, historians have determined that most were used to identify someone involved with an object (owner, craftsmen, or merchant). It is also possible that the seals, and other examples of the Indus script, were protective in nature, operating as a talisman. However, without the ability to read the symbols, how the seals and other objects with writing were used to convey information is a matter of speculation. It is hard to understand how a text is used if one cannot read the content. In the excerpt below, historian Thomas Trautmann, a leading specialist on ancient India, provides an overview of the mysterious Harappan seals.

Source: *India: Brief History of a Civilization.* Thomas R. Trautmann. New York: Oxford University Press, 2011, pp. 22-27

The most intriguing artifacts of the Indus sites are rectangular **steatite** seals, because of the writing on them. These seals, little more than an inch square, generally bear an incised image, beautifully carved, of which the humped bull is a common type (see Figure 3-1); other animals (tiger, elephant), composite mythological beasts, and the rare human form are figured on other seals. They also bear a short inscription across the top, in a script that has defied many attempts to decipher it (see Figure 3-2). This script contains more than four hundred signs, too many to be purely alphabetic or syllabic because no language is known to have more than a hundred phonemes. Although many of the signs are obviously pictographic, other elements act as modifiers, perhaps as word endings, andothers are clearly numerals. The seals were meant to be pressed into soft clay as a mark of ownership, in all likelihood. The inscriptions are short, presumably recording little more than the owner's name. The language of the script is unknown; a Dravidian language would be our best guess because of islands of Dravidian language in the Indus and Ganga valleys, but other languages cannot be ruled out. We do not have a bilingual inscription, like the Rosetta Stone by which the Egyptian hieroglyphics were deciphered, or the Greek and Prakrit inscriptions on coins by which the inscriptions of Ashoka were read. However, because the Indus people were involved with seagoing trade with other literate people, especially the Elamites and perhaps the Mesopotamians, there is a chance that a bilingual inscription will be found one day. It is clear that the Indus people were literate, and that their script became of Ashoka have not convinced the community of scholars.

Figure 3–1

Figure 3–2

---

steatite: a type of metamorphic rock

Religion

Our inability to read the Indus inscriptions has hampered the analysis of Indus religion. There is a strong temptation to interpret the material finds of the Indus Civilization by means of the known content of historic Hinduism, on the assumption that some elements of the Indus culture must have continued and shaped that of historic India, but we need to be cautious. Certain Indus objects lend themselves to the idea that the religion of their makers might be ancestral to certain specific features of historic Hinduism. Three groups of such objects are of interest to this hypothesis.

First there are a number of cheaply made terracotta figurines of women heavily ornamented with necklaces, earrings, and fan-shaped headdresses. It is natural to think that these are votive figures, mass produced for popular worship, and that their function is to promote the fertility of crops, livestock, and humans. Mother goddess figurines are commonplace all across Neolithic Western Asia, and even prehistoric Europe. It is reasonable to hypothesize that the Indus figurines depict the local version of this cult, and that this is the prototype of the Great Goddess of Hinduism, the wife of Shiva. On the other hand it is entirely possible that these images are not objects of worship but toys for children.

Second, there are the seals with their **theriomorphic, anthropomorphic,** and composite images, which might well represent divinities because of their nonnaturalform. On one of the seals we find a man with a horned headdress, perhaps three-faced, seated with the soles of his feet touching, hands on knees, surrounded by two gazelles, a buffalo, a rhinoceros, an elephant, and a tiger. John Marshall, who first expounded the theory of Indus survivals in Hinduism, called this figure "Proto-Shiva." The Shiva of later Hinduism is indeed called "Lord of Beasts," which seems appropriate to the figure on the seal, surrounded as he is by various animals (see Figure 3-3). The posture of the figure, which cannot be imitated without considerable practice and much muscular discomfort, suggests the postures of *yoga* and another of Shiva's epithets, "Lord of Yogis"….

Indus religion appears to have had images of divinities (the existence of temples is not proven), embracing a pantheon partly animal and partly human in form. The case for seeing here an early form of the "Shiva complex"—*yoga*, Shiva Lord of Beasts, his spouse the Great Goddess, and emphasis on the functions and organs of generation and fertility—can be regarded as a reasonable hypothesis to be tested by further research.

Figure 3–3

---

theriomorphic: having the form of a beast
anthromorphic: having the form of a human

Reading and Discussion Questions

1. The author suggests that the seals were used to identify either the owner or the merchant of trade goods. What does this say about the economy of Harappa?
2. The scarcity of metal seals, and the dominance of clay seals, suggests something of how they were used. Discuss the possible implications of relying on cheaper, easier to manufacture seals rather than using more expensive metals.
3. Why does Trautmann caution that we should not be tempted "to interpret the material finds of the Indus Civilization by means of the known content of historic Hinduism"?

3.2   The Code of Manu

The *Manu Smriti,* or *Code of Manu,* dates from c. 200 B.C.E. to 200 C.E., and is the most famous of the *smriti,* or law codes, based on the *Vedas,* which had reached their final form about a thousand years before this text. The *Manu Smriti* is important not only for the specific laws that follow this speculative introduction, but also for what it reveals about interpretation and implementation of the Vedic texts evolved in India over time. Tradition attributes the *Manu Smriti* (which contains laws but it much more than just a law code) to Brahman, the ultimate creative principle of the universe. The excerpt presented below is from the beginning of the *Manu Smriti,* and describes Manu's creation, and retells a creation story

Source: from *Laws of Manu: Translated with Extracts from Seven Commentaries,* G. Bühler, ed. (Oxford: Oxford University Press, 1886), pp. 2-3

But in the beginning he assigned their several names, actions, and conditions (created beings), even according to the words of the Veda.

He, the Lord, also created the class of the gods, who are endowed with life, and whose nature is action; and the subtle class of the Sadhyas, and the eternal sacrifice.

But from fire, wind, and the sun he drew forth the threefold eternal Veda, called Rik, Yaius, and Saman, for the due performance of the sacrifice.

Time and the divisions of time, the lunar mansions and the planets, the rivers, the oceans, the mountains, plains, and uneven ground,

Austerity, speech, pleasure, desire, and anger, this whole creation he likewise produced, as he desired to call these beings into existence... .

Whatever he assigned to each at the (first) creation, noxiousness or harmlessness, gentleness or ferocity, virtue or sin, truth or falsehood, that clung (afterwards) spontaneously to it.

As at the change of the seasons each season of its own accord assumes its distinctive marks, even so corporeal beings (resume in new births) their (appointed) course of action.

But for the sake of the prosperity of the worlds, he created the Brahman, the Kshatriya, the Vaishya, and the Shudra to proceed from his mouth, his arms, his thighs, and his feet....

To Brahmans he assigned teaching and studying (the Veda), sacrificing for their own benefit and for others, giving and accepting (of alms).

The Kshatriya he commanded to protect the people, to bestow gifts, to offer sacrifices, to study (the Veda), and to abstain from attaching himself to sensual pleasures....

The Vaishya to tend cattle, to bestow gifts, to offer sacrifices, to study (the Veda), to trade, to lend money, and to cultivate land.

One occupation only the lord prescribed to the Shudra, to serve meekly even these (other) three castes.

Reading and Discussion Questions

1. One of the features of the acts of creation as described here is the tension between the parts and the whole: each act of creation involves taking a singularity and dividing it into lesser singularities. Discuss what this might mean for the relationship between humanity and the divine.
2. Hierarchies are key element of this creation story; in what order are things created? What is the significance of that order?
3. What does this text reveal about how the *Vedas* were used in Indian society?

3.3   Hymn to Creation from *The Rig Veda*

The *Rig Veda* is the oldest of the Vedic texts, and consists of 1028 hymns. It was transmitted orally for centuries, and probably assumed its present shape c. 1200 B.C.E. There are three other *Vedas*, two of which contain material from the *Rig Veda*, thus making the *RigVeda* the foundational text for the entire Vedic tradition and its successors, including Buddhism, Jainism, and Hinduism. Most of the hymns in the *Rig Veda* relate to the rituals of the Aryan religion, although a few explore more theoretical questions "Purusha" can be translated as "cosmic giant".

Source: *Sources of Indian Tradition.* Theodore de Bary, ed. (New York: Columbia University Press, 1958).

Hymn to Creation

Thousand-headed Purusha, thousand-eyed, thousand-footed he, having pervaded the earth on all sides, still extends ten fingers beyond it.

Purusha alone is all this-whatever has been and whatever is going to be. Further, he is the lord of immortality and also of what grows on account of food.

Such is his greatness; greater, indeed, than this is Purusha. All creatures constitute but one quarter of him, his three-quarters are the immortal in the heaven.

With his three-quarters did Purusha rise up; one quarter of him again remains here. With it did he variously spread out on all sides over what eats and what eats not.

From him was Viraj born, from Viraj evolved Purusha. He, being born, projected himself behind the earth as also before it.

When the gods performed the sacrifice with Purusha as the oblation [an offering made to a deity], then the spring was its clarified butter, the summer the sacrificial fuel, and the autumn the oblation.

The sacrificial victim, namely, Purusha, born at the very beginning, they sprinkled with sacred water upon the sacrificial grass. With him as oblation the gods performed the sacrifice, and also the Sadhyas [a class of semidivine beings] and the rishis [ancient seers].

From that wholly offered sacrificial oblation were born the verses and the sacred chants; from it were born the meters; the sacrificial formula was born from it.

From it horses were born and also those animals who have double rows [i.e., upper and lower] of teeth; cows were born from it, from it were born goats and sheep.

When they divided Purusha, in how many different portions did they arrange him? What became of his mouth, what of his two arms? What were his two thighs and his two feet called?

His mouth became the brahman; his two arms were made into the rajanya; his two thighs the vaishyas; from his two feet the shudra was born.

The moon was born from the mind, from the eye the sun was born; from the mouth Indra and Agni, from the breath the wind was born.

From the navel was the atmosphere created, from the head the heaven issued forth; from the two feet was born the earth and the quarters [the cardinal directions] from the ear. Thus did they fashion the worlds.

Seven were the enclosing sticks in this sacrifice, thrice seven were the fire-sticks made, when the gods, performing the sacrifice, bound down Purusha, the sacrificial victim.

With this sacrificial oblation did the gods offer the sacrifice. These were the first norms [dharma] of sacrifice. These greatnesses reached to the sky wherein live the ancient Sadhyas and gods.

Reading and Discussion Questions

1. Why are there so many paired concepts in the "Hymn of Creation," such as "non-existence nor existence," "death and immortality," etc. What is the *Veda* trying to say about existence in terms of pairings?
2. Why is sacrifice necessary for the creation of humanity, the gods, and the order of things?
3. Hymns are generally defined as songs of praise; in what ways to these texts "praise" and what is being praised?
4. Can the foundations of the caste system be gleaned from this passage? If so, how?

Chapter 4 Agrarian Patterns and the Mandate of Heaven in Ancient China

5000 – 481 BCE

China has had one of the most continuous cultures in world history. The first Neolithic villages developed along the Yellow River c. 10,000 B.C.E. and established a prototype of customs that continues to this day. To this prototype have been added further characteristics now considered typical of Chinese culture, such as reverence for ancestors, a writing system, and eventually Confucianism. Chinese historians have divided their own history into a series of dynasties, each one conferring onto that Neolithic prototype its own distinctive touches that once added, remain a permanent part of the culture. The Pan Gu myth, a creation story, may seem far removed from where China ends up, yet in the Pan Gu story one can see glimpses of the overall pattern of development for China: villages emerge along the "yellow earth" fed by the river the Chinese call the River of Sorrows, and like Pan Gu, China just kept growing until it reached its full imperial size.

Chinese writing began at least in the Shang period; some historians believe that symbols on Neolithic pottery represent a precursor to the actual writing system, but the Shang samples are the earliest known pieces of a systematic approach to a written language. The Shang pieces are the famous "Oracle Bones." These were animal bones (usually the scapula of oxen or a tortoise shell) on which divinatory questions were asked; the bones were heated using a hot poker to produce cracks that were interpreted as the answer. In addition to the physical evidence of writing, these bones are a invaluable resource on Shang culture and ritual practice. A few examples are included in this chapter.

Most of the oracle bones contain questions from the upper classes of Shang society, as one had to have status and wealth in order to have access to the priestly class capable of writing and reading the oracles. It is not surprisingly that most of our written sources from the next dynasty, the Zhou, also originate with the higher social class. The oracles were addressed to a combination of spiritual and divine figures, from gods to the spirits of ancestors. Responses and sometimes confirmation of the validity of the responses were also sometimes written on the bones. Ancestors were integral to all aspects of Shang, and subsequent Zhou, culture. The political system was no exception to this; the oracle bone clearly reveal that rulers consulted ancestors and spirits for advice on matters of state. In the Zhou period (1122-256 B.C.E.), another method of political advice was introduced: Confucianism. It would not replace the use of ancestor divination. As is typical of Chinese culture, the pattern of retaining the original belief and adding to it another layer of belief.

4.1 Shang Oracle Bones

Chinese writing begins with the "Oracle Bones" of the Shang dynasty, c. 1766 – 1122 B.C.E. The selections included here offer an overview of the kinds of questions and answers will the Shang asked on the bones. There are three parties involved in the oracles, the diviners who asked the question, the king who has a question to be answered, and the spirits or powers that will provide the answer. The oracle bones are thus symbolic of intersection of the earthly and the divine that characterized how the Shang understood the world."Di" refers to the High God, one of the powers of nature that governed the Shang natural world.

Source: "Oracle Bone Inscriptions of the Late Shang Dynasty," from *Sources of Chinese Tradition,* Second Edition, Volume I: From Earliest Times to 1600, W. Theodore de Bary and Irene Bloom, eds. (New York: Columbia University Press, 1999), 6-17.

1. Crack-making on *bingxu* (day 23), (we) divined: "Today it will not rain."
2. Crack-making on *renwu* (day 19), Chu (the diviner) divined: "Today there will not be the coming of bad news from the border regions,"
3. Crack-making on *yichou* (day 2): "Today, *yichou*, we offer one penned sheep to Ancestor Xin, promise five cattle."
4A. Crack-making on *gengzi* (day 37): "(We) order Fu to inspect Lin."
4B. "It should be Qin whom we order to inspect Lin."
4C. "It should be Bing whom we order to inspect Lin."
5A. Divined: "On the next day, *jiawu* (day 31), (we) should not make offering to Ancestor [Yi] (the twelfth king)."
5B. Divined: "On the next day, *jiawu*, (we) should make offering to Ancestor Yi."
6. On *dingmao* (day 4) divined: "If the king joins with Zhi [Guo] (an important Shang general) to attack the Shaofang, he will receive [assistance]." Cracked in the temple of Ancestor Yi (the twelfth king). Fifth moon.
7A. Divined: "If the king dances (for rain), there will be approval."
7B. Divined: "The king should not dance (for rain, for if he does, there will not be approval)."
8. Crack-making on *yiwei* (day 32), Gu divined: "Father Yi (the twentieth Shang king, Xiao Yi, the father of Wu Ding) is harming the king."
9A. Divined: "Grandfather Ding (the fifteenth king, father of Xiao Yi) is harming the king."
9B. Divined: ''It is not Grandfather Ding who is harming the king."
10. Divined: "There is a sick tooth; it is not Father Yi (= Xiao Yi, as above) who is harming (it/him)."
11. Crack-making on *dingchou* (day 14), Bin divined: "In praying for harvest to Shang Jia (the predynastic founder of the royal lineage) we offer in holocaust three small penned lambs and split open three cattle."
12A. "It is Shang Jia who is harming the rain."
12B. "It is not Shang Jia who is harming the rain."
13A. On *jisi* (day 6), the king cracked and divined: "[This] season, Shang will receive [harvest]." The king read the cracks and said: "Auspicious."
13B. "The Eastern Lands will receive harvest."
13C. "The Southern Lands will receive harvest." (The king read the cracks and said:) "Auspicious."
13D. "The Western Lands will receive harvest." (The King read the cracks and said:) "Auspicious"
13E. "The Northern Lands will receive harvest." (The King read the cracks and said:) "Auspicious"
14. On *xinsi* (day 18) divined: "(We) will pray for a child to Mother Geng and Mother Bing and offer a bull, a ram, and a white boar."
15A. Crack-making on *jidshen* (day 21). Que divined: "Lady Hao's (a consort of Wu Ding's) childbearing will be good." (Prognostication:) The king read the cracks and said: "If it be on a *ding*-day that she give birth, there will be prolonged luck." (Verification:) (After) thirty-one days, on *jiayin* (day 51), she gave birth; it was not good; it was a girt.
15B. (Prognostication:) The king read the cracks and said: "If it be a *ding*-(day) childbearing, it will be good; if (it be) a *geng*-day (childbearing), there will be prolonged luck; if it be a *renxu* (day 59) (childbearing), it will not be lucky.

16. Crack-making on *renyin* (day 39), Xing divined: "The king hosts Da Ceng's (the fifth king's) consort, Mother Ren, and performs the *xie*-ritual; there will be no trouble."
17. Crack-making on *xinsi* (day 18), divined: "The king hosts Wu Ding's (the twenty-first king's) consort, Mother Xin, and performs the *zai*-ritual; there will be no trouble."
18A. Divined: "Cheng (= Da Yi, the first king) will be hosted by Di."
18B. Divined: "Cheng will not be hosted by Di."
18C. Divined: "Da Jia (the third king) will be hosted by Cheng.
18D. Divined: "Da Jia will not be hosted by Cheng."
18E. Divined: "Da [Jia] will be hosted by Di."
18F. Divined: "Da Jia will not be hosted by Di."
19A. Crack-making on *renzi* (day 49), Zheng divined: "If we build a settlement, Di will not obstruct (but) approve." Third moon.
19B. Crack-making on *guichou* (day 50), Zheng divined: "If we do not build a settlement, Di will approve."
20A. Crack-making on *xinchou* (day 38), Que divined: "Di approves the king (doing something?)."
20B. Divined: "Di does not approve the king (doing something?)."
21A. Crack-making on *wuzi* (day 25). Que divined: "Di, when it comes to the fourth moon, will order the rain."
21B. Divined: "Di will not, when it comes to the present fourth moon, order the rain."
21C. (Prognostication:) The king read the cracks and said: "On the *ding*-day (e.g., *dingyou* [day 34] it will rain; if not, it will be a *xim*-day (e.g. *xichou* [day 38] (that it rains)."
21D. (Verification:) "(After) ten days, on *dingyou* (day 34), it really did rain."
22A. Divined: "It is Di who is harming our harvest." Second moon.
22B. Divined: "It is not Di who is harming our harvest."
23. [Divined:] "The Fang (enemy) are harming and attacking (us); it is Di who orders (them) to make disaster for us." Third moon."
24A. Divined: "(Because) the Fang are harming and attacking (us, we) will raise men.
24B. Divined: "It is not Di who orders (the Fang) to make disaster for us."
25. Crack-making on, *jiachen* (day 41), Zheng divined: "If we attack the Mafang (another enemy group), Di will confer assistance on us." First moon.
26A. Crack-making on *bingwu* (day 43) divined: "It is the Mountain Power that is harming the rain."
26B. "It is the (Yellow) River Power that is harming the rain."
27. "On the present *xin*-day, if the king hunts, the whole day (he) will have no disasters and it will not rain."
28. "If the king goes to hunt. the whole day he will not encounter the Great Winds."
29. Crack-making on *renwu* (day 19): "To the (Yellow) River Power (we) pray for rain and offer a holocaust."
30. Crack-making on *xinwei* (day 8): "To the Mountain Power, (we) pray for rain."
31A. Crack-making on *Jiawu* (day 31), Que divined: "On the next day, *yiwei* (day 32), (we) should make offering to Ancestor Yi (the twelfth king)."
31B. "On the next day, *yiwei*, (we) [should not] make offering to Ancestor Yi."
32A. Crack-making on *guiwei* (day 20), Que divined: "On the the next day, *jiashen* (day 21), the king should host Shang Jia (the predynastic founder) and offer the (*jia*-) day cult." (Prognostication:) The King read the cracks and said: "Auspicious. We should host (Shang Jia)." (Verification "(We) really did host (Shang Jia)."
32B. Divined: "On the next day, *jiashen*, the king should not host Shang Jia and offer the (*jia*-) day cult."
33. Crack-making on *yihai* (day 12), Xing divined: "The king hosts Xiao Yi (the twentieth king) and performs the *xie*-ritual; he will have no fault." Eleventh moon."
34. Crack-making on *dingsi* (day 54), divined: "The king hosts the fouth Ancestor Ding (the fifteenth king) and performs the *xie*-day ritual; he will have no fault."

35.   On *guiwei* (day 20) the king made cracks in the Hui encampment and divined: "In the (next) ten days, there will be no disasters." (Prognostication:) The king read the cracks and said: "Auspicious." (Postface:) It was in the fifth moon, (for the week starting on the) *jiashen* (day 21) (on which we) offered the *ji*-ritual to Ancestor Jia (the twenty-third king) and the *xie*-day ritual to Xiang Jia (the seventeenth king).

36.   On *dingwei* (day 44) divined: "It should be tonight that (we) perform the *you*-cutting sacrifice and perform an exorcism." Cracked in the temple of Father Ding (i.e., Wu Ding).

37.   Divined: "(We) pray for Lady Hao (one of Wu Ding's consorts) to Father Yi (the twentieth king and Wu Ding's father)."

38.   Crack-making on *guiyou* (day 10): "To Father Jia (the seventeenth king), we pray for (good) hunting."

39A. Crack-making on *jimao* (dav 16), Que divined: "It will not rain."

39B. Crack-making on jimao, Que divined: "It will rain." (Prognostication:) The king read the cracks (and said): "If it rains, it will be on a *ren*-day." (Verification:) On *renwu* (day 19), it really did rain.

40.   Crack-making; on *guisi* (day 30), Que divined: "In the (next) ten days there will be no disasters" (Prognostication:) The king read the cracks and said: "There will be calamities; there will he (someone) bringing alarming news." (Verification:) When it came to the fifth day, *dingyou* (day 34), there really was (someone) bringing alarming news, from the west. Zhi Cuo reported and said: "The Tufang have attacked in our eastern borders and have seized two settlements. The Congfang likewise invaded the fields of our western borders.

41.   On *renzi* (day 49), (the king) made cracks and divined:"(We) will hunt at Wu; going and coming hack there will be no disasters." (Prognostication:) The king read the cracks and said: "Auspicious." This was used. (Verification:) (We) caught one wild buffalo; one tiger; seven foxes.

Reading and Discussion Questions

1.   Several of the oracles concern a royal childbirth. What is the anxiety about childbirth that preoccupied kings?

2.   Sometimes the answer is that Di does not want a king to do something; what power might Di have to influence the king?

3.   What do the oracle bones reveal about the lives of royal women? Consider both the references to women and the lack of references to women.

4.   It is clear from these inscriptions that the Shang had a sophisticated understanding of how time operated. In what ways was the measurement of time related to ritual?

4.2   Ancestor Worship and Human Sacrifice from the *Shi Jing*

China has a remarkable poetic history. Perhaps because the writing system was established during the Shang Dynasty (the earliest sample dates from c. 1400 B.C.E), the Chinese had a long time to develop a poetic tradition. The Chinese valued poetry so highly that the *Books of Songs* (the *Shih ching*) an anthology of poems from all aspects of Zhou society, was one of the five definitive Confucian classics that formed the backbone of Chinese culture and education for centuries.

During the Zhou period, families, both noble and common, sacrificed to their ancestors. These sacrifices were of the utmost importance and any neglect would bring about misfortune and calamity, for ancestors had the power to aid or punish their descendants.

Human sacrifice was practiced extensively during the Shang dynasty and to a lesser extent down to the third century BCE. The third selection decries the practice that "takes all our good men" in following the king in death. Duke Mu of Qin died in 621 BCE. The last selection is a conversation between a Zhou king and his minister and demonstrates the Chinese belief in the close interaction between the spirit world and the political environment.

The king could not afford to lose the favor and protection of Heaven.

Source: *The Book of Songs: The Ancient Chinese Classic of Poetry*, Arthur Waley, trans.(London: Allen/Unwin, 1937).

GLORIOUS ANCESTORS

Ah, the glorious ancestors

Endless, their blessings,

Boundless their gifts are extended;

To you, too, they needs must reach.

We have brought them clear wine;

They will give victory.

Here, too, is soup well seasoned,

Well prepared, well mixed.

Because we come in silence,

Setting all quarrels aside,

They make safe for us a ripe old age,

We shall reach the withered cheek, we shall go on and on.

With our leather-bound naves, our bronzeclad yokes,

With eight bells a-jangle

We come to make offering.

The charge put upon us is vast and mighty,

From Heaven dropped our prosperity,

Good harvests, great abundance.

They come [the ancestors], they accept,

They send down blessings numberless.

They regard the paddy-offerings, the offerings of first-fruits

That Tang's descendant brings.

HUMAN SACRIFICE

"Kio" sings the oriole

As it lights on the thorn-bush.

Who went with Duke Mu to the grave?

Yanxi of the clan Ziju.

Now this Yanxi

Was the pick of all our men;

But as he drew near the tomb-hole

His limbs shook with dread.

That blue one, Heaven,

Takes all our good men.

Could we but ransom him

There are a hundred would give their lives.

"Kio" sings the oriole

As it lights on the thorn-bush.

Who went with Duke Mu to the grave?

Zhonghang of the clan Ziju. Now this Zhonghang
Was the sturdiest of all our men;
But as he drew near the tomb-hole
His limbs shook with dread.
That blue one, Heaven,
Takes all our good men.
Could we but ransom him
There are a hundred would give their lives.
"Kio" sings the oriole
As it lights on the thorn-bush.
Who went with Duke
Mu to the grave?
Zhenhu of the clan Ziju.
Now this Quan-hu
Was the strongest of all our men;
But as he drew near the tomb-hole
His limbs shook with dread.
That blue one, Heaven,
Takes all our good men.
Could we but ransom him
There are a hundred would give their lives.

Reading and Discussion Questions

1. What role did spirits play in the lives of the Chinese?
2. Why was it important to placate them?
3. How was human sacrifice regarded by the Chinese?

4.3   Pan Gu: A Chinese Creation Myth

One of the most primal needs of individuals and of societies is to understand how things came to be. All cultures, therefore, have creation stories. Often these are among the first stories produced by a culture. The story of Pan Gu is just such a story. Its origin is uncertain, although it probably dates from the Western Zhou dynasty (1122 – 771 B.C.E.). The myth combines elements that are common to other creation myths. These common elements include a supernatural being that separates sky from land, a giant that supports the sky, and a divine figure who dismemberment creates the individual elements of the world. The version printed here is a modern retelling of the myth.

Source: "Pan Gu: The Creation of the World: The Separation of Earth and Sky," from *World of Chinese Myths,* by Chen Jianing and Yang Yang. Beijing: Beijing Language and Culture University Press, 1995; pp. 5-6.

1. The Creation of the World: the Separation of Earth and Sky

During Summer night when we are gazing at the star filled sky and the new moon we can't help contemplating the vastness of the universe. Does it ever end and if it *ever* does, where and what is beyond that end? If there is no end what does infinity look like? Who dominates this endless universe: Who is the creator? Because of humanity's limited understanding, these questions are still unanswered. Despite this, or perhaps because of this, all the world's peoples have creation myths. In Chinese myth. Pan Gu created the world.

In the beginning, the universe was chaos. The atmosphere formed into an enormous *egg*. Inside the massive egg, the god, Pan Gu, grew. One day, after sleeping for about 18.000 years, he woke up. When he opened his eyes, darkness surrounded him. Dispirited by the blackness, he waved the axe in his hand and with a thundering sound the egg broke. The lighter part of the atmosphere slowly rose, becoming the blue sky. The heavier part sank lowly, becoming the yellow earth. Upon the separation of sky and earth. Pan Gu set foot on the earth and supported the sky with his head. keeping the earth and sky separate. Every day the sky rose one *zhang* (3.3 metres) higher, the earth became one *zhang* thicker, and at the same time. Pan Gu grew one *zhang*. Thus passed another 18,000 years with the sky becoming much higher and the earth much thicker. As the sky expanded, Pan Gu grew to 90,000 *li* (45,000 kilometres). He stood there like a tall pillar, supporting the sky and the earth.

Many many years passed this way, but finally, exhausted, he felt that his support was no longer necessary, thinking that the sky and the earth were forever separated. Exhausted, he died. His dying breath became the winds and clouds, his voice the roaring thunder, his left eye the sun and the right eye the moon. His body formed the four edges of the earth and high mountains. His muscle's turned into rich soil and his blood flowed as rivers and lakes. His veins and sinew became roads and his hair became the bright stars in the sky. His skin and fine body hair became beautiful flowers, grass and trees. His teeth and bone became hard stone and glittering metal and his marrow became jade and pearls. Even his sweat became rain drops. Thus, by his death, Pan Gu gave us a colourful world.

Reading and Discussion Questions

1. Notice the specific details of the created world that reflect the real geography of China. Identify some of those elements and discuss.
2. How is the act of creation through the dismemberment of a god a distinctly agricultural creation myth? What elements in the story suggest a culture moving beyond agricultural villages to a more urbanized landscape?
3. Compare this myth to the "Creation" story from the *Laws of Manu* in Chapter 3. What might explain the common details?
4. Does the story indicate where Pan Gu originated?
5. In this origin myth, only the natural world is created; the creation of humans had their own story. Can you identify details in the story that indicate human culture to come?

4.4   The Announcement to the Duke of Shao

The "Announcement to the Duke of Shao" comes from the *Book of History* (*ShuChing*). The background to the excerpt is that King Ch'eng, the third Zhou king, sent the Duke of Shao to determine it Lo would be an acceptable site for a capital. The Duke of Shao and the Duke of Chou were advisors to the king; it is the Duke of Chou who makes this announcement to the Shao.

The "Announcement" is less concerned with the question of whether Lo is a suitable site for a capital than with defending the legitimacy of Zhou rule and in paying reverence to the rules of Xia and Yin, two states that proceeded the Zhou Dynasty.

Source: "Announcement to the Duke of Shao" from *Sources of Chinese History*, Vol. I, ed. W. Theodore de Bary, Wing-Tsit Chan, and Burton Watson. (New York: Columbia University Press, 1964), pp. 10-12.

In the second month, third quarter, sixth day *i-wei* the king in the morning proceeded from Chou and arrived in Feng. The Grand Guardian, the Duke of Shao, preceded the Duke of Chou to inspect the site. In the third month, the day *mou-shen*, the third day after the first appearance of the new moon on *ping-wu*, the Grand Guardian arrived in the morning at Lo and consulted the tortoise oracle about the site. When he had obtained the oracle he planned and laid out the city. On the third day *Keng-hsuü*, the Grand Guardian with all the Yin people started work on the emplacements at the bend of the Lo River, and on the fifth day *chia-yin* the emplacements were determined. The next day *i-mao*, the Duke of Chou arrived in the morning at Lo and thoroughly inspected the plans for the new city. On the third day *ling-ssu*, he sacrificed two oxen as victims on the suburban altar, and on the next day *mou-wu* he sacrificed to the God of the Soil in the new city one ox, one sheep, and one pig. On the seventh day *chia-tzu* the Duke of Chou by written documents gave charges to all the rulers of the states of the Hou, Tien, and Nan zones in the Yin realm. When orders had been given to the Yin multitude they arose with vigor to do their work. The Grand Guardian then together with all the ruling princes of the states went out and took gifts and entered again and gave them to the Duke of Chou. The Duke of Chou said: "I salute and bow down my head and I extol the king and your Grace. I make an announcement to all Yin and managers of affairs. Oh, august

Heaven, the Lord-on-High, has changed his principal son [i.e., the ruler] and this great state Yin's mandate. Now that the king has received the mandate, unbounded is the grace, but also unbounded is the solicitude. Oh, how can he be but careful! Heaven has removed and made an end to the great state Yin's mandate. There are many former wise kings of Yin in Heaven, and the later kings and people here managed their mandate. But in the end [under the last king] wise and good men lived in misery so that, leading their wives and carrying their children, wailing and calling to Heaven, they went to where no one could come and seize them. Oh, Heaven had pity on the people of the four quarters, and looking with affection and giving its mandate, it employed the zealous ones [i.e., the leaders of the Chou]. May the king now urgently pay careful attention to his virtue. Look at the ancient predecessors, the lords of Hsia; Heaven indulged them and cherished and protected them. They strove to comprehend the obedience to Heaven; but in these times they have lost their mandate. Now a young son is the successor; may he not neglect the aged elders. Then he will comprehend our ancient men's virtue, nay still more it will occur that he is able to comprehend and endeavor to follow Heaven.... May the king come and take over the work of the Lord on-High, and himself manage the government in the center of the land. I, Tan, say: having made the great city, he shall from here be a counter part to august Heaven. He shall carefully sacrifice to the upper and lower spirits, and from here centrally govern .... We should not fail to mirror ourselves in the lords of Hsia; we likewise should not fail to mirror ourselves in the lords of Yin. We do not presume to know and say that the lords of Hsia undertook Heaven's mandate so as to have it for so-and-so many years; we do not presume to know and say that it could not have been prolonged. It was that they did not reverently attend to their virtue, and so they prematurely renounced their mandate. We do not presume to know and say that the lords of Yin received Heaven's mandate for so-and-so many years; we do not know and say that it could not have been prolonged. It was that they did not reverently attend to their virtue and so they prematurely threw away their mandate. Now the king has succeeded to and received their mandate. We should then also remember the mandates of these two states and in succeeding to them equal their merits.... Being king, his position will be that of a leader in virtue; the small people will then imitate him in all the world.... May those above and below [i.e., the king and his servants] labor and be anxiously careful; may they say: we have received Heaven's mandate, may it grandly equal the span of years of the lords of Hsia and not miss the span of years of the lords of Yin."

Reading and Discussion Questions:

1. Confucianism is focused on hierarchy and order. How is that reflected in this excerpt? Consider the order things happened and how information is transmitted.
2. According to this document, what is the "mandate of Heaven" and how does Heaven chose to whom it will give the mandate?
3. What lessons have the Zhou learned from the Hsia and Yin states?
4. What behavior is expected of the king?

Origins Apart: The Americas and Oceania

As the title of this chapter indicates, the story of the Americas and Oceania (also known as Polynesia or the Pacific Islands) are the story of people who are "apart." Traditionally these cultures have been viewed by historians as "apart" from the larger, dominant narrative of Eurasia, both geographically and developmentally. This view uses the pattern of development in Eurasia as a standard, or model, against which other cultures are assessed. Far too often that assessment has meant judgment. It is now clear that although the Americas and Oceania were separated from Eurasia geographically (Oceania less so), they followed the same basic patterns of development, from foraging to settled agriculture to increasingly complex social structures and methods for organizing populations. In the Americas this latter pattern was made manifest in the city, typical of the Eurasian model. It this sense, the Americas and Oceania are not "apart" at all, but further examples of the patterns exhibited elsewhere.

It is also clear that in the Americas and Oceania there are deviations from those same patterns, such as the lack of cities in Oceania (in spite of population sizes that would have supported urban centers), the lack of writing in most of the Americas and all of Oceania, and a few technological differences (the lack of the wheel limited or no metallurgy). However, even in this there is not a complete "apartness," for although the Americas and Oceania developed differently from Eurasia, they developed a pattern of their own and were very much connected to one another. Furthermore, the islands of Oceania were very much connected to Eurasia, as that was the point of origin for the original settlers.Finally, one must acknowledge how very connected these societies were to one another, through trade in material goods as well as migration of people. Historians are still trying to understand how these societies connect; the lack of written evidence has led many historians down paths of speculative dead-ends, as is reflected in the excerpt in this chapter from Thor Heyerdahl, who had a controversial theory about how Oceania might have connected to the Americas. It is important to observe the process by which the theories of history change with new evidence or new interpretations of old evidence.

This chapter introduces the mixed patterns of the Americas and Oceania: the patterns that are typical of all societies and the patterns that are unique to their regions. It also explores the diversity with which those patterns have materialized, from the large elevated monuments of the Americas to the rich oral tales in the Pacific Islands. The sources in this chapter explore that mixed pattern and reflect both the "apartness" of the Americas and Oceania and the connectedness of these cultures as well. A prominent historian's description of a large urban center in Mesoamerica is followed by a selection of primary sources from a variety of American and Polynesian cultures. Some of the stories are foundation stories, such as how the first people came to discover and settle New Zealand. Other sources reveal the astounding ability of early Polynesians to sail across vast stretches of the Pacific Ocean without the assistance of any modern navigational technology. A common theme that is found in many of the sources involves how humans have adapted to, and interacted with, their environments. Several of these are modern retellings of tales that were only available orally for centuries; that fact alone indicates something of the difficulty in studying a society that was complex but non-literate.

5.1 The Wealth of La Venta

This source is obviously not a primary source; it is an account by one of the foremost archaeologists and historians of pre-Columbian Mesoamerica of the wealth of La Venta. La Venta was the secondOlmec urban center. Founded c. 900 B.C.E., when the first city of San Lorenzo was abandoned for reasons that are not yet understood, La Ventaitself collapsed c. 600 B.C.E. for equally mysterious reasons.

Although evidence of Olmec writing was very recently discovered, it has not yet been translated and therefore we must for the moment treat the Olmec as a non-literate society. Coe's description of the physical remains of La Venta gives us a glimpse of what was there as well as what is still there. This source should give you some idea of both the historical Olmec and the dilemmas faced by historians who are trying to re-create the history of non-literate societies. Coe emphasizes that the Olmec were wealthy and had a mature culture (as one would expect from a second city).

Source: "Wealth of La Venta," from *America's First Civilization,* Michael Coe. (New York: American Heritage Publishing Co., Inc., 1968), pp. 63-70.

La Venta's greatest wealth and power were reached during its two final building phases. According to the most recent radiocarbon dates, this would have been after 800 B.C., but before its final abandonment, perhaps around 400 B.C. To this stage in the history of La Venta belong some of the finest offerings and burials ever found in the New World. Many of these are either placed exactly on the center line running through the site, or in relation to it, and the offerings themselves are often laid out so that their own long axis conforms with this center line orientation.

One of the very richest such deposits was Offering No. 2, found in 1955, which has no fewer than fifty-one polished celts, mostly of jade or serpentine. Five of them are finely engraved with typically Olmec designs. Once more, we are reminded of the incredible waste that the burial of these laboriously manufactured articles must represent. Why did they do it? For the gods? or, more prosaically, as a display of the wealth that the Olmec leaders possessed?

Apparently in certain cases they knew where these offering had been put. For this statement we have the testimony of Offering No. 4. The goddess of archaeological fortune in her usual capriciousness decreed that this would come to light in the late afternoon during the 1955 Drucker-Heizer expedition just before the regular shift ended. "It was necessary to expose, record, photograph, and remove the find in the few hours of remaining daylight" because of fear of looting overnight. Offering No. 4 was hit upon under the floor of the Ceremonial Court. Sixteen figurines of jade or serpentine and six celts of the same materials had been arranged in a little group that is obviously meant to be a scene from real life. The figurines are typically Olmec, depicting men with loincloths and with bald or shaven heads that have been deformed in childhood by binding. One rather eroded figure stands with his back to a line of celts; the others are arranged about him and face him. As the excavators, Drucker and Heizer, say, "We can only wonder."

But this is not the end of the story. After the offering had been originally placed and covered up, a series of floors of brightly colored clays—orange, rose, yellow, and white—was laid down over the entire court. Then, no one knows how many years later, somebody dug a pit down through these floors as far as the tops of the figurines and celts; and then, just as mysteriously, filled the pit up again. Why did they do this? Clearly, they had kept some sort of record of where this offering was and had seemingly been rechecking to make sure it was still there.

Burials have been mentioned. These might better be called "tombs," for the rival in richness some of the famous tombs of Old World archaeology. Most of them were uncovered by the Stirling expeditions of 1942 and 1943, for they belong to the final building phases of La Venta and thus lie near the surface. Unfortunately, the extremely acid soil of La Venta over the centuries has eaten away all traces of skeletons; nothing is left but the most imperishable of the loot buried with the deal Olmec lord. The three best-stocked sepulchers were in Mount A-2 on the north side of the Ceremonial Court and again naturally along the center line. The northernmost one is indeed curious, for it was built of gigantic basalt columns that in their natural form imitate tombs of wooden logs. On the limestone-slab floor were found the bundled remains of what had probably been two infants, surrounded (as in all La Venta burials) with brilliant red pigment. When these children, who must have been princes among their own people, were laid to rest, they were accompanied by a treasure-trove in jade: four figurines (one a seated woman with a tiny hematite mirror fragment on her breast), a jade clamshell, beads, ear ornaments, an awl-like object that probably was used to draw sacrificial blood, a jade sting-ray spine, and a pair of jade hands. Also in the same tomb were put a magnetite mirror and the tooth of an extinct giant shark.

Just to the south of this tomb was another, this time a sandstone sarcophagus. Again there was little or no trace of bones, but since it is big enough to contain an adult body and pigment covered its floor, it was surely a tomb. Its exterior was carved with a fearsome representation of a flame-browed werejaguar, while in its clay-filled cavity were found more beautiful jades: paper-thin ear spools (somewhat circular, outflaring objects set into the ear lobe), a serpentine figurine, and another "awl" for ceremonial bloodletting.

Then La Venta comes to an end. The cause and nature of its fate is lost in mystery, a mystery that we shall also see at the great Olmec center of San Lorenzo. All construction comes to a halt, no more tombs are built and stocked, no more offerings are made beneath its multi-colored floors. Its rulers and people are gone, and year after year the nortes come howling in from the coast, shrouding the ruins of La Venta in drift sands. Olmec civilization had died.

Everything at La Venta is exotic, in the sense that it was brought from somewhere else. Even the brightly colored clays had been specially selected and brought to the island, for they are not indigenous. Likewise, the jade and serpentine (ton after ton of the latter) came from a distance and as yet unknown source. But the greatest wonder if that most of the volcanic basali used in their monuments can only have come from the Tuxtla Mountains, sixty miles due west of La Venta.

Dr. Howell Williams is the leading expert on volcanoes. He has long been intrigued by the Olmec "problem" and in 1960 he began explorations and studies with Robert Heizer that have largely solved the mystery of the rock source of the Olmec carvings at La Venta. By making thin sections of small pieces of rock taken from these monuments, it is possible tocompare them under magnification with samples from identified lava flows in the Tuxtlas. It now seems thatmost of the La Venta carvings are made from basalt in the region of the Cerro Cinte-pee, an ancient cone among the many that make up the Tuxtla range. The lower slopes of these mountains are strewn with gigantic boulders of exactly the same kind of basalt. Apparently, the Olmec came here and either carved them on the spot or brought them to La Venta for working. Some are certainly large enough to make a fair-sized Colossal Head, and possibly their natural shape suggested the idea of the huge heads in the first place.

If this question has been answered, an even larger one remains. How did they ever get the stones to La Venta from the Tuxtlas? The engineering problems involved would be formidable even today. Certainly part of the jour-ney could have been on enormous rafts, floating down the westernmost feeder streams of the Coatzacoalcos River, then along the coast, east to the mouth of the Tonalá. But they would have had to have been dragged at least twenty-five miles overland to reach navigable waters within the Coatzacoalcos drainage. Remember that the Colossal Heads, for instance, weigh an average of eighteen tons each. The problem was indeed formi-dable.

During the fourth and last building stage at La Venta, the rulers suddenly hit upon a new architectural device: they surrounded the Ceremonial Court with a kind of fence made up of huge columns of prismatic basalt. We have also seen the use of such columns in the large tomb to its north. Where did they get these? As one flies along the jungle-covered coastline of the Tuxtla region, prismatic basalt can be seen in its natural state, the columns breaking off from the lava fields that once reached the sea. If this really was their source, the quarrying must have been a fearsome operation carried out from rafts, for this coast is often lashed by a heavy surf. One wonders how many great Olmec stones now rest on the bottom of the sea.

Resding and Discussion Questions

1. Coe's description of La Venta's wealth focuses on burials found there, and the grave goods they contained. What are the limitations in using grave sites as evidence for how people of the past lived?
2. Noticeably missing from the gravesites were human remains, which did not survive the highly acidic soil of the area. Does that fact give us any possible clue about the ultimate failure of La Venta, and of San Lorenzo before it?
3. What evidence does Coe present about the nature of Olmec trade?

5.2   The Mound Builder Cultures of North America: Poverty Point

The following excerpt illustrates many of the issues involved in studying the mound builder cultures of the North American Midwest and East. Although the purpose of some mounds is clearly that of gravesites, the purpose of other mounds is still unclear. The excerpt also offers a glimpse at historians at work. The anthropologists mentioned in this excerpt, working with the same evidence, present different theories about the meaning of Poverty Point, Louisiana. Notice how they speak to one another through their theories.

Source: "Poverty Point Mounds," from *Mound Builders of Ancient America: The Archaeology of a Myth,* Robert Silverberg. (Greenwich, CT: New York Graphic Society Ltd., 1968), 256-260.

Several ideas have been proposed by way of tracing the supposed Mexican intrusion into the Ohio Valley. One suggestion is that the puzzling Poverty Point site in northern Louisiana may have been a way station for migrants on their way from Mexico to Ohio. At Poverty Point, near the town of Floyd, in West Carroll Parish, a cluster of six mounds stands close to the banks of Bayou Mason. The largest mound is a flat-topped T-shaped structure 70 feet in height; the other mounds are from 1 to 21 feet high, and the entire group is laid out in a vague semicircle.

The Poverty Point mounds were first mentioned by Samuel H. Lockett in the Smithsonian Institution Annual Report for 1872, and received their earliest detailed examination about fifty years later when Clarence B. Moore spied them from his steamboat, *Gopher.* But little attention was paid to them until recent times, when aerial photographs of the group were taken for mapping purposes by the Mississippi River Commission of the U.S. Army Engineers. In 1953, these photographs were studied by James A. Ford, then on the staff of the American Museum of Natural History in New York. Ford was able to detect an unusual geometrical arrangement of the mounds that had eluded previous observers.

It seemed to him that the worn ridges that arc today's Poverty Point mounds once constituted a set of six concentric octagons, the outermost one three fourths of a mile across; at some distant time in the past, a shift in the channel of the Arkansas River had washed away the eastern half of the octagons. In the report that Ford and C. H. Webb published in 1956 as one of the Anthropological Papers of the American Museum of Natural History, the speculation is offered that "if the concentric octagonal ridges were completed to the east in symmetrical fashion, the total length of ridge constructed would approximate 11.2 miles. Six feet high by eighty feet across the base is a conservative estimate of the average original dimensions of the ridge cross-section. A simple calculation gives the figure of about 530,000 cubic yards of earth," a mass "over thirty-five times the cubage"' of the pyramid of Cheops in Egypt. The largest mound of this structure, Ford says, "is easily the most spectacular of the accomplishments of these people. It measures 700 by 800 feet at the base and rises to 70 feet above the surrounding plain ... it can be estimated that the finished mound required something over three million man-hours of labor."

Yet Ford thinks the entire huge structure was constructed in a single concerted effort: "The few examples of chronological information that have been secured from excavations in various parts of the earthwork suggest that probably all of it was built and inhabited at about the same time. It is obvious that the figure was constructed according to an integrated plan that probably would not have prevailed if the town had grown by accretion over a long span of time." He estimates a population of several thousand, and calculates that it must have taken twenty million 50-pound basket-loads of soil to build the earthworks. From this he draws the conclusion "that this community must have been rather strictly organized. While a religious motivation may ultimately explain the large amount of earth construction, this effort was obviously well-controlled. The geometrical arrangement of the town ... [is clearly the result] of central planning and direction. It is difficult to visualize how in a loosely organized society this quantity of essentially non-productive labor could have been expended."

Radiocarbon dates for Poverty Point fell between 1200 and 100 B.C. Ford and Webb, who thought that the site represented a southern colonial offshoot of the Adena or Hopewell mound-building cultures, preferred an 800-600 B.C. date for the flourishing of the community, which would place it several centuries after the emergence of Adena. Bur the artifacts found at Poverty Point arc mostly of Archaic type; the site would be pure Late Archaic but for the presence of those astonishing earthworks. No Adena or Hopewell material has been found. And, though it seems impossible that such vast works could have been constructed without the support of an agricultural economy, no traces of farming have been detected at Poverty Point; its inhabitants did not even have pots to cook in, but prepared their food by heating balls of baked clay and throwing them into baskets or other containers of water that could not be placed over a fire.

Several possibilities exist: that Poverty Point was an indigenous Louisiana nonagricultural community which somehow took to building immense earthworks, or that there was influence from Ohio, or that the site represents a settlement of northward-bound migrants who eventually reached the Ohio Valley and established the Adena Culture. A more eccentric theory was propounded in 1930 by Henry Shetrone. Misinterpreting the baked clay balls used in cooking as "gambling cones" of a sort employed by certain Western Indian tribes, Shetrone suggested, possibly facetiously, that "considering the almost complete absence of potsherds and other ordinary domestic accumulations, perhaps the Poverty Point site is all that remains of an aboriginal Monte Carlo, curiously well named if prehistoric gambling led to the same financial state as in modern times." More likely, Poverty Point was a sacred ceremonial city-but for whom? And when?

Another possible stopping-off place for Ohio-bound Mexicans has been pointed out in southern Louisiana on the shores of Lake Pontchartrain. Here was the home of the Tchefuncte Culture, first described by James A. Ford and George I. Quimby in 1945. They wrote at that time, "Tchefuncte and Adena are easily distinguishable by a majority of traits which they do not hold in common.... Indeed, it is surprising that there are any similarities between Tchefuncte and Adena, considering their spatial separation and environmental difference. We believe, however, that there is a fundamental similarity between the two cultures. But which way the influences flowed-from north to south or south to north-remains unsettled.

A substantial school of archaeologists finds the Mexican hypothesis, including suggested Louisiana way stations, unacceptable. Webb and Baby, advocates of a Mexican origin, note that "it should be obvious that the ancestral Adena people could come from one of two, and perhaps both, directions, i.e., south and north," and a northern origin is now frequently postulated. Don Dragoo, whose excavation of the Cresap Mound armed him with such an extraordinary perspective on the whole range of Adena development, has pointed out that most of the "Mexican" traits found in Adena mounds come from late Adena mounds and are absent from those he has identified as early ones. "If we are to find the origin of Adena," he asks, "must we not look at the early stages of this culture? How can we use traits that are present in the late stage of a culture, but not present in the early stage, as indicators of origin? Are we to believe that the Adena people had all these ideas with them when they arrived from Middle America but that they did not use them for several hundred years? On the basis of the evidence as I see it, those who have looked towards Middle America for the origin of Adena culture have done so with almost a complete disregard for the facts of the chronological development of Adena culture in the Ohio Valley."

He questions the resemblances Webb and his collaborators have seen between Adena practices and the burial and skull-deformation customs of early Mexico. He objects that the supposedly ancestral Mexican cultures had welldeveloped pottery techniques, using styles unlike any known for early Adena, and though he finds the Mexican theory "romantic and thought-provoking," he declares that "the time has come for serious consideration of other possible sources for the roots of Adena."

Dragoo finds signs of prototypical Adena in certain Late Archaic sites in the Northeast and in the lower Great Lakes area. In this he bases much of his thinking on the work of the New York archaeologist William A. Ritchie, who had found evidence of a formalized burial cult at the Muskalonge Lake and Red Lakes sites in New York. At these Archaic settlements, burial of bundled bones, cremations, and flexed bodies decorated with red ocher had been practiced in small sandy knolls. Although mound building itself was unknown among these people, Ritchie saw a "basic core of religiosity" in them, and "certain ideas possibly germinal to the development of the burial cult."

From New York, Dragoo traces the influence of this "basic core of religiosity" into Archaic cultures to the west, among them the Red Ocher Culture of Illinois and surrounding states, which practiced burial in low artificial mounds on natural prominences, and the Glacial Kame Culture of north-estern Ohio, northeastern Indiana, and southern Michigan, which buried its dead in kames, or natural knolls of gravel and sand deposited by glaciers in Pleistocene times. He sees a "coalescence of ideas and practices concerning the disposal of the dead that had developed in several widely scattered Archaic populations." Thus he regards Adena more as a case of spontaneous local generation than of open invasion from a distant land. This, Dragoo recognizes, is a radical approach; he is forced to explain away the fact that Adena people had pottery, while the other burial-cult peoples of the East did not, by terming pottery an independent development among the Adenas, and he copes with the complication of the distinctive Adena physique by saying that "if, as Snow believes ... the picture of Adena man is based upon the individuals of a selected group then our picture is not truly a representative cross-section of the Adena population." He believes that when more skulls have been recovered from early Adena mounds, few of them will display the conspicuous chins and rounded crania of the "honored dead" of late Adena on which current physical assessments have been based.

Reading and Discussion Questions
1. What evidence does Ford present to defend his theory that the Poverty Point mounds were built by one highly organized community? How do anthropologists "prove" such theories about non-literate societies?
2. Why is it important for historians to determine if Poverty Point represents an indigenous culture or one connected to Adena and Hopewell? What are the implications in either theory?
3. In addition to the mounds themselves, the author of this excerpt used another kind of historical evidence: writings by others historians from the nineteenth and twentieth centuries. What are the complications in using other historians as history?

5.3   A Polynesian Creation Myth

The "Children of Heaven and Earth" is a Polynesian creations myth. As with many Polynesian myths, versions of it can be found throughout Oceania; this particular version is from the Maori of New Zealand. As New Zealand was one of the last of the Pacific Islands to be settled, it might be tempting to read this as the "final" version of the myth. Yet these myths are never finished; each island had their own versions of them, and as people migrated between islands, and continued to trade with one another, the versions were shared, passed back and forth, altered in subtle ways by time and experience. Mythology such as this is as alive as the culture that creates it.

"Children of Heaven and Earth" begins with Rangi and Papa, Heaven and Earth, the "source from which, in the beginning, all things originated" and tells of how they came together to create all things. Creation results in the separation of Heaven and Earth by their offspring, who go on to fright with one another.

Source: "Children of Heaven and Earth" from *Polynesian Mythology: And Ancient Traditional History of the Maori as Told by Their Priests and Chiefs*. Sir George Grey. (Christchurch: Whitcombe and Tombs., Ltd., 1854), 1-8, 9.

Men had but one pair of primitive ancestors; they sprang from the vast heaven that exists above us, and from the earth which lies beneath us. According to the traditions of our race, Rangi and Papa, or Heaven and Earth, were the source from which, in the beginning, all things originated. Darkness then rested upon the heaven and upon the earth, and they still both clave together, for they had not yet been rent apart; and the children they had begotten were ever thinking amongst themselves what might be the difference between darkness and light; they knew that beings had multiplied and increased, and yet light had never broken upon them, but it ever continued dark. Hence these sayings are found in our ancient religious services: 'There was darkness from the first division of time, unto the tenth, to the hundredth, to the thousandth', that is, for a vast space of time; and these divisions of times were considered as beings, and were each termed 'a Po'; and on their account there was as yet no world with its bright light, but darkness only for the beings which existed.

At last the beings who had been begotten by Heaven and Earth, worn out by the continued darkness, consulted amongst themselves, saying: 'Let us now determine what we should do with Rangi and Papa, whether it would be better to slay them or to rend them apart.' Then spoke Tu-matauenga, the fiercest of the children of Heaven and Earth: 'It is well, let us slay them.'

Then spake Tane-mahuta, the father of forests and of all things that inhabit them, or that are constructed from trees: 'Nay, not so. It is better to rend them apart, and to let the heaven stand far above us, and the earth lie under our feet. Let the sky become as a stranger to us, but the earth remain close to us as our nursing mother.'

Hence, also, these sayings of old are found in our prayers: 'Darkness, darkness, light, light, the seeking, the searching, in chaos, in chaos'; these signified the way in which the offspring of heaven and earth sought for some mode of dealing with their parents, so that human beings might increase and live.

So, also, these sayings of old time. 'The multitude, the length', signified the multitude of the thoughts of the children of Heaven and Earth, and the length of time they considered whether they should slay their parents, that human beings might be called into existence; for it was in this manner that they talked and consulted amongst themselves.

But at length their plans having been agreed on, lo, Rongo-ma-tane, the god and father of the cultivated food of man, rises up, that he may rend apart the heavens and the earth; he struggles, but he rends them not apart. Lo, next, Tangaroa, the god and father of fish and reptiles, rises up, that he may rend apart the heavens and the earth; he also struggles, but he rends them not apart. Lo, next, Haumia-tikitiki, the god and father of the food of man which springs without cultivation, rises up and struggles, but ineffectually. Lo, then, Tu-matauenga, the god and father of fierce human beings, rises up and struggles, but he, too, fails in his efforts. Then, at last, slowly uprises Tane-mahuta, the god and mother of forests, of birds, and of insects, and he struggles with his parents; in vain he strives to rend them apart with his hands and arms. Lo, he pauses; his head is now firmly planted on his mother the earth, his feet he raises up and rests against his father the skies, he strains his back and limbs with mighty effort. / Now are rent apart Rangi and Papa, and with cries and groans of woe they shriek aloud: 'Wherefore slay you thus your parents? Why commit you so dreadful a crime as to slay us, as to rend your parents apart?' But Tane-mahuta pauses not, he regards not their shrieks and cries; far, far beneath him he presses down the earth; far, far above him he thrusts up the sky.

Hence these sayings of olden time: 'It was the fierce thrusting of Tane which tore the heaven from the earth, so that they were rent apart, and darkness was made manifest, and so was the light.'

No sooner was heaven rent from earth than the multitude of human beings were discovered whom they had begotten, and who had hitherto lain concealed between the bodies of Rangi and Papa.

Then, also, there arose in the breast of Tawhiri-ma-tea, the god and father of winds and storms, a fierce desire to wage war with his brothers, because they had rent apart their common parents. He from the first had refused to consent to his mother being torn from her lord and children; it was his brothers alone that wished for this separation, and desired that Papa-tu-a-nuku, or the Earth alone, should be left as a parent for them.

The god of hurricanes and storms dreads also that the world should become too fair and beautiful, so he rises, follows his father to the realm above, and hurries to the sheltered hollows in the boundless skies; there he hides and clings, and nestling in this place of rest he consults long with his parent, and as the vast Heaven listens to the suggestions of Tawhiri-ma-tea, thoughts and plans are formed in his breast, and Tawhiri-ma-tea also understands what he should do. Then by himself and the vast Heaven were begotten his numerous brood, and they rapidly increased and grew. Tawhiri-ma-tea despatches one of them to the westward, and one to the southward, and one to the eastward, and one to the northward; and he gives corresponding names to himself and to his progeny the mighty winds.

He next sends forth fierce squalls, whirlwinds, dense clouds, massy clouds, dark clouds, gloomy thick clouds, fiery clouds, clouds which precede hurricanes, clouds of fiery black, clouds reflecting glowing red light, clouds wildly drifting from all quarters and wildly bursting, clouds of thunder storms, and clouds hurriedly flying. In the midst of these Tawhiri-ma-tea himself sweeps wildly on. Alas! alas! then rages the fierce hurricane; and whilst Tane-mahuta and his gigantic forests still stand, unconscious and unsuspecting, the blast of the breath of the mouth of Tawhiri-ma-tea smites them, the gigantic trees are snapt off right in the middle; alas! alas! they are rent to atoms, dashed to the earth, with boughs and branches torn and scattered, and lying on the earth, trees and branches all alike left for the insect, for the grub, and for loathsome rottenness.

From the forests and their inhabitants Tawhiri-ma-tea next swoops down upon the seas, and lashes in his wrath the ocean. Ah! ah! waves steep as cliffs arise, whose summits are so lofty that to look from them would make the beholder giddy; these soon eddy in whirlpools, and Tangaroa, the god of ocean, and father of all that dwell therein, flies affrighted through his seas; but before he fled, his children consulted together how they might secure their safety, for Tangaroa had begotten Punga, and he had begotten two children, Ika-tere, the father of fish, and Tu-te-wehiwehi, or Tu-te-wanawana, the father of reptiles.

When Tangaroa fled for safety to the ocean, then Tu-te-wehiwehi and Ika-tere, and their children, disputed together as to what they should do to escape from the storms, and Tu-te-wehiwehi and his party cried aloud: 'Let us fly inland'; but Ika-tere and his party cried aloud: 'Let us fly to the sea.' Some would not obey one order, some would not obey the other, and they escaped in two parties: the party of Tu-te-wehiwehi, or the reptiles, hid themselves ashore; the party of Punga rushed to the sea. This is what, in our ancient religious services, is called the separation of Tawhiri-ma-tea.

Hence these traditions have been handed down: 'Ika-tere, the father of things which inhabit water, cried aloud to Tu-te-wehiwehi: "Ho, ho, let us all escape to the sea."

'But Tu-te-wehiwehi shouted in answer: "Nay, nay, let us rather fly inland."

'Then Ika-tere warned him, saying: "Fly inland, then; and the fate of you and your race will be, that when they catch you, before you arc cooked, they will singe off your scales over a lighted wisp of dry fern."

'But Tu-te-wehiwehi answered him, saying: "Seek safety, then, in the sea; and the future fate of your race will be, that when they serve out little baskets of cooked vegetable food to each person, you will be laid upon the top of the food to give a relish to it."

'Then without delay these two races of beings, separated. The fish fled in confusion to the sea, the reptiles sought safety in the forests and scrubs.'

Tangaroa, enraged at some of his children deserting him, and, being sheltered by the god of the forests on dry land, has ever since waged war on his brother Tane, who, in return, has waged war against him.

Hence Tane supplies the offspring of his brother Tu-matauenga with canoes, with spears and with fish-hooks made from his trees, and with nets woven from his fibrous plants, that they may destroy the offspring of Tangaroa; whilst Tangaroa, in return, swallows up the offspring of Tane, overwhelming canoes with the surges of his sea, swallowing up the lands, trees, and houses that are swept off by floods, and ever wastes away, with his lapping waves, the shores that confine him, that the giants of the forests may be washed down and swept out into his boundless ocean, that he may then swallow up the insects, the young birds, and the various animals which inhabit them.-all which things are recorded in the prayers which were offered to these gods.

Tawhiri-ma-tea next rushed on to attack his brothers Rongo-ma-tane and Haumia-tikitiki, the gods and progenitors of cultivated and uncultivated food; but Papa, to save these for her other children, caught them up, and hid them in a place of safety; and so well were these children of hers concealed by their mother Earth, that Tawhiri-ma-tea sought for them in vain.

Tawhiri-ma-tea having thus vanquished all his other brothers, next rushed against Tu-matauenga, to try his strength against his; he exerted all his force against him, but he could neither shake him nor prevail against him. What did Tu-matauenga care for his brother's wrath? he was the only one of the whole party of brothers who had planned the destruction of their parents, and had shown himself brave and fierce in war; his brothers had yielded at once before the tremendous assaults of Tawhiri-ma-tea and his progeny-Tane-mahuta and his offspring had been broken and torn in pieces-Tangaroa and his children had fled to the depths of the ocean or the recesses of the shore-Rongo-ma-tane and Haumia-tikitiki had been hidden from him in the earth but Tu-matauenga, or man, still stood erect and unshaken upon the breast of his mother Earth; and now at length the hearts of Heaven and of the god of storms became tranquil, and their passions were assuaged.

Thus Tu-mataucnga devoured all his brothers, and consumed the whole of them, in revenge for their having deserted him and left him to fight alone against Tawhiri-ma-tea and Rangi.

When his brothers had all thus been overcome by Tu', he assumed several nam.es, namely, Tu-ka-riri, Tu-ka-nguha, Tu-ka-taua, Tu-whaka-heke-tangata, Tu-mata-wha-iti, and Tu-mata-uenga; he assumed one name for each of his attributes displayed in the victories over his brothers. Four of his brothers were entirely deposed by him, and became his food; but one of them, Tawhiri-ma-tea, he could not vanquish or make common, by eating him for food, so he, the last born child of Heaven and Earth, was left as an enemy for man, and still, with a rage equal to that of Man, this elder brother ever attacks him in storms and hurricanes, endcavouring to destroy him alike by sea and land.

Reading and Discussion Questions

1. There are many things "created" in this story, including human beings. Discuss the creation of humans; do all the brothers agree on the creation of humans? Is the creation of humans a significant moment in the story?
2. What is the significance of the numerous incidents of intra-familial violence in the Polynesian creation myth? Is the violence meant to reflect literal violence in Polynesian society or is it a metaphor for something else in their world?
3. Compare this creation myth with that of the Aryans of India, the Creation Hymn from the Rig Veda in Chapter 3. How do the two myths compare in terms of creating vis-à-vis destruction?
4. As the Polynesians were a non-literate people, they had to transmit their tales orally. Although the version presented here is not exactly the oral tale, as the very act of writing it down changes it, what elements in the tale reveal its original oral nature?

5.4   Reed Chart from the Marshall Islands, South Pacific

Traditional Micronesian and Polynesian maps of the Pacific, such as this example here from the Marshall Islands, shows sea lanes across the ocean in the form of linked reeds between islands and atolls symbolized by small shells. Each straight stick represents regular currents or waves around the low lying atolls while the curved sticks depict ocean swells.

Reading and Discussion Questions

1. How does this map demonstrate the ability of Pacific Islanders to overcome environmental challenges despite the isolation from other cultures?
2. Do the migrations of Pacific Islanders across the Pacific parallel the expansion of other societies in different parts of the globe during this period? Are their common patterns?

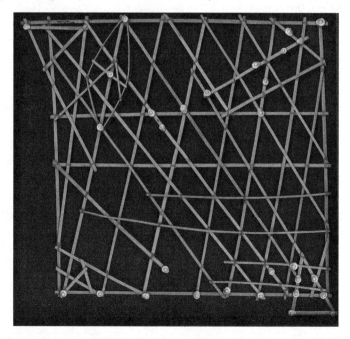

Source: Library of Congress

Chiefdoms and Early States in Africa and the Americas

Chapter 6

600 BCE – 600 CE

Africa and the Americas may be separated by the vastness of the Atlantic Ocean, but both exhibited a similar pattern of development: agriculture, villages, chiefdoms, and kingdoms. The surface details may differ, such as the reliance on iron in Nubia along the Nile and the lack of iron in the Americas, and the pace of development in the Americas was significantly slower than in Africa, but the overall pattern is similar enough to raise questions about the fundamental characteristics of human cultures.

In addition to the larger pattern of development, each of the regions discussed in this chapter also had their own regional patterns, such as the pattern of kingdom-building, competition with neighboring states, conquest, and re-building, exhibited by Nubia. Located south of Egypt, Nubia was a frequent rival of Egypt and of Aksum, another large kingdom in east Africa. In 350 C.E. Ezana, king of Aksum, conquered the Nubian capital of Meroe.

Across the Atlantic, the basic pattern of the development of chiefdoms and kingdoms is best represented by the Maya of Mesoamerica. In the central Yucatan of what is now Guatemala, Maya villages began the process of developing into kingdoms, going through the same stages that the villages of Kush undertook centuries before; by 600 B.C.E., Kush was beginning its third kingdom (Meroe) just as Maya was beginning its first. In both regions, agriculture was the foundation upon which these kingdoms were built. Although we have fewer written sources for the Maya compared to the wealth of material for Kush and Aksum, there are two key texts: the *Popol Vuh* and *Chilam Balam*, one of which, the *Popol Vuh*, is excerpted here.

Sometimes described as the Mayan book of creation, the *PopolVuh* contains the both Mayan mythology as well as hints at the political history of the Mayan people as they established their kingdom in Guatemala. Excerpts from two of the pivotal episodes in the *Popol Vuh* are presented here, the creation of the world and of humanity in one, and in the other, the sacrifice of the Hero Twins in the ballgame with the lords of Xibalba, the underworld.

6.1 The Gold Mines of Nubia

The societies and trade along the Red Sea (or "Erythraean Sea" as the Greeks called it), was well documented by writers of many different cultures, evidence of the intensive exchange in goods and ideas in the region. One of the most sought after trade item was gold. In the second century B.C.E., a Greek historian named Agatharchides of Cnidus vividly described the dangerous circumstances under which gold was mined in Nubia.

Source: Agatharchides of Cnidus, "The Gold Mines of Lower Nubia," from *Ancient African Civilizations: Kush and Axum*, Stanley Burstein, ed. (New Jersey: Markus Wiener Publishers, 1997), pp. 49-52.

Near the furthest point of Egypt and the neighboring regions of Arabia and Aithiopia there is a place that has many large old mines. There such gold is collected with great suffering and expense.

The land is naturally black with seams and veins of quartz that are remarkable for their whiteness and surpass all stones that shine brilliantly. Those in charge of the mining obtain the gold with a multitude of workers.

For the kings of Egypt collect together and consign to the gold mines those condemned for crimes and prisoners of war, and in addition, those who have been the victims of unjust accusations and sent to prison because of their wrath, sometimes themselves alone and sometimes together with their whole families. Thus, at the same time, they exact punishment frorn those condemned and obtain great revenues from their labor. Those convicts, who are numerous and bound with fetters, work at their tasks continuously during the day and throughout the whole night, being allowed no respite at all and rigorously prevented from all possibility of escape. For barbarian soldiers, who speak different languages, are appointed to be guards so that the prisoners cannot corrupt any of their warders through human conversation or some human appeal. They pursue their task in the mountains where the gold is found. They light wood fires on the stone outcrops, which are jagged and extremely hard, and crumble them with the heat.

Having heated the hardest part of the earth which contains the gold and broken it into small pieces, they carry on their work with their hands. Tens of thousands of unfortunate men crush with iron sledges the rock that has been fragmented and can be broken up with little effort. A technician, who evaluates the rock, is in charge of the whole process and gives assignments to the workers. Of those sentenced to this misery, the men distinguished by their bodily strength break up the quartz rock with iron hammers, not by applying skill to their tasks but by brute force. They also excavate galleries, not in a straight line but whichever way goes the vein of the gleaming rock.

As they work in darkness because of the twists and turns of the galleries, these men wear lamps fastened on their foreheads. Often forcing their bodies to conform to the peculiarities of the rock, they throw down on the floor the fragments they have quarried. They do this continuously in response to the brutality and blows of the overseers.

Young boys, who go down through the galleries to the areas of rock that have been excavated, laboriously pick up the rock that is being dug out bit by bit and carry it outside to a place near the entrance. Men over thirty years of age take it from them and pound a fixed amount of the quarried rock on stone mortars with iron pestles until they reduce it to the size of a vetch seed. The women and older men receive from them the seed sized rock and cast it into stone mills, several of which stand in a line; and standing beside them, two or three to a handle, they grind it until they reduce the portion given them to a flour-like state. Since there is general neglect of their bodies and they have no garment to cover their shame, it is impossible for an observer to not pity the wretches because of the extremity of their suffering. For they meet with no respite at all, not the sick, the injured, the aged, not a woman by reason of her weakness, but all are compelled by blows to strive at their tasks until, exhausted by the abuse they suffered, they die in their miseries. For this reason the poor wretches think that the future always will be more fearful than the present because of the extreme severity of their punishment, and they consider death more desirable than life.

Finally, the technicians, after collecting the ground-up rock, bring the process to its final conclusion. For they rub the processed quartz on a flat slightly inclined board while Pouring on water. Then the earthy portion which has been flushed out by the water flows away following the inclination of the board, but the part that contains the gold remains behind on the wood because of its weight. Doing this repeatedly, they at first rub it lightly with their hand, and later washing it with porous sponges, they skim off with these the loose and earthy portions until only the pure particles of gold remain.

Finally, other technicians gather up the gold that has collected, and pack it according to a fixed measure and weight into pottery vessels. They mix in a lump of lead of a size proportionate to the amount of gold and pieces of salt and, in addition, they add a little tin and barley bran. Having covered it with a close fitting lid and thoroughly sealed it with clay, they bake it in a kiln for five days and an equal number of nights continuously. Then, after allowing it to cool, they find in the jars none of the other substances, but they obtain pure gold with only a small amount having been lost.

The death of numerous men in the mines brings our exposition to the conclusion already stated, namely, that, as its nature clearlv demonstrates, the origin of gold is laborious, its preservation is uncertain, it is most zealously sought after, and its use lies between pleasure and pain. For the manner in which it is mined is extremely ancient. For the nature of the mines was discovered by the first rulers of the region, but their working was suspended when the Aithiopians...invaded Egypt in force and garrisoned its cities for many years and (again) during the supremacy of the Medes and Persians. Even in our time bronze chisels are found in the gold mines excavated by those rulers because the use of iron was not yet known at that tirne. Human bones in unbelievable numbers are also found since, as was likely to have happened, many cave-ins occurred in the unstable galleries with their brittle walls, given the great extent of the excavations and their reaching in their deepest sections the sea itself.

Reading and Discussion Questions

1. Agatharchides' concludes his description of the mining of gold with a reference to the "ancient" manner in which gold was excavated. What evidence does he offer that the methods had not changed in centuries?
2. Who did the actual mining of the gold and why were they chosen for this job?
3. Agatharchides refers to "technicians" who perform specific tasks, such as weighing and packing the gold. What information does this convey about labor specialization and social class?
4. How is the labor of gold mining divided by gender?
5. What role do the Egyptian kings play in the gold mining?

6.2 *Periplus of the Erythraean Sea:* Travel and Trade in the Red Sea and Indian Ocean

The evidence for cultural and economic exchange between Aksum, Nubia, Arabia, East Africa and the wider Indian Ocean Basin intensifies signifcantly by 1000 B.C.E. The *Periplus of the Erythraen Sea*, from about 100 C.E., offers a detailed guide to the lands south and east of Egypt's border, their natural resources, potential for trade, and inhabitants.

Source: W.H. Schoff (tr. & ed.), *The Periplus of the Erythraean Sea: Travel and Trade in the Indian Ocean by a Merchant of the First Century* (London, Bombay & Calcutta 1912)

4. Below Ptolemais of the Hunts, at a distance of about three thousand **stadia** there is Adulis, a port established by law, lying at the inner end of a bay that runs in toward the south. Before the harbor lies the so-called Mountain Island, about two hundred stadia seaward from the very head of the bay, with the shores of the mainland close to it on both sides. Ships bound for this port now anchor here because of attacks from the land. They used formerly to anchor at the very head of the bay, by an island called Diodorus, close to the shore, which could be reached on foot from the land; by which means the barbarous natives attacked the island. Opposite Mountain Island, on the mainland twenty stadia from shore, lies Adulis, a

---

stadia: A stadia is 608 feet, so 3000 stadia is about 200 miles

fair-sized village, from which there is a three-days' journey to Coloe, an inland town and the first market for ivory. From that place to the city of the people called Auxumites there is a five days' journey more; to that place all the ivory is brought from the country beyond the Nile through the district called Cyeneum, and thence to Adulis. Practically the whole number of elephants and rhinoceros that are killed live in the places inland, although at rare intervals they are hunted on the seacoast even near Adulis. Before the harbor of that markettown, out at sea on the right hand, there lie a great many little sandy islands called Alalaei, yielding tortoiseshell, which is brought to market there by the Fish-Eaters.

5.   And about eight hundred stadia beyond there is another very deep bay, with a great mound of sand piled up at the right of the entrance; at the bottom of which the opsian stone is found, and this is the only place where it is produced. These places, from the Calf-Eaters to the other Berber country, are governed by Zoscales; who is miserly in his ways and always striving for more, but otherwise upright, and acquainted with Greek literature.

6.   There are imported into these places, undressed cloth made in Egypt for the Berbers; robes from Arsinoe; cloaks of poor quality dyed in colors; double-fringed linen mantles; many articles of flint glass, and others of murrhine, made in Diospolis; and brass, which is used for ornament and in cut pieces instead of coin; sheets of soft copper, used for cooking-utensils and cut up for bracelets and anklets for the women; iron, which is made into spears used against the elephants and other wild beasts, and in their wars. Besides these, small axes are imported, and adzes and swords; copper drinking-cups, round and large; a little coin for those coming to the market; wine of Laodicea and Italy, not much; olive oil, not much; for the king, gold and silver plate made after the fashion of the country, and for clothing, military cloaks, and thin coats of skin, of no great value. Likewise from the district of Ariaca across this sea, there are imported Indian iron, and steel, and Indian cotton cloth; the broad cloth called monache and that called sagmatogene, and girdles, and coats of skin and mallow-colored cloth, and a few muslins, and colored lac. There are exported from these places ivory, and tortoiseshell and rhinoceros-horn. The most from Egypt is brought to this market from the month of January to September, that is, from Tybi to Thoth; but seasonably they put to sea about the month of September.

7.   From this place the Arabian Gulf trends toward the east and becomes narrowest just before the Gulf of Avalites. After about four thousand stadia, for those sailing eastward along the same coast, there are other Berber market-towns, known as the 'far-side' ports; lying at intervals one after the other, without harbors but having roadsteads where ships can anchor and lie in good weather. The first is called Avalites; to this place the voyage from Arabia to the far-side coast is the shortest. Here there is a small market-town called Avalites, which must be reached by boats and rafts. There are imported into this place, flint glass, assorted; juice of sour grapes from Diospolis; dressed cloth, assorted, made for the Berbers; wheat, wine, and a little tin. There are exported from the same place, and sometimes by the Berbers themselves crossing on rafts to Ocelis and Muza on the opposite shore, spices, a little ivory, tortoise-shell, and a very little myrrh, but better than the rest. And the Berbers who live in the place are very unruly.

8.   After Avalites there is another market-town, better than this, called Malao, distant a sail of about eight hundredstadia. The anchorage is an open roadstead, sheltered by a spit running out from the east. Here the natives are more peaceable. There are imported into this place the things already mentioned, and many tunics, cloaks from Arsinoe, dressed and dyed; drinking-cups, sheets of soft copper in small quantity, iron, and gold and silver coin, not much. There are exported from these places myrrh, a little frankincense, the harder cinnamon, duaca, Indian copal and macir, which are imported into Arabia; and slaves, but rarely.

9.   Two days' sail, or three, beyond Malao is the market-town of Mundus, where the ships lie at anchor more safely behind a projecting island close to the shore. There are imported into this place the things previously set forth, and from it likewise are exported the merchandise already stated, and the incense called mocrotu. And the traders living here are more quarrelsome.

10. Beyond Mundus, sailing toward the east, after another two days' sail, or three, you reach Mosyllum, on a beach, with a bad anchorage. There are imported here the same things already mentioned, also silver plate, a very little iron, and glass. There are shipped from the place a great quantity of cinnamon, (so that this markettown requires ships of larger size), and fragrant gums, spices, a little tortoise shell, and mocrotu, (poorer, than that of Mundus), frankincense, (the far-side), ivory and myrrh in small quantities.

11. Sailing along the coast beyond Mosyllum, after a two days' course you come to the so-called Little Nile River, and a fine spring, and a small laurel-grove, and Cape Elephant. Then the shore recedes into a bay, and has a river, called Elephant, and a large laurel-grove called Acannae; where alone is produced the far-side frankincense, in great quantity and of the best grade.

12. Beyond this place, the coast trending toward the south, there is the Market and Cape of Spices, an abrupt promontory, at the very end of the Berber coast toward the east. The anchorage is dangerous at times from the ground-swell, because the place is exposed to the north. A sign of an approaching storm which is peculiar to the place, is that the deep water becomes more turbid and changes its color. When this happens they all run to a large promontory called Tabae, which offers safe shelter. There are imported into this market town the things already mentioned; and there are produced in it cinnamon (and its different varieties, gizir, asypha, areho, iriagia, and moto) and frankincense.

13. Beyond Tabae, after four hundred stadia, there is the village of Pano. And then, after sailing four hundred stadia along a promontory, toward which place the current also draws you, there is another market-town called Opone, into which the same things are imported as those already mentioned, and in it the greatest quantity of cinnamon is produced, (the arebo and moto), and slaves of the better sort, which are brought to Egypt in increasing numbers; and a great quantity of tortoiseshell, better than that found elsewhere.

14. The voyage to all these farside market-towns is made from Egypt about the month of July, that is Epiphi. And ships are also customarily fitted out from the places across this sea, from Ariaca and Barygaza, bringing to these far-side market-towns the products of their own places; wheat, rice, clarified butter, sesame oil, cotton cloth, (the monache and the sagmatogene), and girdles, and honey from the reed called sacchari. Some make the voyage especially to these market-towns, and others exchange their cargoes while sailing along the coast. This country is not subject to a King, but each market-town is ruled by its separate chief.

15. Beyond Opone, the shore trending more toward the south, first there are the small and great bluffs of Azania; this coast is destitute of harbors, but there are places where ships can lie at anchor, the shore being abrupt; and this course is of six days, the direction being south-west. Then come the small and great beach for another six days' course and after that in order, the Courses of Azania, the first being called Sarapion and the nextNicon; and after that several rivers and other anchorages, one after the other, separately a rest and a run for each day, seven in all, until the Pyralax islands and what is called the channel; beyond which, a little to the south of south-west, after two courses of a day and night along the Ausanitic coast, is the island Menuthias, about three hundred stadia from the mainland, low and and wooded, in which there are rivers and many kinds of birds and the mountain-tortoise. There are no wild beasts except the crocodiles; but there they do not attack men. In this place there are sewed boats, and canoes hollowed from single logs, which they use for fishing and catching tortoise. In this island they also catch them in a peculiar wav, in wicker baskets, which they fasten across the channel-opening between the breakers.

16. Two days' sail beyond, there lies the very last market-town of the continent of Azania, which is called Rhapta; which has its name from the sewed boats (rhaptonploiarion) already mentioned; in which there is ivory in great quantity, and tortoise-shell. Along this coast live men of piratical habits, very great in stature, and under separate chiefs for each place. The Mapharitic chief governs it under some ancient right that subjects it to the sovereignty of the state that is become first in Arabia. And the people of Muza now hold it under his authority, and send thither many large ships; using Arab captains and agents, who are familiar with the natives and intermarry with them, and who know the whole coast and understand the language.

17. There are imported into these markets the lances made at Muza especially for this trade, and hatchets and daggers and awls, and various kinds of glass; and at some places a little wine, and wheat, not for trade, but to serve for getting the good-will of the savages. There are exported from these places a great quantity of ivory, but inferior to that of Adulis, and rhinoceros-horn and tortoise-shell (which is in best demand after that from India), and a little palm-oil.

18. And these markets of Azania are the very last of the continent that stretches down on the right hand from Berenice; for beyong these places the unexplored ocean curves around toward the west, and running along by the regions to the south of Aethiopia and Libya and Africa, it mingles with the western sea.

19. Now to the left of Berenice, sailing for two or three days from Mussel Harbor eastward across the adjacent gulf, there is another harbor and fortified place, which is called White Village, from which there is a road to Petra, which is subject to Malichas, King of the Nabataeans. It holds the position of a market-town for the small vessels sent there from Arabia; and so a centurion is stationed there as a collector of one-fourth of the merchandise imported, with an armed force, as a garrison.

20. Directly below this place is the adjoining country of Arabia, in its length bordering a great distance on the Erythraean Sea. Different tribes inhabit the country, differing in their speech, some partially, and some altogether. The land next the sea is similarly dotted here and there with caves of the Fish-Eaters, but the country inland is peopled by rascally men speaking two languages, who live in villages and nomadic camps, by whom those sailing off the middle course are plundered, and those surviving shipwrecks are taken for slaves. And so they too are continually taken prisoners by the chiefs and kings of Arabia; and they are called Carnaites. Navigation is dangerous along this whole coast of Arabia, which is without harbors, with bad anchorages, foul, inaccessible because of breakers and rocks, and terrible in every way. Therefore we hold our course down the middle of the gulf and pass on as fast as possible by the country of Arabia until we come to the Burnt Island; directly below which there are regions of peaceful people, nomadic, pasturers of cattle, sheep and camels.

21. Beyond these places, in a bay at the foot of the left side of this gulf, there is a place by the shore called Muza, a market-town established by law, distant altogether from Berenice for those sailing southward, about twelve thousand stadia. And the whole place is crowded with Arab shipowners and seafaring men, and is busy with the affairs of commerce; for they carry on a trade with the far-side coast and with Barygaza, sending their own ships there.

22. Three days inland from this port there is a city called Saua, in the midst of the region called Mapharitis; and there is a vassal-chief named Cholaebus who lives in that city.

23. And after nine days more there is Saphar, the metropolis, in which lives Charibael, lawful king of two tribes, theHomerites and those living next to them, called the Sabaites; through continual embassies and gifts, he is a friend of the Emperors.

24. The market-town of Muza is without a harbor, but has a good roadstead and anchorage because of the sandy bottom thereabouts, where the anchors hold safely. The merchandise imported there consists of purple cloths, both fine and coarse; clothing in the Arabian style, with sleeves; plain, ordinary, embroidered, or interwoven with gold; saffron, sweet rush, muslins, cloaks, blankets (not many), some plain and others made in the local fashion; sashes of different colors, fragrant ointments in moderate quantity, wine and wheat, not much. For the country produces grain in moderate amount, and a great deal of wine. And to the King and the Chief are given horses and sumpter-mules, vessels of gold and polished silver, finely woven clothing and copper vessels. There are exported from the same place the things produced in the country: selected myrrh, and the Gebanite-Minaean stacte, alabaster and all the things already mentioned from Avalites and the far-side coast. The voyage to this place is made best about the month of September, that is Thoth; but there is nothing to prevent it even earlier.

25. After sailing beyond this place about three hundred stadia, the coast of Arabia and the Berber country about the Avalitic gulf now coming close together, there is a channel, not long in extent, which forces the sea together and shuts it into a narrow strait, the passage through which, sixty stadia in length, the island

Diodorus divides. Therefore the course through it is beset with rushing currents and with strong winds blowing down from the adjacent ridge of mountains. Directly on this strait by the shore there is a village of Arabs, subject to the same chief, called Ocelis; which is not so much a market-town as it is an anchorage and watering-place and the first landing for those sailing into the gulf.

Reading and Discussion Questions

1. What picture of emerges of the lands described in the *Periplus*? How pervasive are cross-cultural connections?
2. How many different peoples are described in the *Periplus*? Do they appear to be participants in a shared zone of trade and exchange?

6.3   The *Popol Vuh*

The *Popol Vuh* was originally written in Mayan hieroglyphs, of the K'iche (also spelled Quiche) Maya (one of several distinct Maya dialects). The current text is an English translation of a Spanish translation made in the sixteenth century, and therefore represents several layers of interpretation of the original. Although it may have existed earlier, the version of the *Popol Vuh* that has survived dates from the late Mayan period, after the seventh century C.E.

The *Popol Vuh* (the name means "Council Book") begins, appropriately enough, at the beginning, when nothing existed except the sky, sea, and the Sovereign Plumed Serpent. The natural world is created first, and then animals are brought into being, including humans. Notice that there are several references to corn (maize) in this excerpt, an indication of how important corn was to Mesoamerican cultures such as the Maya.

Source: "Creation" from *Popol Vuh: The Definitive Edition of the Mayan Book of the Dawn of Life and the Glories of Gods and Kings.* Dennis Tedlock, trans. (New York: Simon & Schuster, Inc., 1985), 71-73, 79-85.

This is the beginning of the ancient word, here in this place called *Quiché*. Here we shall inscribe, we shall implant the Ancient Word, the potential and source for everything done in the citadel of Quiché, in the nation of Quiché people.

And here we shall take up the demonstration, revelation, and account of how things were put in shadow and brought to light as is said in the words of Quiché. They accounted for everything and did it, as enlightened beings, in enlightened words. We shall write about this now amid the preaching of God, **in Christendom now**. We shall bring it out because there is no longera place to see it, a Council Book, a place to see "The Light That Came from Beside the Sea," the account of "Our Place in the Shadows," a place to see "The Dawn of Life,"as it is called. There is the original book and ancient writing, but the one who reads and assesses it has a hidden identity. It takes a long performance and account to complete the lighting of all the sky-earth:

This is the account, here it is: Now it still ripples, now it still murmurs, ripples, it sighs, still hums, and it is empty under the sky.

Here follow the first words, the first eloquence:

There is not yet one person, one animal, bird, fish, crab, tree, rock, hollow, canyon, meadow, forest. Only the sky alone is there; the face of the earth is not clear. Only the sea alone is pooled under all the sky; there is noth-

---

in Christendom now: the writer of the *Popol Vuh* confirms he is writing after his world has been conquered by Christians, in this case, by Spanish Conquistadors. He is recording a past that stretches back before his experience.

ing whatever gathered together. It is at rest; not a single thing stirs. It is held back, kept at rest under the sky.

Whatever there is that might be is simply not there: only the pooled water, only the calm sea, only it alone is pooled.

Whatever might be is simply not there: only murmurs, ripples, in the dark, in the night. Only the Maker, Modeler alone, Sovereign Plumed Serpent, the Bearers, Begetters are in the water, a glittering light. They are there, they are enclosed in **quetzal feathers**, in blue-green.

Thus the name, "Plumed Serpent." They are great knowers, great thinkers in their very being.

And of course there is the sky, and there is also the Heart of Sky. This is the name of the god, as it is spoken.

And then came his word, he came here to the Sovereign Plumed Serpent, here in the blackness, in the early dawn. He spoke with the Sovereign Plumed Serpent, and they talked, then they thought, then they worried. They agreed with each other, they joined their wordstheir thoughts. Then it was clear, then they reached accord in the light, and then humanity was clear, when they conceived the growth, the generation of trees, of bushes, and the growth of life, of humankind, in the blackness, in the early dawn, all because of the Heart of Sky, named Hurricane. Thunderbolt Hurricane comes first, the second is Newborn Thunderbolt, and the third is Sudden Thunderbolt.

So there were three of them, as Heart of Sky, who came to the Sovereign Plumed Serpent, when the dawn of life was conceived:

"How should the sowing be, and the dawning?Who is to be the provider, nurturer?

"Let it be this way, think about it: this water should be removed, emptied out for the formation of the earth's own plate and platform, then should come the sowing, the dawning of the sky-earth. But there will be no high daysand no bright praise for our work, our design, until the rise of the human work, the human design," they said.

And then the earth arose because of them, it was simply their word that brought it forth. For the forming of the earth they said "Earth." It arose suddenly, just like a cloud, like a mist, now forming, unfolding.

Then the mountains were separated from the water, all at once the great mountains came forth. By their genius alone, by their cutting edge alone they carried out the conception of the mountain-plain, whose face grew instant groves of cypress and pine.

And the Plumed Serpent was pleased with this:

"It was good that you came, Heart of Sky, Hurricane, and Newborn Thunderbolt, Sudden Thunderbolt. Our work, our design will turn out well," they said.

And the earth was formed first, the mountain-plain. The channels of water were separated; their branches wound their ways among the mountains. The waters were divided when the great mountains appeared. The sky was set apart, and the earth was set apart in the midst of the waters.

Reading and Discussion Questions

1. Many creation myths involve the use of speech. Why do you think the Maya thought speech was so powerful?
2. What elements of nature are represented in the creation story? What is the importance of those particular aspects of nature?
3. Why do the first attempts at creating humans fail? What does that fact imply about the power of the creator gods? What might it imply about human nature?

---

quetzal feathers: The iridescent blue and green tail feathers were treasured components of royal clothing throughout Mesoamerica.

6.4   "The Creation" by Diego Rivera

This painting by Mexican artist Diego Rivera (1886-1957), was created in 1931 as an illustration for an English translation of the Popol Vuh. Titled "The Creation," it tells its story pictorially—evoking the way the early, authentic text of the Popol Vuh used hieroglyphic images, rather than alphabetic words. Though of European rather than Mesoamerican ancestry, Rivera in his work represented the less-appreciated members of society. He is well-known as the painter of several monumental murals celebrating workers and is also controversial as a left-wing social activist.

Reading and Discussion Questions

1. Diego Rivera's painting is thousands of years older than the *Popol Vuh*. What does this say about the reception of foundational myths in modern societies?
2. What particular elements from the *Popol Vuh* are portrayed in Rivera's painting?

Source: Library of Congress

Chapter 7   Persia, Greece, and Rome

Undoubtedly, one of the most significant series of interactions in world history began in the fifth century B.C.E., with the first wars between the Achaemenid Persian Empire and the Greek city-states. These wars, along with other, more peaceful, exchanges of items and ideas, had an immediate impact on the development of both civilizations. Furthermore, these interactions continue to influence relations between Europe and the Middle East to this day, as it also continued to shape the relationship betweentheir successor states: Rome in the west, and in the east, the Parthians and then the Sasanians. The sources in this chapter explore the various individual cultures and states of this interaction, from the One of the most detailed descriptions of the Persian Achaemenid Empire and culture comes from Herodotus, a Greek writer who lived in Halicarnassus, a Greek city in Anatolia. Herodotus wrote during the wars between Greece and Persia, and in addition to wanting to understand the causes of the wars, he was also curious about the Persians in general. Herodotus's use of inquiry, and his emphasis on sources and cause essentially invented the discipline of history. His methodology was adopted and adapted by the second of the founding fathers of Greek history writing, Thucydides, and by numerous historians thereafter.

Zoroastrianism is a religion that worships Ahura Mazda, a creator god of light and good. It was a religion that either was or became monotheistic; it certainly has many beliefs in common with the more explicitly monotheistic religions of Judaism, Christianity, and Islam. Many Zoroastrian ideas, such as the struggle between the forces of good and evil, the concept of the apocalypse, and the promise of a savior figure, link Zoroastrianism to the three later monotheistic faiths. There is a text from early Christianity in this chapter that illustrates a Roman emperor's role in shaping that faith, much as the Achaemenid Persian emperors had influence over the practices of Zoroastrianism.

In addition to the religious legacy, the Achaemenid Persians were profoundly important for world history because of their model of empire building. Herodotus, in his excerpt, notes that the Persians were open to the customs of other cultures; without losing their own traditions, they were tolerant of others over whom they had imperial power. Another aspect of the Persian approach to empire that will have lasting influence is their concept of power.Achaemenid Persians called their rulers "*shahinshah*" or "king of kings" to indicate their exalted status as rulers over many diverse cultures, peoples, and even over other kings. Two *shahinshahs* were particularly exalted: Cyrus the Great (550 – 530 B.C.E.) and Darius the Great (522 – 486 B.C.E.). Cyrus, the second of that name, expanded his rule from that of king of the Persians to emperor of a large empire that contained Mesopotamia, Persia, Lydia, and Ionia. The latter two regions brought Persia directly into contact with the Greek city-states located there. Darius restored the Achaemenid dynasty to power by defeating an interloper who had seized the throne. Both men are represented here by key texts that illustrate the degree of their power. After conquering Babylon in 539 B.C.E., Cyrus issued a declaration promising freedom of religious worship. Although the Persians were Zoroastrians, and in particular, the Achaemenids allied themselves with the Zoroastrianism, they did not enforce their religious system on the many peoples they conquered. Similarly, in his list of accomplishments, Darius promised to not be oppressive in his rule.

7.1   Darius I of Persia: the Behistan Inscription

Darius I, the Great (522 – 486 B.C.E.) personified the Achaemenid title of "shahinshah," or "king of kings." To defend his status as shahinshah, Darius had a list of his accomplishments inscribed on a cliff side in Behistan in Iran. The inscription, written in three different forms of cuneiform, was accompanied by a massive relief carving that depicted Darius leading a line of the captives. The list details Darius's victory over Gaumata, a magician (or Magian) who had usurped the throne of Persia from Cambyses. Gaumata pretended to be Bardiya, the son of Cyrus and brother to Cambyses, the emperor Gaumata challenged. Darius worshipped Ahuramazda, the main god of Zoroastrianism.

Source: "Achievements of Darius," from the Behistan Inscription of King Darius, from *A Sourcebook of Ancient History*, ed. George Willis Botsford and Lillie Shaw Botsford. (New York: Macmillan Company, 1927), 57-59.

A great god is Ahuramazda who created this excellent work which one sees; who created happiness for man; who bestowed wisdom and energy upon Darius the king. Says Darius the king: by the favor of Ahuramazda I am of such a kind that I am a friend to what is right, I am no friend to what is wrong. It is not my wish that to the weak is done wrong because of the mighty, it is not my wish that the weak is hurt because of the mighty, that the mighty is hurt because of the weak. What is right, that is my wish. I am no friend of the man who is a follower of the lie. I am not hot-tempered. When I feel anger rising, I keep that under control by my thinking power. I control firmly my impulses. The man who co-operates, him do I reward according to his co-operation. He who does harm, him I punish according to the damage. It is not my wish that a man does harm, it is certainly not my wish that a man if he causes damage be not punished. What a man says against a man, that does not convince me, until I have heard testimony from both parties. What a man does or performs according to his powers, satisfies me, therewith I am satisfied and it gives me great pleasure and I am very satisfied and I give much to faithful men.

I am trained with both hands and feet. As a horseman I am a good horseman. As a bowman I am a good bowman, both afoot and on horseback. As a spearman I am a good spearman, both afoot and on horseback. And the skills which Ahuramazda has bestowed upon me, and I have had the strength to use them, by the favour of Ahuramazda, what has been done by me, I have done with these skills which Ahuramazda has bestowed upon me.

Reading and Discussion Questions
1. With the list, Darius is trying to establish that he is the legitimate king of Persia. Find evidence in the list of accomplishments that serve that purpose.
2. According to Darius, what makes him worthy of being king?
3. How does the inscription indicate the extent of the Achaemenid empire?

7.2   Herodotus on the Battle of Thermopylae (480 B.C.E.)

Herodotus (c. 484-c.425 B.C.) is generally recognized as the "Father of History." Following the tradition of the Homeric epics, Herodotus sets out to chronicle the great and heroic deeds of men. Unlike Homer, however, Herodotus writes of the historic past in an attempt to understand the causes and origins of the war between the Greeks and Persians that culminated in the early years of his life. In this selection, Herodotus chronicles the desperate stand of the Spartans at Thermopylae, as the Greeks struggled with an overwhelmingly large Persian invasion force.

Source: G. Rawlinsn, *The History of Herodotus* (New York: E. P. Dutton, 1910)

Book VII

As far as this point then, and on land, as far as Thermopylae, the armament of Xerxes had been free from mischance; and the numbers were still, according to my reckoning, of the following amount. First there was the ancient complement of the twelve hundred and seven vessels which came with the king from Asia- the contingents of the nations severally- amounting, if we allow to each ship a crew of two hundred men, to 241,400. Each of these vessels had on board, besides native soldiers, thirty fighting men, who were either Persians, Medes, or Sacans; which gives an addition of 36,210. To these two numbers I shall further add the crews of the penteconters; which may be reckoned, one with another, at fourscore men each. Of such vessels there were (as I said before) three thousand; and the men on board them accordingly would be 240,000. This was the sea force brought by the king from Asia; and it amounted in all to 517,610 men. The number of the foot soldiers was 1,700,000; that of the horsemen 80,000; to which must be added the Arabs who rode on camels, and the Libyans who fought in chariots, whom I reckon at 20,000. The whole number, therefore, of the land and sea forces added together amounts to 2,317,610 men. Such was the force brought from Asia, without including the camp followers, or taking any account of the provision- ships and the men whom they had on board.

To the amount thus reached we have still to add the forces gathered in Europe, concerning which I can only speak from conjecture. The Greeks dwelling in Thrace, and in the islands off the coast of Thrace, furnished to the fleet one hundred and twenty ships; the crews of which would amount to 24,000 men. Besides these, footmen were furnished by the Thracians, the Paeonians, the Eordians, the Bottiaeans, by the Chalcidean tribes, by the Brygians, the Pierians, the Macedonians, the Perrhaebians the Enianians, the Dolopians, the Magnesians, the Achaeans and by all the dwellers upon the Thracian sea-board; and the forces of these nations amounted, I believe, to three hundred thousand men. These numbers, added to those of the force which came out of Asia, make the sum of the fighting men 2,641,610.

Such then being the number of the fighting men, it is my belief that the attendants who followed the camp, together with the crews of the corn-barks, and of the other craft accompanying the army, made up an amount rather above than below that of the fighting men. However I will not reckon them as either fewer or more, but take them at an equal number. We have therefore to add to the sum already reached an exactly equal amount. This will give 5,283,220 as the whole number of men brought by Xerxes, the son of Darius, as far as Sepias and Thermopylae.

Such then was the amount of the entire host of Xerxes. As for the number of the women who ground the corn, of the concubines, and the eunuchs, no one can give any sure account of it; nor can the baggage-horses and other sumpter-beasts, nor the Indian hounds which followed the army, be calculated, by reason of their multitude. Hence I am not at all surprised that the water of the rivers was found too scant for the army in some instances; rather it is a marvel to me how the provisions did not fail, when the numbers were so great. For I find on calculation that if each man consumed no more than a **choenix** of corn a day, there must have been used daily by the army 110,340 medimni, and this without counting what was eaten by the women, the eunuchs, the sumpter-beasts, and the hounds. Among all this multitude of men there was not one who, for beauty and stature, deserved more than Xerxes himself to wield so vast a power. . . .

The Greeks who at this spot awaited the coming of Xerxes were the following:- From Sparta, three hundred men-at-arms; from Arcadia, a thousand Tegeans and Mantineans, five hundred of each people; a hundred and twenty Orchomenians, from the Arcadian Orchomenus; and a thousand from other cities: from Corinth, four

---

choenix: unit of measure equal to approximately one quart

hundred men; from Phlius, two hundred; and from Mycenae eighty. Such was the number from the Peloponnese. There were also present, from Boeotia, seven hundred Thespians and four hundred Thebans.

Besides these troops, the Locrians of Opus and the Phocians had obeyed the call of their countrymen, and sent, the former all the force they had, the latter a thousand men. For envoys had gone from the Greeks at Thermopylae among the Locrians and Phocians, to call on them for assistance, and to say- "They were themselves but the vanguard of the host, sent to precede the main body, which might every day be expected to follow them. The sea was in good keeping, watched by the Athenians, the Eginetans, and the rest of the fleet. There was no cause why they should fear; for after all the invader was not a god but a man; and there never had been, and never would be, a man who was not liable to misfortunes from the very day of his birth, and those misfortunes greater in proportion to his own greatness. The assailant therefore, being only a mortal, must needs fall from his glory." Thus urged, the Locrians and the Phocians had come with their troops to Trachis.

The various nations had each captains of their own under whom they served; but the one to whom all especially looked up, and who had the command of the entire force, was the Lacedaemonian, Leonidas. Now Leonidas was the son of Anaxandridas, who was the son of Leo, who was the son of Eurycratidas, who was the son of Anaxander, who was the son of Eurycrates, who was the son of Polydorus, who was the son of Alcamenes, who was the son of Telecles, who was the son of Archelaus, who was the son of Agesilaus, who was the son of Doryssus, who was the son of Labotas, who was the son of Echestratus, who was the son of Agis, who was the son of Eurysthenes, who was the son of Aristodemus, who was the son of Aristomachus, who was the son of Cleodaeus, who was the son of Hyllus, who was the son of Hercules.

Leonidas had come to be king of Sparta quite unexpectedly.

Having two elder brothers, Cleomenes and Dorieus, he had no thought of ever mounting the throne. However, when Cleomenes died without male offspring, as Dorieus was likewise deceased, having perished in Sicily, the crown fell to Leonidas, who was older than Cleombrotus, the youngest of the sons of Anaxandridas, and, moreover, was married to the daughter of Cleomenes. He had now come to Thermopylae, accompanied by the three hundred men which the law assigned him, whom he had himself chosen from among the citizens, and who were all of them fathers with sons living. On his way he had taken the troops from Thebes, whose number I have already mentioned, and who were under the command of Leontiades the son of Eurymachus. The reason why he made a point of taking troops from Thebes, and Thebes only, was that the Thebans were strongly suspected of being well inclined to the Medes. Leonidas therefore called on them to come with him to the war, wishing to see whether they would comply with his demand, or openly refuse, and disclaim the Greek alliance. They, however, though their wishes leant the other way, nevertheless sent the men.

The force with Leonidas was sent forward by the Spartans in advance of their main body, that the sight of them might encourage the allies to fight, and hinder them from going over to the Medes, as it was likely they might have done had they seen that Sparta was backward. They intended presently, when they had celebrated the Carneian festival, which was what now kept them at home, to leave a garrison in Sparta, and hasten in full force to join the army. The rest of the allies also intended to act similarly; for it happened that the Olympic festival fell exactly at this same period. None of them looked to see the contest at Thermopylae decided so speedily; wherefore they were content to send forward a mere advanced guard. Such accordingly were the intentions of the allies.

The Greek forces at Thermopylae, when the Persian army drew near to the entrance of the pass, were seized with fear; and a council was held to consider about a retreat. It was the wish of the Peloponnesians generally that the army should fall back upon the Peloponnese, and there guard the Isthmus. But Leonidas, who saw with what indignation the Phocians and Locrians heard of this plan, gave his voice for remaining where they were, while they sent envoys to the several cities to ask for help, since they were too few to make a stand against an army like that of the Medes.

While this debate was going on, Xerxes sent a mounted spy to observe the Greeks, and note how many they were, and see what they were doing. He had heard, before he came out of Thessaly, that a few men were assembled at this place, and that at their head were certain Lacedaemonians, under Leonidas, a descendant of Hercules. The horseman rode up to the camp, and looked about him, but did not see the whole army; for such as were on the further side of the wall (which had been rebuilt and was now carefully guarded) it was not possible for him to behold; but he observed those on the outside, who were encamped in front of the rampart. It chanced that at this time the Lacedaemonians held the outer guard, and were seen by the spy, some of them engaged in gymnastic exercises, others combing their long hair. At this the spy greatly marvelled, but he counted their number, and when he had taken accurate note of everything, he rode back quietly; for no one pursued after him, nor paid any heed to his visit. So he returned, and told Xerxes all that he had seen.

Upon this, Xerxes, who had no means of surmising the truth- namely, that the Spartans were preparing to do or die manfully- but thought it laughable that they should be engaged in such employments, sent and called to his presence Demaratus the son of Ariston, who still remained with the army. When he appeared, Xerxes told him all that he had heard, and questioned him concerning the news, since he was anxious to understand the meaning of such behaviour on the part of the Spartans. Then Demaratus said-

"I spake to thee, O king! concerning these men long since, when we had but just begun our march upon Greece; thou, however, didst only laugh at my words, when I told thee of all this, which I saw would come to pass. Earnestly do I struggle at all times to speak truth to thee, sire; and now listen to it once more. These men have come to dispute the pass with us; and it is for this that they are now making ready. 'Tis their custom, when they are about to hazard their lives, to adorn their heads with care. Be assured, however, that if thou canst subdue the men who are here and the Lacedaemonians who remain in Sparta, there is no other nation in all the world which will venture to lift a hand in their defence. Thou hast now to deal with the first kingdom and town in Greece, and with the bravest men."

Then Xerxes, to whom what Demaratus said seemed altogether to surpass belief, asked further "how it was possible for so small an army to contend with his?"

"O king!" Demaratus answered, "let me be treated as a liar, if matters fall not out as I say."

But Xerxes was not persuaded any the more. Four whole days he suffered to go by, expecting that the Greeks would run away. When, however, he found on the fifth that they were not gone, thinking that their firm stand was mere impudence and recklessness, he grew wroth, and sent against them the Medes and Cissians, with orders to take them alive and bring them into his presence. Then the Medes rushed forward and charged the Greeks, but fell in vast numbers: others however took the places of the slain, and would not be beaten off, though they suffered terrible losses. In this way it became clear to all, and especially to the king, that though he had plenty of combatants, he had but very few warriors. The struggle, however, continued during the whole day.

Then the Medes, having met so rough a reception, withdrew from the fight; and their place was taken by the band of Persians under Hydarnes, whom the king called his "Immortals": they, it was thought, would soon finish the business. But when they joined battle with the Greeks, 'twas with no better success than the Median detachment- things went much as before- the two armies fighting in a narrow space, and the barbarians using shorter spears than the Greeks, and having no advantage from their numbers. The Lacedaemonians fought in a way worthy of note, and showed themselves far more skillful in fight than their adversaries, often turning their backs, and making as though they were all flying away, on which the barbarians would rush after them with much noise and shouting, when the Spartans at their approach would wheel round and face their pursuers, in this way destroying vast numbers of the enemy. Some Spartans likewise fell in these encounters, but only a very few. At last the Persians, finding that all their efforts to gain the pass availed nothing, and that, whether they attacked by divisions or in any other way, it was to no purpose, withdrew to their own quarters.

During these assaults, it is said that Xerxes, who was watching the battle, thrice leaped from the throne on which he sat, in terror for his army.

Next day the combat was renewed, but with no better success on the part of the barbarians. The Greeks were so few that the barbarians hoped to find them disabled, by reason of their wounds, from offering any further resistance; and so they once more attacked them. But the Greeks were drawn up in detachments according to their cities, and bore the brunt of the battle in turns- all except the Phocians, who had been stationed on the mountain to guard the pathway. So, when the Persians found no difference between that day and the preceding, they again retired to their quarters.

Now, as the king was in great strait, and knew not how he should deal with the emergency, Ephialtes, the son of Eurydemus, a man of Malis, came to him and was admitted to a conference. Stirred by the hope of receiving a rich reward at the king's hands, he had come to tell him of the pathway which led across the mountain to Thermopylae; by which disclosure he brought destruction on the band of Greeks who had there withstood the barbarians. This Ephialtes afterwards, from fear of the Lacedaemonians, fled into Thessaly; and during his exile, in an assembly of the Amphictyons held at Pylae, a price was set upon his head by the Pylagorae. When some time had gone by, he returned from exile, and went to Anticyra, where he was slain by Athenades, a native of Trachis. Athenades did not slay him for his treachery, but for another reason, which I shall mention in a later part of my history: yet still the Lacedaemonians honoured him none the less. Thus then did Ephialtes perish a long time afterwards.

Besides this there is another story told, which I do not at all believe- to wit, that Onetas the son of Phanagoras, a native of Carystus, and Corydallus, a man of Anticyra, were the persons who spoke on this matter to the king, and took the Persians across the mountain. One may guess which story is true, from the fact that the deputies of the Greeks, the Pylagorae, who must have had the best means of ascertaining the truth, did not offer the reward for the heads of Onetas and Corydallus, but for that of Ephialtes of Trachis; and again from the flight of Ephialtes, which we know to have been on this account. Onetas, I allow, although he was not a Malian, might have been acquainted with the path, if he had lived much in that part of the country; but as Ephialtes was the person who actually led the Persians round the mountain by the pathway, I leave his name on record as that of the man who did the deed.

Great was the joy of Xerxes on this occasion; and as he approved highly of the enterprise which Ephialtes undertook to accomplish, he forthwith sent upon the errand Hydarnes, and the Persians under him. The troops left the camp about the time of the lighting of the lamps. The pathway along which they went was first discovered by the Malians of these parts, who soon afterwards led the Thessalians by it to attack the Phocians, at the time when the Phocians fortified the pass with a wall, and so put themselves under covert from danger. And ever since, the path has always been put to an ill use by the Malians.

The course which it takes is the following:- Beginning at the Asopus, where that stream flows through the cleft in the hills, it runs along the ridge of the mountain (which is called, like the pathway over it, Anopaea), and ends at the city of Alpenus- the first Locrian town as you come from Malis- by the stone called Melampygus and the seats of the Cercopians. Here it is as narrow as at any other point.

The Persians took this path, and, crossing the Asopus, continued their march through the whole of the night, having the mountains of Oeta on their right hand, and on their left those of Trachis. At dawn of day they found themselves close to the summit. Now the hill was guarded, as I have already said, by a thousand Phocian men-at-arms, who were placed there to defend the pathway, and at the same time to secure their own country. They had been given the guard of the mountain path, while the other Greeks defended the pass below, because they had volunteered for the service, and had pledged themselves to Leonidas to maintain the post.

The ascent of the Persians became known to the Phocians in the following manner:- During all the time that they were making their way up, the Greeks remained unconscious of it, inasmuch as the whole mountain was covered with groves of oak; but it happened that the air was very still, and the leaves which the Persians stirred with their feet made, as it was likely they would, a loud rustling, whereupon the Phocians jumped up and flew to seize their arms. In a moment the barbarians came in sight, and, perceiving men arming themselves, were greatly amazed; for they had fallen in with an enemy when they expected no opposition. Hydarnes, alarmed at the sight, and fearing lest the Phocians might be Lacedaemonians, inquired of Ephialtes to what nation these troops belonged. Ephialtes told him the exact truth, whereupon he arrayed his Persians for battle. The Phocians, galled by the showers of arrows to which they were exposed, and imagining themselves the special object of the Persian attack, fled hastily to the crest of the mountain, and there made ready to meet death; but while their mistake continued, the Persians, with Ephialtes and Hydarnes, not thinking it worth their while to delay on account of Phocians, passed on and descended the mountain with all possible speed.

The Greeks at Thermopylae received the first warning of the destruction which the dawn would bring on them from the seer Megistias, who read their fate in the victims as he was sacrificing. After this deserters came in, and brought the news that the Persians were marching round by the hills: it was still night when these men arrived. Last of all, the scouts came running down from the heights, and brought in the same accounts, when the day was just beginning to break. Then the Greeks held a council to consider what they should do, and here opinions were divided: some were strong against quitting their post, while others contended to the contrary. So when the council had broken up, part of the troops departed and went their ways homeward to their several states; part however resolved to remain, and to stand by Leonidas to the last.

It is said that Leonidas himself sent away the troops who departed, because he tendered their safety, but thought it unseemly that either he or his Spartans should quit the post which they had been especially sent to guard. For my own part, I incline to think that Leonidas gave the order, because he perceived the allies to be out of heart and unwilling to encounter the danger to which his own mind was made up. He therefore commanded them to retreat, but said that he himself could not draw back with honour; knowing that, if he stayed, glory awaited him, and that Sparta in that case would not lose her prosperity. For when the Spartans, at the very beginning of the war, sent to consult the oracle concerning it, the answer which they received from the Pythoness was "that either Sparta must be overthrown by the barbarians, or one of her kings must perish." The prophecy was delivered in hexameter verse, and ran thus:-

O ye men who dwell in the streets of broad Lacedaemon!

Either your glorious town shall be sacked by the children of Perseus, Or, in exchange, must all through the whole Laconian country

Mourn for the loss of a king, descendant of great Heracles.

He cannot be withstood by the courage of bulls nor of lions,

Strive as they may; he is mighty as Jove; there is nought that shall stay him,

Till he have got for his prey your king, or your glorious city. The remembrance of this answer, I think, and the wish to secure the whole glory for the Spartans, caused Leonidas to send the allies away. This is more likely than that they quarrelled with him, and took their departure in such unruly fashion.

To me it seems no small argument in favour of this view, that the seer also who accompanied the army, Megistias, the Acarnanian- said to have been of the blood of Melampus, and the same who was led by the appearance of the victims to warn the Greeks of the danger which threatened them- received orders to retire (as it is certain he did) from Leonidas, that he might escape the coming destruction. Megistias, however, though bidden to depart, refused, and stayed with the army; but he had an only son present with the expedition, whom he now sent away.

So the allies, when Leonidas ordered them to retire, obeyed him and forthwith departed. Only the Thespians and the Thebans remained with the Spartans; and of these the Thebans were kept back by Leonidas as hostages, very much against their will. The Thespians, on the contrary, stayed entirely of their own accord, refusing to retreat, and declaring that they would not forsake Leonidas and his followers. So they abode with the Spartans, and died with them. Their leader was Demophilus, the son of Diadromes.

At sunrise Xerxes made libations, after which he waited until the time when the forum is wont to fill, and then began his advance. Ephialtes had instructed him thus, as the descent of the mountain is much quicker, and the distance much shorter, than the way round the hills, and the ascent. So the barbarians under Xerxes began to draw nigh; and the Greeks under Leonidas, as they now went forth determined to die, advanced much further than on previous days, until they reached the more open portion of the pass. Hitherto they had held their station within the wall, and from this had gone forth to fight at the point where the pass was the narrowest. Now they joined battle beyond the defile, and carried slaughter among the barbarians, who fell in heaps. Behind them the captains of the squadrons, armed with whips, urged their men forward with continual blows. Many were thrust into the sea, and there perished; a still greater number were trampled to death by their own soldiers; no one heeded the dying. For the Greeks, reckless of their own safety and desperate, since they knew that, as the mountain had been crossed, their destruction was nigh at hand, exerted themselves with the most furious valour against the barbarians.

By this time the spears of the greater number were all shivered, and with their swords they hewed down the ranks of the Persians; and here, as they strove, Leonidas fell fighting bravely, together with many other famous Spartans, whose names I have taken care to learn on account of their great worthiness, as indeed I have those of all the three hundred. There fell too at the same time very many famous Persians: among them, two sons of Darius, Abrocomes and Hyperanthes, his children by Phratagune, the daughter of Artanes. Artanes was brother of King Darius, being a son of Hystaspes, the son of Arsames; and when he gave his daughter to the king, he made him heir likewise of all his substance; for she was his only child.

Thus two brothers of Xerxes here fought and fell. And now there arose a fierce struggle between the Persians and the Lacedaemonians over the body of Leonidas, in which the Greeks four times drove back the enemy, and at last by their great bravery succeeded in bearing off the body. This combat was scarcely ended when the Persians with Ephialtes approached; and the Greeks, informed that they drew nigh, made a change in the manner of their fighting. Drawing back into the narrowest part of the pass, and retreating even behind the cross wall, they posted themselves upon a hillock, where they stood all drawn up together in one close body, except only the Thebans. The hillock whereof I speak is at the entrance of the straits, where the stone lion stands which was set up in honour of Leonidas. Here they defended themselves to the last, such as still had swords using them, and the others resisting with their hands and teeth; till the barbarians, who in part had pulled down the wall and attacked them in front, in part had gone round and now encircled them upon every side, overwhelmed and buried the remnant which was left beneath showers of missile weapons.

Thus nobly did the whole body of Lacedaemonians and Thespians behave; but nevertheless one man is said to have distinguished himself above all the rest, to wit, Dieneces the Spartan. A speech which he made before the Greeks engaged the Medes, remains on record. One of the Trachinians told him, "Such was the number of the barbarians, that when they shot forth their arrows the sun would be darkened by their multitude." Dieneces, not at all frightened at these words, but making light of the Median numbers, answered "Our Trachinian friend brings us excellent tidings. If the Medes darken the sun, we shall have our fight in the shade." Other sayings too of a like nature are reported to have been left on record by this same person.

Next to him two brothers, Lacedaemonians, are reputed to have made themselves conspicuous: they were named Alpheus and Maro, and were the sons of Orsiphantus. There was also a Thespian who gained greater glory than any of his countrymen: he was a man called Dithyrambus, the son of Harmatidas.

The slain were buried where they fell; and in their honour, nor less in honour those who died before Leonidas sent the allies away, an inscription was set up, which said:-

Here did four thousand men from Pelops' land

Against three hundred myriads bravely stand. This was in honour of all. Another was for the Spartans alone:-

Go, stranger, and to Lacedaemon tell

That here, obeying her behests, we fell. This was for the Lacedaemonians. The seer had the following:-

The great Megistias' tomb you here may view,

Whom slew the Medes, fresh from Spercheius' fords.

Well the wise seer the coming death foreknew,

Yet scorned he to forsake his Spartan lords.

These inscriptions, and the pillars likewise, were all set up by the Amphictyons, except that in honour of Megistias, which was inscribed to him (on account of their sworn friendship) by Simonides, the son of Leoprepes.

Two of the three hundred, it is said, Aristodemus and Eurytus, having been attacked by a disease of the eyes, had received orders from Leonidas to quit the camp; and both lay at Alpeni in the worst stage of the malady. These two men might, had they been so minded, have agreed together to return alive to Sparta; or if they did not like to return, they might have gone both to the field and fallen with their countrymen. But at this time, when either way was open to them, unhappily they could not agree, but took contrary courses. Eurytus no sooner heard that the Persians had come round the mountain than straightway he called for his armour, and having buckled it on, bade his helot lead him to the place where his friends were fighting. The helot did so, and then turned and fled; but Eurytus plunged into the thick of the battle, and so perished. Aristodemus, on the other hand, was faint of heart, and remained at Alpeni. It is my belief that if Aristodemus only had been sick and returned, or if both had come back together, the Spartans would have been content and felt no anger; but when there were two men with the very same excuse, and one of them was chary of his life, while the other freely gave it, they could not but be very wroth with the former.

This is the account which some give of the escape of Aristodemus. Others say that he, with another, had been sent on a message from the army, and, having it in his power to return in time for the battle, purposely loitered on the road, and so survived his comrades; while his fellow-messenger came back in time, and fell in the battle.

When Aristodemus returned to Lacedaemon, reproach and disgrace awaited him; disgrace, inasmuch as no Spartan would give him a light to kindle his fire, or so much as address a word to him; and reproach, since all spoke of him as "the craven." However he wiped away all his shame afterwards at the battle of Plataea.

Another of the three hundred is likewise said to have survived the battle, a man named Pantites, whom Leonidas had sent on an embassy into Thessaly. He, they say, on his return to Sparta, found himself in such disesteem that he hanged himself.

The Thebans under the command of Leontiades remained with the Greeks, and fought against the barbarians, only so long as necessity compelled them. No sooner did they see victory inclining to the Persians, and the Greeks under Leonidas hurrying with all speed towards the hillock, than they moved away from their companions, and with hands upraised advanced towards the barbarians, exclaiming, as was indeed most true- "that they for their part wished well to the Medes, and had been among the first to give earth and water to the king; force alone had brought them to Thermopylae; and so they must not be blamed for the slaughter which had befallen the king's army." These words, the truth of which was attested by the Thessalians, sufficed to obtain the Thebans the grant of their lives. However, their good fortune was not without some drawback; for several of them were slain by the barbarians on their first approach; and the rest, who were the greater number, had the royal mark branded upon their bodies by the command of Xerxes- Leontiades, their captain, being the first to suffer. (This man's son, Eurymachus, was afterwards slain by the Plataeans, when he came with a band Of 400 Thebans, and seized their city.)

Thus fought the Greeks at Thermopylae. . .

Reading and Discussion Questions

1. How does Herodotus portray Xerxes? Leonidas? For Herodotus, what is the chief character flaw of Xerxes? How does this contrast with how the Greeks are portrayed?
2. Why are the Persians described as "barbarians"? Herodotus is considered by many historians the first writer to contrast the European democratic tradition with "Oriental despotism". What evidence in the passage above supports or refutes this statement?

7.3   Anaximander, "On Nature"

Anaximander, a sixth century B.C.E. philosopher, mathematician, and astronomer, was one of a school of philosophers in Miletus, Ionia. Little is known of his life, and one brief piece of his writing has survived; as with many early philosophers, his ideas are known from other writers. It is known that he studied with Thales, who postulated that the world was composed of one basic material element, water. In contrast, Anaximander thought the universe was not reducible to a material element but was instead cause by the "infinite."

Source: Anaximander. "On Nature," from *The Classical Greek Reader,* ed. Kenneth J. Atchity (New York: Henry Holt and Company, 1996), 73.

1. The first principle of all other things is infinite. ... From this the heavens and the world, in them arise.
2. This first principle is eternal and does not grow old, and it surrounds all the worlds.
3. Motion is eternal, and as a result of it the heavens arise.
4. "Immortal" and "indestructible" surround all and direct all.
5. [To that they return when they are destroyed] of necessity; for ... they suffer punishment and give satisfaction to one another for injustice.
6. Existing opposites are separated from the unit·.
7. Things come into being not by change in the nature of the element, but by the separation of the opposites which the eternal motion causes.
8. The earth is a heavenly body, controlled by no other power, and keeping its position because it is the same distance from all things; the form of it is curved, cylindrical like a stone column; it has two faces: One of these is the ground beneath our feet, and the other is opposite to it.
9. The stars are a circle of fire, separated from the fire about the world, and surrounded by air. There are

certain breathing-holes like the holes of a flute through which we see the stars; so that when the holes arc stopped up, there are eclipses.

10.   The moon is sometimes full and sometimes in other phases as these holes are stopped up or open.

11.   The circle of the sun is twenty-seven times that of the moon, but the circles of the fixed stars are lower.

12.   Animals come into being through vapors raised by the sun.

13.   Man, however, came into being from another animal, namely the fish, for at first he was like a fish.

14.   Winds are due to a separation of the lightest vapors and the motion of the masses of these vapors and moisture comes from the vapor raised by the sun from them; and lightning occurs when a wind falls upon clouds and separates them.

15.   The soul is like air in its nature.

Reading and Discussion Questions

1.   How is Anaximander a precursor to evolutionary thought?

2.   What does Anaximander mean by the "first principle" and how did it work?

3.   One of the Greeks' innovations in both religion and science was their emphasis on observation; how does Anaximander represent that approach?

4.   Anaximander is credited with being the first "monist:" a believer in an impersonal first principle. Discuss what that means, using evidence from the text.

7.4   Plutarch on Julius Caesar

Plutarch (c. 46 – 120 CE) was the most important Greek writer of his age. He is best known for his *Lives of Noble Greeks and Romans*. In the *Lives* he attempted to present moral lessons by describing the lives of famous Greeks and Romans who exemplified specific virtues.

The subject of this selection from Plutarch's *Lives* is Gaius Julius Caesar (102 B.C.E.–44 B.C.E.). In this particular piece by Plutarch, it is believed that the opening paragraphs of this story, likely describing Caesar's birth and youth, are lost. Caesar is a key figure in Rome's transformation from republic to empire. Through a series of political alliances and military actions, he would rise into power and prominence – ultimately gaining full power through civil war in 49 B.C. and naming himself dictator for life. Under his rule, Rome underwent extensive changes through social and political reforms. His actions, however, clashed with many in the empire, including friend Marcus Junius Brutus, and would ultimately lead to his assassination on the Ides of March (March 15) in 44 B.C.E.

Source: Plutarch, *The Parallel Lives*. Translated by Bernadotte Perrin (London: Loeb Classical Library, 1919)

After these matters had been finished and he had been declared consul for the fourth time, Caesar made an expedition into Spain against the sons of Pompey. These were still young, but had collected an army of amazing numbers and displayed a boldness which justified their claims to leadership, so that they beset Caesar with the greatest peril. The great battle was joined near the city of Munda, and here Caesar, seeing his own men hard pressed and making a feeble resistance, asked in a loud voice as he ran through the armed ranks whether they felt no shame to take him and put him in the hands of boys. With difficulty and after much strenuous effort he repulsed the enemy and slew over thirty thousand of them, but he lost one thousand of his own men, and those the very best.

[...]

This was the last war that Caesar waged; and the triumph that was celebrated for it vexed the Romans as nothing else had done. For it commemorated no victory over foreign commanders or barbarian kings, but the utter annihilation of the sons and the family of the mightiest of the Romans, who had fallen upon misfortune; and it was not meet for Caesar to celebrate a triumph for the calamities of his country, priding himself upon actions which had no defence before gods or men except that they had been done under necessity, and that too although previously he had sent neither messenger nor letters to announce to the people a victory in the civil wars, but had scrupulously put from him the fame arising there from.

However, the Romans gave way before the good fortune of the man and accepted the bit, and regarding the monarchy as a respite from the evils of the civil wars, they appointed him dictator for life. This was confessedly a tyranny, since the monarchy, besides the element of irresponsibility, now took on that of permanence. It was Cicero who proposed the first honours for him in the senate, and their magnitude was, after all, not too great for a man; but others added excessive honours and vied with one another in proposing them, thus rendering Caesar odious and obnoxious even to the mildest citizens because of the pretension and extravagance of what was decreed for him. It is thought, too, that the enemies of Caesar no less than his flatterers helped to force these measures through, in order that they might have as many pretexts as possible against him and might be thought to have the best reasons for attempting his life. For in all other ways, at least, after the civil wars were over, he showed himself blameless; and certainly it is thought not inappropriate that the temple of Clemency was decreed as a thank-offering in view of his mildness. For he pardoned many of those who had fought against him, and to some he even gave honours and offices besides, as to Brutus and Cassius, both of whom were now praetors. The statues of Pompey, which had been thrown down, he would not suffer to remain so, but set them up again, at which Cicero said that in setting up Pompey's statues Caesar firmly fixed his own.

[…]

As for the nobles, to some of them he promised consulships and praetorships in the future, others he appeased with sundry other powers and honours, and in all he implanted hopes, since he ardently desired to rule over willing subjects. Therefore, when Maximus the consul died, he appointed Caninius Revilius consul for the one day still remaining of the term of office. To him, as we are told, many were going with congratulations and offers of escort, whereupon Cicero said: "Let us make haste, or else the man's consulship will have expired."

Caesar's many successes, however, did not divert his natural spirit of enterprise and ambition to the enjoyment of what he had laboriously achieved, but served as fuel and incentive for future achievements, and begat in him plans for greater deeds and a passion for fresh glory, as though he had used up what he already had. What he felt was therefore nothing else than emulation of himself, as if he had been another man, and a sort of rivalry between what he had done and what he purposed to do. For he planned and prepared to make an expedition against the Parthians; and after subduing these and marching around the **Euxine** by way of Hyrcania, the Caspian sea, and the Caucasus, to invade Scythia; and after overrunning the countries bordering on Germany and Germany itself, to come back by way of Gaul to Italy, and so to complete this circuit of his empire, which would then be bounded on all sides by the ocean. During this expedition, moreover, he intended to dig through the isthmus of Corinth, and had already put Anienus in charge of this work; he intended also to divert the Tiber just below the city into a deep channel, give it a bend towards Circeium, and make it empty into the sea at Terracina, thus contriving for merchantmen a safe as well as an easy passage to Rome; and besides this, to convert marshes about Pomentinum and Setia into a plain which many thousands of men could cultivate; and further, to build moles which should barricade the sea where it was nearest to Rome, to clear away the hidden dangers on the shore of Ostia, and then construct harbours and roadsteads sufficient for the great fleets that would visit them. And all these things were in preparation.

———
Euxine: the Black Sea

[...]

But the most open and deadly hatred towards him was produced by his passion for the royal power. For the multitude this was a first cause of hatred, and for those who had long smothered their hate, a most specious pretext for it. And yet those who were advocating this honour for Caesar actually spread abroad among the people a report that from the Sibylline books it appeared that Parthia could be taken if the Romans went up against it with a king, but otherwise could not be assailed; and as Caesar was coming down from Alba into the city they ventured to hail him as king. But at this the people were confounded, and Caesar, disturbed in mind, said that his name was not King, but Caesar, and seeing that his words produced an universal silence, he passed on with no very cheerful or contented looks. Moreover, after sundry extravagant honours had been voted him in the senate, it chanced that he was sitting above the rostra, and as the praetors and consuls drew near, with the whole senate following them, he did not rise to receive them, but as if he were dealing with mere private persons, replied that his honours needed curtailment rather than enlargement. This vexed not only the senate, but also the people, who felt that in the persons of the senators the state was insulted, and in a terrible dejection they went away at once, all who were not obliged to remain, so that Caesar too, when he was aware of his mistake, immediately turned to go home, and drawing back his toga from his neck, cried in loud tones to his friends that he was ready to offer his throat to any one who wished to kill him. But afterwards he made his disease an excuse for his behaviour, saying that the senses of those who are thus afflicted do not usually remain steady when they address a multitude standing, but are speedily shaken and whirled about, bringing on giddiness and insensibility. However, what he said was not true; on the contrary, he was very desirous of rising to receive the senate; but one of his friends, as they say, or rather one of his flatterers, Cornelius Balbus, restrained him, saying: "Remember that thou art Caesar, and permit thyself to be courted as a superior."

There was added to these causes of offence his insult to the tribunes. It was, namely, the festival of the Lupercalia, of which many write that it was anciently celebrated by shepherds, and has also some connection with the Arcadian Lycaea. At this time many of the noble youths and of the magistrates run up and down through the city naked, for sport and laughter striking those they meet with shaggy thongs. And many women of rank also purposely get in their way, and like children at school present their hands to be struck, believing that the pregnant will thus be helped to an easy delivery, and the barren to pregnancy. These ceremonies Caesar was witnessing, seated upon the rostra on a golden throne, arrayed in triumphal attire. And Antony was one of the runners in the sacred race; for he was consul. Accordingly, after he had dashed into the forum and the crowd had made way for him, he carried a diadem, round which a wreath of laurel was tied, and held it out to Caesar. Then there was applause, not loud, but slight and preconcerted. But when Caesar pushed away the diadem, all the people applauded; and when Antony offered it again, few, and when Caesar declined it again, all, applauded. The experiment having thus failed, Caesar rose from his seat, after ordering the wreath to be carried up to the Capitol; but then his statues were seen to have been decked with royal diadems. So two of the tribunes, Flavius and Maryllus, went up to them and pulled off the diadems, and after discovering those who had first hailed Caesar as king, led them off to prison. Moreover, the people followed the tribunes with applause and called them Brutuses, because Brutus was the man who put an end to the royal succession and brought the power into the hands of the senate and people instead of a sole ruler. At this, Caesar was greatly vexed, and deprived Maryllus and Flavius of their office, while in his denunciation of them, although he at the same time insulted the people, he called them repeatedly Brutes and Cymaeans.

Under these circumstances the multitude turned their thoughts towards Marcus Brutus, who was thought to be a descendant of the elder Brutus on his father's side, on his mother's side belonged to the Servilii, another illustrious house, and was a son-in law and nephew of Cato. The desires which Brutus felt to attempt of his own accord the abolition of the monarchy were blunted by the favours and honours that he had received from Caesar. For not only had his life been spared at Pharsalus after Pompey's flight, and the lives of many of his friends at his entreaty, but also he had great credit with Caesar. He had received the most honourable of the praetorships for the current year, and was to be consul three years later, having been preferred to Cassius, who was a rival candidate. For Caesar, as we are told, said that Cassius urged the juster claims to the office, but that for his own part he could not pass Brutus by. Once, too, when certain persons were actually accusing Brutus to him, the conspiracy being already on foot, Caesar would not heed them, but laying his hand upon his body said to the accusers: "Brutus will wait for this shrivelled skin," implying that Brutus was worthy to rule because of his virtue, but that for the sake of ruling he would not become a thankless villain. Those, however, who were eager for the change, and fixed their eyes on Brutus alone, or on him first, did not venture to talk with him directly, but by night they covered his praetorial tribune and chair with writings, most of which were of this sort: "Thou art asleep, Brutus," or, "Thou art not Brutus." When Cassius perceived that the ambition of Brutus was somewhat stirred by these things, he was more urgent with him than before, and pricked him on, having himself also some private grounds for hating Caesar; these I have mentioned in the Life of Brutus. Moreover, Caesar actually suspected him, so that he once said to his friends: "What, think ye, doth Cassius want? I like him not over much, for he is much too pale." And again, we are told that when Antony and Dolabella were accused to him of plotting revolution, Caesar said: "I am not much in fear of these fat, long-haired fellows, but rather of those pale, thin ones," meaning Brutus and Cassius.

[…]

The following story, too, is told by many. A certain seer warned Caesar to be on his guard against a great peril on the day of the month of March which the Romans call the Ides; and when the day had come and Caesar was on his way to the senate-house, he greeted the seer with a jest and said: "Well, the Ides of March are come," and the seer said to him softly: "Ay, they are come, but they are not gone." Moreover, on the day before, when Marcus Lepidus was entertaining him at supper, Caesar chanced to be signing letters, as his custom was, while reclining at table, and the discourse turned suddenly upon the question what sort of death was the best; before any one could answer Caesar cried out: "That which is unexpected." After this, while he was sleeping as usual by the side of his wife, all the windows and doors of the chamber flew open at once, and Caesar, confounded by the noise and the light of the moon shining down upon him, noticed that Calpurnia was in a deep slumber, but was uttering indistinct words and inarticulate groans in her sleep; for she dreamed, as it proved, that she was holding her murdered husband in her arms and bewailing him.

Some, however, say that this was not the vision which the woman had; but that there was attached to Caesar's house to give it adornment and distinction, by vote of the senate, a gable-ornament, as Livy says, and it was this which Calpurnia in her dreams saw torn down, and therefore, as she thought, wailed and wept. At all events, when day came, she begged Caesar, if it was possible, not to go out, but to postpone the meeting of the senate; if, however, he had no concern at all for her dreams, she besought him to inquire by other modes of divination and by sacrifices concerning the future. And Caesar also, as it would appear, was in some suspicion and fear. For never before had he perceived in Calpurnia any womanish superstition, but now he saw that she was in great distress. And when the seers also, after many sacrifices, told him that the omens were unfavourable, he resolved to send Antony and dismiss the senate.

But at this juncture Decimus Brutus, surnamed Albinus, who was so trusted by Caesar that he was entered in his will as his second heir, but was partner in the conspiracy of the other Brutus and Cassius, fearing that if Caesar should elude that day, their undertaking would become known, ridiculed the seers and chided Caesar for laying himself open to malicious charges on the part of the senators, who would think themselves mocked at;

for they had met at his bidding, and were ready and willing to vote as one man that he should be declared king of the provinces outside of Italy, and might wear a diadem when he went anywhere else by land or sea; but if some one should tell them at their session to be gone now, but to come back again when Calpurnia should have better dreams, what speeches would be made by his enemies, or who would listen to his friends when they tried to show that this was not slavery and tyranny? But if he was fully resolved (Albinus said) to regard the day as inauspicious, it was better that he should go in person and address the senate, and then postpone its business. While saying these things Brutus took Caesar by the hand and began to lead him along. And he had gone but a little way from his door when a slave belonging to someone else, eager to get at Caesar, but unable to do so for the press of numbers about him, forced his way into the house, gave himself into the hands of Calpurnia, and bade her keep him secure until Caesar came back, since he had important matters to report to him.

[…]

Well, then, Antony, who was a friend of Caesar's and a robust man, was detained outside by Brutus Albinus, who purposely engaged him in a lengthy conversation; but Caesar went in, and the senate rose in his honour. Some of the partisans of Brutus took their places round the back of Caesar's chair, while others went to meet him, as though they would support the petition which Tillius Cimber presented to Caesar in behalf of his exiled brother, and they joined their entreaties to his and accompanied Caesar up to his chair. But when, after taking his seat, Caesar continued to repulse their petitions, and, as they pressed upon him with greater importunity, began to show anger towards one and another of them, Tillius seized his toga with both hands and pulled it down from his neck. This was the signal for the assault. It was Casca who gave him the first blow with his dagger, in the neck, not a mortal would, nor even a deep one, for which he was too much confused, as was natural at the beginning of a deed of great daring; so that Caesar turned about, grasped the knife, and held it fast. At almost the same instant both cried out, the smitten man in Latin: "Accursed Casca, what does thou?" and the smiter, in Greek, to his brother: "Brother, help!"

So the affair began, and those who were not privy to the plot were filled with consternation and horror at what was going on; they dared not fly, nor go to Caesar's help, nay, nor even utter a word. But those who had prepared themselves for the murder bared each of them his dagger, and Caesar, hemmed in on all sides, whichever way he turned confronting blows of weapons aimed at his face and eyes, driven hither and thither like a wild beast, was entangled in the hands of all; for all had to take part in the sacrifice and taste of the slaughter. Therefore Brutus also gave him one blow in the groin. And it is said by some writers that although Caesar defended himself against the rest and darted this way and that and cried aloud, when he saw that Brutus had drawn his dagger, he pulled his toga down over his head and sank, either by chance or because pushed there by his murderers, against the pedestal on which the statue of Pompey stood. And the pedestal was drenched with his blood, so that one might have thought that Pompey himself was presiding over this vengeance upon his enemy, who now lay prostrate at his feet, quivering from a multitude of wounds. For it is said that he received twenty-three; and many of the conspirators were wounded by one another, as they struggled to plant all those blows in one body.

Caesar thus done to death, the senators, although Brutus came forward as if to say something about what had been done, would not wait to hear him, but burst out of doors and fled, thus filling the people with confusion and helpless fear, so that some of them closed their houses, while others left their counters and places of business and ran, first to the place to see what had happened, then away from the place when they had seen. Antony and Lepidus, the chief friends of Caesar, stole away and took refuge in the houses of others. But Brutus and his partisans, just as they were, still warm from the slaughter, displaying their daggers bare, went all in a body out of the senate-house and marched to the Capitol, not like fugitives, but with glad faces and full of confidence, summoning the multitude to freedom, and welcoming into their ranks the most distinguished of those who met them. Some also joined their number and went up with them as though they had shared in the deed, and laid claim to the glory of it, of whom were Caius Octavius and Lentulus Spinther. These men, then, paid the penalty for their imposture later, when they were put to death by Antony and the **young Caesar**, without even enjoying the fame for the sake of which they died, owing to the disbelief of their fellow men. For even those who punished them did not exact a penalty for what they did, but for what they wished they had done....

Reading and Discussion Questions

1. How is Caesar depicted by Plutarch? Is his murder portrayed as something he deserved?
2. How is kingship portrayed by Plutarch? Republican principles?
3. Plutarch wrote when the Roman Empire was its height. Is Plutarch's biography of Julius Caesar a commentary on the nature of imperial rule?

7.5   Eusebius on Constantine the Great

Constantine I became caesar in 306 C.E.; by 312 he had established himself as an emperor and defeated his most powerful rival for power. Secure in his political power, Constantine quickly turned to matters of religion. He was responsible for issuing the Edict of Milan, along with Lucinius (a co-emperor and another rival) in 313. This Edict officially made Christianity legal within the empire. This was only the first of many steps Constantine took to promote Christianity.

Constantine also took on a leadership role in relation to the church. In 325, Constantine summoned a church council at Nicaea, to combat heresy and define a statement of belief, or a creed. Eusebius, Bishop of Caesarea, recorded the events of the council and the creed in his *Ecclesiastical History,* one of the most important sources for the history of early Christianity although very much a believer's history.

Source: Eusebius, *The Life of the Blessed Emperor Constantine.* (London: Samuel Bagster and Sons, 1844), 120-126

The Vision of Constantine I the Great

Now, Constantine looked upon all the world as one vast body. But he observed that the head of it all, the imperial city of the Roman Empire, was oppressed by a tyrannous slavery. He had at first left the task of its protection to the rulers of the other parts of the Empire. After all, they were older than he was. But when none of these was able to provide help, when those attempting to do so were stopped in a disastrous manner, he declared that life was not worth living as long as he saw the imperial city thus afflicted. He therefore began preparations to overthrow the tyranny.

He knew well that he needed more powerful help than he could get from his army. This was on account of the evil practices and magical tricks which were so favored by the tyrant. Constantine therefore sought the help of God. Armed men and soldiers were of secondary importance when compared with God's aid, he believed, and he considered that the assistance of God was invincible and unshakable. But on which god could he depend as an ally? That was his problem. As he pondered the question, a thought occurred to him. Of his numerous imperial predecessors, those who had put their hopes in a multitude of gods and had served them

---

young Caesar: Octavian, distant relative of Julius Caesar and the first Roman emperor, who assumed the title "Augustus".

with libations and sacrificial offerings were first of all deceived by flattering prophecies, by oracles promising success to them, and still had come to a bad end. None of their gods stood by them or warned them of the catastrophe about to afflict them. On the other hand, his own father, who had been the only one to follow the opposite course and denounce their error, had given honor to almighty God throughout his life and had found in Him a savior, a protector of his Empire, and the provider of all good things.

As he pondered this matter, he reflected that those who had trusted in a multitude of gods had been brought low by many forms of death. They had left neither family nor offspring, stock, name, nor memorial among men. But the God of his father had given him clear and numerous indications of His power. Constantine furthermore considered the fact that those who had earlier sought to campaign against the tyrant and had gone to battle accompanied by a great number of gods had suffered a disgraceful end. One of them shamefully retreated from an encounter without striking a blow. The other was fair game for death and was killed among his own soldiers. Constantine thought of all these things, and decided that it would be stupid to join in the empty worship of those who were no gods and to stray from truth after observing all this positive evidence. He decided that only the God of his father ought to be worshiped.

He prayed to Him, therefore. He asked Him and besought Him to say Who He was and to stretch forth a hand to him in his present situation. As he prayed in this fashion and as he earnestly gave voice to his entreaties, a most marvelous sign appeared to the Emperor from God. It would have been hard to believe if anyone else had spoken of it. But a long time later the triumphant Emperor himself described it to the writer of this work. This was when I had the honor of knowing him and of being in his company. When he told me the story, he swore to its truth. And who could refuse to believe it, especially when later evidence showed it to have been genuine?

Around noontime, when the day was already beginning to decline, he saw before him in the sky the sign of a cross of light. He said it was above the sun and it bore the inscription, "Conquer with this." The vision astounded him, as it astounded the whole army which was with him on this expedition and which also beheld the miraculous event.

He said he became disturbed. What could the vision mean? He continued to ponder and to give great thought to the question, and night came on him suddenly. When he was asleep, the Christ of God appeared to him and He brought with Him the sign which had appeared in the sky. He ordered Constantine to make a replica of this sign which he had witnessed in the sky, and he was to use it as a protection during his encounters with the enemy.

In the morning he told his friends of this extraordinary occurrence. Then he summoned those who worked with gold or precious stones, and he sat among them and described the appearance of the sign. He told them to represent it in gold and precious stones.

It was made in the following way. There was a long spear, covered with gold, and forming the shape of the Cross through having a transverse bar overlaying it. Over it all there was a wreath made of gold and precious stones. Within it was the symbol of the Savior's name, two letters to show the beginning of Christ's name. And the letter *P* was divided at the center by *X*. Later on, the Emperor adopted the habit of wearing these insignia on his helmet. . . .

The Emperor regularly used this saving symbol as a protection against every contrary and hostile power. Copies of it were carried by his command at the head of all his armies.

Constantine's Victory Over Maxentius at the Milvian Bridge

Constantine was the leading emperor in rank and dignity, and he was the first to show pity on the victims of tyranny at Rome. He prayed the God of heaven and Jesus Christ, the Savior of all, to be his allies, and with all his forces he marched to restore to the Romans their ancient liberty. Maxentius, of course, relied more upon the devices of magic than on the goodwill of his subjects. Indeed, he lacked the courage to go even beyond the city gates. Instead, he employed a numberless crowd of heavy-armed soldiers and countless legionary bands to secure every place, every region, and every city which had been enslaved by him in the neighborhood of Rome and throughout Italy. But the Emperor, who trusted in the alliance of God, attacked the first, second, and third of the tyrant's armies and easily captured them. He advanced over a great part of Italy and drew very close to Rome itself.

Forestalling the need to fight Romans on account of the tyrant, God Himself, as though using chains, dragged the tyrant far away from the gates of the city. Just as in the days of Moses himself and of the ancient godly race of Hebrews, "He cast into the sea the chariots and the host of Pharaoh, his chosen horsemen and his captains, and they sank in the Red Sea and the deep concealed them." In the same way, Maxentius, with the armed soldiers and guards who surrounded him, "sank into the depths like a stone." This happened while he was fleeing before the God-sent power of Constantine and while he was crossing the river that lay before his path. By joining the boats together, he had efficiently bridged this river, and yet by doing so he had forged an instrument of destruction for himself. . . . For the bridge over the river broke down and the passage across collapsed. At once the boats, men and all, sank into the deep, and the first to go was that most wicked man himself.

Reading and Discussion Questions

1. How does Eusebius portray pagan Rome? How is the omen Constantine received before the Battle of Milvian Bridge portrayed by Eusebius as coming from the Christian god? Is there a motive behind Eusebius's glorification of Constantine's victory this way?
2. Do you believe the political and military realties were more complex than Eusebisu would have his readers believe?

7.6   The Tondo of St. Mamai

Thrown to the lions in 275 C.E. by the Romans for refusing to recant his Christian beliefs, St. Mamai is an important martyr in the iconography of Georgia, a Caucasian kingdom that embraced Christianity early in the 4th century. This gilded silver medallion, made in Georgia in the eleventh century, depicts the saint astride a lion while he bears a cross in one hand, symbolizing his triumphant victory over death and ignorance.

Reading and Discussion Questions

1. How does this medallion show the emergence of a new religious civilization in late antiquity in the West?
2. Find a map that shows Georgia in the 11th century C.E., the time when this medallion was made. What about the context of this period makes the symbolism of this artwork particularly powerful?

Source: Courtesy of the Kekelidze Institute of Manuscripts, Tbilisi, Georgia

Empires and Visionaries in India

India underwent many religious and cultural changes during the Mauryan (322 – 185 B.C.E.) and Gupta (322 – 550) Empires, and the period in between. Both of these were religious empires. The Mauryan Empire supported Brahmanism and Jainism, until the third Mauryan emperor re-created himself as a Buddhist ruler. The Gupta dynasty supported Hinduism, and it turn was supported by the religion's emphasis on the ruler as personally connected to gods such as Vishnu. The Gupta were also witnesses to the transformation of Vedic Brahmanism into true Hinduism. In addition to the religious developments, these were also important empires in that they represented rare moments of political unification for a significant portion of the Indian subcontinent. Chandragupta Maurya created a model for state building in northern Indian that would be copied by the subsequent Gupta dynasty, yet not again until the Muslims came in and created the Delhi Sultanate and Mughal Empires much later. The tendency of the Indian region to decentralize politically is matched by the religious diversity. Cultural unity was provided by the widespread prevalence of the caste system and a core of shared beliefs, such as reincarnation, a common pantheon of gods, shared languages, and a search for spiritual truth.

The specifics of that truth did vary from tradition to tradition. The religious concepts introduced in the *Vedas*, and opened up by the *Upanishads* and great *Mahabharata* and *Ramayana* epics were, by the fifth century B.C.E., no longer sufficient to satisfy the spiritual needs of most of the believers. Rituals performed by the elite for the elite, by the Brahmin (priests) for the nobility, excluded the majority of India's population, even thought they too were trapped in the same pattern of *karma – samsara*. Thus, a few centuries before Chandragupta Maurya first unified his way across north India, Buddhism and Jainism offered their own alternatives to the Vedic Brahmanism. Mauryan rulers traveled down these same alternative religious paths. After his conversion, Ashoka dedicated himself to *dharma* and became an advocate for its principles of right conduct and moral living. Two generations before Ashoka, his grandfather Chandragupta Maurya renounced his title to take on the ascetic life of the Jains.

8.1   The *Dhammapada*

The *Dhammapada* is sometimes referred to as the "Path of Virtue" and is a compilation of brief aphorisms credited to the Buddha. It can be read, and used, as both a metaphysical exploration of the Buddhist understanding of *dharma* as well as a pragmatic guide to living as a Buddhist.

Source: Buddha, "Excerpts from the Dhammapada," translated by F. Max Müller, 1886

THE TWIN VERSES

All that we are is the result of what we have thought: it is founded on our thoughts, it is made up of our thoughts. If a man speaks or acts with an evil thought, pain follows him, as the wheel follows the foot of the ox that draws the carriage.

All that we are is the result of what we have thought: it is founded on our thoughts, it is made up of our thoughts. If a man speaks or acts with a pure thought, happiness follows him, like a shadow that never leaves him.

'He abused me, he beat me, he defeated me, he robbed me,'—in those who harbour such thoughts hatred will never cease.

'He abused me, he beat me, he defeated me, he robbed me,'—in those who do not harbour such thoughts hatred will cease.

For hatred does not cease by hatred at any time: hatred ceases by love, this is an old rule.

The world does not know that we must all come to an end here; —but those who know it, their quarrels cease at once. He who lives looking for pleasures only, his senses uncontrolled, immoderate in his food, idle, and weak,

Mâra (the tempter) will certainly overthrow him, as the wind throws down a weak tree.

He who lives without looking for pleasures, his senses well controlled, moderate in his food, faithful and strong, him Mâra will certainly not overthrow, any more than the wind throws down a rocky mountain. He who wishes to put on the yellow dress without having cleansed himself from sin, who disregards also temperance and truth, is unworthy of the yellow dress.

They who imagine truth in untruth, and see untruth in truth, never arrive at truth, but follow vain desires. They who know truth in truth, and untruth in untruth, arrive at truth, and follow true desires. As rain breaks through an ill-thatched house, passion will break through an unreflecting mind. As rain does not break through a well thatched house, passion will not break through a well reflecting mind. The evildoer mourns in this world, and he mourns in the next; he mourns in both. He mourns and suffers when he sees the evil of his own work.

The virtuous man delights in this world, and he delights in the next; he de lights in both. He delights and rejoices when he sees the purity of his own work.

The evildoer suffers in this world, and he suffers in the next; he suffers in both. He suffers when he thinks of the evil he has done; he suffers more when going on the evil path.

The virtuous man is happy in this world, and he is happy in the next; he is happy in both. He is happy when he thinks of the good he has done; he is still more happy when going on the good path.

The thoughtless man, even if he can recite a large portion (of the law), but is not a doer of it, has no share in the priesthood, but is like a cowherd counting the cows of others.

The follower of the law, even if he can recite only a small portion (of the law), but, having forsaken passion and hatred and foolishness, possesses true knowledge and serenity of mind, he, caring for nothing in this world or that to come, has indeed a share in the priesthood.

CHAPTER III
Thought

As a fletcher makes straight his arrow, a wise man makes straight his trembling and unsteady thought, which is difficult to guard, difficult to hold back.

As a fish taken from his watery home and thrown on the dry ground, our thought trembles all over in order to escape the dominion of Mâra (the tempter).

It is good to tame the mind, which is difficult to hold in and flighty, rushing wherever it listeth; a tamed mind brings happiness.

Let the wise man guard his thoughts, for they are difficult to perceive, very artful, and they rush wherever they list; thoughts well guarded bring happiness.

Those who bridle their mind which travels far, moves about alone, is without a body, and hides in the chamber (of the heart), will be free from the bonds of Mâra (the tempter).

If a man's thoughts are unsteady, if he does not know the true law, if his peace of mind is troubled, his knowledge will never be perfect.

If a man's thoughts are not dissipated, if his mind is not perplexed, if he has ceased to think of good or evil, then there is no fear for him while he is watchful.

Before long, alas! this body will lie on the earth, despised, without understanding, like a useless log.

Whatever a hater may do to a hater, or an enemy to an enemy, a wrongly directed mind will do us greater mischief.

Not a mother, not a father will do so much, nor any other relative; a well directed mind will do us greater service.

CHAPTER V
The Fool

Long is the night to him who is awake; long is a mile to him who is tired; long is life to the foolish who do not know the true law.

If a traveller does not meet with one who is his better, or his equal, let him firmly keep to his solitary journey; there is no companionship with a fool.

'These sons belong to me, and this wealth belongs to me,' with such thoughts a fool is tormented. He himself does not belong to himself; how much less sons and wealth?

The fool who knows his foolishness is wise at least so far. But a fool who thinks himself wise, he is called a fool indeed.

If a fool be associated with a wise man even all his life, he will perceive the truth as little as a spoon perceives the taste of soup.

If an intelligent man be associated for one minute only with a wise man, he will soon perceive the truth as the tongue perceives the taste of soup.

Fools of little understanding have themselves for their greatest enemies, for they do evil deeds which must bear biller fruits.

That deed is not well done of which a man must repent, and the reward of which he receives crying and with a tearful face.

No, that deed is well done of which a man does not repent, and the reward of which he receives gladly and cheerfully.

As long as the evil deed done does not bear fruit, the fool thinks it is like honey; but when it ripen s, then the fool suffers grief.

Let a fool month after month eat his food (like an ascetic) with the tip of a blade of Kusa grass, yet is he not worth the sixteenth particle of those who have well weighed the law?

An evil deed, like newly drawn milk, does not turn (suddenly); smouldering, like tire covered by ashes, it follows the fool.

CHAPTER VI
The Wise Man

If you see an intelligent man who tells you where true treasures are to be found, who shows what is to be avoided, and administers reproofs, follow that wise man; it will be better, not worse, tor those who follow him.

Let him admonish, let him teach, let him forbid what is improper! —he will be beloved of the good, by the bad he will be hated.

Do not have evildoers for friends, do not have low people for friends; have virtuous people for friends, have for friends the best of men. He who drinks in the law lives happily with a serene mind; the sage rejoices always in the law, as preached by the elect (Ariyas).

Well makers lead the water (wherever they like); fletchers bend the arrow; carpenters bend a log of wood; wise people fashion themselves.

As a solid rock is not shaken by the wind, wise people falter not amidst blame and praise.

Wise people, after they have listened to the laws, become serene, like a deep, smooth, and still lake.

Good people walk on whatever befall s, the good do not prattle, longing for pleasure; whether touched by happiness or sorrow wise people never appear elated or depressed.

If, whether for his own sake, or for the sake of others, a man wishes neither for a son, nor for wealth, nor for lordship, and if he does not wish for his own success by unfair means, then he is good, wise, and virtuous.

CHAPTER IX
Evil

If a man would hasten towards the good, he should keep his thought away from evil; if a man does what is good slothfully, his mind delights in evil. If a man commits a sin, let him not do it again; let him not delight in sin; pain is the outcome of evil.

If a man does what is good, let him do it again; let him delight in it; happiness is the outcome of good. Even an evildoer sees happiness as long as his evil deed has not ripened; but when his evil deed has ripened, then does the evildoer see evil.

Even a good man sees evil days, as long as his good deed has not ripened; but when his good deed has ripened, then does the good man see happy days.

Let no man think lightly of evil, saying in his heart, It will not come nigh unto me. Even by the tailing of water-drops a water-pot is filled; the fool becomes full of evil, even if he gathers it little by little.

Let no man think lightly of good, saying in his heart. It will not come nigh unto me. Even by the falling of water-drops a water-pot is tilled; the wise man becomes full of good, even if he gathers it little by little. Let a man avoid evil deeds, as a merchant, if he has few companions and carries much wealth, avoids a dangerous road; as a man who loves life avoids poison.

If a man offend a harmless, pure, and innocent person, the evil falls back upon that fool, like light dust thrown up against the wind.

Some people are born again; evildoers go to hell; righteous people go to heaven; those who are free from all worldly desires attain Nirvana.

CHAPTER XIII
The World

Do not follow the evil law! Do not live on in thoughtlessness! Do not follow false doctrine! Be not a friend of the world.

Rouse thyself! Do not be idle! Follow the law of virtue! The virtuous rest in bliss in this world and in the next.

Follow the law of virtue; do not follow that of sin. The virtuous rests in bliss in this world and in the next.

Look upon the world as a bubble, look upon it as a mirage; the king of death does not see him who thus looks down upon the world. Come, look at this glittering world, like unto a royal chariot; the foolish are immersed in it, but the wise do not touch it.

He who formerly was reckless and afterwards became sober, brightens up this world, like the moon when freed from clouds.

He whose evil deeds are covered by good deeds, brightens up this world, like the moon when freed from clouds.

This world is dark, few only can see here; a few only go to heaven, like birds escaped from the net. The swans go on the path of the sun, they go through the ether by means of their miraculous power; the wise are led out of this world, when they have conquered Mâra and his train.

If a man has transgressed one law, and speaks lies, and scoffs at another world, there is no evil he will not do.

The uncharitable do not go to the world of the gods; fools only do not praise liberality; a wise man rejoices in liberality, and through it becomes blessed in the other world.

Better than sovereignty over the earth, better than going to heaven, better than lordship over all worlds, is the reward of the first step in holiness.

CHAPTER XIV
The Buddha

He whose conquest is not conquered again, into whose conquest no one in this world enters, by what track can you lead him, the Awakened, the Omniscient, the trackless?

Even the gods envy those who are awakened and not forgetful, who are given to meditation, who are wise, and who delight in the repose of retirement (from the world).

Difficult (to obtain) is the conception of men, difficult is the life of mortals, difficult is the hearing of the True Law, difficult is the birth of the Awakened (the attainment of Buddhahood).

Not to commit any sin, to do good, and to purify one's mind, that is the teaching of (all) the Awakened.

The Awakened call patience the highest penance, long suffering the highest Nirvana; for he is not an anchorite who strikes others, he is not an ascetic who insults others. Not to blame, not to strike, to live restrained under the law, to be moderate in eating, to sleep and sit alone, and to dwell on the highest thoughts,-this is the teaching of the Awakened.

There is no satisfying lusts, even by a shower of gold pieces; he who knows that lusts have a short taste and cause pain, he is wise. Even in heavenly pleasures he finds no satisfaction, the disciple who is fully awakened delights only in the destruction of all desires.

Men, driven by fear, go to many a refuge, to mountains and forests, to groves and sacred trees. But that is not a sate refuge, that is not the best refuge; a man is not delivered from all pains after having gone to that refuge.

He who takes refuge with Buddha, the Law, and the Church; he who, with clear understanding, sees the four holy truths: Pain, the origin of pain, the destruction of pain, and the eightfold holy way that leads to the quieting of pain.

That is the safe refuge, that is the best refuge; having gone to that refuge, a man is delivered from all pain. A supernatural person (a Buddha) is not easily found, he is not born everywhere. Wherever such a sage is born, that race prospers.

Happy is the arising of the awakened, happy is the teaching of the True Law, happy is peace in the church, happy is the devotion of those who are at peace. He who pays homage to those who deserve homage, whether the awakened (Buddha) or their disciples, those who have overcome the host (of evils), and crossed the flood of sorrow, he who pays homage to such as have found deliverance and know no fear, his merit can never be measured by anybody.

CHAPTER XVI
Pleasure

He who gives himself to vanity, and does not give himself to meditation, forgetting the real aim (of life) and grasping at pleasure, will in time envy him who has exerted himself in meditation. Let no man ever look for what is pleasant, or what is unpleasant. Not to see what is pleasant is pain, and it is pain to see what is unpleasant.

Let, therefore, no man love anything; loss of the beloved is evil. Those who love nothing, and hate nothing, have no fetters.

From affection comes grief, from affection comes fear; he who is free from affection knows neither grief nor fear.

From lust comes grief, from lust comes fear; he who is free from lust knows neither grief nor fear. From love comes grief, from love comes fear; he who is free from love knows neither grief nor fear.

From greed comes grief, from greed comes fear; he who is free from greed knows neither grief nor fear. He who possesses virtue and intelligence, who is just, speaks the truth, and does what is his own business, him the world will hold dear.

CHAPTER XVII
Anger

Let a man leave anger, let him forsake pride, let him overcome all bondage! No sufferings befall the man who is not attached to name and form, and who calls nothing his own.

He who holds back rising anger like a rolling chariot, him J call a real driver; other people are but holding the rein s.

Let a man overcome anger by love, let him overcome evil by good; let him overcome the greedy by liberality, the liar by truth!

Speak the truth, do not yield to anger; give, if thou art asked for little; by these three steps thou wilt go near the gods.

The sages who injure nobody, and who always control their body, they will go to the unchangeable place (Nirvana), where, if they have gone, they will suffer no more.

Those who are ever watchful, who study day and night, and who strive after Nirvana their passions will come to an end.

This is an old saying, O Atula, this is not only of today: 'They blame him who sits silent, they blame him who speaks much, they also blame him who says little; there is no one on earth who is not blamed.'

There never was, there never will be, nor is there now, a man who is always blamed, or a man who is always praised.

But he whom those who discriminate praise continually day after day, as without blemish, wise, rich in knowledge and virtue, who would dare to blame him like a coin made of gold from the Gambž river? Even the gods praise him, he is praised even by Brahman.

Beware of bodily anger, and control thy body! Leave the sins of the body, and with thy body practice virtue!

Beware of the anger of the tongue, and control thy tongue! Leave the sins of the tongue, and practice virtue with thy tongue!

Beware of the anger of the mind, and control thy mind! Leave the sins of the mind, and practice virtue with they mind!

CHAPTER XVIII
Impurity

Thou art now like a sere leaf, the messengers of death have come near to thee; thou standest at the door of thy departure, and thou hast no provision for thy journey.

Make thyself an island, work hard, be wise! When thy impurities are blown away, and thou art free from guilt, thou wilt enter into the heavenly world of the elect.

Thy life has come to an end, thou art come near to death, there is no resting place for thee on the road, and thou hast no provision for thy journey.

Make thyself an island, work hard, be wise! When thy impurities are blown away, and thou art free from guilt, thou wilt not enter again into birth and decay.

Let a wise man blow off the impurities of his self, as a smith blows off the impurities of silver, one by one, little by little, and from time to time.

As the impurity which springs from the iron, when it springs from it, destroys it; thus do a transgressor's own works lead him to the evil path.

The taint of prayers is non-repetition; the taint of houses, non-repair; the taint of the body is sloth; the taint of a watchman, thoughtlessness.

Bad conduct is the taint of woman, greediness the taint of a benefactor; tainted are all evil ways, in this world and in the next.

But there is a taint worse than all taints,—ignorance is the greatest taint. O mendicants! throw off that taint, and become taintless!

Life is easy to live for a man who is without shame, a crow hero, a mischief-maker, an insulting, bold, and wretched fellow.

But life is hard to live for a modest man, who always looks for what is pure, who is disinterested, quiet, spotless, and intelligent.

He who destroys life, who speaks untruth, who in this world takes what is not given him, who goes to another man's wife.

And the man who gives himself to drinking intoxicating liquors, he, even in this world, digs up his own root.

O man, know this, that the unrestrained are in a bad state; take care that greediness and vice do not bring thee to grief for a long time!

The world gives according to their faith or according to their pleasure; if a man frets about the food and the drink given to others, he will find no rest either by day or by night. He in whom that feeling is destroyed, and taken out with the very root, finds rest by day and by night.

The fault of others is easily perceived, but that of oneself is difficult to perceive; a man Winnows his neighbour's faults like chaff, but his own fault he hides, as a cheat hides the bad die from the gambler.

CHAPTER XXII
The Downward Course

He who says what is not, goes to hell; he also who, having done a thing, says I have not done it. After death both are equal, they are men with evil deeds in the next world.

Many men whose shoulders are covered with the yellow gown are ill-conditioned and unrestrained; such evildoers by their evil deeds go to hell. Better it would be to swallow a heated iron ball, like flaring fire, than that a bad unrestrained fellow should live on the charity of the land.

Four things does a reckless man gain who covets his neighbour's wife,-a bad reputation, an uncomfortable bed, thirdly, punishment, and lastly, hell. There is bad reputation, and the evil way (to hell), there is the short pleasure of the frightened in the arms of the frightened, and the king imposes heavy punishment; therefore let no man think of his neighbour's wife. As a grass blade, if badly grasped, cuts the arm, badly-practised asceticism leads to hell. An act carelessly performed, a broken vow, and hesitating obedience to discipline, all this brings no great reward.

If anything is to be done, let a man do it, let him attack it vigorously! A careless pilgrim only scatters the dust of his passions more widely. An evil deed is better left undone, for a man repents of it afterwards; a good deed is better done, for having done it, one does not repent.

Like a well guarded frontier fort, with defences within and without, so let a man guard himself Not a moment should escape, for they who allow the right moment to pass, suffer pain when they are in hell. They who are ashamed of what they ought not to be ashamed of, and are not ashamed of what they ought to be ashamed of~ such men, embracing false doctrines, enter the evil path.

They who fear when they ought not to fear, and fear not when they ought to fear, such men, embracing false doctrines, enter the evil path. They who forbid when there is nothing to be forbidden, and forbid not when there IS something to be forbidden, such men, embracing false doctrines, enter the evil path. They who know what is forbidden as forbidden, and what is not forbidden as not forbidden, such men, embracing the true doctrine, enter the good path.

CHAPTER XXIV
Thirst

The thirst of a thoughtless man grows like a creeper; he runs from life to life, like a monkey seeking fruit in the forest.

Whomsoever this fierce thirst overcomes, full of poison, in this world, his sufferings Increase like the abounding B'rana grass.

He who overcomes this fierce thirst, difficult to be conquered in this world, sufferings fall off from him, like water drops from a lotus leaf.

This salutary word I tell you, 'Do ye, as many as are here assembled, dig up the root of thirst, as he who wants the sweet-scented Us'ra root must dig up the B'rana grass, that Mâra (the tempter) may not crush you again and again, as the stream crushes the reeds.'

As a tree, even though it has been cut down, is firm so long as its root is safe, and grows again, thus, unless the feeders of thirst are destroyed, this pain (of life) will return again and again.

He whose thirst running towards pleasure is exceeding strong in the thirty-six channels, the waves will carry away that misguided man, viz, his desires which are set on passion.

The channels run everywhere, the creeper (of passion) stands sprouting; if you see the creeper springing up, cut its root by means of know ledge.

A creature's pleasures are extravagant and luxurious; sunk in lust and looking for pleasure, men undergo (again and again) birth and decay.

Men, driven on by thirst, run about like a snared hare; held in fetters and bonds, they undergo pain for a long time, again and again.

Men, driven on by thirst, nm about like a snared hare; let therefore the mendicant drive out thirst, by striving after passionlessness for himself.

He who having got rid of the forest (of lust) (i.e. after having reached Nirvana) gives himself over to forest life (i.e. to lust), and who, when removed from the forest (i.e. from lust), runs to the forest (i.e. to lust), look at that man! Though free, he runs into bondage.

Wise people do not call that a strong feller which is made of iron, wood, or hemp; far stronger is the care for precious stones and rings, for sons and a wife.

That fetter wise people call strong which drags down, yields, but is difficult to undo; after having cut this at last, people leave the world, free from cares, and leaving desires and pleasures behind.

Those who are slaves to passions, run down with the stream (of desires), as a spider runs down the web which he has made himself; when they have cut this, at last, wise people leave the world, free from cares, leaving all affection behind.

Give up what is before, give up what is behind, give up what is in the middle, when thou goest to the other shore of existence; if thy mind is altogether free, thou wilt not again enter into birth and decay. If a man is tossed about by doubts, full of strong passions, and yearning only for what is delightful, his thirst will grow more and more, and he will indeed make his fetters strong. If a man delights in quieting doubts, and, always reflecting, dwells on what is not delightful (the impurity of the body, etc.). he certainly will remove, nay, he will cut the fetter of Mâra.

He who has reached the consummation, who does not tremble, who is without thirst and without sin, he has broken all the thorns of life; this will be his last body.

Reading and Discussion Questions

1. According to the *Dhammapada*, the fool wanders "about doing evil deeds." Is the fool malicious in his evil deeds? What makes his deeds morally evil?
2. In Chapter XXIV, "Thirst (or Craving)" the Buddha uses analogies of nature to illustrate what he means by craving, analogies of plants and animals. What is the Buddha implying in connecting craving to nature?
3. Why is the Buddha "not easily found," as stated in Chapter XIV? What are the qualities that make one a Buddha?

8.2   Kautilya, "The Duties of Government Superintendents"

Kautilya was a political advisor to the first Mauryan king, Chandragupta Maurya, who in c. 321 B.C.E. created a vast empire across northern India. Kautilya wrote this treatise to guide Chandragupta and his successors, but his text was influential on subsequent states and empires as well. In this excerpt, Kautilya describes how a village should be organized and run; it reflects the pragmatic approach Kautilya had toward politics in general. Although written later than the other material in this chapter, it is another example of the far reach of Vedic influence.

Source: Translated by R. Shamasastry, 1915.

BOOK II, "THE DUTIES OF GOVERNMENT SUPERINTENDENTS"
CHAPTER I. FORMATION OF VILLAGES.
Either by inducing foreigners to immigrate (paradesapraváhanena) or by causing the thickly-populated centres of his own kingdom to send forth the excessive population (svadésábhishyandavámanénavá), the king may construct villages either on new sites or on old ruins (bhútapúrvamavá).

Villages consisting each of not less than a hundred families and of not more than five-hundred families of agricultural people of sudra caste, with boundaries extending as far as a krósa (2250 yds.) or two, and capable of protecting each other shall be formed. Boundaries shall be denoted by a river, a mountain, forests, bulbous plants (grishti), caves, artificial buildings (sétubandha), or by trees such as sálmali (silk cotton tree), samí (Acacia Suma), and kshíravriksha (milky trees).

There shall be set up a stháníya (a fortress of that name) in the centre of eight-hundred villages, a drónamukha in the centre of four-hundred villages, a khárvátika in the centre of two-hundred villages and sangrahana in the midst of a collection of ten villages.

There shall be constructed in the extremities of the kingdom forts manned by boundary-guards (antapála) whose duty shall be to guard the entrances into the kingdom. The interior of the kingdom shall be watched by trapkeepers (vágurika), archers (sábara), hunters (pulinda), chandálas, and wild tribes (aranyachára).

Those who perform sacrifices (ritvik), spiritual guides, priests, and those learned in the Vedas shall be granted Brahmadaya lands yielding sufficient produce and exempted from taxes and fines (adandkaráni).

Superintendents, Accountants, Gopas, Sthánikas, Veterinary Surgeons (Aníkastha), physicians, horse-trainers, and messengers shall also be endowed with lands which they shall have no right to alienate by sale or mortgage.

Lands prepared for cultivation shall be given to tax-payers (karada) only for life (ekapurushikáni).

Unprepared lands shall not be taken away from those who are preparing them for cultivation.

Lands may be confiscated from those who do not cultivate them; and given to others; or they may be cultivated by village labourers (grámabhritaka) and traders (vaidehaka), lest those owners who do not properly cultivate them might pay less (to the government). If cultivators pay their taxes easily, they may be favourably supplied with grains, cattle, and money.

The king shall bestow on cultivators only such favour and remission (anugrahaparihárau) as will tend to swell the treasury, and shall avoid such as will deplete it.

A king with depleted treasury will eat into the very vitality of both citizens and country people. Either on the occasion of opening new settlements or on any other emergent occasions, remission of taxes shall be made.

He shall regard with fatherly kindness those who have passed the period of remission of taxes.

He shall carry on mining operations and manufactures, exploit timber and elephant forests, offer facilities for cattlebreeding and commerce, construct roads for traffic both by land and water, and set up market towns (panyapattana).

He shall also construct reservoirs (sétu) filled with water either perennial or drawn from some other source. Or he may provide with sites, roads, timber, and other necessary things those who construct reservoirs of their own accord. Likewise in the construction of places of pilgrimage (punyasthána) and of groves.

Whoever stays away from any kind of cooperative construction (sambhúyasetubhandhát) shall send his servants and bullocks to carry on his work, shall have a share in the expenditure, but shall have no claim to the profit.

The king shall exercise his right of ownership (swámyam) with regard to fishing, ferrying and trading in vegetables (haritapanya) in reservoirs or lakes (sétushu).

Those who do not heed the claims of their slaves (dása), hirelings (áhitaka), and relatives shall be taught their duty.

The king shall provide the orphans, (bála), the aged, the infirm, the afflicted, and the helpless with maintenance.

He shall also provide subsistence to helpless women when they are carrying and also to the children they give birth to.

Elders among the villagers shall improve the property of bereaved minors till the latter attain their age; so also the property of Gods.

When a capable person other than an apostate (patita) or mother neglects to maintain his or her child, wife, mother, father, minor brothers, sisters, or widowed girls (kanyávidhaváscha), he or she shall be punished with a fine of twelve panas.

When, without making provision for the maintenance of his wife and sons, any person embraces asceticism, he shall be punished with the first amercement; likewise any person who converts a woman to asceticism (pravrá-jayatah).

Whoever has passed the age of copulation may become an ascetic after distributing the properties of his own acquisition (among his sons); otherwise, he will be punished.

No ascetic other than a vánaprastha (forest-hermit), no company other than the one of local birth (sájáta-danyassanghah), and no guilds of any kind other than local cooperative guilds (sámutthávika danyassa-mayánubandhah) shall find entrance into the villages of the kingdom. Nor shall there be in villages buildings (sáláh) intended for sports and plays. Nor, in view of procuring money, free labour, commodities, grains, and liquids in plenty, shall actors, dancers, singers, drummers, buffoons (vágjívana), and bards (kusílava) make any disturbance to the work of the villagers; for helpless villagers are always dependent and bent upon their fields.

The king shall avoid taking possession of any country which is liable to the inroads of enemies and wild tribes and which is harassed by frequent visitations of famine and pestilence. He shall also keep away from expensive sports.

He shall protect agriculture from the molestation of oppressive fines, free labor, and taxes (dandav-ishtikarábádhaih); herds of cattle from thieves, tigers, poisonous creatures and cattle-disease.

He shall not only clear roads of traffic from the molestations of courtiers (vallabha), of workmen (kármika), of robbers, and of boundary-guards, but also keep them from being destroyed by herds of cattle.

Thus the king shall not only keep in good repair timber and elephant forests, buildings, and mines created in the past, but also set up new ones.

Reading and Discussion Questions

1. How is the concept of *dharma*, of acting appropriately to one's varna or caste, reflected in this excerpt?
2. How is this political treatise influenced by the spiritual culture, i.e., the *Vedas*, in which it was written?
3. Chandragupta's empire was geographically vast; how does Kautilya address the difficulty in ruling such a large state?

8.3   Faxien, A Record of Buddhist Countries

Faxien (circa 334-415 C.E.) was a Chinese monk who, with several companions, traveled the Silk Road to India and returned via the Indian Ocean trade route between 399 and 413 C.E.. Their successful quest to obtain Buddhist scriptures helped to disseminate the religion throughout East Asia. Faxien also recorded his travels, which provide an invaluable depiction of central and south Asia of the time.

Source: Faxien, *A Record of Buddhist Kingdoms: Being an Account by the Chinese Monk Faxien of His Travels in India and Ceylon*, trans. by James Legge, 1886.

CHAPTER XVI

ON TO MATHURA OR MUTTRA.CONDITION AND CUSTOMS OF CENTRAL INDIA; OF THE MONKS, VIHARAS, AND MONASTERIES.

From this place they traveled southeast, passing by a succession of very many monasteries, with a multitude of monks, who might be counted by myriads. After passing all these places, they came to a country named Ma-t' aou-lo. They still followed the course of the P'oo-nariver, on the banks of which, left and right, there were twenty monasteries, which might contain three thousand monks; and (here) the Law of Buddha was still more flourishing. Everywhere, from the Sandy Desert, in all the countries of India, the kings had been firm believers in that Law. When they make their offerings to a community of monks, they take off their royal caps, and along with their relatives and ministers, supply them with food with their own hands. That done, (the king) has a carpet spread for himself on the ground, and sits down in front of the chairman; - they dare not presume to sit on couches in front of the community. The laws and ways, according to which the kings presented their offerings when Buddha was in the world, have been handed down to the present day.

All south from this is named the Middle Kingdom. In it the cold and heat are finely tempered, and there is neither hoarfrost nor snow. The people are numerous and happy; they have not to register their households, or attend to any magistrates and their rules; only those who cultivate the royal land have to pay (a portion of) the grain from it. If they want to go, they go; if they want to stay on, they stay. The king governs without decapitation or (other) corporal punishments. Criminals are simply fined, lightly or heavily, according to the circumstances (of each case). Even in cases of repeated attempts at wicked rebellion, they only have their right hands cut off. The king's body-guards and attendants all have salaries. Throughout the whole country the people do not kill any living creature, nor drink intoxicating liquor, nor eat onions or garlic. The only exception is that of the Chandalas. That is the name for those who are (held to be) wicked men, and live apart from others. When they enter the gate of a city or a market-place, they strike a piece of wood to make themselves known, so that men know and avoid them, and do not come into contact with them. In that country, they do not keep pigs and fowls, and do not sell live cattle; in the markets there are no butchers' shops and no dealers in intoxicating drink. In buying and selling commodities they use cowries. Only the Chandalas are fishermen and hunters, and sell flesh meat.

After Buddha attained to pari-nirvana, the kings of the various countries and the heads of the Vaisyas built **viharas** for the priests, and endowed them with fields, houses, gardens, and orchards, along with the resident populations and their cattle, the grants being engraved on plates of metal, so that afterwards they were handed down from king to king, without any daring to annul them, and they remain even to the present time.

The regular business of the monks is to perform acts of meritorious virtue, and to recite their Sutras and sit wrapped in meditation. When stranger monks arrive (at any monastery), the old residents meet and receive them, carry for them their clothes and alms-bowl, give them water to wash their feet, oil with which to anoint them, and the liquid food permitted out of the regular hours. When (the stranger) has enjoyed a very brief rest, they further ask the number of years that he has been a monk, after which he receives a sleeping apartment with its appurtenances, according to his regular order, and everything is done for him which the rules prescribe.

Where a community of monks resides, they erect topes to Sariputtra, to Mahamaudgalyayana, and to Ananda, and also topes (in honour) of the Abhidharma, the Vinaya, and the Sutras. A month after the (annual season

---

vihara: Buddhist monastery

of) rest, the families which are looking out for blessing stimulate one another to make offerings to the monks, and send round to them the liquid food which may be taken out of the ordinary hours. All the monks come together in a great assembly, and preach the Law; after which offerings are presented at the tope of Sariputtra, with all kinds of flowers and incense. All through the night lamps are kept burning, and skilful musicians are employed to perform.

When Sariputtra was a great Brahman, he went to Buddha, and begged (to be permitted) to quit his family (and become a monk). The great Mugalan and the great Kasyapa also did the same. The bhikshunis for the most part make their offerings at the tope of Ananda, because it was he who requested the World-honoured one to allow females to quit their families (and become nuns). The Sramaneras mostly make their offerings to Rahula. The professors of the Abhidharma make their offerings to it; those of the Vinaya to it. Every year there is one such offering, and each class has its own day for it. Students of the mahayana present offerings to the Prajna-paramita, to Manjusri, and to Kwan-she-yin. When the monks have done receiving their annual tribute (from the harvests), the Heads of the Vaisyas and all the Brahmans bring clothes and other such articles as the monks require for use, and distribute among them. The monks, having received them, also proceed to give portions to one another. From the nirvana of Buddha, the forms of ceremony, laws, and rules, practiced by the sacred communities, have been handed down from one generation to another without interruption.

From the place where (the travelers) crossed the Indus to Southern India, and on to the Southern Sea, a distance of forty or fifty thousand **li**, all is level plain. There are no large hills with streams (among them); there are simply the waters of the rivers.

Reading and Discussion Questions

1. What picture of India emerges from Faxien's descriptions?
2. Based on Faxien's description, what role do monasteries and monks play in the life of the country?

8.4   The Status of Women in Ancient India

Hindu beliefs, as expressed in the Vedic literature, placed Indian women in a thoroughly subservient position within the caste system. Women's lives were circumscribed by rigid laws, and even in death they could not guarantee escape from domination by men. The *Law of Manu*, which date to roughly 500 B.C.E., is an important Vedic scripture comprising nearly 3000 verses. It offers one of the clearest statements of dharma as its relates to Hindu women.

Source: *The Law of Manu: The Sacred Books of the East*. Edited by F. Max Müller. (Oxford: Clarendon Press, 1886)

Selections from *The Law of Manu*

By a girl, by a young woman, or even by an aged one, nothing must be done independently, even in her own house.

In childhood a female must be subject to her father, in youth to her husband, when her lord is dead to her sons; a woman must never be independent.

---

li: a traditional Chinese unit of measure, roughly equal to half a kilometer.

She must not seek to separate herself from her father, husband, or sons; by leaving them she would make both (her own and her husband's) families contemptible.

She must always be cheerful, clever in (the management of her) household affairs, careful in cleaning her utensils, and economical in expenditure.

Him to whom her father may give her, or her brother with the father's permission, she shall obey as long as he lives, and when he is dead, she must not insult (his memory).

For the sake of procuring good fortune to (brides), the recitation of benedictory texts and the sacrifice to the Lord of creatures are used at weddings; (but) the betrothal (by the father or guardian) is the cause of (the husband's) dominion (over his wife).

The husband who wedded her with sacred texts, always gives happiness to his wife, both in season and out of season, in this world and in the next.

Though destitute of virtue, or seeking pleasure (elsewhere), or devoid of good qualities (yet) a husband must be constantly worshipped as a god by a faithful wife.

No sacrifice, no vow, no fast must be performed by women apart (from their husbands); if a wife obeys her husband, she will for that (reason alone) be exalted in heaven.

A faithful wife, who desires to dwell (after death) with her husband, must never do anything that might displease him who took her hand, whether he be alive or dead.

At her pleasure let her emaciate her body by (living on) pure flowers, roots, and fruit; but she must never even mention the name of another man after her husband has died.

Until death let her be patient (of hardships), self-controlled, and chaste, and strive (to fulfil) that most excellent duty which (is prescribed) for wives who have one husband only.

Many thousands of Brahmanas who were chaste from their youth, have gone to heaven without continuing their race.

A virtuous wife who after the death of her husband constantly remains chaste, reaches heaven, though she have no son, just like those chaste men.

But a woman who from a desire to have offspring violates her duty towards her (deceased) husband, brings on herself disgrace in this world, and loses her place with her husband (in heaven).

Offspring begotten by another man is here not (considered lawful), nor (does offspring begotten) on another man's wife (belong to the begetter), nor is a second husband anywhere prescribed for virtuous women.

She who cohabits with a man of higher caste, forsaking her own husband who belongs to a lower one, will become contemptible in this world, and is called a remarried woman.

By violating her duty towards her husband, a wife is disgraced in this world, (after death) she enters the womb of a jackal, and is tormented by diseases (the punishment of) her sin.

She who, controlling her thoughts, words, and deeds, never slights her lord, resides (after death) with her husband (in heaven), and is called a virtuous (wife).

In reward of such conduct, a female who controls her thoughts, speech, and actions, gains in this (life) highest renown, and in the next (world) a place near her husband.

Reading and Discussion Questions

1. What rights are accorded to Hindu women in *The Law of Manu*?
2. Compare this document with document 9.4 Ban Zhao, "Admonitions for Women". What are the similarities and differences between the status of women in India compared to women in China?

8.5   Jain Cosmological Map

Jainism was founded by Vardhamana Mahavira ("the great hero") in India in the sixth century B.C.E. Among other adaptations from Hindu culture, from which it emanated, Jainism has its own version of geography and cosmology. This cosmological map shows the world of human habitation as a central continent with mountain ranges and rivers, surrounded by a series of concentric oceans (with swimmers and fish) and ring-shaped continents.

Reading and Discussion Questions

1. What kind of world view and conception of the cosmos is expressed by this map?
2. At the center of the map is Mount Meru, a mythical mountain in northern India where Mahavira was annointed. Why do mountains enjoy special significance in many religions?

Source: Library of Congress

Chapter 9 China: Imperial Unification and Perfecting the Moral Order

722 B.C.E. – 618 C.E.

China entered into its most dynamic intellectual period in the sixth century B.C.E., during the Zhou dynasty. Confucianism, Legalism, and Daoism, the three foundational philosophical schools, were introduced during that period, and the process of refining these ideas began almost immediately. Much of China's intellectual endeavors in the future will be linked in some way to one or more of these systems (with the addition of Buddhism in the Han Dynasty, c. third century C.E.). The few centuries immediately following the sixth century BCE was also a period of dramatic political events, which would also have a lasting legacy for China. The Zhou dynasty ended in a prolonged period of chaos, in which no one dynasty was able to dominate the region that is known as "China." This Warring States Period, from 403 – 221 B.C.E. was not the longest period of disunity China will have, and is most notable for came next. In 221 B.C.E. the Qin Dynasty created the first unified Chinese empire, and introduced the idea of an imperial state to China, an ideal that China will never again step away from. The subsequent dynasties of imperial China, including the Han Dynasty of 202 B.C.E. – 220 C.E., would strive to exceed the geographic hegemony of the Qin Dynasty.

The documents in this chapter reflect both the philosophical dynamism and the political turbulence of the centuries from the Zhou to the end of the Later Han, roughly the eighth century B.C.E. to the third century C.E.

9.1 Han Fei-tzu, "Selections on Legalism,"

Although Han Fei-tzu (d. 233 B.C.E.) began his studies as a Confucianist, he was a protégé of Hsun Tzu, one of Confucius's more cynical successors. Thus Han Fei-tzu switched to Legalism, which was less concerned with theories and more concerned with the practical fundamentals of that interaction. Over time, what began as expediency became more deliberate and exhaustive in its attempts to regularize all aspects of civic behavior and thought.

Source: Han Fei-tzu, "Selections on Legalism," from *The Four Books*. James Legge, ed. and trans. (Shanghai: The Chinese Book Company, 1930), 437-442.

HAVING REGULATIONS

No country is permanently strong. Nor is any country permanently weak. If conformers to law are strong, the country is strong; if conformers to law are weak, the country is weak....

Any ruler able to expel private crookedness and uphold public law finds the people safe and the state in order; and any ruler able to expunge private action and act on public law finds his army strong and his enemy weak. So, find out men following the discipline of laws and regulations, and place them above the body of officials. Then the sovereign cannot be deceived by anybody with fraud and falsehood....

Therefore, the intelligent sovereign makes the law select men and makes no arbitrary promotion himself. He makes the law measure merits and makes no arbitrary regulation himself. In consequence, able men cannot be obscured, bad characters cannot be disguised, falsely praised fellows cannot be advanced, wrongly defamed people cannot be degraded. To govern the state by law is to praise the right and blame the wrong.

The law does not fawn on the noble....Whatever the law applies to, the wise cannot reject nor can the brave defy. Punishment for fault never skips ministers, reward for good never misses commoners. Therefore, to correct the faults of the high, to rebuke the vices of the low, to suppress disorders, to decide against mistakes, to subdue the arrogant, to straighten the crooked, and to unify the folkways of the masses, nothing could match the law. To warn the officials and overawe the people, to rebuke obscenity and danger, and to forbid falsehood and deceit, nothing could match penalty. If penalty is severe, the noble cannot discriminate against the humble. If law is definite, the superiors are esteemed and not violated. If the superiors are not violated, the sovereign will become strong and able to maintain the proper course of government. Such was the reason why the early kings esteemed Legalism and handed it down to posterity. Should the lord of men discard law and practice selfishness, high and law would have no distinction.

THE TWO HANDLES

The means whereby the intelligent ruler controls his ministers are two handles only. The two handles are chastisement and commendation. What are meant by chastisement and commendation? To inflict death or torture upon culprits is called chastisement; to bestow encouragements or rewards on men of merit is called commendation.

Ministers are afraid of censure and punishment but fond of encouragement and reward. Therefore, if the lord of men uses the handles of chastisement and commendation, all ministers will dread his severity and turn to his liberality. The villainous ministers of the age are different. To men they hate they would by securing the handle of chastisement from the sovereign ascribe crimes; on men they love they would by securing the handle of commendation. From the sovereign bestow rewards. Now supposing the lord of men placed the authority of punishment and the profit of reward not in his hands but let the ministers administer the affairs of reward and punishment instead, then everybody in the country would fear the ministers and slight the ruler and turn to the ministers and away from the ruler. This is the calamity of the ruler's loss of the handles of chastisement and commendation.

Reading and Discussion Questions

1. How do Legalists distinguish between public and private concerns? Which has priority and why?
2. How do Legalists such as Han Fei-tzu view the ordinary Chinese citizen? What accounts for this attitude?
3. Why were Han Fei-Tzu's views on government so influential during a period when China was undergoing political upheaval?

9.2   Confucius, Selections from the *Analects*

Although Confucius may have been a fertile thinker, he was not a prolific writer. There is only collection of materials attributed to "the Master:" the *Analects*. Confucius did not write these; they were gathered from his immediate followers, and read as a collection of profound musings on politics, morality, personal behavior, family, and culture.

There is little about Confucius's personal life in the *Analects*, and little is known of him from contemporary sources. Traditional versions of his life story say that he was born in the sixth century B.C.E., and was an itinerant political advisor. He was, technically speaking, a failure in his lifetime, unable to find permanent employment with any one of the Zhou vassal kingdoms. History would prove him greatly successful, however.

The following excerpts give a broad overview of the basic Confucian tenets encapsulated in the *Analects*, including the Master's thoughts on filial piety and the *junzi*, or "superior man."

Source: Confucius, "Selections from the Analects I," from *The Four Books*. James Legge, ed. and trans. (Shanghai: The Chinese Book Company, 1930), 13, 16, 19, 33, 161-162, 245-248.

FILIAL PIETY

The Master said, "A youth, when at home, should be filial, and, abroad, respectful to his elders. He should be earnest and truthful. He should overflow in love to all, and cultivate the friendship of the good. When he has time and opportunity, after the performance of these things, he should employ them in polite studies." Mang I asked what filial piety was. The Master said, "It is not being disobedient." Soon after, as Fan Chi was driving him, the Master told him, saying, "Mangsun asked me what filial piety was, and I answered him, - Ônot being disobedient.'" Fan Chi said, "What did you mean?" The Master replied, "That parents, when alive, should be served according to propriety; that, when dead, they should be buried according to propriety; and that they should be sacrificed to according to propriety." The Master said, "In serving his parents, a son may remonstrate with them, but gently; when he sees that they do not incline to follow his advice, he shows an increased degree of reverence, but does not abandon his purpose; and should they punish him, he does not allow himself to murmur."

EDUCATION

The Master said, "If the scholar be not grave, he will not call forth any veneration, and his learning will not be solid."

The Master said, "If a man keeps cherishing his old knowledge, so as continually to be acquiring new, he may be a teacher of others."

The Master said, "The accomplished scholar is not a utensil."

The Master said, "Learning without thought is labor lost; thought without learning is perilous."

The Master said, "Yu, shall I teach you what knowledge is? When you know a thing, to hold that you know it; and when you do not know a thing, to allow that you do not know it; this is knowledge."

The Master said, "They who know the truth are not equal to those who love it, and they who love it are not equal to those who delight in it."

The Master said, "The scholar who cherishes the love of comfort is not fit to be deemed a scholar."

When the Master went to Wei, Zan Yu acted as driver of his carriage. The Master observed, "How numerous are the people!" Yu said, "Since they are so numerous, what more shall be done for them?" "Enrich them," was the reply. "And when they have been enriched, what more shall be done?" The Master said, "Teach them."

GOVERNMENT

The Master said, "To rule a country of a thousand chariots, there must be reverent attention to business, and sincerity; economy in expenditure, and love for men; and the employment of the people at the proper seasons."

The Master said, "He who exercises government by means of his virtue may be compared to the north polar star, which keeps its place and all the stars turn towards it."

The Master said, "If the people be led by laws, and uniformity sought to be given them by punishment, they will try to avoid the punishment, but have no sense of shame. If they be led by virtue, and uniformity sought to be given them by the rules of propriety, they will have the sense of shame, and moreover will become good."

Ji Kang asked how to cause the people to reverence their ruler, to be faithful to him, and to go on to nerve themselves to virtue. The Master said, "Let him preside over them with gravity; then they will reverence him. Let him be filial and kind to all; then they will be faithful to him. Let him advance the good and teach the incompetent; then they will eagerly seek to be virtuous."

Zigong asked about government. The Master said, "The requisites of government are that there be sufficiency of food, sufficiency of military equipment, and the confidence of the people in their ruler." Zigong said, "If it cannot be helped, and one of these must be dispensed with, which of the three should be foregone first?" "The military equipment," said the Master. Zigong again asked, "If it cannot be helped, and one of the remaining two must be dispensed with, which of them should be foregone?" The Master answered, "Part with the food. From of old, death has been the lot of all men; but if the people have no faith in their rulers, there is no standing for the State."

Ji Kang asked Confucius about government, saying, "What do you say to killing the unprincipled for the good of the principled?" Confucius replied, "Sir, in carrying on your government, why should you use killing at all? Let your evinced desires be for what is good, and the people will be good. The relation between superiors and inferiors is like that between the wind and the grass. The grass must bend, when the wind blows across it."

The Master said, "When a prince's personal conduct is correct, the government is effective without the issuing of orders. If his personal conduct is not correct, he may issue orders, but they will not be followed."

Zizhang asked Confucius, saying, "In what way should a person in authority act in order that he may conduct government properly?" The Master replied, "Let him honor the five excellent, and banish away the four bad, things; then may he conduct government properly." Zizhang said, "What are meant by the five excellent things?"

The Master said, "When the person in authority is beneficent without great expenditure; when he lays tasks on the people without their repining; when he pursues what he desires without being covetous; when he maintains a dignified ease without being proud; when he is majestic without being fierce."

Zizhang then asked, "What are meant by the four bad things?" The Master said, "To put the people to death without having instructed them; this is called cruelty. To require from them, suddenly, the full tale of work, without having given them warning; this is called oppression. To issue orders as if without urgency, at first, and, when the time comes, to insist on them with severity; this is called injury. And, generally, in the giving pay or rewards to men, to do it in a stingy way; this is called acting the part of a mere official."

RELIGION

The Master said, "He who offends against Heaven has none to whom he can pray."

Ji Lu asked about serving the spirits of the dead. The Master said, "While you are not able to serve men, how can you serve their spirits?" Ji Lu added, "I venture to ask about death." He was answered, "While you do not know life, how can you know about death?"

The Master said, "Alas! there is no one that knows me." Zi Gong said, "What do you mean by thus saying - that no one knows you?" The Master replied, "I do not murmur against Heaven. I do not grumble against men. My studies lie low, and my penetration rises high. But there is Heaven; that knows me!"

The Master said, "I would prefer not speaking." Zi Gong said, "If you, Master, do not speak, what shall we, your disciples, have to record?" The Master said, "Does Heaven speak? The four seasons pursue their courses, and all things are continually being produced, but does Heaven say anything?"

The Master said, "Without recognizing the ordinances of Heaven, it is impossible to be a superior man."

VIRTUE AND GOODNESS

The Master said, "Fine words and an insinuating appearance are seldom associated with true virtue."

The Master said, "See what a man does. Mark his motives. Examine in what things he rests. How can a man conceal his character?"

The Master said, "I do not know how a man without truthfulness is to get on. How can a large carriage be made to go without the cross-bar for yoking the oxen to, or a small carriage without the arrangement for yoking the horses?"

The Master said, "To see what is right and not to do it is want of courage."

The Master said, "If the will be set on virtue, there will be no practice of wickedness."

The Master said, "Riches and honors are what men desire. If virtue cannot be obtained in the proper way, they should not be held. Poverty and meanness are what men dislike. If virtue cannot be obtained in the proper way, they should be avoided."

The Master said, "I have not seen a person who loved virtue, or one who hated what was not virtuous. He who loved virtue, would esteem nothing above it. He who hated what is not virtuous, would practice virtue in such a way that he would not allow anything that is not virtuous to approach his person. Is any one able for one day to apply his strength to virtue? I have not seen the case in which his strength would be insufficient."

The Master said, "A man should say, I am not concerned that I have no place, I am concerned how I may fit myself for one. I am not concerned that I am not known, I seek to be worthy to be known."

The Master said, "When we see men of worth, we should think of equaling them; when we see men of a contrary character, we should turn inwards and examine ourselves."

The Master said, "Virtue is not left to stand alone. He who practices it will have neighbors."

The Master said, "Let the will be set on the path of duty. Let every attainment in what is good be firmly grasped. Let perfect virtue be accorded with. Let relaxation and enjoyment be found in the polite arts."

The Master said, "With coarse rice to eat, with water to drink, and my bended arm for a pillow; I have still joy in the midst of these things. Riches and honors acquired by unrighteousness are to me as a floating cloud."

The Master said, "Is virtue a thing remote? I wish to be virtuous, and lo! virtue is at hand."

The Master said, "Respectfulness, without the rules of propriety, becomes laborious bustle; carefulness, without the rules of propriety, becomes timidity; boldness, without the rules of propriety, becomes insubordination; straightforwardness, without the rules of propriety, becomes rudeness."

The Master said, "Can men refuse to assent to the words of strict admonition? But it is reforming the conduct because of them which is valuable. Can men refuse to be pleased with words of gentle advice? But it is unfolding their aim which is valuable. If a man be pleased with these words, but does not unfold their aim, and assents to those, but does not reform his conduct, I can really do nothing with him."

The Master said, "Hold faithfulness and sincerity as first principles. Have no friends not equal to yourself. When you have faults, do not fear to abandon them."

The Master said, "The commander of the forces of a large State may be carried off, but the will of even a common man cannot be taken from him."

The Master said, "The wise are free from perplexities; the virtuous from anxiety; and the bold from fear."

The Master said, "To go beyond is as wrong as to fall short."

Zhong Gong asked about perfect virtue. The Master said, "It is, when you go abroad, to behave to every one as if you were receiving a great guest; to employ the people as if you were assisting at a great sacrifice; not to do to others as you would not wish done to yourself to have no murmuring against you in the country, and none in the family."

Fan Chi asked about benevolence. The Master said, "It is to love all men." He asked about knowledge. The Master said, "It is to know all men."

Fan Chi asked about perfect virtue. The Master said, "It is, in retirement, to be sedately grave; in the management of business, to be reverently attentive; in intercourse with others, to be strictly sincere. Though a man go among rude, uncultivated tribes, these qualities may not be neglected."

Zigong asked, saying, "What do you say of a man who is loved by all the people of his neighborhood?"

The Master replied, "We may not for that accord our approval of him." "And what do you say of him who is hated by all the people of his neighborhood?" The Master said, "We may not for that conclude that he is bad. It is better than either of these cases that the good in the neighborhood love him, and the bad hate him."

The Master said, "He who speaks without modesty will find it difficult to make his words good."

Someone said, "What do you say concerning the principle that injury should be recompensed with kindness?"

The Master said, "With what then will you recompense kindness? Recompense injury with justice, and recompense kindness with kindness."

Zigong asked, saying, "Is there one word which may serve as a rule of practice for all one's life?" The Master said, "Is not RECIPROCITY such a word? What you do not want done to yourself, do not do to others."

The Master said, "Virtue is more to man than either water or fire. I have seen men die from treading on water and fire, but I have never seen a man die from treading the course of virtue."

Confucius said, "There are three friendships which are advantageous, and three which are injurious. Friendship with the upright; friendship with the sincere; and friendship with the man of much observation; these are advantageous. Friendship with the man of specious airs; friendship with the insinuatingly soft; and friendship with the glib-tongued; these are injurious."

Confucius said, "There are three things men find enjoyment in which are advantageous, and three things they find enjoyment in which are injurious. To find enjoyment in the discriminating study of ceremonies and music; to find enjoyment in speaking of the goodness of others; to find enjoyment in having many worthy friends; these are advantageous. To find enjoyment in extravagant pleasures; to find enjoyment in idleness and sauntering; to find enjoyment in the pleasures of feasting; these are injurious."

Zigong asked Confucius about perfect virtue. Confucius said, "To be able to practice five things everywhere under Heaven constitutes perfect virtue." He begged to ask what they were, and was told, "Gravity, generosity of soul, sincerity, earnestness, and kindness. If you are grave, you will not be treated with disrespect. If you are generous, you will win all. If you are sincere, people will repose trust in you. If you are earnest, you will accomplish much. If you are kind, this will enable you to employ the services of others."

Reading and Discussion Questions

1. What are the priorities of the state, according to Confucius, and how are they to be reconciled if there are limited resources?
2. Perhaps the single most important Confucian idea is filial piety. What did Confucius mean by that phrase, and how did it work in the public sphere?
3. What is the purpose of ceremony for Confucius?
4. Why are so many of the ideas in the *Analects* presented as lists?

9.3   Laozi, excerpt from the *Daode Jing*, "The Unvarying Way"

"Laozi" is a title meaning "Old Child;" little is known about the historical reality that lay behind that accolade. It is perhaps fitting that Laozi is a mysterious figure, as the *dao* that he spoke of was equally enigmatic. If there was a Laozi, he probably lived in the early seventh century B.C.E., which would make him a near contemporary of Confucius. That is also appropriate, as both schools of thought deal with similar concepts, such as the *dao*, although they have vastly different understandings of what those terms mean. For Laozi and the Daoists, the *dao* was a universal force that transcends all. It is essentially unknowable. For Confucius, the *dao* was a recognizable and knowable force that governed the world and led humanity to strive for moral behavior. The following verses are taken from the *Daode Jing*, the classic of Daoist thought.

Source: Lao Tzu. "The Unvarying Way." Tao TeChing, trans. by Arthur Waley, 1934

The Unvarying Way

The unvarying way that can be preached is not the enduring and unchanging way. The name that can be namedis not the enduring and unchanging name.We look at it, and we do not see it, and we name it 'the invisible.' We listen to it, and we do not hear it, and wename it 'the inaudible.' We try to grasp it, and do not get hold of it, and we name it 'the intangible.' With these three qualities, it cannot be made the subject of description; blended together they are a unity.The unvarying way is all pervading, it may be found on the left or the right.The unvarying way is hidden, and has no name; but it is the way things are, which is skillful at imparting to all things what they need to make them complete. All things depend on it and it does not desert them. Ambitionless, it may be found in the smallest things. Itclothes all things, but does not act as a master. Always without desire, it may be called insignificant. All things return to it; it may be named great.

Heaven and earth under its guidance unite together and send down the sweet dew, which, without the directionsof men, reaches equally everywhere as of its own accord. Likewise, the relation of the unvarying way to all the world is like that of the great rivers and seas to the streamsfrom the valleys.There is nothing in the world more soft and weak than water, and yet there is nothing better for attacking things that are firm and strong. There is nothing so effectual for causing change. Water has the highest excellence. It benefits all things, and occupies without striving the low place which allmen dislike. Hence it is close to the way things are.The unvarying way relies on non-action, and so there is nothing which it does not do.The way things are is to act without thinking of acting; to conduct affairs without feeling the trouble of them; to taste without consuming; it considers what is small as great, and a few as many; and it recompenses injury withkindness.The unvarying way moves by contraries, and weakness marks the course of its action. As soon as the way is expressed in a creative act, it has a name. When it once has that name, men can know how to come into equilibrium with it. When they know how to come to equilibrium, they can be free from risk of failure and error.

Reading and Discussion Questions

1. How does Laozi use oppositions to convey the unknowability of the Dao?
2. Why is Daoism presented in verses that are open to various interpretations? Compare how Doaism is presented with how Confucius explained his principles in the previous source
3. If the Dao cannot fully be perceived, is it possible to define any of its characteristics?

9.4   Ban Zhao, "Admonitions for Women"

Ban Zhao was the daughter and sister of prominent Han historians. She was born in the first century of the common era, during the Later Han Dynasty, and is thus the last of the writers included in this chapter. Her "Admonitions for Women" takes a very Confucian approach to defining appropriate behavior. If Confucius and Mencius were trying to create the *junzi*, or superior man, then Ban Zhao was attempting to craft the female version of that.

In addition to this text, Ban Zhao also completed a history of the Former Han begun by her father and brother, and worked as a tutor at the Han court, educating the women of the Han dynasty. Thus she was a professional historian and educator, and unusual occupation for women.

Source: "Admonitions for Women," from *Sources of Chinese Tradition: From Earliest Times to 1600,* Second Edition. Wm. Theodore de Bary and Irene Bloom, eds. (New York: Columbia University Press, 1999), 823-824

Humility

… Let a woman retire late to bed, but rise early to her duties; let her not dread tasks by day or by night. Let her not refuse to perform domestic duties whether easy or difficult. That which must be done, let her finish completely, tidily, and systematically. [When a woman follows such rules as these] then she may be said to be industrious.

Let a woman be composed in demeanor and upright in bearing in the service of her husband. Let her live in purity and quietness [of spirit] and keep watch over herself. Let her not love gossip and silly laughter. Let her cleanse, purify, and arrange in order the wine and the food for the offerings to the ancestors. [Observing such principles as these] is what it means to continue the ancestral rites. …

Husband and Wife

If a husband be unworthy, then he possesses nothing by which to control his wife. If a wife be unworthy, then she possesses nothing with which to serve her husband. If a husband does not control his wife, then he loses his authority. If a wife does not serve her husband, then right principles [the natural order] are neglected and destroyed. As a matter of fact, in practice these two [the controlling of women by men and the serving of men by women] work out in the same way.

Now examine the gentlemen of the present age. They only know that wives must be controlled and that the husband's authority must be maintained. They therefore teach their boys to read books and [study] histories. But they do not in the least understand how husbands and masters are to be served or how rites and right principles are to be maintained.

Yet only to teach men and not to teach women — is this not ignoring the reciprocal relation between them? According to the *Rites*, book learning begins at the age of eight, and at the age of fifteen one goes to school. Why, however, should this principle not apply to girls as well as boys?

Respect and Compliance

As yin and yang are not of the same nature, so man and woman differ in behavior. The virtue of yang is firmness; yin is manifested in yielding. Man is honored for strength; a woman is beautiful on account of her gentleness. Hence there arose the common saying, "A man born as a wolf may, it is feared, become a woman; a woman born as a mouse may, it is feared, become a tigress."

Now for self-cultivation there is nothing like respectfulness. To avert harshness there is nothing like compliance. Consequently it can be said that the Way of respect and compliance is for women the most important element in ritual decorum. …

[If a wife] does not restrain her contempt for her husband, then it will be followed by scolding and shouting [from him]. [If a husband] does not restrain his anger, then there is certain to be beating [of the wife]. The correct relationship between husband and wife is based upon harmony and intimacy, and [conjugal] love is grounded in proper union. If it comes to blows, how can the proper relationship be preserved? If sharp words are spoken, how can [conjugal] love exist? If love and proper relationship are both destroyed, then husband and wife are parted.

Womanly Behavior

In womanly behavior there are four things [to be considered]: womanly virtue, womanly speech, womanly appearance, and womanly work. …

To guard carefully her chastity, to control circumspectly her behavior, in every motion to exhibit modesty, and to model each act on the best usage: this may be called womanly virtue.

To choose her words with care, to avoid vulgar language, to speak at appropriate times, and not to be offensive to others may be called womanly speech.

To wash and scrub dirt and grime, to keep clothes and ornaments fresh and clean, to wash the head and bathe the body regularly, and to keep the person free from disgraceful filth may be called womanly appearance.

With wholehearted devotion to sew and weave, not to love gossip and silly laughter, in cleanliness and order [to prepare] the wine and food for serving guests may be called womanly work.

Reading and Discussion Questions:

1. How is Ban Zhao interpreting the Confucian ideals of appropriate behavior and filial piety for women? Does she see them as essentially different for women than for men?
2. Compare Ban Zhao's list of proper women's behavior with Confucius's lists for the proper behavior of the "superior man" or the *junzi*, from the excerpt of the *Analects*.
3. Compare and contrast Ban Zhao's admonitions with the rules for Hindu women expressed in document 8.4

Islamic Civilization and Byzantium

Chapter 10

600 – 1300

In the seventh century, a new world religion and a tremendously successful culture emerged from a hitherto little known region, Arabia. In 610, a merchant from Mecca named Muhammad began to receive revelations from the god Allah, via a messenger and archangel, Gabriel (Jabril in the Islamic tradition). Two years later Muhammad became a messenger as well and started to share his revelations with first family, then associates, then to any and all that would listen. The message was deceptively simple: there is only one god, and He is merciful and wise. Of course, that message became more complex and more nuanced as more revelations emerged, and Islam evolved into an equally complex and nuanced religion. The sources in this chapter reflect that evolution, as well as the full participation of Islam as a culture in world far beyond Arabia.

In a somewhat similar fashion, the Byzantine Empire succeeded the Roman Empire around 640 when the emperors, under attack by the Arabs, reorganized their military forces and redefined the inherited Christian theology. This Christianity acquired its specific eastern identity by becoming clearly separate from the other Christianities outside the Byzantine Empire, such as Catholic western European, Syrian and Egyptian Monophysitic, and Asian Nestorian Christianities. Byzantium recovered politically and culturally in the mid-900s, and the empire changed into a commonwealth when Russian Kiev converted to eastern Christianity. Unfortunately, the recovery lasted only a century. The Seljuk Muslim Turks conquered most Anatolian provinces of Byzantium (1071–1176), and the Venetians conquered Constantinople in the Fourth Crusade (1204–1261). Byzantium recovered thereafter for another two and a half centuries and even flourished culturally, but after 1453 the center of eastern Christian civilization would shift northward to Russia.

10.1 The *Quran*: "The Five Pillars," from Surah 2, ("The Cow")

The *Quran* is the holy text of Islam. Muslims believe that it was revealed to Muhammad by the archangel Gabriel, at the behest of Allah. Muhammad, in turn, revealed what had been revealed to him to his followers, and ordered that each revelation be written down. A copy of the full text was written down in 633, when the Caliph Abu Bakr was determined to preserve it before the original followers of Muhammad died; copies of the text were distributed by the Caliph Uthman in 645. Thus the *Quran* was born of a process of recitation (the meaning of the term "*Quran*") and writing. Every Muslim not only reads the *Quran*; many Muslims memorize it as an act of piety, and it has been the single defining source of Muslim traditions, beliefs, practices, and history of the faith.

Although there will be several different interpretations of Islam, and how to be a Muslim, over the centuries, one set of beliefs held in common by all Muslims are the Five Pillars, five ritual observances that all who are devout are expected to perform. These Five Pillars are presented in the second Surah, or chapter, of the *Quran*, called *The Cow*.

Source: http://quod.lib.umich.edu/k/koran/browse.htm

[2.1] Alif Lam Mim.

[2.2] This Book, there is no doubt in it, is a guide to those who guard (against evil).

[2.3] Those who believe in the unseen and keep up prayer and spend out of what We have given them.

[2.4] And who believe in that which has been revealed to you and that which was revealed before you and they are sure of the hereafter.

[2.5] These are on a right course from their Lord and these it is that shall be successful.

[2.6] Surely those who disbelieve, it being alike to them whether you warn them, or do not warn them, will not believe.

[2.7] Allah has set a seal upon their hearts and upon their hearing and there is a covering over their eyes, and there is a great punishment for them.

[2.8] And there are some people who say: We believe in Allah and the last day; and they are not at all believers.

[2.9] They desire to deceive Allah and those who believe, and they deceive only themselves and they do not perceive.

[2.10] There is a disease in their hearts, so Allah added to their disease and they shall have a painful chastisement because they lied.

[2.11] And when it is said to them, Do not make mischief in the land, they say: We are but peace-makers.

[2.12] Now surely they themselves are the mischief makers, but they do not perceive.

[2.13] And when it is said to them: Believe as the people believe they say: Shall we believe as the fools believe? Now surely they themselves are the fools, but they do not know.

[2.14] And when they meet those who believe, they say: We believe; and when they are alone with their Shaitans, they say: Surely we are with you, we were only mocking.

[2.15] Allah shall pay them back their mockery, and He leaves them alone in their inordinacy, blindly wandering on.

[2.16] These are they who buy error for the right direction, so their bargain shall bring no gain, nor are they the followers of the right direction.

[2.17] Their parable is like the parable of one who kindled a fire but when it had illumined all around him, Allah took away their light, and left them in utter darkness– they do not see.

[2.18] Deaf, dumb (and) blind, so they will not turn back.

[2.19] Or like abundant rain from the cloud in which is utter darkness and thunder and lightning; they put their fingers into their ears because of the thunder peal, for fear of death, and Allah encompasses the unbelievers.

[2.20] The lightning almost takes away their sight; whenever it shines on them they walk in it, and when it becomes dark to them they stand still; and if Allah had pleased He would certainly have taken away their hearing and their sight; surely Allah has power over all things.

[2.21] O men! serve your Lord Who created you and those before you so that you may guard (against evil).

[2.22] Who made the earth a resting place for you and the heaven a canopy and (Who) sends down rain from the cloud then brings forth with it subsistence for you of the fruits; therefore do not set up rivals to Allah while you know.

[2.23] And if you are in doubt as to that which We have revealed to Our servant, then produce a chapter like it and call on your witnesses besides Allah if you are truthful.

[2.24] But if you do (it) not and never shall you do (it), then be on your guard against the fire of which men and stones are the fuel; it is prepared for the unbelievers.

[2.25] And convey good news to those who believe and do good deeds, that they shall have gardens in which rivers flow; whenever they shall be given a portion of the fruit thereof, they shall say: This is what was given to us before; and they shall be given the like of it, and they shall have pure mates in them, and in them, they shall abide.

[2.26] Surely Allah is not ashamed to set forth any parable– (that of) a gnat or any thing above that; then as for those who believe, they know that it is the truth from their Lord, and as for those who disbelieve, they say: What is it that Allah means by this parable: He causes many to err by it and many He leads aright by it! but He does not cause to err by it (any) except the transgressors,

[2.27] Who break the covenant of Allah after its confirmation and cut asunder what Allah has ordered to be joined, and make mischief in the land; these it is that are the losers.

[2.28] How do you deny Allah and you were dead and He gave you life? Again He will cause you to die and again bring you to life, then you shall be brought back to Him.

[2.29] He it is Who created for you all that is in the earth, and He directed Himself to the heaven, so He made them complete seven heavens, and He knows all things.

[2.30] And when your Lord said to the angels, I am going to place in the earth a khalif, they said: What! wilt Thou place in it such as shall make mischief in it and shed blood, and we celebrate Thy praise and extol Thy holiness? He said: Surely I know what you do not know.

[2.31] And He taught Adam all the names, then presented them to the angels; then He said: Tell me the names of those if you are right.

[2.32] They said: Glory be to Thee! we have no knowledge but that which Thou hast taught us; surely Thou art the Knowing, the Wise.

[2.33] He said: O Adam! inform them of their names. Then when he had informed them of their names, He said: Did I not say to you that I surely know what is ghaib in the heavens and the earth and (that) I know what you manifest and what you hide?

[2.34] And when We said to the angels: Make obeisance to Adam they did obeisance, but Iblis (did it not). He refused and he was proud, and he was one of the unbelievers.

[2.35] And We said: O Adam! Dwell you and your wife in the garden and eat from it a plenteous (food) wherever you wish and do not approach this tree, for then you will be of the unjust.

[2.36] But the Shaitan made them both fall from it, and caused them to depart from that (state) in which they were; and We said: Get forth, some of you being the enemies of others, and there is for you in the earth an abode and a provision for a time.

[2.37] Then Adam received (some) words from his Lord, so He turned to him mercifully; surely He is Oft-returning (to mercy), the Merciful.

[2.38] We said: Go forth from this (state) all; so surely there will come to you a guidance from Me, then whoever follows My guidance, no fear shall come upon them, nor shall they grieve.

[2.39] And (as to) those who disbelieve in and reject My communications, they are the inmates of the fire, in it they shall abide.

[2.40] O children of Israel! call to mind My favor which I bestowed on you and be faithful to (your) covenant with Me, I will fulfill (My) covenant with you; and of Me, Me alone, should you be afraid.

[2.41] And believe in what I have revealed, verifying that which is with you, and be not the first to deny it, neither take a mean price in exchange for My communications; and Me, Me alone should you fear.

[2.42] And do not mix up the truth with the falsehood, nor hide the truth while you know (it).

[2.43] And keep up prayer and pay the poor-rate and bow down with those who bow down.

[2.44] What! do you enjoin men to be good and neglect your own souls while you read the Book; have you then no sense?

[2.45] And seek assistance through patience and prayer, and most surely it is a hard thing except for the humble ones,

[2.46] Who know that they shall meet their Lord and that they shall return to Him.

[2.47] O children of Israel! call to mind My favor which I bestowed on you and that I made you excel the nations.

[2.48] And be on your guard against a day when one soul shall not avail another in the least, neither shall intercession on its behalf be accepted, nor shall any compensation be taken from it, nor shall they be helped.

[2.49] And when We delivered you from Firon's people, who subjected you to severe torment, killing your sons and sparing your women, and in this there was a great trial from your Lord.

[2.50] And when We parted the sea for you, so We saved you and drowned the followers of Firon and you watched by.

[2.51] And when We appointed a time of forty nights with Musa, then you took the calf (for a god) after him and you were unjust.

[2.52] Then We pardoned you after that so that you might give thanks.

[2.53] And when We gave Musa the Book and the distinction that you might walk aright.

[2.54] And when Musa said to his people: O my people! you have surely been unjust to yourselves by taking the calf (for a god), therefore turn to your Creator (penitently), so kill your people, that is best for you with your Creator: so He turned to you (mercifully), for surely He is the Oft-returning (to mercy), the Merciful.

[2.55] And when you said: O Musa! we will not believe in you until we see Allah manifestly, so the punishment overtook you while you looked on.

[2.56] Then We raised you up after your death that you may give thanks.

[2.57] And We made the clouds to give shade over you and We sent to you manna and quails: Eat of the good things that We have given you; and they did not do Us any harm, but they made their own souls suffer the loss.

[2.58] And when We said: Enter this city, then eat from it a plenteous (food) wherever you wish, and enter the gate making obeisance, and say, forgiveness. We will forgive you your wrongs and give more to those who do good (to others).

[2.59] But those who were unjust changed it for a saying other than that which had been spoken to them, so We sent upon those who were unjust a pestilence from heaven, because they transgressed.

[2.60] And when Musa prayed for drink for his people, We said: Strike the rock with your staff So there gushed from it twelve springs; each tribe knew its drinking place: Eat and drink of the provisions of Allah and do not act corruptly in the land, making mischief.

[2.61] And when you said: O Musa! we cannot bear with one food, therefore pray Lord on our behalf to bring forth for us out of what the earth grows, of its herbs and its cucumbers and its garlic and its lentils and its onions. He said: Will you exchange that which is better for that which is worse? Enter a city, so you will have what you ask for. And abasement and humiliation were brought down upon them, and they became deserving of Allah's wrath; this was so because they disbelieved in the communications of Allah and killed the prophets unjustly; this was so because they disobeyed and exceeded the limits.

[2.62] Surely those who believe, and those who are Jews, and the Christians, and the Sabians, whoever believes in Allah and the Last day and does good, they shall have their reward from their Lord, and there is no fear for them, nor shall they grieve.

[2.63] And when We took a promise from you and lifted the mountain over you: Take hold of the law (Tavrat) We have given you with firmness and bear in mind what is in it, so that you may guard (against evil).

[2.64] Then you turned back after that; so were it not for the grace of Allah and His mercy on you, you would certainly have been among the losers.

[2.65] And certainly you have known those among you who exceeded the limits of the Sabbath, so We said to them: Be (as) apes, despised and hated.

[2.66] So We made them an example to those who witnessed it and those who came after it, and an admonition to those who guard (against evil).

[2.67] And when Musa said to his people: Surely Allah commands you that you should sacrifice a cow; they said: Do you ridicule us? He said: I seek the protection of Allah from being one of the ignorant.

[2.68] They said: Call on your Lord for our sake to make it plain to us what she is. Musa said: He says, Surely she is a cow neither advanced in age nor too young, of middle age between that (and this); do therefore what you are commanded.

[2.69] They said: Call on your Lord for our sake to make it plain to us what her color is. Musa said: He says,

Surely she is a yellow cow; her color is intensely yellow, giving delight to the beholders.

[2.70] They said: Call on your Lord for our sake to make it plain to us what she is, for surely to us the cows are all alike, and if Allah please we shall surely be guided aright.

[2.71] Musa said: He says, Surely she is a cow not made submissive that she should plough the land, nor does she irrigate the tilth; sound, without a blemish in her. They said: Now you have brought the truth; so they sacrificed her, though they had not the mind to do (it).

[2.72] And when you killed a man, then you disagreed with respect to that, and Allah was to bring forth that which you were going to hide.

[2.73] So We said: Strike the (dead body) with part of the (Sacrificed cow), thus Allah brings the dead to life, and He shows you His signs so that you may understand.

[2.74] Then your hearts hardened after that, so that they were like rocks, rather worse in hardness; and surely there are some rocks from which streams burst forth, and surely there are some of them which split asunder so water issues out of them, and surely there are some of them which fall down for fear of Allah, and Allah is not at all heedless of what you do.

[2.75] Do you then hope that they would believe in you, and a party from among them indeed used to hear the Word of Allah, then altered it after they had understood it, and they know (this).

[2.76] And when they meet those who believe they say: We believe, and when they are alone one with another they say: Do you talk to them of what Allah has disclosed to you that they may contend with you by this before your Lord? Do you not then understand?

[2.77] Do they not know that Allah knows what they keep secret and what they make known?

[2.78] And there arc among them illiterates who know not the Book but only lies, and they do but conjecture.

[2.79] Woe, then, to those who write the book with their hands and then say: This is from Allah, so that they may take for it a small price; therefore woe to them for what their hands have written and woe to them for what they earn.

[2.80] And they say: Fire shall not touch us but for a few days. Say: Have you received a promise from Allah, then Allah will not fail to perform His promise, or do you speak against Allah what you do not know?

[2.81] Yeal whoever earns evil and his sins beset him on every side, these are the inmates of the fire; in it they shall abide.

[2.82] And (as for) those who believe and do good deeds, these are the dwellers of the garden; in it they shall abide.

[2.83] And when We made a covenant with the children of Israel: You shall not serve any but Allah and (you shall do) good to (your) parents, and to the near of kin and to the orphans and the needy, and you shall speak to men good words and keep up prayer and pay the poor-rate. Then you turned back except a few of you and (now too) you turn aside.

[2.84] And when We made a covenant with you: You shall not shed your blood and you shall not turn your people out of your cities; then you gave a promise while you witnessed.

[2.85] Yet you it is who slay your people and turn a party from among you out of their homes, backing each other up against them unlawfully and exceeding the limits; and if they should come to you, as captives you would ransom them– while their very turning out was unlawful for you. Do you then believe in a part of the Book and disbelieve in the other? What then is the re ward of such among you as do this but disgrace in the life of this world, and on the day of resurrection they shall be sent back to the most grievous chastisement, and Allah is not at all heedless of what you do.

[2.86] These are they who buy the life of this world for the hereafter, so their chastisement shall not be lightened nor shall they be helped.

[2.87] And most certainly We gave Musa the Book and We sent apostles after him one after another; and We gave Isa, the son of Marium, clear arguments and strengthened him with the holy spirit, What! whenever then an apostle came to you with that which your souls did not desire, you were insolent so you called some liars and some you slew.

[2.88] And they say: Our hearts are covered. Nay, Allah has cursed them on account of their unbelief; so little it is that they believe.

[2.89] And when there came to them a Book from Allah verifying that which they have, and aforetime they used to pray for victory against those who disbelieve, but when there came to them (Prophet) that which they did not recognize, they disbelieved in him; so Allah's curse is on the unbelievers.

[2.90] Evil is that for which they have sold their souls–that they should deny what Allah has revealed, out of envy that Allah should send down of His grace on whomsoever of His servants He pleases; so they have made themselves deserving of wrath upon wrath, and there is a disgraceful punishment for the unbelievers.

[2.91] And when it is said to them, Believe in what Allah has revealed, they say: We believe in that which was revealed to us; and they deny what is besides that, while it is the truth verifying that which they have. Say: Why then did you kill Allah's Prophets before if you were indeed believers?

[2.92] And most certainly Musa came to you with clear arguments, then you took the calf (for a god) in his absence and you were unjust.

[2.93] And when We made a covenant with you and raised the mountain over you: Take hold of what We have given you with firmness and be obedient. They said: We hear and disobey. And they were made to imbibe (the love of) the calf into their hearts on account of their unbelief Say: Evil is that which your belief bids you if you are believers.

[2.94] Say: If the future abode with Allah is specially for you to the exclusion of the people, then invoke death if you are truthful.

[2.95] And they will never invoke it on account of what their hands have sent before, and Allah knows the unjust.

[2.96] And you will most certainly find them the greediest of men for life (greedier) than even those who are polytheists; every one of them loves that he should be granted a life of a thousand years, and his being granted a long life will in no way remove him further off from the chastisement, and Allah sees what they

[2.97] Say: Whoever is the enemy of Jibreel–for surely he revealed it to your heart by Allah's command, verifying that which is before it and guidance and good news for the believers.

[2.98] Whoever is the enemy of Allah and His angels and His apostles and Jibreel and Meekaeel, so surely Allah is the enemy of the unbelievers.

[2.99] And certainly We have revealed to you clear communications and none disbelieve in them except the transgressors.

[2.100] What! whenever they make a covenant, a party of them cast it aside? Nay, most of them do not believe.

[2.101] And when there came to them an Apostle from Allah verifying that which they have, a party of those who were given the Book threw the Book of Allah behind their backs as if they knew nothing.

[2.102] And they followed what the Shaitans chanted of sorcery in the reign of Sulaiman, and Sulaiman was not an unbeliever, but the Shaitans disbelieved, they taught men sorcery and that was sent down to the two angels at Babel, Harut and Marut, yet these two taught no man until they had said, "Surely we are only a trial, therefore do not be a disbeliever." Even then men learned from these two, magic by which they might cause a separation between a man and his wife; and they cannot hurt with it any one except with Allah's permission, and they learned what harmed them and did not profit them, and certainly they know that he who bought it should have no share of good in the hereafter and evil was the price for which they sold their souls, had they but known this.

[2.103] And if they had believed and guarded themselves (against evil), reward from Allah would certainly have been better; had they but known (this).

[2.104] O you who believe! do not say Raina and say Unzurna and listen, and for the unbelievers there is a painful chastisement.

[2.105] Those who disbelieve from among the followers of the Book do not like, nor do the polytheists, that the good should be sent down to you from your Lord, and Allah chooses especially whom He pleases for His mercy, and Allah is the Lord of mighty grace.

[2.106] Whatever communications We abrogate or cause to be forgotten, We bring one better than it or like it. Do you not know that Allah has power over all things?

[2.107] Do you not know that Allah's is the kingdom of the heavens and the earth, and that besides Allah you have no guardian or helper?

[2.108] Rather you wish to put questions to your Apostle, as Musa was questioned before; and whoever adopts unbelief instead of faith, he indeed has lost the right direction of the way.

[2.109] Many of the followers of the Book wish that they could turn you back into unbelievers after your faith, out of envy from themselves, (even) after the truth has become manifest to them; but pardon and forgive, so that Allah should bring about His command; surely Allah has power over all things.

[2.110] And keep up prayer and pay the poor-rate and whatever good you send before for yourselves, you shall find it with Allah; surely Allah sees what you do.

[2.111] And they say: None shall enter the garden (or paradise) except he who is a Jew or a Christian. These are their vain desires. Say: Bring your proof if you are truthful.

[2.112] Yes! whoever submits himself entirely to Allah and he is the doer of good (to others) he has his reward from his Lord, and there is no fear for him nor shall he grieve.

[2.113] And the Jews say: The Christians do not follow anything (good) and the Christians say: The Jews do not follow anything (good) while they recite the (same) Book. Even thus say those who have no knowledge, like to what they say; so Allah shall judge between them on the day of resurrection in what they differ.

[2.114] And who is more unjust than he who prevents (men) from the masjids of Allah, that His name should be remembered in them, and strives to ruin them? (As for) these, it was not proper for them that they should have entered them except in fear; they shall meet with disgrace in this world, and they shall have great chastisement in the hereafter.

[2.115] And Allah's is the East and the West, therefore, whither you turn, thither is Allah's purpose; surely Allah is Amplegiving, Knowing.

[2.116] And they say: Allah has taken to himself a son. Glory be to Him; rather, whatever is in the heavens and the earth is His; all are obedient to Him.

[2.117] Wonderful Originator of the heavens and the earth, and when He decrees an affair, He only says to it, Be, so there it is.

[2.118] And those who have no knowledge say: Why does not Allah speak to us or a sign come to us? Even thus said those before them, the like of what they say; their hearts are all alike. Indeed We have made the communications clear for a people who are sure.

[2.119] Surely We have sent you with the truth as a bearer of good news and as a warner, and you shall not be called upon to answer for the companions of the flaming fire.

[2.120] And the Jews will not be pleased with you, nor the Christians until you follow their religion. Say: Surely Allah's guidance, that is the (true) guidance. And if you follow their desires after the knowledge that has come to you, you shall have no guardian from Allah, nor any helper.

[2.121] Those to whom We have given the Book read it as it ought to be read. These believe in it; and whoever disbelieves in it, these it is that are the losers.

[2.122] O children of Israel, call to mind My favor which I bestowed on you and that I made you excel the nations.

[2.123] And.be on your guard against a day when no soul shall avail another in the least neither shall any compensation be accepted from it, nor shall intercession profit it, nor shall they be helped.

[2.124] And when his Lord tried Ibrahim with certain words, he fulfilled them. He said: Surely I will make you an Imam of men. Ibrahim said: And of my offspring? My covenant does not include the unjust, said He.

[2.125] And when We made the House a pilgrimage for men and a (place of) security, and: Appoint for your-selves a place of prayer on the standing-place of Ibrahim. And We enjoined Ibrahim and Ismail saying: Purify My House for those who visit (it) and those who abide (in it) for devotion and those who bow down (and) those who prostrate themselves.

[2.126] And when Ibrahim said: My Lord, make it a secure town and provide its people with fruits, such of them as believe in Allah and the last day. He said: And whoever disbelieves, I will grant him enjoyment for a short while, then I will drive him to the chastisement of the fire; and it is an evil destination.

[2.127] And when Ibrahim and Ismail raised the foundations of the House: Our Lord! accept from us; surely Thou art the Hearing, the Knowing:

[2.128] Our Lord! and make us both submissive to Thee and (raise) from our offspring a nation submitting to Thee, and show us our ways of devotion and turn to us (mercifully), surely Thou art the Oft-returning (to mercy), the Merciful.

[2.129] Our Lord! and raise up in them an Apostle from among them who shall recite to them Thy communica-tions and teach them the Book and the wisdom, and purify them; surely Thou art the Mighty, the Wise.

[2.130] And who forsakes the religion of Ibrahim but he who makes himself a fool, and most certainly We chose him in this world, and in the hereafter he is most surely among the righteous.

[2.131] When his Lord said to him, Be a Muslim, he said: I submit myself to the Lord of the worlds.

[2.132] And the same did Ibrahim enjoin on his sons and (so did) Yaqoub. O my sons! surely Allah has chosen for you (this) faith, therefore die not unless you are Muslims.

[2.133] Nay! were you witnesses when death visited Yaqoub, when he said to his sons: What will you serve after me? They said: We will serve your God and the God of your fathers, Ibrahim and Ismail and Ishaq, one God only, and to Him do we submit.

[2.134] This is a people that have passed away; they shall have what they earned and you shall have what you earn, and you shall not be called upon to answer for what they did.

[2.135] And they say: Be Jews or Christians, you will be on the right course. Say: Nay! (we follow) the religion of Ibrahim, the Hanif, and he was not one of the polytheists.

[2.136] Say: We believe in Allah and (in) that which had been revealed to us, and (in) that which was revealed to Ibrahim and Ismail and Ishaq and Yaqoub and the tribes, and (in) that which was given to Musa and Isa, and (in) that which was given to the prophets from their Lord, we do not make any distinction between any of them, and to Him do we submit.

[2.137] If then they believe as you believe in Him, they are indeed on the right course, and if they turn back, then they are only in great opposition, so Allah will suffice you against them, and He is the Hearing, the Knowing.

[2.138] (Receive) the baptism of Allah, and who is better than Allah in baptising? and Him do we serve.

[2.139] Say: Do you dispute with us about Allah, and He is our Lord and your Lord, and we shall have our deeds and you shall have your deeds, and we are sincere to Him.

[2.140] Nay! do you say that Ibrahim and Ismail and Yaqoub and the tribes were Jews or Christians? Say: Are you better knowing or Allah? And who is more unjust than he who conceals a testimony that he has from Allah? And Allah is not at all heedless of what you do.

[2.141] This is a people that have passed away; they shall have what they earned and you shall have what you earn, and you shall not be called upon to answer for what they did.

[2.142] The fools among the people will say: What has turned them from their qiblah which they had? Say: The East and the West belong only to Allah; He guides whom He likes to the right path.

[2.143] And thus We have made you a medium (just) nation that you may be the bearers of witness to the people and (that) the Apostle may be a bearer of witness to you; and We did not make that which you would have to be the qiblah but that We might distinguish him who follows the Apostle from him who turns back upon his heels, and this was surely hard except for those whom Allah has guided aright; and Allah was not going to make your faith to be fruitless; most surely Allah is Affectionate, Merciful to the people.

[2.144] Indeed We see the turning of your face to heaven, so We shall surely turn you to a qiblah which you shall like; turn then your face towards the Sacred Mosque, and wherever you are, turn your face towards it, and those who have been given the Book most surely know that it is the truth from their Lord; and Allah is not at all heedless of what they do.

[2.145] And even if you bring to those who have been given the Book every sign they would not follow your qiblah, nor can you be a follower of their qiblah, neither are they the followers of each other's qiblah, and if you follow their desires after the knowledge that has come to you, then you shall most surely be among the unjust.

[2.146] Those whom We have given the Book recognize him as they recognize their sons, and a party of them most surely conceal the truth while they know (it).

[2.147] The truth is from your Lord, therefore you should not be of the doubters.

[2.148] And every one has a direction to which he should turn, therefore hasten to (do) good works; wherever you are, Allah will bring you all together; surely Allah has power over all things.

[2.149] And from whatsoever place you come forth, turn your face towards the Sacred Mosque; and surely it is the very truth from your Lord, and Allah is not at all heedless of what you do.

[2.150] And from whatsoever place you come forth, turn your face towards the Sacred Mosque; and wherever you are turn your faces towards it, so that people shall have no accusation against you, except such of them as are unjust; so do not fear them, and fear Me, that I may complete My favor on you and that you may walk on the right course.

[2.151] Even as We have sent among you an Apostle from among you who recites to you Our communications and purifies you and teaches you the Book and the wisdom and teaches you that which you did not know.

[2.152] Therefore remember Me, I will remember you, and be thankful to Me, and do not be ungrateful to Me.

[2.153] O you who believe! seek assistance through patience and prayer; surely Allah is with the patient.

[2.154] And do not speak of those who are slain in Allah's way as dead; nay, (they are) alive, but you do not perceive.

[2.155] And We will most certainly try you with somewhat of fear and hunger and loss of property and lives and fruits; and give good news to the patient,

[2.156] Who, when a misfortune befalls them, say: Surely we are Allah's and to Him we shall surely return.

[2.157] Those are they on whom are blessings and mercy from their Lord, and those are the followers of the right course.

[2.158] Surely the Safa and the Marwa are among the signs appointed by Allah; so whoever makes a pilgrimage to the House or pays a visit (to it), there is no blame on him if he goes round them both; and whoever does good spontaneously, then surely Allah is Grateful, Knowing.

[2.159] Surely those who conceal the clear proofs and the guidance that We revealed after We made it clear in the Book for men, these it is whom Allah shall curse, and those who curse shall curse them (too).

[2.160] Except those who repent and amend and make manifest (the truth), these it is to whom I turn (mercifully); and I am the Oft-returning (to mercy), the Merciful.

[2.161] Surely those who disbelieve and die while they are disbelievers, these it is on whom is the curse of Allah and the angels and men all;

[2.162] Abiding in it; their chastisement shall not be lightened nor shall they be given respite.

2.163] And your God is one God! there is no god but He; He is the Beneficent, the Merciful.

[2.164] Most surely in the creation of the heavens and the earth and the alternation of the night and the day, and the ships that run in the sea with that which profits men, and the water that Allah sends down from the cloud, then gives life with it to the earth after its death and spreads in it all (kinds of) animals, and the changing of the winds and the clouds made subservient between the heaven and the earth, there are signs for a people who understand.

[2.165] And there are some among men who take for themselves objects of worship besides Allah, whom they love as they love Allah, and those who believe are stronger in love for Allah and O, that those who are unjust had seen, when they see the chastisement, that the power is wholly Allah's and that Allah is severe in requiting (evil).

[2.166] When those who were followed shall renounce those who followed (them), and they see the chastisement and their ties are cut asunder.

[2.167] And those who followed shall say: Had there been for us a return, then we would renounce them as they have renounced us. Thus will Allah show them their deeds to be intense regret to them, and they shall not come forth from the fire.

[2.168] O men! eat the lawful and good things out of what is in the earth, and do not follow the footsteps of the Shaitan; surely he is your open enemy.

[2.169] He only enjoins you evil and indecency, and that you may speak against Allah what you do not know.

[2.170] And when it is said to them, Follow what Allah has revealed, they say: Nay! we follow what we found our fathers upon. What! and though their fathers had no sense at all, nor did they follow the right way.

[2.171] And the parable of those who disbelieve is as the parable of one who calls out to that which hears no more than a call and a cry; deaf, dumb (and) blind, so they do not understand.

[2.172] O you who believe! eat of the good things that We have provided you with, and give thanks to Allah if Him it is that you serve.

[2.173] He has only forbidden you what dies of itself, and blood, and flesh of swine, and that over which any other (name) than (that of) Allah has been invoked; but whoever is driven to necessity, not desiring, nor exceeding the limit, no sin shall be upon him; surely Allah is Forgiving, Merciful.

[2.174] Surely those who conceal any part of the Book that Allah has revealed and take for it a small price, they eat nothing but fire into their bellies, and Allah will not speak to them on the day of resurrection, nor will He purify them, and they shall have a painful chastisement.

[2.175] These are they who buy error for the right direction and chastisement for forgiveness; how bold they are to encounter fire.

[2.176] This is because Allah has revealed the Book with the truth; and surely those who go against the Book are in a great opposition.

[2.177] It is not righteousness that you turn your faces towards the East and the West, but righteousness is this that one should believe in Allah and the last day and the angels and the Book and the prophets, and give away wealth out of love for Him to the near of kin and the orphans and the needy and the wayfarer and the beggars and for (the emancipation of) the captives, and keep up prayer and pay the poor-rate; and the performers of their promise when they make a promise, and the patient in distress and affliction and in time of conflicts–these are they who are rue (to themselves) and these are they who guard (against evil).

[2.178] O you who believe! retaliation is prescribed for you in the matter of the slain, the free for the free, and the slave for the slave, and the female for the female, but if any remission is made to any one by his (aggrieved) brother, then prosecution (for the bloodwit) should be made according to usage, and payment should be made to him in a good manner; this is an alleviation from your Lord and a mercy; so whoever exceeds the limit after this he shall have a painful chastisement.

[2.179] And there is life for you in (the law of) retaliation, O men of understanding, that you may guard yourselves.

[2.180] Bequest is prescribed for you when death approaches one of you, if he leaves behind wealth for parents and near relatives, according to usage, a duty (incumbent) upon those who guard (against evil).

[2.181] Whoever then alters it after he has heard it, the sin of it then is only upon those who alter it; surely Allah is Hearing, Knowing.

[2.182] But he who fears an inclination to a wrong course or an act of disobedience on the part of the testator, and effects an agreement between the parties, there is no blame on him. Surely Allah is Forgiving, Merciful.

[2.183] O you who believe! fasting is prescribed for you, as it was prescribed for those before you, so that you may guard (against evil).

[2.184] For a certain number of days; but whoever among you is sick or on a journey, then (he shall fast) a (like) number of other days; and those who are not able to do it may effect a redemption by feeding a poor man; so whoever does good spontaneously it is better for him; and that you fast is better for you if you know.

[2.185] The month of Ramazan is that in which the Quran was revealed, a guidance to men and clear proofs of the guidance and the distinction; therefore whoever of you is present in the month, he shall fast therein, and whoever is sick or upon a journey, then (he shall fast) a (like) number of other days; Allah desires ease for you, and He does not desire for you difficulty, and (He desires) that you should complete the number and that you should exalt the greatness of Allah for His having guided you and that you may give thanks.

[2.186] And when My servants ask you concerning Me, then surely I am very near; I answer the prayer of the suppliant when he calls on Me, so they should answer My call and believe in Me that they may walk in the right way.

[2.187] It is made lawful to you to go into your wives on the night of the fast; they are an apparel for you and you are an apparel for them; Allah knew that you acted unfaithfully to yourselves, so He has turned to you (mercifully) and removed from you (this burden); so now be in contact with them and seek what Allah has ordained for you, and eat and drink until the whiteness of the day becomes distinct from the blackness of the night at dawn, then complete the fast till night, and have not contact with them while you keep to the mosques; these are the limits of Allah, so do not go near them. Thus does Allah make clear His communications for men that they may guard (against evil).

[2.188] And do not swallow up your property among yourselves by false means, neither seek to gain access thereby to the judges, so that you may swallow up a part of the property of men wrongfully while you know.

[2.189] They ask you concerning the new moon. Say: They are times appointed for (the benefit of) men, and (for) the pilgrimage; and it is not righteousness that you should enter the houses at their backs, but righteousness is this that one should guard (against evil); and go into the houses by their doors and be careful (of your duty) to Allah, that you may be successful.

[2.190] And fight in the way of Allah with those who fight with you, and do not exceed the limits, surely Allah does not love those who exceed the limits.

[2.191] And kill them wherever you find them, and drive them out from whence they drove you out, and persecution is severer than slaughter, and do not fight with them at the Sacred Mosque until they fight with you in it, but if they do fight you, then slay them; such is the recompense of the unbelievers.

[2.192] But if they desist, then surely Allah is Forgiving, Merciful.

[2.193] And fight with them until there is no persecution, and religion should be only for Allah, but if they desist, then there should be no hostility except against the oppressors.

[2.194] The Sacred month for the sacred month and all sacred things are (under the law of) retaliation; whoever then acts aggressively against you, inflict injury on him according to the injury he has inflicted on you and be careful (of your duty) to Allah and know that Allah is with those who guard (against evil).

[2.195] And spend in the way of Allah and cast not yourselves to perdition with your own hands, and do good (to others); surely Allah loves the doers of good.

[2.196] And accomplish the pilgrimage and the visit for Allah, but if, you are prevented, (send) whatever offering is easy to obtain, and do not shave your heads until the offering reaches its destination; but whoever among you is sick or has an ailment of the head, he (should effect) a compensation by fasting or alms or sacrificing, then when you are secure, whoever profits by combining the visit with the pilgrimage (should take) what offering is easy to obtain; but he who cannot find (any offering) should fast for three days during the pilgrimage and seven days when you return; these (make) ten (days) complete; this is for him whose family is not present in the Sacred Mosque, and be careful (of your duty) to Allah, and know that Allah is severe in requiting (evil).

[2.197] The pilgrimage is (performed in) the well-known months; so whoever determines the performance of the pilgrimage therein, there shall be no intercourse nor fornication nor quarrelling amongst one another; and whatever good you do, Allah knows it; and make provision, for surely the provision is the guarding of oneself, and be careful (of your duty) to Me, O men of understanding.

[2.198] There is no blame on you in seeking bounty from your Lord, so when you hasten on from "Arafat", then remember Allah near the Holy Monument, and remember Him as He has guided you, though before that you were certainly of the erring ones.

[2.199] Then hasten on from the Place from which the people hasten on and ask the forgiveness of Allah; surely Allah is Forgiving, Merciful.

[2.200] So when you have performed your devotions, then laud Allah as you lauded your fathers, rather a greater lauding. But there are some people who say, Our Lord! give us in the world, and they shall have no resting place.

[2.201] And there are some among them who say: Our Lord! grant us good in this world and good in the here-after, and save us from the chastisement of the fire.

[2.202] They shall have (their) portion of what they have earned, and Allah is swift in reckoning.

[2.203] And laud Allah during the numbered days; then whoever hastens off in two days, there is no blame on him, and whoever remains behind, there is no blame on him, (this is) for him who guards (against evil), and be careful (of your duty) to Allah, and know that you shall be gathered together to Him.

[2.204] And among men is he whose speech about the life of this world causes you to wonder, and he calls on Allah to witness as to what is in his heart, yet he is the most violent of adversaries.

[2.205] And when he turn,s back, he runs along in the land that he may cause mischief in it and destroy the tilth and the stock, and Allah does not love mischief-making.

[2.206] And when it is said to him, guard against (the punish ment of) Allah; pride carries him off to sin, there-fore hell is sufficient for him; and certainly it is an evil resting place.

[2.207] And among men is he who sells himself to seek the pleasure of Allah; and Allah is Affectionate to the servants.

[2.208] O you who believe! enter into submission one and all and do not follow the footsteps of Shaitan; surely he is your open enemy.

[2.209] But if you slip after clear arguments have come to you, then know that Allah is Mighty, Wise.

[2.210] They do not wait aught but that Allah should come to them in the shadows of the clouds along with the angels, and the matter has (already) been decided; and (all) matters are returned to Allah.

[2.211] Ask the Israelites how many a clear sign have We given them; and whoever changes the favor of Allah after it has come to him, then surely Allah is severe in requiting (evil).

[2.212] The life of this world is made to seem fair to those who disbelieve, and they mock those who believe, and those who guard (against evil) shall be above them on the day of resurrection; and Allah gives means of subsistence to whom he pleases without measure.

[2.213] (All) people are a single nation; so Allah raised prophets as bearers of good news and as warners, and He revealed with them the Book with truth, that it might judge between people in that in which they dif-fered; and none but the very people who were given it differed about it after clear arguments had come to them, revolting among themselves; so Allah has guided by His will those who believe to the truth about which they differed and Allah guides whom He pleases to the right path.

[2.214] Or do you think that you would enter the garden while yet the state of those who have passed away before you has not come upon you; distress and affliction befell them and they were shaken violently, so that the Apostle and those who believed with him said: When will the help of Allah come? Now surely the help of Allah is nigh!

[2.215] They ask you as to what they should spend. Say: Whatever wealth you spend, it is for the parents and the near of kin and the orphans and the needy and the wayfarer, and whatever good you do, Allah surely knows it.

[2.216] Fighting is enjoined on you, and h is an object of dislike to you; and it may be that you dislike a thing while it is good for you, and it may be that you love a thing while it is evil for you, and Allah knows, while you do not know.

[2.217] They ask you concerning the sacred month about fighting in it. Say: Fighting in it is a grave matter, and hindering (men) from Allah's way and denying Him, and (hindering men from) the Sacred Mosque and turning its people out of it, are still graver with Allah, and persecution is graver than slaughter; and they will not cease fighting with you until they turn you back from your religion, if they can; and whoever of you turns back from his religion, then he dies while an unbeliever– these it is whose works shall go for nothing in this world and the hereafter, and they are the inmates of the fire; therein they shall abide.

[2.218] Surely those who believed and those who fled (their home) and strove hard in the way of Allah these hope for the mercy of Allah and Allah is Forgiving, Merciful.

[2.219] They ask you about intoxicants and games of chance. Say: In both of them there is a great sin and means of profit for men, and their sin is greater than their profit. And they ask you as to what they should spend. Say: What you can spare. Thus does Allah make clear to you the communications, that you may ponder

[2.220] On this world and the hereafter. And they ask you concerning the orphans Say: To set right for them (their affairs) is good, and if you become co-partners with them, they are your brethren; and Allah knows the mischief-maker and the pacemaker, and if Allah had pleased, He would certainly have caused you to fall into a difficulty; surely Allah is Mighty, Wise.

[2.221] And do not marry the idolatresses until they believe, and certainly a believing maid is better than an idolatress woman, even though she should please you; and do not give (believing women) in marriage to idolaters until they believe, and certainly a believing servant is better than an idolater, even though he should please you; these invite to the fire, and Allah invites to the garden and to forgiveness by His will, and makes clear His communications to men, that they may be mindful.

[2.222] And they ask you about menstruation. Say: It is a discomfort; therefore keep aloof from the women during the menstrual discharge and do not go near them until they have become clean; then when they have cleansed themselves, go in to them as Allah has commanded you; surely Allah loves those who turn much (to Him), and He loves those who purify themselves.

[2.223] Your wives are a tilth for you, so go into your tilth when you like, and do good beforehand for yourselves, and be careful (of your duty) to Allah, and know that you will meet Him, and give good news to the believers.

[2.224] And make not Allah because of your swearing (by Him) an obstacle to your doing good and guarding (against evil) and making peace between men, and Allah is Hearing, Knowing.

[2.225] Allah does not call you to account for what is vain in your oaths, but He will call you to account for what your hearts have earned, and Allah is Forgiving, Forbearing.

[2.226] Those who swear that they will not go in to their wives should wait four months; so if they go back, then Allah is surely Forgiving, Merciful.

[2.227] And if they have resolved on a divorce, then Allah is surely Hearing, Knowing.

[2.228] And the divorced women should keep themselves in waiting for three courses; and it is not lawful for them that they should conceal what Allah has created in their wombs, if they believe in Allah and the last day; and their husbands have a better right to take them back in the meanwhile if they wish for reconciliation; and they have rights similar to those against them in a just manner, and the men are a degree above them, and Allah is Mighty, Wise.

[2.229] Divorce may be (pronounced) twice, then keep (them) in good fellowship or let (them) go with kindness; and it is not lawful for you to take any part of what you have given them, unless both fear that they cannot keep within the limits of Allah; then if you fear that they cannot keep within the limits of Allah, there is no blame on them for what she gives up to become free thereby. These are the limits of Allah, so do not exceed them and whoever exceeds the limits of Allah these it is that are the unjust.

[2.230] So if he divorces her she shall not be lawful to him afterwards until she marries another husband; then if he divorces her there is no blame on them both if they return to each other (by marriage), if they think that they can keep within the limits of Allah, and these are the limits of Allah which He makes clear for a people who know.

[2.231] And when you divorce women and they reach their prescribed time, then either retain them in good fellowship or set them free with liberality, and do not retain them for injury, so that you exceed the limits, and whoever does this, he indeed is unjust to his own soul; and do not take Allah's communications for a mockery, and remember the favor of Allah upon you, and that which He has revealed to you of the Book and the Wisdom, admonishing you thereby; and be careful (of your duty to) Allah, and know that Allah is the Knower of all things.

[2.232] And when you have divorced women and they have ended– their term (of waiting), then do not prevent them from marrying their husbands when they agree among themselves in a lawful manner; with this is admonished he among you who believes in Allah and the last day, this is more profitable and purer for you; and Allah knows while you do not know.

[2.233] And the mothers should suckle their children for two whole years for him who desires to make complete the time of suckling; and their maintenance and their clothing must be– borne by the father according to usage; no soul shall have imposed upon it a duty but to the extent of its capacity; neither shall a mother be made to suffer harm on account of her child, nor a father on account of his child, and a similar duty (devolves) on the (father's) heir, but if both desire weaning by mutual consent and counsel, there is no blame on them, and if you wish to engage a wet-nurse for your children, there is no blame on you so long as you pay what you promised for according to usage; and be careful of (your duty to) Allah and know that Allah sees what you do.

[2.234] And (as for) those of you who die and leave wives behind, they should keep themselves in waiting for four months and ten days; then when they have fully attained their term, there is no blame on you for what they do for themselves in a lawful manner; and Allah is aware of what you do.

[2.235] And there is no blame on you respecting that which you speak indirectly in the asking of (such) women in marriage or keep (the proposal) concealed within your minds; Allah knows that you win mention them, but do not give them a promise in secret unless you speak in a lawful manner, and do not confirm the marriage tie until the writing is fulfilled, and know that Allah knows what is in your minds, therefore beware of Him, and know that Allah is Forgiving, Forbearing.

[2.236] There is no blame on you if you divorce women when you have not touched them or appointed for them a portion, and make provision for them, the wealthy according to his means and the straitened in circumstances according to his means, a provision according to usage; (this is) a duty on the doers of good (to others).

[2.237] And if you divorce them before you have touched them and you have appointed for them a portion, then (pay to them) half of what you have appointed, unless they relinquish or he should relinquish in whose hand is the marriage tie; and it is nearer to righteousness that you should relinquish; and do not neglect the giving of free gifts between you; surely Allah sees what you do.

[2.238] Attend constantly to prayers and to the middle prayer and stand up truly obedient to Allah.

[2.239] But if you are in danger, then (say your prayers) on foot or on horseback; and when you are secure, then remember Allah, as. He has taught you what you did not know.

[2.240] And those of you who die and leave wives behind, (make) a bequest in favor of their wives of maintenance for a year without turning (them) out, then if they themselves go away, there is no blame on you for what they do of lawful deeds by themselves, and Allah is Mighty, Wise.

[2.241] And for the divorced women (too) provision (must be made) according to usage; (this is) a duty on those who guard (against evil).

[2.242] Allah thus makes clear to you His communications that you may understand.

[2.243] Have you not considered those who went forth from their homes, for fear of death, and they were thousands, then Allah said to them, Die; again He gave them life; most surely Allah is Gracious to people, but most people are not grateful.

[2.244] And fight in the way of Allah, and know that Allah is Hearing, Knowing.

[2.245] Who is it that will offer of Allah a goodly gift, so He will multiply it to him manifold, and Allah straitens and amplifies, and you shall be returned to Him.

[2.246] Have you not considered the chiefs of the children of Israel after Musa, when they said to a prophet of theirs: Raise up for us a king, (that) we may fight in the way of Allah. He said: May it not be that you would not fight if fighting is ordained for you? They said: And what reason have we that we should not fight in the way of Allah, and we have indeed been compelled to abandon our homes and our children. But when fighting was ordained for them, they turned back, except a few of them, and Allah knows the unjust.

[2.247] And their prophet said to them: Surely Allah has raised Talut to be a king over you. They said: How can he hold kingship over us while we have a greater right to kingship than he, and he has not been granted an abundance of wealth? He said: Surely Allah has chosen him in preference to you, and He has increased him abundantly in knowledge and physique, and Allah grants His kingdom to whom He pleases, and Allah is Amplegiving, Knowing.

[2.248] And the prophet said to them: Surely the sign of His kingdom is, that there shall come to you the chest in which there is tranquillity from your Lord and residue of the relics of what the children of Musa and the children of Haroun have left, the angels bearing it; most surely there is a sign in this for those who believe.

[2.249] So when Talut departed with the forces, he said: Surely Allah will try you with a river; whoever then drinks from it, he is not of me, and whoever does not taste of it, he is surely of me, except he who takes with his hand as much of it as fills the hand; but with the exception of a few of them they drank from it. So when he had crossed it, he and those who believed with him, they said: We have today no power against Jalut and his forces. Those who were sure that they would meet their Lord said: How often has a small party vanquished a numerous host by Allah's permission, and Allah is with the patient.

[2.250] And when they went out against Jalut and his forces they said: Our Lord, pour down upon us patience, and make our steps firm and assist us against the unbelieving people.

[2.251] So they put them to flight by Allah's permission. And Dawood slew Jalut, and Allah gave him kingdom and wisdom, and taught him of what He pleased. And were it not for Allah's repelling some men with others, the earth would certainly be in a state of disorder; but Allah is Gracious to the creatures.

[2.252] These are the communications of Allah: We recite them to you with truth; and most surely you are (one) of the apostles.

[2.253] We have made some of these apostles to excel the others among them are they to whom Allah spoke, and some of them He exalted by (many degrees of) rank; and We gave clear miracles to Isa son of Marium, and strengthened him with the holy spirit. And if Allah had pleased, those after them would not have fought one with another after clear arguments had come to them, but they disagreed; so there were some of them who believed and others who denied; and if Allah had pleased they would not have fought one with another, but Allah brings about what He intends.

[2.254] O you who believe! spend out of what We have given you before the day comes in which there is no bargaining, neither any friendship nor intercession, and the unbelievers– they are the unjust.

[2.255] Allah is He besides Whom there is no god, the Everliving, the Self-subsisting by Whom all subsist; slumber does not overtake Him nor sleep; whatever is in the heavens and whatever is in the earth is His; who is he that can intercede with Him but by His permission? He knows what is before them and what is behind them, and they cannot comprehend anything out of His knowledge except what He pleases, His knowledge extends over the heavens and the earth, and the preservation of them both tires Him not, and He is the Most High, the Great.

[2.256] There is no compulsion in religion; truly the right way has become clearly distinct from error; therefore, whoever disbelieves in the Shaitan and believes in Allah he indeed has laid hold on the firmest handle, which shall not break off, and Allah is Hearing, Knowing.

[2.257] Allah is the guardian of those who believe. He brings them out of the darkness into the light; and (as to) those who disbelieve, their guardians are Shaitans who take them out of the light into the darkness; they are the inmates of the fire, in it they shall abide.

[2.258] Have you not considered him (Namrud) who disputed with Ibrahim about his Lord, because Allah had given him the kingdom? When Ibrahim said: My Lord is He who gives life and causes to die, he said: I give life and cause death. Ibrahim said: So surely Allah causes the sun to rise from the east, then make it rise from the west; thus he who disbelieved was confounded; and Allah does not guide aright the unjust people.

[2.259] Or the like of him (Uzair) who passed by a town, and it had fallen down upon its roofs; he said: When will Allah give it life after its death? So Allah caused him to die for a hundred years, then raised him to life. He said: How long have you tarried? He said: I have tarried a day, or a part of a day. Said He: Nay! you have tarried a hundred years; then look at your food and drink– years have not passed over it; and look at your ass; and that We may make you a sign to men, and look at the bones, how We set them together, then clothed them with flesh; so when it became clear to him, he said: I know that Allah has power over all things.

[2.260] And when Ibrahim said: My Lord! show me how Thou givest life to the dead, He said: What! and do you not believe? He said: Yes, but that my heart may be at ease. He said: Then take four of the birds, then train them to follow you, then place on every mountain a part of them, then call them, they will come to you flying; and know that Allah is Mighty, Wise.

[2.261] The parable of those who spend their property in the way of Allah is as the parable of a grain growing seven ears (with) a hundred grains in every ear; and Allah multiplies for whom He pleases; and Allah is Ample-giving, Knowing

[2.262] (As for) those who spend their property in the way.of Allah, then do not follow up what they have spent with reproach or injury, they shall have their reward from their Lord, and they shall have no fear nor shall they grieve.

[2.263] Kind speech and forgiveness is better than charity followed by injury; and Allah is Self-sufficient, For-bearing.

[2.264] O you who believe! do not make your charity worthless by reproach and injury, like him who spends his property to be seen of men and does not believe in Allah and the last day; so his parable is as the parable of a smooth rock with earth upon it, then a heavy rain falls upon it, so it leaves it bare; they shall not be able to gain anything of what they have earned; and Allah does not guide the unbelieving people.

[2.265] And the parable of those who spend their property to seek the pleasure of Allah and for the certainty 'of their souls is as the parable of a garden on an elevated ground, upon which heavy rain falls so it brings forth its fruit twofold but if heavy rain does not fall upon it, then light rain (is sufficient); and Allah sees what you do.

[2.266] Does one of you like that he should have a garden of palms and vines with streams flowing beneath it; he has in it all kinds of fruits; and old age has overtaken him and he has weak offspring, when, (lo!) a whirlwind with fire in it smites it so it becomes blasted; thus Allah makes the communications clear to you, that you may reflect.

[2.267] O you who believe! spend (benevolently) of the good things that you earn and or what We have brought forth for you out of the earth, and do not aim at what is bad that you may spend (in alms) of it, while you would not take it yourselves unless you have its price lowered, and know that Allah is Self-sufficient, Praiseworthy.

[2.268] Shaitan threatens you with poverty and enjoins you to be niggardly, and Allah promises you forgiveness from Himself and abundance; and Allah is Ample-giving, Knowing.

[2.269] He grants wisdom to whom He pleases, and whoever is granted wisdom, he indeed is given a great good and none but men of understanding mind.

[2.270] And whatever alms you give or (whatever) vow you vow, surely Allah knows it; and the unjust shall have no helpers.

[2.271] If you give alms openly, it is well, and if you hide it and give it to the poor, it is better for you; and this will do away with some of your evil deeds; and Allah is aware of what you do.

[2.272] To make them walk in the right way is not incumbent on you, but Allah guides aright whom He pleases; and whatever good thing you spend, it is to your own good; and you do not spend but to seek Allah's pleasure; and whatever good things you spend shall be paid back to you in full, and you shall not be wronged.

[2.273] (Alms are) for the poor who are confined in the way of Allah– they cannot go about in the land; the ignorant man thinks them to be rich on account of (their) abstaining (from begging); you can recognise them by their mark; they do not beg from men importunately; and whatever good thing you spend, surely Allah knows it.

[2.274] (As for) those who spend their property by night and by day, secretly and openly, they shall have their reward from their Lord and they shall have no fear, nor shall they grieve.

[2.275] Those who swallow down usury cannot arise except as one whom Shaitan has prostrated by (his) touch does rise. That is because they say, trading is only like usury; and Allah has allowed trading and forbidden usury. To whomsoever then the admonition has come from his Lord, then he desists, he shall have what has already passed, and his affair is in the hands of Allah; and whoever returns (to it)– these arc the inmates of the fire; they shall abide in it.

[2.276] Allah does not bless usury, and He causes charitable deeds to prosper, and Allah does not love any ungrateful sinner.

[2.277] Surely they who believe and do good deeds and keep up prayer and pay the poor-rate they shall have their reward from their Lord, and they shall have no fear, nor shall they grieve.

[2.278] O you who believe! Be careful of (your duty to) Allah and relinquish what remains (due) from usury, if you are believers.

[2.279] But if you do (it) not, then be apprised of war from Allah and His Apostle; and if you repent, then you shall have your capital; neither shall you make (the debtor) suffer loss, nor shall you be made to suffer loss.

[2.280] And if (the debtor) is in straitness, then let there be postponement until (he is in) ease; and that you remit (it) as alms is better for you, if you knew.

[2.281] And guard yourselves against a day in which you shall be returned to Allah; then every soul shall be paid back in full what it has earned, and they shall not be dealt with unjustly.

[2.282] O you who believe! when you deal with each other in contracting a debt for a fixed time, then write it down; and let a scribe write it down between you with fairness; and the scribe should not refuse to write as Allah has taught him, so he should write; and let him who owes the debt dictate, and he should be careful of (his duty to) Allah, his Lord, and not diminish anything from it; but if he who owes the debt is unsound in understanding, or weak, or (if) he is not able to dictate himself, let his guardian dictate with fairness; and call in to witness from among your men two witnesses; but if there are not two men, then one man and two women from among those whom you choose to be witnesses, so that if one of the two errs, the second of the two may remind the other; and the witnesses should not refuse when they are summoned; and be not averse to writing it (whether it is) small or large, with the time of its falling due; this is more equitable in the sight of Allah and assures greater accuracy in testimony, and the nearest (way) that you may not entertain doubts (afterwards), except when it is ready merchandise which you give and take among yourselves from hand to hand, then there is no blame on you in not writing it down; and have witnesses when you barter with one another, and let no harm be done to the scribe or to the witness; and if you do (it) then surely it will be a transgression in you, and be careful of (your duty) to Allah, Allah teaches you, and Allah knows all things.

[2.283] And if you are upon a journey and you do not find a scribe, then (there may be) a security taken into possession; but if one of you trusts another, then he who is trusted should deliver his trust, and let him be careful (of his duty to) Allah, his Lord; and do not conceal testimony, and whoever conceals it, his heart is surely sinful; and Allah knows what you do.

[2.284] Whatever is in the heavens and whatever is in the earth is Allah's; and whether you manifest what is in your minds or hide it, Allah will call you to account according to it; then He will forgive whom He pleases and chastise whom He pleases, and Allah has power over all things.

[2.285] The apostle believes in what has been revealed to him from his Lord, and (so do) the believers; they all believe in Allah and His angels and His books and His apostles; We make no difference between any of His apostles; and they say: We hear and obey, our Lord! Thy forgiveness (do we crave), and to Thee is the eventual course.

[2.286] Allah does not impose upon any soul a duty but to the extent of its ability; for it is (the benefit of) what it has earned and upon it (the evil of) what it has wrought: Our Lord! do not punish us if we forget or make a mistake; Our Lord! do not lay on us a burden as Thou didst lay on those before us, Our Lord do not impose upon us that which we have not the strength to bear; and pardon us and grant us protection and have mercy on us, Thou art our Patron, so help us against the unbelieving people.

Reading and Discussion Questions

1. This section of the *Quran* speaks of repentance; how are ritual acts of the Five Pillars acts of repentance?
2. Under what circumstances is a devout Muslim not required to complete any one of the Five Pillars?
3. Why is the month of Ramadan the month of fasting? What makes this month worthy of that level of devotion?
4. What does the Five Pillars say in regard to how Muslims are to treat non-believers?
5. Why are prayers offered facing the Sacred Mosque? What is the Sacred Mosque?

10.2 Al-Ghazali, excerpt from *Confessions*

Originally from Persia (Iran), Abd al-Hamid al-Ghazali (1058–1111 C.E.) was an educated scholar living and working in Baghdad, the cosmopolitan center of the Muslim world at that time. Midway through his career, however, Ghazali changed course and took up the Sufi mystic path of contemplation and writing. His scholarly background helped him reconcile orthodox Islam with the individualism of Sufism.

Source: Abd al-Hamid al-Ghazali, *Confessions* (1100), trans. by Claude Field (E. P. Dutton, 1909).

Glory be to God, whose praise should precede every writing and every speech! May the blessings of God rest on Mohammed, his Prophet and his Apostle, on his family and companions, by whose guidance error is escaped!

You have asked me, O brother in the faith, to expound the aim and the mysteries of religious sciences, the boundaries and depths of theological doctrines. You wish to know my experiences while disentangling truth lost in the medley of sects and divergencies of thought, and how I have dared to climb from the low levels of traditional belief to the topmost summit of assurance. You desire to learn what I have borrowed, first of all from scholastic theology; and secondly from the method of the Ta'limites, who, in seeking truth, rest upon the authority of a leader; and why, thirdly, I have been led to reject philosophic systems; and finally, what I have accepted of the doctrine of the Sufis, and the sum total of truth which I have gathered in studying every variety of opinion. You ask me why, after resigning at Baghdad a teaching post, which attracted a number of hearers, I have, long afterward, accepted a similar one at Nishapur. Convinced as I am of the sincerity, which prompts your inquiries, I proceed to answer them, invoking the help and protection of God.

Know then, my brothers (may God direct you in the right way), that the diversity in beliefs and religions, and the variety of doctrines and sects which divide men, are like a deep ocean strewn with shipwrecks, from which very few escape safe and sound. Each sect, it is true, believes itself in possession of the truth and of salvation, "each party," as the Quransaith, "rejoices in its own creed"; but as the chief of the apostles, whose word is always truthful, has told us, "My people will be divided into more than seventy sects, of whom only one will be saved." This prediction, like all others of the Prophet, must be fulfilled.

From the period of adolescence, that is to say, previous to reaching my twentieth year to the present time when I have passed my fiftieth, I have ventured into this vast ocean; I have fearlessly sounded its depths, and like a resolute diver, I have penetrated its darkness and dared its dangers and abysses. I have interrogated the beliefs of each sect and scrutinized the mysteries of each doctrine, in order to disentangle truth from error and orthodoxy from heresy. I have never met one who maintained the hidden meaning of the Quran without investigating the nature of his belief. nor a partisan of its exterior sense without inquiring into the results of his doctrine. There is no philosopher whose system I have not fathomed, nor theologian the intricacies of whose doctrine I have not followed out.

Sufism has no secrets into which I have not penetrated; the devout adorer of Deity has revealed to me the aim of his austerities; the atheist has not been able to conceal from me the real reason of his unbelief. The thirst for knowledge was innate in me from an early age; it was like a second nature implanted by God, without any will on my part. No sooner had I emerged from boyhood than I had already broken the fetters of tradition and freed myself from hereditary beliefs.

Having noticed how easily the children of Christians become Christians, and the children of Muslims embrace Islam, and remembering also the traditional saying ascribed to the Prophet, "Every child has in him the germ of Islam, then his parents make him Jew, Christian, or Zarathustrian," I was moved by a keen desire to learn what was this innate disposition in the child, the nature of the accidental beliefs imposed on him by the authority of his parents and his masters, and finally the unreasoned convictions which he derives from their instructions.

Struck with the contradictions which I encountered in endeavoring to disentangle the truth and falsehood of these opinions, I was led to make the following reflection: "The search after truth being the aim which I propose to myself, I ought in the first place to ascertain what are the bases of certitude." In the next place I recognized that certitude is the clear and complete knowledge of things, such knowledge as leaves no room for doubt nor possibility of error and conjecture, so that there remains no room in the mind for error to find an entrance. In such a case it is necessary that the mind, fortified against all possibility of going astray, should embrace such a strong conviction that, if, for example, any one possessing the power of changing a stone into gold, or a stick into a serpent, should seek to shake the bases of this certitude, it would remain firm and immovable. Suppose, for instance, a man should come and say to me, who am firmly convinced that ten is more than three, "No; on the contrary, three is more than ten, and, to prove it, I change this rod into a serpent," and supposing that he actually did so, I should remain none the less convinced of the falsity of his assertion, and although his miracle might arouse my astonishment, it would not instill any doubt into my belief.

I then understood that all forms of knowledge which do not unite these conditions (imperviousness to doubt, etc.) do not deserve any confidence, because they are not beyond the reach of doubt, and what is not impregnable to doubt cannot constitute certitude.

Reading and Discussion Questions

1. How does Ghazali expand the conception of Islam so that it is focused not just on the technicalities of law, but on personal commitment to God?
2. What steps does Ghazali propose for reducing the uncertainty Muslims face in thinking and experiencing God?

10.3 Al-Farabi on the Perfect Society

One of the most important thinkers of early Islamic civilization was Abu Nasr Muhammad al-Farabi (c. 870-950 C.E.). Of Turkish descent, al-Farabi lived for most of his in the city of Baghdad, where he became a student of philosophy, instructed by teachers immersed in the classical Greek tradition as it had been developed during the Hellenistic age. Although he was a noted philosopher in his own time, al-Farabi shunned fame and publicity, preferring to live a secluded and austere life.

The influence of classical Greek philosophy on al-Farabi, particularly of Plato, Aristotle, and the neo-Platonists, is evident throughout his writings, including his book, *The Perfect State*. Although the title of this work indicates its subject to be politics, al-Farabi turns to his description of the ideal state only in Chapter 15, after he has grounded his views in a full theory both of metaphysics (including theology and natural science) and psychology, employing arguments from analogy as the basis for his political conclusions.

But al-Farabi's thought was not just derivative from the Greeks. As a Muslim he added a further dimension to the philosopher-king concept. The ideal ruler must also be a prophet. Not only is such a ruler an individual of high intelligence but one of an intellect of "divine quality" who can look into the future and warn "of things to come."

Source: Richard Walzer, trans., *Al-Farabi on the Perfect State* (Oxford: Oxford University Press, 1985).

Chapter 15 Perfect Associations and Perfect Ruler; Faulty Associations

1. In order to preserve himself and to attain his highest perfections every human being is by his very nature in need of many things which he cannot provide all by himself, he is indeed in need of people who each supply him with some particular need of his. Everybody finds himself in the same relation to everybody in this respect. Therefore man cannot attain the perfection, for the sake of which his inborn nature has been given to him, unless many (societies of) people who co-operate come together who each supply everybody else with some particular need of his, so that as a result of the contribution of the whole community all the things are brought together which everybody needs in order to preserve himself and to attain perfection. Therefore human individuals have come to exist in great numbers, and have settled in the inhabitable region of the earth, so that human societies have come to exist in it, some of which are perfect, others imperfect.

2. There are three kinds of perfect society, great, medium and small. The great one is the union of all the societies in the inhabitable world; the medium one the union of one nation in one part of the inhabitable world; the small one the union of the people of a city in the territory of any nation whatsoever. Imperfect are the union of people in a village, the union of people in a quarter, then the union in a street, eventually the union in a house, the house being the smallest union of all. Quarter and village exist both for the sake of the city, but the relation of the village to the city is one of service whereas the quarter is related to the city as a part of it; the street is a part of the quarter, the house a part of the street. The city is a part of the territory of a nation, the nation a part of all the people of the inhabitable world.

3. The most excellent good and the utmost perfection is, in the first instance, attained in a city, not in a society which is less complete than it. But since good in its real sense is such as to be attainable through choice and will, and evils are also due to will and choice only, a city may be established to enable its people to cooperate in attaining some aims that are evil. Hence felicity is not attainable in every city. The city, then, in which people aim through association at co-operating for the things by which felicity in its real and true sense can be attained, is the excellent city, and the society in which there is a co-operation to acquire felic-ity is the excellent society; and the nation in which all of its cities co-operate for those things through which felicity is attained is the excellent nation. In the same way, the excellent universal state will arise only when all the nations in it co-operate for the purpose of reaching felicity.

4. The excellent city resembles the perfect and healthy body, all of whose limbs co-operate to make the life of the animal perfect and to preserve it in this state. Now the limbs and organs of the body are different and their natural endowments and faculties are unequal in excellence, there being among them one ruling organ, namely the heart, and organs which are close in rank to that ruling organ, each having been given by nature a faculty by which it performs its proper function in conformity with the natural aim of that ruling organ. Other organs have by nature faculties by which they perform their functions according to the aims of those organs which have no intermediary between themselves and the ruling organ; they are in the second rank. Other organs, in turn, perform their functions according to the aim of those which are in the second rank, and so on until eventually organs are reached which only serve and do not rule at all.

    The same holds good in the case of the city. Its parts are different by nature, and their natural dispositions are unequal in excellence: there is in it a man who is the ruler, and there are others whose ranks are close to the ruler, each of them with a disposition and a habit through which he performs an action in conformity with the intention of that ruler; these are the holders of the first ranks. Below them are people who perform their actions in accordance with the aims of those people; they are in the second rank. Below them in turn are people who perform their actions according to the aims of the people mentioned in the second instance, and the parts of the city continue to be arranged in this way, until eventually parts are reached which perform their actions according to the aims of others, while there do not exist any people who per-form their actions according to their aims; these, then, are the people who serve without being served in turn, and who are hence in the lowest rank and at the bottom of the scale.

    But the limbs and organs of the body are natural, and the dispositions which they have are natural faculties, whereas, although the parts of the city are natural, their dispositions and habits, by which they perform their actions in the city, are not natural but voluntary, notwithstanding that the parts of the city are by nature provided with endowments unequal in excellence which enable them to do one thing and not another. But they are not parts of the city by their inborn nature alone but rather by the voluntary habits which they acquire such as the arts and their likes; to the natural faculties which exist in the organs and limbs of the body correspond the voluntary habits and dispositions in the parts of the city.

5. The ruling organ in the body is by nature the most perfect and most complete of the organs in itself and in its specific qualification, and it also has the best of everything of which another organ has a share as well; beneath it, in turn, are other organs which rule over organs inferior to them, their rule being lower in rank than the rule of the first and indeed subordinate to the rule of the first; they rule and are ruled.

    In the same way, the ruler of the city is the most perfect part of the city in his specific qualification and has the best of everything which anybody else shares with him; beneath him are people who are ruled by him and rule others.

    The heart comes to be first and becomes then the cause of the existence of the other organs and limbs of the body, and the cause of the existence of their faculties in them and of their arrangement in the ranks proper to them, and when one of its organs is out of order, it is the heart which provides the means to remove that disorder. In the same way the ruler of this city must come to be in the first instance, and will subsequently be the cause of the rise of the city and its parts and the cause of the presence of the voluntary habits of its parts and of their arrangement in the ranks proper to them; and when one part is out of order he provides it with the means to remove its disorder.

The parts of the body close to the ruling organ perform of the natural functions, in agreement—by nature—with the aim of the ruler, the most noble ones; the organs beneath them perform those functions which are less noble, and eventually the organs are reached which perform the meanest functions. In the same way the parts of the city which are close in authority to the ruler of the city perform the most noble voluntary actions, and those below them less noble actions, until eventually the parts are reached which perform the most ignoble actions. The inferiority of such actions is sometimes due to the inferiority of their matter, although they may be extremely useful, like the action of the bladder and the action of the lower intestine in the body; sometimes it is due to their being of little use; at other times it is due to their being very easy to perform. This applies equally to the city and equally to every whole which is composed by nature of well ordered coherent parts: they have a ruler whose relation to the other parts is like the one just described.

6.   This applies also to all existents. For the relation of the First Cause to the other existents is like the relation of the king of the excellent city to its other parts. For the ranks of the immaterial existents are close to the First. Beneath them are the heavenly bodies, and beneath the heavenly bodies the material bodies. All these existents act in conformity with the First Cause, follow it, take it as their guide and imitate it; but each existent does that according to its capacity, choosing its aim precisely on the strength of its established rank in the universe: that is to say the last follows the aim of that which is slightly above it in rank, equally the second existent, in turn, follows what is above itself in rank, and in the same way the third existent has an aim which is above it. Eventually existents are reached which are linked with the First Cause without any intermediary whatsoever. In accordance with this order of rank all the existents permanently follow the aim of the First Cause. Those which are from the very outset provided with all the essentials of their existence are made to imitate the First (Cause) and its aim from their very outset, and hence enjoy eternal bliss and hold the highest ranks; but those which are not provided from the outset with all the essentials of their existence, are provided with a faculty by which they move towards the expected attainment of those essentials and will then be able to follow the aim of the First (Cause). The excellent city ought to be arranged in the same way: all its parts ought to imitate in their actions the aim of their first ruler according to their rank.

7.   The ruler of the excellent city cannot just be any man, because rulership requires two conditions: (a) he should be predisposed for it by his inborn nature, (b) he should have acquired the attitude and habit of will for rulership which will develop in a man whose inborn nature is predisposed for it. Nor is every art suitable for rulership; most of the arts, indeed, are rather suited for service within the city, just as most men are by their very nature born to serve. Some of the arts rule certain (other) arts while serving others at the same time, whereas there are other arts which, not ruling anything at all, only serve. Therefore the art of ruling the excellent city cannot just be any chance art, nor due to any chance habit whatever. For just as the first ruler in a genus cannot be ruled by anything in that genus, (for instance the ruler of the limbs cannot be ruled by any other limb, and this holds good for any ruler of any composite whole), so the art of the ruler in the excellent city of necessity cannot be a serving art at all and cannot be ruled by any other art, but his art must be an art towards the aim of which all the other arts tend, and for which they strive in all the actions of the excellent city.

8.   That man is a person over whom nobody has any sovereignty whatsoever. He is a man who has reached his perfection and has become actually intellect and actually being thought (intelligized), his representative faculty having by nature reached its utmost perfection in the way stated by us; this faculty of his is predisposed by nature to receive, either in waking life or in sleep, from the Active Intellect the particulars, either as they are or by imitating them, and also the intelligibles, by imitating them. His Passive Intellect

will have reached its perfection by [having apprehended] all the intelligibles, so that none of them is kept back from it, and it will have become actually intellect and actually being thought. Indeed any man whose Passive Intellect has thus been perfected by [having apprehended] all the intelligibles and has become actually intellect and actually being thought, so that the intelligible in him has become identical with that which thinks in him, acquires an actual intellect which is superior to the Passive Intellect and more perfect and more separate from matter than the Passive Intellect. It is called the 'Acquired Intellect' and comes to occupy a middle position between the Passive Intellect and the Active Intellect, nothing else being between it and the Active Intellect. The Passive Intellect is thus like matter and substratum for the Acquired Intellect, and the Acquired Intellect like matter and substratum for the Active Intellect, and the rational faculty, which is a natural disposition, is a matter underlying the Passive Intellect which is actually intellect.

9. The first stage, then, through which man becomes man is the coming to be of the receptive natural disposition which is ready to become actually intellect; this disposition is common to all men. Between this disposition and the Active Intellect are two stages, the Passive Intellect which has become actually intellect, and [the rise of] the Acquired Intellect. There are thus two stages between the first stage of being a man and the Active Intellect. When the perfect Passive Intellect and the natural disposition become one thing in the way the compound of matter and form is one-and when the form of the humanity of this man is taken as identical with the Passive Intellect which has become actually intellect, there will be between this man and the Active Intellect only one stage. And when the natural disposition is made the matter of the Passive Intellect which has become actually intellect, and the Passive Intellect the matter of the Acquired Intellect, and the Acquired Intellect the matter of the Active Intellect, and when all this is taken as one and the same thing, then this man is the man on whom the Active Intellect has descended.

10. When this occurs in both parts of his rational faculty, namely the theoretical and the practical rational faculties, and also in his representative faculty, then it is this man who receives Divine Revelation, and God Almighty grants him Revelation through the mediation of the Active Intellect, so that the emanation from God Almighty to the Active Intellect is passed on to his Passive Intellect through the mediation of the Acquired Intellect, and then to the faculty of representation. Thus he is, through the emanation from the Active Intellect to his Passive Intellect, a wise man and a philosopher and an accomplished thinker who employs an intellect of divine quality, and through the emanation from the Active Intellect to his faculty of representation a visionary prophet: who warns of things to come and tells of particular things which exist at present.

11. This man holds the most perfect rank of humanity and has reached the highest degree of felicity. His soul is united as it were with the Active Intellect, in the way stated by us. He is the man who knows every action by which felicity can be reached. This is the first condition for being a ruler. Moreover, he should be a good orator and able to rouse [other people's] imagination by well-chosen words. He should be able to lead people well along the right path to felicity and to the actions by which felicity is reached. He should, in addition, be of tough physique, in order to shoulder the tasks of war.

This is the sovereign over whom no other human being has any sovereignty whatsoever; he is the Imam; he is the first sovereign of the excellent city, he is the sovereign of the excellent nation, and the sovereign of the universal state.

But this state can only be reached by a man in whom twelve natural qualities are found together, with which he is endowed by birth. (1) One of them is that he should have limbs and organs which are free from deficiency and strong, and that they will make him fit for the actions which depend on them; when he intends to perform an action with one of them, he accomplishes it with ease. (2) He should by nature be good at understanding and perceiving everything said to him, and grasp it in his mind according to what the speaker intends and what the thing itself demands. (3) He should be good at retaining what he comes to know and see and hear and apprehend in general, and forget almost nothing. (4) He should be well provided with ready intelligence and very bright; when he sees the slightest indication of a thing, he should grasp it in the way indicated. (5) He should have a fine diction, his tongue enabling him to explain to perfection all that is in the recess of his mind. (6) He should be fond of learning and acquiring knowledge, be devoted to it and grasp things easily, without finding the effort painful, nor feeling discomfort about the toil which it entails. (7) He should by nature be fond of truth and truthful men and hate falsehood and liars. (8) He should by nature not crave for food and drink and sexual intercourse, and have a natural aversion to gambling and hatred of the pleasures which these pursuits provide.

(9) He should be proud of spirit and fond of honour, his soul being by his nature above everything ugly and base, and rising naturally to the most lofty things. (10) Dirham and dinar and the other worldly pursuits should be of little amount in his view. (11) He should by nature be fond of justice and of just people, and hate oppression and injustice and those who practice them, giving himself and others their due, and urging people to act justly and showing pity to those who are oppressed by injustice; he should lend his support to what he considers to be beautiful and noble and just; he should not be reluctant to give in nor should he be stubborn and obstinate if he is asked to do justice; but he should be reluctant to give in if he is asked to do injustice and evil altogether. (12) He should be strong in setting his mind firmly upon the thing which, in his view, ought to be done, and daringly and bravely carry it out without fear and weak-mindedness.

13. Now it is difficult to find all these qualities united in one man, and, therefore, men endowed with this nature will be found one at a time only, such men being altogether very rare. Therefore if there exists such a man in the excellent city who, after reaching maturity, fulfils the six aforementioned conditions - or five of them if one excludes the gift of visionary prophecy through the faculty of representation - he will be the sovereign. Now when it happens that, at a given time, no such man is to be found but there was previously an unbroken succession of sovereigns of this kind, the laws and the customs which were introduced will be adopted and eventually firmly established.

The next sovereign, who is the successor of the first sovereigns, will be someone in whom those [twelve] qualities are found together from the time of his birth and his early youth and who will, after reaching his maturity, be distinguished by the following six qualities: (1) He will be a philosopher. (2) He will know and remember the laws and customs (and rules of conduct) with which the first sovereigns had governed the city, conforming in all his actions to all their actions. (3) He will excel in deducing a new law by analogy where no law of his predecessors has been recorded, following for his deductions the principles laid down by the first Imams. (4) He will be good at deliberating and be powerful in his deductions to meet new situations for which the first sovereigns could not have laid down any law; when doing this he will have in mind the good of the city. (5) He will be good at guiding the people by his speech to fulfill the laws of the first sovereigns as well as those laws which he will have deduced in conformity with their principles after their time. (6) He should be of tough physique in order to shoulder the tasks of war, mastering the serving as well as the ruling military art. When one single man who fulfills all these conditions cannot be found but there are two, one of whom is a philosopher and the other fulfills the remaining conditions, the two of them will be the sovereigns of this city.

But when all these six qualities exist separately in different men, philosophy in one man and the second quality in another man and so on, and when these men are all in agreement, they should all together be the excellent sovereigns. But when it happens, at a given time, that philosophy has no share in the government, though every other condition may be present in it, the excellent city will remain without a king, the ruler actually in charge of this city will not be a king, and the city will be on the verge of destruction; and if it happens that no philosopher can be found who will be attached to the actual ruler of the city, then, after a certain interval, this city will undoubtedly perish.

Reading and Discussion Questions

1. What arguments does Farabi use to describe the perfect state and the perfect ruler?
2. Compare Farabi's descriptions of the perfect society with Confucius's (document 9.2) and with Kautilya's (document 8.2). What are the similarities and differences?
3. How does Farabi ground his arguments in Aristotlean thought and logic?

10.4 Ibn Fadlan's Account of the Rus

Ibn Fadlan was a tenth-century Arab chronicler. In 921 C.E., the Caliph of Baghdad sent Ibn Fadlan on an embassy to the King of the Bulgars of the Middle Volga (present-day Russia). Ibn Fadlan wrote an account of his journey: the *Risala*. During the course of his journey, Ibn Fadlan met a people called the Rus, acting as traders in the Bulgar capital.

Source: Smyser, H.M. "Ibn Fadlan's Account of the Rus with Some Commentary and Some Allusions to Beowulf." *Franciplegius: Medieval and Linguistic Studies in Honor of Francis Peabody Magoun, Jr.* eds. Jess B. Bessinger Jr. and Robert P. Creed. (New York: New York University Press. 1925), pp. 92-119.

I have seen the Rus as they came on their merchant journeys and encamped by the Volga. I have never seen more perfect physical specimens, tall as date palms, blonde and ruddy; they wear neither tunics nor caftans, but the men wear a garment which covers one side of the body and leaves a hand free.

Each man has an axe, a sword, and a knife and keeps each by him at all times. The swords are broad and grooved, of Frankish sort. Every man is tattooed from fingernails to neck with dark green trees, figures, etc.

Each woman wears on either breast a box of iron, silver, copper or gold; the value of the box indicates the wealth of the husband. Each box has a ring from which hangs a knife. The women wear neck rings of gold and silver, one for each 10,000 dirhams which her husband is worth; some women have many. Their most prized ornaments are beads of green glass of the same make as ceramic objects one finds on their ships. They trade beads among themselves and they pay an exaggerated price for them, for they buy them for a dirham apiece. They string them as necklaces for their women.

In place of gold the Rus use sable skins. No standard measure is known in the land; they buy and sell by dry measure. They are very fond of pork and many of them who have assumed the garb of Muslims miss it very much....

...I heard that at the deaths of their chief personages they did many things, of which the least was cremation, and I was interested to learn more. At last I was told of the death of one of their outstanding men. They placed him in a grave and put a roof over it for ten days, while they cut and sewed garments for him.

They burn the deceased in this fashion: they leave him for the first ten days in a grave. His possessions they divide into three parts: one part for his daughters and wives; another for garments to clothe the corpse; another part covers the cost of the intoxicating drink which they consume in the course of ten days, uniting sexually with women and playing musical instruments. Meanwhile, the slave girl who gives herself to be burned with him, in these ten days drinks and indulges in pleasure; she decks her head and her person with all sorts of ornaments and fine dress and so arrayed gives herself to the men.

When a great personage dies, the people of his family ask his young women and men slaves, "Who among you will die with him?" One answers, "I." Once he or she has said that, the thing is obligatory: there is no backing out of it. Usually it is one of the girl slaves who do this.

When the man of whom I have spoken died, his girl slaves were asked, "Who will die with him?" One answered, "I." She was then put in the care of two young women, who watched over her and accompanied her everywhere, to the point that they occasionally washed her feet with their own hands. Garments were being made for the deceased and all else was being readied of which he had need. Meanwhile the slave drinks every day and sings, giving herself over to pleasure.

When the day arrived on which the man was to be cremated and the girl with him, I went to the river on which was his ship. I saw that they had drawn the ship onto the shore, and that they had erected four posts of birch wood and other wood, and that around the ship was made a structure like great ship's tents out of wood. Then they pulled the ship up until it was on this wooden construction. Then they began to come and go and to speak words which I did not understand, while the man was still in his grave and had not yet been brought out. The tenth day, having drawn the ship up onto the river bank, they guarded it. In the middle of the ship they prepared a dome or pavilion of wood and covered this with various sorts of fabrics. Then they brought a couch and put it on the ship and covered it with a mattress of Greek brocade. Then came an old woman whom they call the Angel of Death, and she spread upon the couch the furnishings mentioned. It is she who has charge of the clothes-making and arranging all things, and it is she who kills the girl slave. I saw that she was a strapping old woman, fat and leering.

When they came to the grave they removed the earth from above the wood, then the wood, and took out the dead man clad in the garments in which he had died. I saw that he had grown black from the cold of the country. They put intoxicating drink, fruit, and a stringed instrument in the grave with him. They removed all that. The dead man did not smell bad, and only his color had changed. They dressed him in trousers, stockings, boots, a tunic, and caftan of brocade with gold buttons. They put a hat of brocade and fur on him.

Then they carried him into the pavilion on the ship. They seated him on the mattress and propped him up with cushions. They brought intoxicating drink, fruits, and fragrant plants, which they put with him, then bread, meat, and onions, which they placed before him. Then they brought a dog, which they cut in two and put in the ship. Then they brought his weapons and placed them by his side.

Then they took two horses, ran them until they sweated, then cut them to pieces with a sword and put them in the ship. Next they killed a rooster and a hen and threw them in. The girl slave who wished to be killed went here and there and into each of their tents, and the master of each tent had sexual intercourse with her and said, "Tell your lord I have done this out of love for him."

After that, the group of men who have cohabitated with the slave girl make of their hands a sort of paved way whereby the girl, placing her feet on the palms of their hands, mounts onto the ship.

The men came with shields and sticks. She was given a cup of intoxicating drink; she sang at taking it and drank. The interpreter told me that she in this fashion bade farewell to all her girl companions. Then she was given another cup; she took it and sang for a long time while the old woman incited her to drink up and go into the pavilion where her master lay. I saw that she was distracted; she wanted to enter the pavilion but put her head between it and the boat. Then the old woman seized her head and made her enter the pavilion and entered with her. Thereupon the men began to strike with the sticks on the shields so that her cries could not be heard and the other slave girls would not seek to escape death with their masters. Then six men went into the pavilion and each had intercourse with the girl. Then they laid her at the side of her master; two held her feet and two her hands; the old woman known as the Angel of Death re-entered and looped a cord around her neck and gave the crossed ends to the two men for them to pull. Then she approached her with a broad-bladed dagger, which she plunged between her ribs repeatedly, and the men strangled her with the cord until she was dead.

Reading and Discussion Questions

1. What impression do the Rus make on Ibn Fadlan? Would the pagan customs and sexual rituals have shocked Ibn Fadlan?
2. The Rus did not convert to orthodox Christianity until a few decades after Ibn Fadlan's journey. What was the impact of Russia's conversion to Christianity, especially for the Muslim world?

10.5 John of Damascus, "On Icons."

John of Damascus, d. 754, wrote in defense of images during the first stage of the iconoclast controversy (726-787) in the Byzantine Empire. The Byzantines were torn apart by the dispute over whether icons violated the Biblical prohibition of graven images; it was a schism that had religious and political repercussions, and ultimately led to the loss of authority by the emperor over the church (in 842). It also distracted the Byzantine church from other potential religious developments.

Source: from *A Source Book for Ancient Church History: From the Apostolic Age to the Close of the Concillar Period.* Edited by Joseph Cullen Ayer. (New York: Charles Scribner's Sons, 1913), pp. 691-693.

In the first place, then, before speaking to you, I beseech Almighty God, to whom all things lie open, who knows my small capacity and my genuine intention, to bless the words of my mouth, and to enable me to bridle my mind and direct it to Him, to walk in His presence straightly, not declining to a plausible right hand, nor knowing the left. Then I ask all God's people, the chosen ones of His royal priesthood, with the holy shepherd of Christ's orthodox flock, who represents in his own person Christ's priesthood, to receive my treatise with kindness. They must not dwell on my unworthiness, nor seek for eloquence, for I am only too conscious of my shortcomings. They must consider the thoughts themselves. The kingdom of heaven is not in word but in deed. Conquest is not my object. I raise a hand which is fighting for the truth—a willing hand under the divine guidance. Relying, then, upon substantial truth as my auxiliary, I will enter on my subject matter.

I have taken heed to the words of Truth Himself: "The Lord thy God is one." (Deut. 6.4) And "Thou shalt fear the Lord thy God, and shalt serve Him only, and thou shalt not have strange, gods." (Deut. 6.13) Again, "Thou shalt not make to thyself a graven thing, nor the likeness of anything that is in heaven above, or in the earth beneath" (Ex. 20.4); and "Let them be all confounded that adore graven things." (Ps. 97.7) Again, "The gods that have not made heaven and earth, let them perish." (Jer. 10.11) In this way God spoke of old to the patriarchs through the prophets, and lastly, through His only-begotten Son, on whose account He made the ages. He says, "This is eternal life, that they may know Thee, the only true God, and Jesus Christ whom Thou didst send." (Jn 17.3) I believe in one God, the source of all things, without beginning, uncreated, immortal, everlasting, incomprehensible, bodiless, invisible, uncircumscribed, without form. I believe in one supersubstantialbeing, one divine Godhead in three entities, the Father, the Son, and the Holy Ghost, and I adore Him alone with the worship of latreia. I adore one God, one Godhead but three Persons, God the Father, God the Son made flesh, and God the Holy Ghost, one God. I do not adore creation more than the Creator, but I adore the creature created as I am, adopting creation freely and spontaneously that He might elevate our nature and make us partakers of His divine nature. Together with my Lord and King I worship Him clothed in the flesh, not as if it were a garment or He constituted a fourth person of the Trinity—God forbid. That flesh is divine, and endures after its assumption. Human nature was not lost in the Godhead, but just as the Word made flesh remained the Word, so flesh became the Word remaining flesh, becoming, rather, one with the Word through union. Therefore I venture to draw an image of the invisible God, not as invisible, but as having become visible for our sakes through flesh and blood. I do not draw an image of the immortal Godhead. I paint the visible flesh of God, for it is impossible to represent a spirit, how much more God who gives breath to the spirit.

Now adversaries say: God's commands to Moses the law-giver were, "Thou shalt adore shalt worship him the Lord thy God, and thou alone, and thou shalt not make to thyself a graven thing that is in heaven above, or in the earth beneath."

They err truly, not knowing the Scriptures, for the letter kills whilst the spirit quickens–not finding in the letter the hidden meaning. I could say to these people, with justice, He who taught you this would teach you the following. Listen to the law-giver's interpretation in Deuteronomy: "And the Lord spoke to you from the midst of the fire. You heard the voice of His words, but you saw not any form at all." (Deut. 4.12) And shortly afterwards: "Keep your souls carefully. You saw not any similitude in the day that the Lord God spoke to you in Horeb from the midst of the fire, lest perhaps being deceived you might make you a graven similitude, or image of male and female, the similitude of any beasts that are upon the earth, or birds that fly under heaven." (Deut. 4.15-17) And again, "Lest, perhaps, lifting up thy eyes to heaven, thou see the sun and the moon, and all the stars of heaven, and being deceived by error thou adore and serve them." (Deut. 4.19)

You see the one thing to be aimed at is not to adore a created thing more than the Creator, nor to give the worship of latreia except to Him alone. By worship, consequently, He always understands the worship of latreia. For, again, He says: "Thou shalt not have strange gods other than Me. Thou shalt not make to thyself a graven thing, nor any similitude. Thou shalt not adore them, and thou shalt not serve them, for I am the Lord thy God." (Deut. 5.7-9) And again, "Overthrow their altars, and break down their statues; burn their groves with fire, and break their idols in pieces. For thou shalt not adore a strange god." (Deut. 12.3) And a little further on: "Thou shalt not make to thyself gods of metal." (Ex. 34.17)

You see that He forbids image-making on account of idolatry, and that it is impossible to make an image of the immeasurable, uncircumscribed, invisible God. You have not seen the likeness of Him, the Scripture says, and this was St Paul's testimony as he stood in the midst of the Areopagus: "Being, therefore, the offspring of God, we must not suppose the divinity to be like unto gold, or silver, or stone, the graving of art, and device of man." (Acts 17.29)

These injunctions were given to the Jews on account of their proneness to idolatry. Now we, on the contrary, are no longer in leading strings. Speaking theologically, it is given to us to avoid superstitious error, to be with God in the knowledge of the truth, to worship God alone, to enjoy the fullness of His knowledge. We have passed the stage of infancy, and reached the perfection of manhood. We receive our habit of mind from God, and know what may be imaged and what may not. The Scripture says, "You have not seen the likeness of Him." (Ex. 33.20) What wisdom in the law-giver. How depict the invisible? How picture the inconceivable? How give expression to the limitless, the immeasurable, the invisible? How give a form to immensity? How paint immortality? How localize mystery? It is clear that when you contemplate God, who is a pure spirit, becoming man for your sake, you will be able to clothe Him with the human form. When the Invisible One becomes visible to flesh, you may then draw a likeness of His form. When He who is a pure spirit, without form or limit, immeasurable in the boundlessness of His own nature, existing as God, takes upon Himself the form of a servant in substance and in stature, and a body of flesh, then you may draw His likeness, and show it to anyone willing to contemplate it. Depict His ineffable condescension, His virginal birth, His baptism in the Jordan, His transfiguration on Thabor, His all-powerful sufferings, His death and miracles, the proofs of His Godhead, the deeds which He worked in the flesh through divine power, His saving Cross, His Sepulchre, and resurrection, and ascent into heaven. Give to it all the endurance of engraving and colour. Have no fear or anxiety; worship is not all of the same kind.

Abraham worshipped the sons of Emmor, impious men in ignorance of God, when he bought the double cave for a tomb. (Gen. 23.7; Acts 7.16) Jacob worshipped his brother Esau and Pharao, the Egyptian, but on the point of his staff.(Gen 33.3) He worshipped, he did not adore. Josue and Daniel worshipped an angel of God; (Jos. 5.14) they did not adore him. The worship of latreia is one thing, and the worship which is given to merit another. Now, as we are talking of images and worship, let us analyze the exact meaning of each. An image is a likeness of the original with a certain difference, for it is not an exact reproduction of the original. Thus, the Son is the living, substantial, unchangeable Image of the invisible God (Col. 1.15), bearing in Himself the whole Father, being in all things equal to Him, differing only in being begotten by the Father, who is the Begetter; the Son is begotten. The Father does not proceed from the Son, but the Son from the Father. It is through the Son, though not after Him, that He is what He is, the Father who generates. In God, too, there are representations and images of His future acts,-that is to say, His counsel from all eternity, which is ever unchangeable. That which is divine is immutable; there is no change in Him, nor shadow of change. (James 1.17) Blessed Denis, (the Carthusian [i.e., Pseudo-Dionysius]) who has made divine things in God's presence his study, says that these representations and images are marked out beforehand. In His counsels, God has noted and settled all that He would do, the unchanging future events before they came to pass. In the same way, a man who wished to build a house would first make and think out a plan. Again, visible things are images of invisible and intangible things, on which they throw a faint light. Holy Scripture clothes in figure God and the angels, and the same holy man (Blessed Denis) explains why. When sensible things sufficiently render what is beyond sense, and give a form to what is intangible, a medium would be reckoned imperfect according to our standard, if it did not fully represent material vision, or if it required effort of mind. If, therefore, Holy Scripture, providing for our need, ever putting before us what is intangible, clothes it in flesh, does it not make an image of what is thus invested with our nature, and brought to the level of our desires, yet invisible? A certain conception through the senses thus takes place in the brain, which was not there before, and is transmitted to the judicial faculty, and added to the mental store. Gregory, who is so eloquent about God, says that the mind, which is set upon getting beyond corporeal things, is incapable of doing it. For the invisible things of God since the creation of the world are made visible through images. (Rom. 1.20) We see images in creation which remind us faintly of God, as when, for instance, we speak of the holy and adorable Trinity, imaged by the sun, or light, or burning rays, or by a running fountain, or a full river, or by the mind, speech, or the spirit within us, or by a rose tree, or a sprouting flower, or a sweet fragrance.

Again, an image is expressive of something in the future, mystically shadowing forth what is to happen. For instance, the ark represents the image of Our Lady, Mother of God, so does the staff and the earthen jar. The serpent brings before us Him who vanquished on the Cross the bite of the original serpent; the sea, water, and the cloud the grace of baptism. (I Cor. 10.1)

Again, things which have taken place are expressed by images for the remembrance either of a wonder, or an honour, or dishonour, or good or evil, to help those who look upon it in after times that we may avoid evils and imitate goodness. It is of two kinds, the written image in books, as when God had the law inscribed on tablets, and when He enjoined that the lives of holy men should be recorded and sensible memorials be preserved in remembrance; as, for instance, the earthen jar and the staff in the ark. (Ex. 34.28; Heb. 9.4) So now we preserve in writing the images and the good deeds of the past. Either, therefore, take away images altogether and be out of harmony with God, who made these regulations, or receive them with the language and in the manner which befits them. In speaking of the manner let us go into the question of worship.

Worship is the symbol of veneration and of honour. Let us understand that there are different degrees of worship. First of all the worship of latreia, which we show to God, who alone by nature is worthy of worship.

When, for the sake of God who is worshipful by nature, we honour His saints and servants, as Josue and Daniel worshipped an angel, and David His holy places, when be says, "Let us go to the place where His feet have stood." (Ps. 132.7) Again, in His tabernacles, as when all the people of Israel adored in the tent, and standing round the temple in Jerusalem, fixing their gaze upon it from all sides, and worshipping from that day to this, or in the rulers established by Him, as Jacob rendered homage to Esau, his elder brother, (Gen. 33.3) and to Pharaoh, the divinely established ruler. (Gen. 47.7) Joseph was worshipped by his brothers. (Gen. 50.18) I am aware that worship was based on honour, as in the case of Abraham and the sons of Emmor. (Gen. 23.7) Either, then, do away with worship, or receive it altogether according to its proper measure.

Answer me this question. Is there only one God? You answer, "Yes, there is only one Law-giver." Why, then, does He command contrary things? The cherubim are not outside of creation; why, then, does He allow cherubim carved by the hand of man to overshadow the mercy-scat? Is it not evident that as it is impossible to make an image of God, who is uncircumscribed and impassible, or of one like to God, creation should not be worshipped as God. He allows the image of the cherubim who are circumscribed, and prostrate in adoration before the divine throne, to be made, and thus prostrate to overshadow the mercy-seat. It was fitting that the image of the heavenly choirs should overshadow the divine mysteries. Would you say that the ark and staff and mercy-seat were not made? Are they not produced by the hand of man? Are they not due to what you call contemptible matter? What was the tabernacle itself? Was it not an image? Was it not a type and a figure? Hence the holy Apostle's words concerning the observances of the law, "Who serve unto the example and shadow, of heavenly things." As it was answered to Moses, when he was to finish the tabernacle: "See" (He says), "that thou make all things according to the pattern which was shown thee on the Mount." (Heb. 8.5; Ex. 25.40) But the law was not an image. It shrouded the image. In the words of the same Apostle, "the law contains the shadow of the goods to come, not the image of those things." (Heb. 10.1) For if the law should forbid images, and yet be itself a forerunner of images, what should we say? If the tabernacle was a figure, and the type of a type, why does the law not prohibit image-making? But this is not in the least the case. There is a time for everything. (Eccl. 3.1)

Of old, God the incorporeal and uncircumscribed was never depicted. Now, however, when God is seen clothed in flesh, and conversing with men, (Bar. 3.38) I make an image of the God whom I see. I do not worship matter, I worship the God of matter, who became matter for my sake, and deigned to inhabit matter, who worked out my salvation through matter. I will not cease from honouring that matter which works my salvation. I venerate it, though not as God. How could God be born out of lifeless things? And if God's body is God by union (kaqupostasin), it is immutable. The nature of God remains the same as before, the flesh created in time is quickened by a logical and reasoning soul. I honour all matter besides, and venerate it. Through it, filled, as it were, with a divine power and grace, my salvation has come to me. Was not the thrice happy and thrice blessed wood of the Cross matter? Was not the sacred and holy mountain of Calvary matter? What of the life-giving rock, the Holy Sepulchre, the source of our resurrection: was it not matter? Is not the most holy book of the Gospels matter? Is not the blessed table matter which gives us the Bread of Life? Are not the gold and silver matter, out of which crosses and altar-plate and chalices are made? And before all these things, is not the body and blood of our Lord matter? Either do away with the veneration and worship due to all these things, or submit to the tradition of the Church in the worship of images, honouring God and His friends, and following in this the grace of the Holy Spirit. Do not despise matter, for it is not despicable. Nothing is that which God has made. This is the Manichean heresy. That alone is despicable which does not come from God, but is our own invention, the spontaneous choice of will to disregard the natural law,–that is to say, sin. If, therefore, you dishonour and give up images, because they are produced by matter, consider what the Scripture says: And the Lord spoke to Moses, saying, "Behold I have called by name Beseleel, the son of Uri, the son of Hur, of the tribe of Juda. And

I have filled him with the spirit of God, with wisdom and understanding, and knowledge in all manner of work. To devise whatsoever may be artificially made of gold, and silver, and brass, of marble and precious stones, and variety of wood. And I have given him for his companion, Ooliab, the son of Achisamech, of the tribe of Dan. And I have put wisdom in the heart of every skillful man, that they may make all things which I have commanded thee." (Ex. 31.1-6) [18] And again: "Moses said to all the assembly of the children of Israel: This is the word the Lord hath commanded, saying: Set aside with you first fruits to the Lord. Let every one that is willing and hath a ready heart, offer them to the Lord, gold, and silver, and brass, violet, and purple, and scarlet twice dyed, and fine linen, goat's hair, and ram's skins died red and violet, coloured skins, selim-wood, and oil to maintain lights and to make ointment, and most sweet incense, onyx stones, and precious stones for the adorning of the ephod and the rational. Whosoever of you is wise, let him come, and make that which the Lord hath commanded." (Ex. 35.4-10) See you here the glorification of matter which you make inglorious. What is more insignificant than goat's hair or colours? Are not scarlet and purple and hyacinth colours? Now, consider the handiwork of man becoming the likeness of the cherubim. How, then, can you make the law a pretence for giving up what it orders? If you invoke it against images, you should keep the Sabbath, and practise circumcision. It is certain that "if you observe the law, Christ will not profit you. You who are justified in the law, you [19] are fallen from grace." (Gal. 5.2-4) Israel of old did not see God, but "we see the Lord's glory face to face." (IICor. 3.18)

We proclaim Him also by our senses on all sides, and we sanctify the noblest sense, which is that of sight. The image is a memorial, just what words are to a listening ear. What a book is to the literate, that an image is to the illiterate. The image speaks to the sight as words to the ear; it brings us understanding. Hence God ordered the ark to be made of imperishable wood, and to be gilded outside and in, and the tablets to be put in it, and the staff and the golden urn containing the manna, for a remembrance of the past and a type of the future. Who can say these were not images and far-sounding heralds? And they did not hang on the walls of the tabernacle; but in sight of all the people who looked towards them, they were brought forward for the worship and adoration of God, who made use of them. It is evident that they were not worshipped for themselves, but that the people were led through them to remember past signs, and to worship the God of wonders. They were images to serve as recollections, not divine, but leading to divine things by divine power.

And God ordered twelve stones to be taken out of the Jordan, and specified why. For he says: "When your son asks you the meaning of these stones, tell him how the water left the Jordan by the divine command, and how the ark was saved and the whole people." (Jos. 4.21-22) How, then, shall we not record on image the saving pains and wonders of Christ our Lord, so that when my child asks me, "What is this?" I may say, that God the Word became man, and that for His sake not Israel alone passed through the Jordan, but all the human race gained their original happiness. Through Him human nature rose from the lowest depths of the earth higher than the skies, and in His Person sat down on the throne His Father had prepared for Him.

But the adversary says: "Make an image of Christ or of His mother who bore Him and let that be sufficient." O what folly this is! On your own showing, you are absolutely against the saints. For if you make an image of Christ and not of the saints, it is evident that you do not disown images, but the honour of the saints. You make statues indeed of Christ as of one glorified, whilst you [21] reject the saints as unworthy of honour, and call truth a falsehood. "I live," says the Lord, "and I will glorify those who glorify Me." (I Sam. 2.30) And the divine Apostle: therefore now he is not a servant, but a son. "And if a son, an heir also through God." (Gal. 4.7) Again, "If we suffer with Him, that we also may be glorified:" (Rom. 8.17) you are not waging war against images, but against the saints. St John, who rested on His breast, says, that "we shall be like to Him" (I Jn. 3.2): just as a man by contact with fire becomes fire, not by nature, but by contact and by burning and by participation, so is it, I apprehend, with the flesh of the Crucified Son of God. That flesh, by participation through union with the divine nature, was unchangeably God, not in virtue of grace from God as was the case with each of the prophets, but by the presence of the Fountain Head Himself. God, the Scripture says, stood in the synagogue of the gods, (Ps. 82.1) so that the saints, too, are gods. Holy Gregory takes the words, "God stands in the midst of the gods," to mean that He discriminates their several merits. The saints in their lifetime were filled with the Holy Spirit, and when they are no more, His grace abides with their spirits and with their bodies in their tombs, and also with their likenesses and holy images, not by nature, but by grace and divine power.

God charged David to build Him a temple through his son, and to prepare a place of rest. Solomon, in building the temple, made the cherubim, as the book of Kings says. And he encompassed the cherubim with gold, and all the walls in a circle, and he had the cherubim carved, and palms inside and out, in a circle, not from the sides, be it observed. And there were bulls and lions and pomegranates. (I Kgs. 6.28-29) Is it not more seemly to decorate all the walls of the Lord's house with holy forms and images rather than with beasts and plants? Where is the law declaring "thou shalt not make any graven image"? But Solomon receiving the gift of wisdom, imaging heaven, made the cherubim, and the likenesses of bulls and lions, which the law forbade. Now if we make a statue of Christ, and likenesses of the saints, does not their being filled with the Holy Ghost increase the piety of our homage? As then the people and the temple were purified in blood and in burnt offerings, (Heb. 9.13) so now the Blood of Christ giving testimony under Pontius Pilate, (I Tim. 6.13) and being Himself the first fruits of the martyrs, the Church is built up on the blood of the saints. Then the signs and forms of lifeless animals figured forth the human tabernacle, the martyrs themselves whom they were preparing for God's abode.

We depict Christ as our King and Lord, and do not deprive Him of His army. The saints constitute the Lord's army. Let the earthly king dismiss his army before he gives up his King and Lord. Let him put off the purple before he takes honour away from his most valiant men who have conquered their passions. For if the saints are heirs of God, and co-heirs of Christ, (Rom. 8.17) they will be also partakers of the divine glory of sovereignty. If the friends of God have had a part in the sufferings of Christ, how shall they not receive a share of His glory even on earth? "I call you not servants," our Lord says, "you are my friends." (Jn. 15.15) Should we then deprive them of the honour given to them by the Church? What audacity! What boldness of mind, to fight God and His commands! You, who refuse to worship images, would not worship the Son of [24] God, the Living Image of the invisible God, (Col. 1.15) and His unchanging form. I worship the image of Christ as the Incarnate God; that of Our Lady, the Mother of us all, as the Mother of God's Son; that of the saints as the friends of God. They have withstood sin unto blood, and followed Christ in shedding their blood for Him, who shed His blood for them. I put on record the excellencies and the sufferings of those who have walked in His footsteps, that I may sanctify myself, and be fired with the zeal of imitation. St Basil says, "Honouring the image leads to the prototype." If you raise churches to the saints of God, raise also their trophies. The temple of old was not built in the name of any man. The death of the just was a cause of tears, not of feasting. A man who touched a corpse was considered unclean, (Num. 19.11) even if the corpse was Moses himself. But now the memories of the saints are kept with rejoicings. The dead body of Jacob was wept over, whilst there is joy over the death of Stephen. Therefore, either give up the solemn commemorations of the saints, which are not according to the old law, or accept images which are [25] also against it, as you say. But it is impossible not to keep with rejoicing the memories of the saints. The Holy Apostles and Fathers are at one in enjoining them. From the time that God the Word became flesh He is as we are in everything except sin, and of our nature, without confusion. He has deified our flesh for ever, and we are in very deed sanctified through His Godhead and the union of His flesh with it. And from the time that God, the Son of God, impassible by reason of His Godhead, chose to suffer voluntarily He wiped out our debt, also paying for us a most full and noble ransom. We are truly free through the sacred blood of the Son pleading for us with the Father. And we are indeed delivered from corruption since He descended into hell to the souls detained there through centuries (I Pet. 3.19) and gave the captives their freedom, sight to the blind, (Mt. 12.29) and chaining the strong one. He rose in the plenitude of His power, keeping the flesh of immortality which He had taken for us. And since we have been born again of water and the Spirit, we are truly sons and heirs of God. Hence St Paul calls the faithful holy; (I Cor. 1.2) hence we do not grieve but rejoice over the death of the saints. We are then no longer under grace, (Rom. 6.14) being justified through faith, (Rom. 5.1) and knowing the one true God. The just man is not bound by the law. (I. Tim. 1.9) We are not held by the letter of the law, nor do we serve as children, (Gal. 4.1) but grown into the perfect estate of man we are fed on solid food, not on that which conduces to idolatry. The law is good as a light shining in a dark place until the day breaks. Your hearts have already been illuminated, the living water of God's knowledge has run over the tempestuous seas of heathendom, and we may all know God. The old creation has passed away, and all things are renovated. The holy Apostle Paul said to St Peter, the chief of the Apostles: "If you, being a Jew, live as a heathen and not a Jew, how will you persuade heathens to do as Jews do?" (Gal. 2.14) And to the Galatians: "I will bear witness to every circumcised man that it is salutary to fulfil the whole law." (Gal. 5.3)

Of old they who did not know God, worshipped false gods. But now, knowing God, or rather being known by Him, how can we [27] return to bare and naked rudiments? (Gal. 4.8-9) I have looked upon the human form of God, and my soul has been saved. I gaze upon the image of God, as Jacob did, (Gen. 32.30) though in a different way. Jacob sounded the note of the future, seeing with immaterial sight, whilst the image of Him who is visible to flesh is burnt into my soul. The shadow and winding sheet and relics of the apostles cured sickness, and put demons to flight. (Acts 5.15) How, then, shall not the shadow and the statues of the saints be glorified? Either do away with the worship of all matter, or be not an innovator. Do not disturb the boundaries of centuries, put up by your fathers. (Prov. 22.28)

It is not in writing only that they have bequeathed to us the tradition of the Church, but also in certain unwritten examples. In the twenty-seventh book of his work, in thirty chapters addressed to Amphilochios concerning the Holy Spirit, St Basil says, "In the cherished teaching and dogmas of the Church, we hold some things by written documents; others we have received in mystery from the apostolical tradition." Both are of equal value for the soul's growth. No one will dispute this who has considered even a little the discipline of the Church. For if we neglect unwritten customs, as not having much weight we bury in oblivion the most pertinent facts connected with the Gospel. These are the great Basil's words. How do we know the Holy place of Calvary, or the Holy Sepulchre? Does it not rest on a tradition handed down from father to son? It is written that our Lord was crucified on Calvary, and buried in a tomb, which Joseph hewed out of the rock; (Mt. 27.60) but it is unwritten tradition which identifies these spots, and does more things of the same kind. Whence come the three immersions at baptism, praying with face turned towards the east, and the tradition of the mysteries? Hence St Paul says, "Therefore, brethren, stand fast, and hold the traditions which you have learned either by word, or by our epistle." (II Thess. 2.15) As, then, so much has been handed down in the Church, and is observed down to the present day, why disparage images?

If you bring forward certain practices, they do not inculpate our worship of images, but the worship of heathens who make them idols. Because heathens do it foolishly, this is no reason for objecting to our pious practice. If the same magicians and sorcerers use supplication, so does the Church with catechumens; the former invoke devils, but the Church calls upon God against devils. Heathens have raised up images to demons, whom they call gods. Now we have raised them to the one Incarnate God, to His servants and friends, who are proof against the diabolical hosts.

If, again, you object that the great Epiphanius thoroughly rejected images, I would say in the first place the work in question is fictitious and unauthentic. It bears the name of someone who did not write it, which used to be commonly done. Secondly, we know that blessed Athanasius objected to the bodies of saints being put into chests, and that he preferred their burial in the ground, wishing to set at nought the strange custom of the Egyptians, who did not bury their dead under ground, but set them upon beds and couches. Thus, supposing that he really wrote this work, the great Epiphanius, wishing to correct something of the same kind, ordered that images should not be used. The proof that he did not object to images, is to be found in his own church, which is adorned with images to this day. Thirdly, the exception is not a law to the Church, neither does one swallow make summer, as it seems to Gregory the theologian, and to the truth. Neither can one expression overturn the tradition of the whole Church which is spread throughout the world.

Accept, therefore, the teaching of Scripture and spiritual writers. If the Scripture does call "the idols of heathens silver and gold, and the works of man's hand," (Ps. 135.15) it does not forbid the adoration of inanimate things, or man's handiwork, but the adoration of demons.

We have seen that prophets worshipped angels, and men, and kings, and the impious, and even a staff. David says, "And you adore His footstool." (Ps. 99.5) Isaias, speaking in God's name, says, "The heavens are my throne, and the earth my footstool." (Is. 66.1) Now, it is evident to everyone that the heavens and the earth are created things. Moses, too, and Aaron with all the people adored the work of hands. St Paul, the golden grasshopper of the Church, says in his Epistle to the Hebrews, "But Christ being come, a high priest of the good [31] things to come, by a greater and more perfect tabernacle not made by hand," that is "not of this creation." And, again, "For Jesus is not entered into the Holies made by hands, the patterns of the true; but into heaven itself." (Heb. 9.11, 24) Thus the former holy things, the tabernacle, and everything within it, were made by hands, and no one denies that they were adored.

Reading and Discussion Questions

1. What evidence does John use to defend his belief that images are appropriate to use in worship?
2. What role does Christ play in John's defense of images? How should a devout Christian use images?
3. Do you see any similarities in the problems John is grappling with issues that Ghazali also confronts in document 10.2?

10.6 Arabic Science

Al-Tughrai (1061-1122) was an Arab poet, politician, soldier, and scientist. He served during the reign of the Seljuk sultans and rose to become a grand vizier, but was eventually executed. His *Lanterns of Wisdom and the Keys of Mercy* describes various instruments that weigh, measure, and mix metals and chemical compounds. Shown here are scales for weighing the four known elements at the time—air, water, fire, and earth.

Reading and Discussion Questions

1. How does this document show Arabic science as the adaptation between Islam and the learning of classical and Hellenistic Greece? Compare this image with Anaximander's theories on the universe (document 7.3).
2. Why would books such as this one be of such interest to Muslim rulers? What purpose did they serve?

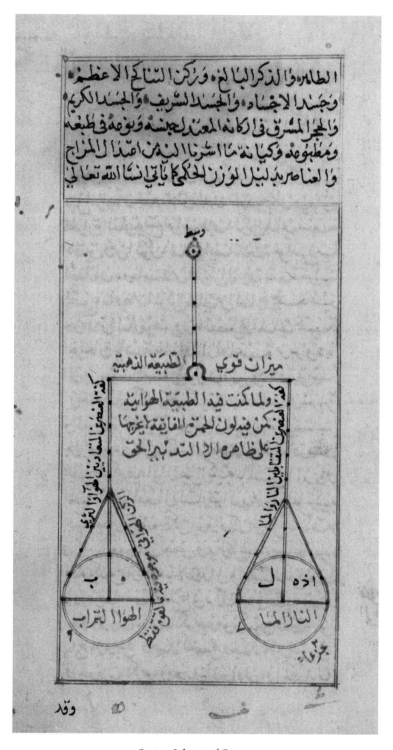

Chapter 11 Innovations and Adaptation in the Western Christian World

600 – 1400

One of the major themes of the European Middle Ages is reform. Perhaps it is the Christian emphasis on repentance; or perhaps it is the Christian belief that time moves in a linear fashion, heading toward something better. Traditionally, that "something better" meant, or so Christians hoped, a heavenly afterlife with God. However, Medieval Christians also believed that the here and now could be improved, made into something better. The many reform movements of the Middle Ages were dichotomous movements, based on the simultaneous and contradictory beliefs in the fallibility and the improvability of humanity. Humans were imperfect and frequently failed, but as they were created in the image of a perfect God, there was always the possibility of progress. It was the fallibility that caused problems to appear, and re-appear, and it was the possibility that encouraged reform. The process of failure and redemption had one glorious side effect, however; it allowed for inventive approaches to human shortcomings and constant adaptation to the promise of salvation that was the core of Medieval Christian belief.

Several of the sources in this chapter are explicit attempts at reform; others are regulations that implicit attempts at pre-emptive reform. The first source is an example of the latter. St. Benedict's *Rule* was a set of regulations for men (and women) who chose to devote their lives entirely to prayer and service to God. The *Rule* regulated monastic houses (hence the name "regular clergy" for monks) and thus was an attempt to institutionalize personal behavior and thought for those who took up the monastic life. Benedict's *Rule* would become tremendously popular, in part because although it emphasized renunciation (essential to monasticism), it was also a moderate and therefore doable.

While not all of Europe was Catholic, or even Christian, the Catholic Church certainly dominated Medieval culture from the fourth century onward, beginning with the conversion of the Roman Emperor Constantine. Constantine's conversion led to the intertwining of state and church in a way that allowed for Christianity (specifically, over time, the Roman Catholic version of it) to be both state supported and state dependent. One area of Medieval life that seemed to require constant reform was church and state relations. Tensions between the two hopelessly entangled institutions escalated in the Investiture Controversy of the eleventh and twelfth centuries. In that dispute, the papacy tried to separate the power of selecting clergy from lay officials, such as the Holy Roman Emperors. The persistence of the struggle to separate the church from state interference is revealed in, "Canto XIX" from Dante's *Inferno*. In this fourteenth century poem, the Italian laments those overly worldly, overly materialist, interests of the church.

Further need for regulation led to the creation of rules for the students at the University of Paris, to curb intellectual and social abuses they had developed, and to rules for the guild of spurriers of London. Essentially university students were also a guild, an organization of craftsmen of a particular skill that governed the economic, social, and religious lives of guild members. Guilds determined what was produced, by whom, and for what prices; guild regulations and the rules for the University of Paris also established the identities of the guild and its members. Establishing identities was also a matter of establishing boundaries of authority, much as the Investiture Controversy and Benedictine *Rule* also established boundaries of authority.

Finally, the last document of the chapter is not about reform, but about what the Medieval person envisioned was the potential punishment for lack of reform and regulation: apocalyptic catastrophe. In 1347 the Black Death made it's appearance in Western Europe; as the Florentine writer Marchione di Coppo Stefani describes it to us, this "very great pestilence" required a new set of civil laws regulating behavior and reforming interactions between patient and doctor, laity and clergy, parent and child, and all aspects of Medieval town life.

11.1   The *Rule* of St. Benedict

Although St. Benedict (c. 480 – 542 C.E.) did not invent Christian monasticism, his *Rule* was synonymous with it throughout the Catholic Middle Ages. Benedict founded his monastery in Monte Cassino, Italy, and designed a set of regulations (known as a "rule") for his monks to follow. The *Rule* governed all aspects of a monk's life: when and how to pray, eat, work, and socialize. Monasteries such as Benedict's were designed to allow men and women (housed separately) to devote themselves to prayer and worship, and to renounce earthly interests as much as humanly possible.

Other monastic groups criticized Benedict's *Rule* as too lenient, in comparison with monastic regulations from Egypt (the birthplace of Christian monasticism) and Ireland, which emphasized physical renunciation and punishment. However, Benedict's *Rule* would succeed in part because it was less onerous than other monastic *Rules*, particularly in the moderation of punishments meted out to the monks for violating the regulations. The *Rule* gained in popularity from the seventh century onward, particularly after Pope Gregory the Great popularized it and associated it with the Roman papacy.

Source: From Migne, *Patrologia Latina* Vol. 66, col. 215ff, translated by Ernest F. Henderson, *Select Historical Documents of the Middle Ages,* (London: George Bell and Sons, 1910)

1. Concerning the Kinds of Monks and Their Manner of Living.

It is manifest that there are four kinds of monks. The cenobites are the first kind; that is, those living in a monastery, serving under a rule or an abbot. Then the second kind is that of the anchorites; that is, the hermits-those who, not by the new fervor of a conversion but by the long probation of life in a monastery, have learned to fight against the devil, having already been taught by the solace of many. They, having been well prepared in the army of brothers for the solitary fight of the hermit, being secure now without the consolation of another, are able, God helping them, to fight with their own hand or arm against the vices of the flesh or of their thoughts.

But a third very bad kind of monks are the sarabaites, approved by no rule, experience being their teacher, as with the gold which is tried in the furnace. But, softened after the manner of lead, keeping faith with the world by their works, they are known through their tonsure to lie to God. These being shut up by twos or threes, or, indeed, alone, without a shepherd, not in the Lord's but in their own sheep-folds-their law is the satisfaction of their desires. For whatever they think good or choice, this they call holy; and what they do not wish, this they consider unlawful. But the fourth kind of we are about to found, therefore, a school for the monks is the kind which is called gyratory. During their whole life they are guests, for three or four days at a time, in the cells of the different monasteries, throughout the various provinces; always wandering and never stationary, given over to the service of their own pleasures and the joys of the palate, and in every way worse than the sarabaites. Concerning the most wretched way of living of all such monks it is better to be silent than to speak. These things therefore being omitted, let us proceed, with the aid of God, to treat of the best kind, the cenobites.

2. What the Abbot Should Be Like

An abbot who is worthy to preside over a monastery ought always to remember what he is called, and carry out with his deeds the name of a Superior. For he is believed to be Christ's representative, since he is called by His name, the apostle saying: "Ye have received the spirit of adoption of sons, whereby we call Abba, Father." And so the abbot should not-grant that he may not-teach, or decree, or order, anything apart from the precept of the Lord; but his order or teaching should be sprinkled with the ferment of divine justice in the minds of his disciples. Let the abbot always be mindful that, at the tremendous judgment of God, both things will be weighed in the balance: his teaching and the obedience of his disciples. And let the abbot know that whatever the father of the family finds of less utility among the sheep is laid to the fault of the shepherd. Only in a case where the whole diligence of their pastor shall have been bestowed on an unruly and disobedient flock, and his whole care given to their morbid actions, shall that pastor, absolved in the judgment of the Lord, be free to say to the Lord with the prophet: "I have not hid Thy righteousness within my heart, I have declared Thy faithfulness and Thy salvation, but they despising have scorned me." And then at length let the punishment for the disobedient sheep under his care be death itself prevailing against them. Therefore, when any one receives the name of abbot, he ought to rule over his disciples with a double teaching; that is, let him show forth all good and holy things by deeds more than by words. So that to ready disciples he may propound the mandates of God in words; but, to the hard-hearted and the more simpleminded, he may show forth the divine precepts by his deeds. But as to all the things that he has taught to his disciples to be wrong, he shall show by his deeds that they are not to be done; lest, preaching to others, he himself shall be found worthy of blame, and lest God may say at some time to him a sinner: "What hast thou to do to declare my statutes or that thou should'st take my covenant in thy mouth. Seeing that thou hatest instruction and casteth my words behind thee; and why beholdest thou the mote that is in thy brother's eye, but considerest not the beam that is in thine own eye?" He shall make no distinction of persons in the monastery. One shall not be more cherished than another, unless it be the one whom he finds excelling in good works or in obedience. A free-born man shall not be preferred to one coming from servitude, unless there be some other reasonable cause. But if, justice demanding that it should be thus, it seems good to the abbot, he shall do this no matter what the rank shall be. But otherwise they shall keep their own places; for whether we be bond or free we are all one in Christ; and, under one God, we perform an equal service of subjection; for God is no respecter of persons. Only in this way is a distinction made by Him concerning us: if we are found humble and surpassing others in good works. Therefore let him (the abbot) have equal charity for all: let the same discipline be administered in all cases according to merit. In his teaching indeed the abbot ought always to observe that form laid down by the apostle when he says: "reprove, rebuke, exhort." That is, mixing seasons with seasons, blandishments with terrors, let him display the feeling of a severe yet devoted master. He should, namely, rebuke more severely the unruly and the turbulent. The obedient, moreover, and the gentle and the patient, he should exhort, that they may progress to higher things. But the negligent and scorners, we warn him to admonish and reprove....

4. The Instruments of Good Works

1. First of all, to love the Lord thy God with all thy heart, with all thy soul, and with all thy strength.
2. Then, to love thy neighbor as thyself.
3. Next, not to kill.
4. Not to commit adultery.
5. Not to steal.
6. Not to covet.
7. Not to bear false witness.
8. To honor all men.
9. Not to do to another what one would not have done to oneself.
10. To deny oneself in order to follow Christ.
11. To chastise the body.
12. Not to seek after luxuries.
13. To love fasting.
14. To refresh the poor.
15. To clothe the naked.
16. To visit the sick.
17. To bury the dead.
18. To help in affliction.
19. To console the sorrowing.
20. To keep aloof from worldly actions.
21. To prefer nothing to the love of Christ.
22. Not to follow the promptings of anger.
23. Not to seek an occasion of revenge.
24. Not to foster deceit in one's heart.
25. Not to make a feigned peace.
26. Not to forsake charity.
27. Not to swear, lest perhaps one perjure oneself.
28. To utter the truth with heart and lips.
29. Not to render evil for evil.
30. To do no wrong to anyone, but to bear patiently any wrong done to oneself.
31. To love one's enemies.
32. Not to speak ill of those who speak ill of us, but rather to speak well of them.
33. To suffer persecution for justice' sake.
34. Not to be proud.
35. Not to be given to wine.
36. Not to be a glutton.
37. Not to be given to sleep.
38. Not to be slothful.
39. Not to be a murmurer.
40. Not to be a detractor.
41. To put one's trust in God.
42. To attribute any good one sees in oneself to God and not to oneself.
43. But always to acknowledge that the evil is one's own, and to attribute it to oneself.
44. To fear the days of judgment.
45. To be in dread of hell.
46. To desire everlasting life with all spiritual longing.
47. To keep death daily before one's eyes.

48. To keep guard at all times over the actions of one's life.
49. To know for certain that God sees one in every place.
50. To dash upon Christ one's evil thoughts the instant they come to one's heart, and to manifest them to one's spiritual father.
51. To keep one's mouth from speech that is wicked or full of guile.
52. Not to love much speaking.
53. Not to speak words that are vain or such as provoke laughter.
54. Not to love much or noisy laughter.
55. To listen willingly to holy reading.
56. To apply oneself frequently to prayer.
57. Daily with tears and sighs to confess one's sins to God in prayer, and to amend these evils for the future.
58. Not to fulfill the desires of the flesh.
59. To hate one's own will.
60. To obey in all things the commands of the Abbot, even though he himself (which God forbid) should act otherwise, being mindful of that precept of the Lord: "What they say, do ye; but what they do, do ye not"
61. Not to wish to be called holy before one is so, but first to be holy that one may be truly so called.
62. To fulfill the commandments of God daily by one's deeds.
63. To love chastity.
64. To hate no man.
65. To have no jealousy or envy.
66. Not to love strife.
67. To fly from vainglory.
68. To reverence one's seniors.
69. To love one's juniors.
70. To pray for one's enemies in the love of Christ.
71. To make peace with those with whom one is at variance before the setting of the sun.
72. And never to despair of God's mercy.

Behold, these are the instruments of the spiritual art, which, if they be constantly employed by day and by night, and delivered up on the day of judgment, will gain for us from the Lord that reward which He Himself has promised: "Eye has not see, nor ear heard, nor has it entered into the heart of man, what things God has prepared for those who love Him." And the workshop in which we are to labor diligently at all these things is the enclosure of the monastery and stability in the community.

Reading and Discussion Questions
1. What powers does the abbot have in relation to the monks? What are his limits?
2. In the *Rule*, Benedict lists a series of "Instruments of Good Works" that lead to spiritual progress. Why does Benedict believe that a monastery is the best place to use these instruments? Which instruments are particularly "monastic"?
3. In general, Christian monks take three vows: poverty, chastity, and obedience. Find an example of each in the excerpts from the Rule and discuss what that vow is meant to achieve for the monk.

11.2 Einhard, *Life of Charlemagne*

Einhard was part of Charlemagne's inner circle of advisors, and was educated in part at Palace School created by Charlemagne. This school was a key element of the Carolingian renaissance of education and learning. As a product of that education, and as a companion of Charlemagne, Einhard was ideally suited to writing a detailed biography of the emperor. *The Life of Charlemagne* is an important example of secular biography from the early MiddleAges.

Source: Einhard, "Life of Charlemagne," Einhard: *The Life of Charlemagne,* translated by Samuel Epes Turner, (New York: Harper & Brothers, 1880)

Extent of Charlemagne's Conquests

Such are the wars, most skillfully planned and successfully fought, which this most powerful king waged during the forty-seven years of his reign. He so largely increased the Frank kingdom, which was already great and strong when he received it at his father's hands, that more than double its former territory was added to it. The authority of the Franks was formerly confined to that part of Gaul included between the Rhine and the Loire, the Ocean and the Balearic Sea; to that part of Germany which is inhabited by the so-called Eastern Franks, and is bounded by Saxony and the Danube, the Rhine and the Saale-this stream separates the Thuringians from the Sorabians; and to the country of the Alemanni and Bavarians. By the wars above mentioned he first made tributary Aquitania, Gascony, and the whole of the region of the Pyrenees as far as the River Ebro, which rises in the land of the Navarrese, flows through the most fertile districts of Spain, and empties into the Balearic Sea, beneath the walls of the city of Tortosa. He next reduced and made tributary all Italy from Aosta to Lower Calabria, where the boundary line runs between the Beneventans and the Greeks, a territory more than a thousand miles" long; then Saxony, which constitutes no small part of Germany, and is reckoned to be twice as wide as the country inhabited by the Franks, while about equal to it in length; in addition, both Pannonias, Dacia beyond the Danube, and Istria, Liburnia, and Dalmatia, except the cities on the coast, which he left to the Greek Emperor for friendship's sake, and because of the treaty that he had made with him. In fine, he vanquished and made tributary all the wild and barbarous tribes dwelling in Germany between the Rhine and the Vistula, the Ocean and the Danube, all of which speak very much the same language, but differ widely from one another in customs and dress. The chief among them are the Welatabians, the Sorabians, the Abodriti, and the Bohemians, and he had to make war upon these; but the rest, by far the larger number, submitted to him of their own accord.

Foreign Relations

He added to the glory of his reign by gaining the good will of several kings and nations; so close, indeed, was the alliance that he contracted with Alfonso [II 791-842] King of Galicia and Asturias, that the latter, when sending letters or ambassadors to Charles, invariably styled himself his man. His munificence won the kings of the Scots also to pay such deference to his wishes that they never gave him any other title than lord or themselves than subjects and slaves: there are letters from them extant in which these feelings in his regard are expressed. His relations with Aaron [ie, Harun Al-Rashid, 786-809], King of the Persians, who ruled over almost the whole of the East, India excepted, were so friendly that this prince preferred his favor to that of all the kings and potentates of the earth, and considered that to him alone marks of honor and munificence were due. Accordingly, when the ambassadors sent by Charles to visit the most holy sepulcher and place of resurrection of our Lord and Savior presented themselves before him with gifts, and made known their master's wishes, he not only granted what was asked, but gave possession of that holy and blessed spot. When they returned, he dispatched his ambassadors with them, and sent magnificent gifts, besides stuffs, perfumes, and other rich products of the Eastern lands. A few years before this, Charles had asked him for an elephant, and he sent the only one that he had. The Emperors of Constantinople, Nicephorus [I 802-811], Michael [I, 811-813], and Leo [V, 813-820], made advances to Charles, and sought friendship and alliance with him by several embassies; and even when the Greeks suspected him of designing to wrest the empire from them, because of his assumption of the title Emperor, they made a close alliance with him, that he might have no cause of offense. In fact, the power of the Franks was always viewed by the Greeks and Romans with a jealous eye, whence the Greek proverb "Have the Frank for your friend, but not for your neighbor."

Public Works

This King, who showed himself so great in extending his empire and subduing foreign nations, and was constantly occupied with plans to that end, undertook also very many works calculated to adorn and benefit his kingdom, and brought several of them to completion. Among these, the most deserving of mention are the basilica of the Holy Mother of God at Aix-la-Chapelle, built in the most admirable manner, and a bridge over the Rhine at Mayence, half a mile long, the breadth of the river at this point. This bridge was destroyed by fire [May, 813] the year before Charles died, but, owing to his death so soon after, could not be repaired, although he had intended to rebuild it in stone. He began two palaces of beautiful workmanship - one near his manor called Ingelheim, not far from Mayence; the other at Nimeguen, on the Waal, the stream that washes the south side of the island of the Batavians. But, above all, sacred edifices were the object of his care throughout his whole kingdom; and whenever he found them falling to ruin from age, he commanded the priests and fathers who had charge of them to repair them, and made sure by commissioners that his instructions were obeyed. He also fitted out a fleet for the war with the **Northmen**; the vessels required for this purpose were built on the rivers that flow from Gaul and Germany into the Northern Ocean. Moreover, since the Northmen continually overran and laid waste the Gallic and German coasts, he caused watch and ward to be kept in all the harbors, and at the mouths of rivers large enough to admit the entrance of vessels, to prevent the enemy from disembarking; and in the South, in Narbonensis and Septimania, and along the whole coast of Italy as far as Rome, he took the same precautions against the Moors, who had recently begun their piratical practices. Hence, Italy suffered no great harm in his time at the hands of the Moors, nor Gaul and Germany from the

Northmen, save that the Moors got possession of the Etruscan town of CivitaVecchia by treachery, and sacked it, and the Northmen harried some of the islands in Frisia off the German coast.

Private Life

Thus did Charles defend and increase as well, as beautify his, kingdom, as is well known; and here let me express my admiration of his great qualities and his extraordinary constancy alike in good and evil fortune. I will now forthwith proceed to give the details of his private and family life.

After his father's death, while sharing the kingdom with his brother, he bore his unfriendliness and jealousy most patiently, and, to the wonder of all, could not be provoked to be angry with him. Later he married a daughter of ofDesiderius, King of the Lombards, at the instance of his mother; but he repudiated her at the end of a year for some reason unknown, and married Hildegard, a woman of high birth, of Suabian origin. He had three sons by her - Charles, Pepin and Louis -and as many daughters - Hruodrud, Bertha, and and Gisela. He had three other daughters besides these - Theoderada, Hiltrud, and Ruodhaid - two by his third wife, Fastrada, a woman of East Frankish (that is to say, of German) origin, and the third by a concubine, whose name for the moment escapes me. At the death of Fastrada [794], he married Liutgard, an Alemannic woman, who bore

---

Northmen: the Vikings

him no children. After her death [Jun 4, 800] he had three concubines - Gersuinda, a Saxon by whom he had Adaltrud; Regina, who was the mother of Drogo and Hugh; and Ethelind, by whom he lead Theodoric. Charles' mother, Berthrada, passed her old age with him in great honor; he entertained the greatest veneration for her; and there was never any disagreement between them except when he divorced the daughter of King Desiderius, whom he had married to please her. She died soon after Hildegard, after living to three grandsons and as many granddaughters in her son's house, and he buried her with great pomp in the Basilica of St. Denis, where his father lay. He had an only sister, Gisela, who had consecrated herself to a religious life from girlhood, and he cherished as much affection for her as for his mother. She also died a few years before him in the nunnery where she passed her life.

Charles and the Education of His Children

The plan that he adopted for his children's education was, first of all, to have both boys and girls instructed in the liberal arts, to which he also turned his own attention. As soon as their years admitted, in accordance with the custom of the Franks, the boys had to learn horsemanship, and to practice war and the chase, and the girls to familiarize themselves with cloth-making, and to handle distaff and spindle, that they might not grow indolent through idleness, and he fostered in them every virtuous sentiment. He only lost three of all his children before his death, two sons and one daughter, Charles, who was the eldest, Pepin, whom he had made King of Italy, and Hruodrud, his oldest daughter. whom he had betrothed to Constantine [VI, 780-802], Emperor of the Greeks. Pepin left one son, named Bernard, and five daughters, Adelaide, Atula, Guntrada, Berthaid and Theoderada. The King gave a striking proof of his fatherly affection at the time of Pepin's death [810]: he appointed the grandson to succeed Pepin, and had the granddaughters brought up with his own daughters. When his sons and his daughter died, he was not so calm as might have been expected from his remarkably strong mind, for his affections were no less strong, and moved him to tears. Again, when he was told of the death of Hadrian [796], the Roman Pontiff, whom he had loved most of all his friends, he wept as much as if he had lost a brother, or a very dear son. He was by nature most ready to contract friendships, and not only made friends easily, but clung to them persistently, and cherished most fondly those with whom he had formed such ties. He was so careful of the training of his sons and daughters that he never took his meals without them when he was at home, and never made a journey without them; his sons would ride at his side, and his daughters follow him, while a number of his body-guard, detailed for their protection, brought up the rear. Strange to say, although they were very handsome women, and he loved them very dearly, he was never willing to marry any of them to a man of their own nation or to a foreigner, but kept them all at home until his death, saying that he could not dispense with their society. Hence, though other-wise happy, he experienced the malignity of fortune as far as they were concerned; yet he concealed his knowledge of the rumors current in regard to them, and of the suspicions entertained of their honor.

Conspiracies Against Charlemagne

By one of his concubines he had a son, handsome in face, but hunchbacked, named Pepin, whom I omitted to mention in the list of his children. When Charles was at war with the Huns, and was wintering in Bavaria [792], this Pepin shammed sickness, and plotted against his father in company with some of the leading Franks, who seduced him with vain promises of the royal authority. When his deceit was discovered, and the conspirators were punished, his head was shaved, and he was suffered, in accordance with his wishes, to devote himself to a religious life in the monastery of Prüm. A formidable conspiracy against Charles had previously been set on foot in Germany, but all the traitors were banished, some of them without mutilation, others after their eyes had been put out. Three of them only lost their lives; they drew their swords and resisted arrest, and, after killing several men, were cut down, because they could not be otherwise overpowered. It is supposed that the cruelty of Queen Fastrada was the primary cause of these plots, and they were both due to Charles' apparent acquiescence in his wife's cruel conduct, and deviation from the usual kindness and gentleness of his disposition. All the rest of his life he was regarded by everyone with the utmost love and affection, so much so that not the least accusation of unjust rigor was ever made against him.

Charlemagne's Treatment of Foreigners

He liked foreigners, and was at great pains to take them under his protection. There were often so many of them, both in the palace and the kingdom, that they might reasonably have been considered a nuisance; but he, with his broad humanity, was very little disturbed by such annoyances, because he felt himself compensated for these great inconveniences by the praises of his generosity and the reward of high renown.

Personal Appearance

Charles was large and strong, and of lofty stature, though not disproportionately tall (his height is well known to have been seven times the length of his foot); the upper part of his head was round, his eyes very large and animated, nose a little long, hair fair, and face laughing and merry. Thus his appearance was always stately and dignified, whether he was standing or sitting; although his neck was thick and somewhat short, and his belly rather prominent; but the symmetry of the rest of his body concealed these defects. His gait was firm, his whole carriage manly, and his voice clear, but not so strong as his size led one to expect. His health was excellent, except during the four years preceding his death, when he was subject to frequent fevers; at the last he even limped a little with one foot. Even in those years he consulted rather his own inclinations than the advice of physicians, who were almost hateful to him, because they wanted him to give up roasts, to which he was accustomed, and to eat boiled meat instead. In accordance with the national custom, he took frequent exercise on horseback and in the chase, accomplishments in which scarcely any people in the world can equal the Franks. He enjoyed the exhalations from natural warm springs, and often practiced swimming, in which he was such an adept that none could surpass him; and hence it was that he built his palace at Aix- la- Chapelle, and lived there constantly during his latter years until his death. He used not only to invite his sons to his bath, but his nobles and friends, and now and then a troop of his retinue or body guard, so that a hundred or more persons sometimes bathed with him.

Dress

He used to wear the national, that is to say, the Frank, dress next his skin, a linen shirt and linen breeches, and above these a tunic fringed with silk; while hose fastened by bands covered his lower limbs, and shoes his feet, and he protected his shoulders and chest in winter by a close-fitting coat of otter or marten skins. Over all he flung a blue cloak, and he always had a sword girt about him, usually one with a gold or silver hilt and belt; he sometimes carried a jewelled sword, but only on great feast-days or at the reception of ambassadors from foreign nations. He despised foreign costumes, however handsome, and never allowed himself to be robed in them, except twice in Rome, when he donned the Roman tunic, chlamys, and shoes; the first time at the request of Pope Hadrian, the second to gratify Leo, Hadrian's successor. On great feast-days he made use of embroidered clothes, and shoes bedecked with precious stones; his cloak was fastened by a golden buckle, and he appeared crowned with a diadem of gold and gems: but on other days his dress varied little from the common dress of the people.

Habits

Charles was temperate in eating, and particularly so in drinking, for he abominated drunkenness in anybody, much more in himself and those of his household; but he could not easily abstain from food, and often complained that fasts injured his health. He very rarely gave entertainments, only on great feast-days, and then to large numbers of people. His meals ordinarily consisted of four courses, not counting the roast, which his huntsmen used to bring in on the spit; he was more fond of this than of any other dish. While at table, he listened to reading or music. The subjects of the readings were the stories and deeds of olden time: he was fond, too, of St. Augustine's books, and especially of the one entitled "The City of God."

He was so moderate in the use of wine and all sorts of drink that he rarely allowed himself more than three cups in the course of a meal. In summer after the midday meal, he would eat some fruit, drain a single cup, put off his clothes and shoes, just as he did for the night, and rest for two or three hours. He was in the habit of awaking and rising from bed four or five times during the night. While he was dressing and putting on his shoes, he not only gave audience to his friends, but if the Count of the Palace told him of any suit in which his judgment was necessary, he had the parties brought before him forthwith, took cognizance of the case, and gave his decision, just as if he were sitting on the Judgment-seat. This was not the only business that he transacted at this time, but he performed any duty of the day whatever, whether he had to attend to the matter himself, or to give commands concerning it to his officers.

Studies

Charles had the gift of ready and fluent speech, and could express whatever he had to say with the utmost clearness. He was not satisfied with command of his native language merely, but gave attention to the study of foreign ones, and in particular was such a master of Latin that he could speak it as well as his native tongue; but he could understand Greek better than he could speak it. He was so eloquent, indeed, that he might have passed for a teacher of eloquence. He most zealously cultivated the liberal arts, held those who taught them in great esteem, and conferred great honors upon them. He took lessons in grammar of the deacon Peter of Pisa, at that time an aged man. Another deacon, Albin of Britain, surnamed Alcuin, a man of Saxon extraction, who was the greatest scholar of the day, was his teacher in other branches of learning. The King spent much time and labour with him studying rhetoric, dialectics, and especially astronomy; he learned to reckon, and used to investigate the motions of the heavenly bodies most curiously, with an intelligent scrutiny. He also tried to write, and used to keep tablets and blanks in bed under his pillow, that at leisure hours he might accustom his hand to form the letters; however, as he did not begin his efforts in due season, but late in life, they met with ill success.

Piety

He cherished with the greatest fervor and devotion the principles of the Christian religion, which had been instilled into him from infancy. Hence it was that he built the beautiful basilica at Aix-la-Chapelle, which he adorned with gold and silver and lamps, and with rails and doors of solid brass. He had the columns and marbles for this structure brought from Rome and Ravenna, for he could not find such as were suitable elsewhere. He was a constant worshipper at this church as long as his health permitted, going morning and evening, even after nightfall, besides attending mass; and he took care that all the services there conducted should be administered with the utmost possible propriety, very often warning the sextons not to let any improper or unclean thing be brought into the building or remain in it. He provided it with a great number of sacred vessels of gold and silver and with such a quantity of clerical robes that not even the doorkeepers who fill the humblest office in the church were obliged to wear their everyday clothes when in the exercise of their duties. He was at great pains to improve the church reading and psalmody, for he was well skilled in both although he neither read in public nor sang, except in a low tone and with others.

Generosity

He was very forward in succoring the poor, and in that gratuitous generosity which the Greeks call alms, so much so that he not only made a point of giving in his own country and his own kingdom, but when he discovered that there were Christians living in poverty in Syria, Egypt, and Africa, at Jerusalem, Alexandria, and Carthage, he had compassion on their wants, and used to send money over the seas to them. The reason that he zealously strove to make friends with the kings beyond seas was that he might get help and relief to the Christians living under their rule.

He cherished the Church of St. Peter the Apostle at Rome above all other holy and sacred places, and heaped its treasury with a vast wealth of gold, silver, and precious stones. He sent great and countless gifts to the popes; and throughout his whole reign the wish that he had nearest at heart was to re-establish the ancient authority of the city of Rome under his care and by his influence, and to defend and protect the Church of St. Peter, and to beautify and enrich it out of his own store above all other churches. Although he held it in such veneration, he only repaired to Rome to pay his vows and make his supplications four times during the whole forty-seven years that he reigned.

Charlemagne Crowned Emperor

When he made his last journey thither, he also had other ends in view. The Romans had inflicted many injuries upon the Pontiff Leo, tearing out his eyes and cutting out his tongue, so that he had been comp lied to call upon the King for help [Nov 24, 800]. Charles accordingly went to Rome, to set in order the affairs of the Church, which were in great confusion, and passed the whole winter there. It was then that he received the titles of Emperor and Augustus [Dec 25, 800], to which he at first had such an aversion that he declared that he would not have set foot in the Church the day that they were conferred, although it was a great feast-day, if he could have foreseen the design of the Pope. He bore very patiently with the jealousy which the Roman emperors showed upon his assuming these titles, for they took this step very ill; and by dint of frequent embassies and letters, in which he addressed them as brothers, he made their haughtiness yield to his magnanimity, a quality in which he was unquestionably much their superior.

Reading and Discussion Questions

1. Much of the *Life* concerns Charlemagne's military victories; why is Einhard particularly interested in describing those? What is he trying to say about Charlemagne?
2. What does the *Life* reveal about Carolingian family relationships, particularly the relationship between fathers and children?
3. The most common form of biography in the early Middle Ages was the hagiography, or biography of a saint. What elements of Einhard's biography of Charlemagne are hagiographic in nature?

11.3   Dante, Canto XIX from the *Inferno*

Dante Alighieri (1265 – 1321) was an Florentine poet who bridges the artistic cultures of the Middle Ages and of the Renaissance. Dante's approach to his poetry foreshadowed the Renaissance with his use of vernacular Italian rather than Latin, and his frequent allusion to classical Greek and Roman literature and history. However, his subject matter was typically Medieval; the *Divine Comedy* trilogy concerns questions of salvation and of humanity's relationship with God. It is designed as an imagined explorations of Hell (*Inferno*), Purgatory, and Paradise, set in the year 1300. Echoing some of the issues of the Investiture Controversy, Dante was also troubled with the church's continued interest in secular matters, and the continued influence of secular leaders over the church. The following Canto from the first part of the *Divine Comedy* is about priests (especially popes) who bribed their way into office. To buy one's office is the sin of simony, named for Simon Magus who in the New Testament *Book of Acts* attempted to buy the power of the Holy Spirit.

Source: *The Inferno of Dante Alighieri* (London: JM Dent and Co., 1900)

O SIMON-MAGUS! O wretched followers of his and robbers ye, who prostitute the things of God, that should be wedded unto righteousness, for gold and, silver! now must the trump sound for you: for ye are in the third chasm.

Already we had mounted to the following grave, on that part of the cliff which hangs right over the middle of the fosse.

O Wisdom Supreme, what art thou showest in heaven, on earth and in the evil world, and how justly thy Goodness dispenses!

I saw the livid stone, on the sides and on the bottom, full of holes, all of one breadth; and each was round.

Not less wide they seemed to me, nor larger, than those that are in my beauteous San Giovanni made for stands to the baptizers;

one of which, not many years ago, I broke to save one that was drowning in it: and be this o, seal to undeceive all men.

From the mouth of each emerged a sinner's feet, and legs up to the calf; and the rest remained within.

The soles of all were both on fire: wherefore the joints quivered so strongly, that they would have snapped in pieces withes and grass-ropes.

As the flaming of things oiled moves only on their outer surface: so was it there, from the heels to the points.

"Master! who is that who writhes himself, quivering more than all his fellows," I said, "and sucked by ruddier flame?"

And he to me: "If thou wilt have me carry thee down there, by that lower bank, thou shalt learn from him about himself and about his wrongs."

And 1: "Whatever pleases thee, to me is grateful: thou art my lord, and knowest that I depart, not from thy will; also thou knowest what is not spoken.

Then we came upon the fourth bulwark; we turned and descended, on the left hand, down there into the perforated and narrow bottom.

The kind Master did not yet depose me from his side, till he brought me to the cleft of him who so lamented with his legs.

"O whoe'er thou be that hast thy upper part beneath, unhappy spirit, planted like a stake!" I began to say; "if thou art able, speak."

I stood, like the friar who is confessing a treacherous assassin that, after being fixed, recalls him and thus delays the death;

and he cried: "Art thou thee already standing, Boniface? art thou there already standing? By several years the writ has lied to me.

Art thou so quickly sated with that wealth, for which thou didst not fear to seize the comely Lady- by deceit, and then make havoc of her? "

I became like those who stand as if bemocked, not comprehending what is answered to them, and unable to reply.

Then Virgil said: "Say to him quickly, 'I am not he, I am not he whom thou thinkest."' And I replied as was enjoined me.

Whereat the spirit quite wrenched his feet; thereafter, sighing and with voice of weeping, he said to me: "Then what askest thou of me?

If to know who I am concerneth thee so much, that thou hast therefore passed the bank, learn that I was clothed with the Great Mantle;

and verily I was a son of the She-bear, so eager to advance the Whelps, that I pursed wealth above, and here myself.

Beneath my head are dragged the others who preceded me in simony, cowering within the fissures of the stone.

I too shall fall down thither, when he comes for whom I took thee when I put the sudden question.

But longer is the time already, that I have baked my feet and stood inverted thus, than he shall stand planted with glowing feet:

for after him, from westward, there shall come a lawless Shepherd, of uglier deeds, fit to cover him and me.

A new Jason will it be, of whom we read in Maccabees; and as to that high priest his king was pliant, so to this shall be like he who governs France.

I know not if here I was too hardy, for I answered him in this strain: "Ahi! now tell me how much treasure Our Lord required of St. Peter, before he put the keys into his keeping? Surely he demanded nought but 'Follow me!"

Nor did Peter, nor the others, ask of Matthias gold or silver, when he was chosen for the office which the guilty soul had lost.

Therefore stay thou here, for thou art justly punished; and keep well the ill–ot money, which against Charles made thee be bold."

And were it not that reverence for the Great Keys thou wieldest in the glad life yet hinders me,

I should use still heavier words: for your avarice grieves the world, trampling on the good, and raising up the wicked.

Shepherds such as ye the Evangelist perceived, when she, that sitteth on the waters, was seen by him committing fornication with the kings;

she that was born with seven heads, and in her ten horns had a witness so long as virtue pleased her spouse.

Ye have made you a god of gold and silver; and wherein do ye differ from the idolater, save that he worships one, and ye a hundred?

Ah Constantine! to how much ill gave birth, not thy conversion, but that **dower** which the first rich Father took from thee!

And whilst I sung these notes to him, whether it was rage or conscience gnawed him, he violently sprawled with both his feet.

———
dower: a gift, specifically, to a wife in the event she survived her husband

And indeed I think it pleased my Guide, with so satisfied a look did he keep listening to the sound of the true words uttered.

Therefore with both his arms he took me; and, when he had me quite upon his breast, remounted by the path where he had descended.

Nor did he weary in holding me clasped to him, till he bore me away to the summit of the arch which is a crossway from the fourth to the fifth rampart.

Here he placidly set down the burden, pleasing to him on the rough steep cliff, which to the goats would be a painful passage; thence another valley was discovered to me.

Reading and Discussion Questions

1. Dante blames the Donation of Constantine for causing simony in the papacy. This was believed to be a donation by the fourth century Constantine the Great of land that became the Papal States. Why does Dante object to the Donation?
2. The Master that guides Dante through hell was the Roman poet Virgil; how is the poetic device of Virgil both Medieval and Renaissance in character?
3. The pope that Dante interviews is Nicholas III, who first assumes Dante is Pope Boniface VIII. However, the poem is set in 1300 and Boniface will not die until 1303; how is Dante using this poem as an opportunity to criticize the contemporary church?
4. The *Divine Comedy* is filled with symbols and metaphors. What is the symbolic meaning of the holes in which the Simoniac popes are buried? What is the meaning of their burial headfirst?

11.4   Regulations for the London Spurrier's Guild, 1347

Craft guilds were organizations that governed individual crafts or artisanal fields. Guilds were created by the practitioners of a craft, and they set standards of product and prices for their craft. Guilds organized their crafts into monopolies, and controlled who could produce a certain good within their town or city. Membership in guilds were highly sought after because they were necessary for employment as craftsmen or artisans. Guilds also offered protection for its members and their families, in case of death or infirmity; they also often provided religious and charitable services for their communities. The following excerpt is from the 1347 guild regulations for the London spurriers' guild. Spurriers make spurs.

ARTICLES OF THE LONDON SPURRJERS, 1347

Be it remembered, that on Tuesday, the morrow of St. Peter's Chains [1 August], in the 19th year of the reign of King Edward the Third etc., the Articles underwritten were read before John Hamond, Mayor, Roger de Depham, Recorder, and the other Aldermen; and seeing that the same were deemed befitting, they were accepted and enrolled, in these words:

"In the first place, that no one of the trade of Spurriers shall work longer than from the beginning of the day until curfew rung out at the Church of St. Sepulchre, outside Newgate; by reason that no man can work so neatly by night as by day.

And many persons of the said trade, who compass how to practice deception in their work, desire to work by night rather than by day: and then they introduce false iron, and iron that has been cracked, for tin, and also, they put gilt on false copper, and cracked.

And further, many of the said trade are wandering about all day, without working at all at their trade; and then, when they have become drunk and frantic, they take to their work, to the annoyance of the sick and of all their neighbourhood, as well as by reason of the broils that arise between them and the strange folks who are dwelling among them.

And then they blow up their fires so vigorously, that their forges begin all at once to blaze; to the great peril of themselves and of all the neighbourhood around. And then too, all the neighbours are much in dread of the sparks, which so vigorously issue forth in all directions from the mouths of the chimneys in their forges.

By reason whereof, it seems unto them that working by night [should be put an end to,] in order such false work and such perils to avoid; and therefore, the Mayor and Aldermen do will, by assent of the good folks of the said trade, and for the common profit, that from henceforth such time for working, and such false work made in the trade, shall be forbidden.

And if any person shall be found in the said trade to do to the contrary hereof, let him be amerced, the first time in 40 d. [pence], one half thereof to go to the use of the Chamber of the Guildhall of London, and the other half to the use of the said trade; the second time, in half a mark, and the third time, in 10 s. [shillings], to the use of the same Chamber and trade; and the fourth time, let him forswear the trade for ever.

"Also, that no one of the said trade shall hang his spurs out on Sunday, or on other days that are Double Feasts; but only a sign indicating his business: and such spurs as they shall so sell, they are to show and sell within their shops, without exposing them without, or opening the doors or windows of their shops, on the pain aforesaid.

"Also, that no one of the said trade shall keep a house or shop to carry on his business, unless he is free of the City; and that no one shall cause to be sold, or exposed for sale, any manner of old spurs for new ones; or shall garnish them, or change them for new ones.

"Also, that no one of the said trade shall take an apprentice for a less term than seven years; and such apprentice shall be enrolled, according to the usages of the said city. "Also, that if anyone of the said trade, who is not a freeman, shall take an apprentice for a term of years, he shall be amerced, as aforesaid. "Also, that no one of the said trade shall receive the apprentice, serving-man, or journeyman, of another in the same trade, during the term agreed upon between his master and him; on the pain aforesaid.

"Also, that no alien of another country, or foreigner of this country, shall follow or use the said trade, unless he is enfranchised before the Mayor, Aldermen, and Chamberlain; and that, by witness and surety of the good folks of the said trade, who will undertake for him as to his loyalty and his good behaviour.

"Also, that no one of the said trade shall work on Saturdays, after **None** has been rung out in the City; and not from that hour until the Monday morning following."

Reading and Discussion Questions

1. Are the regulations about working at night designed to protect craftsmen or their customers?
2. Why are apprentices required to train for seven years before allowed to enroll in the guild?
3. How do towns and cities profit financially from the regulations of the guild?

11.5 Marchione di Coppio Stefani on the Black Death in Florence

The Black Death was an outbreak of the Bubonic plague in Europe, beginning in 1347. Although there had been outbreaks before, the plague had not been present in Europe in centuries. The populace was already weakened by a famine in the first two decades of the century, and was thus especially susceptible to the reappearance of the plague. Unfortunately, fourteenth century Europeans lacked scientific understanding of what caused the deaths; it was usually referred to as the pestilence. The Black Death produced many different responses by people afraid of

---

none: a fixed time of prayer, around 3:00 pm

dying, and many theories as to what caused the many deaths, as evidenced by this account by Marchione di Coppio Stefani of what happened in Florence.

Source: Stefani, Marchione di Coppo. Cronacafiorentina. Rerum Italicarum Scriptores, Vol. 30. ed. *Niccolo Rodolico*. Citta di Castello: 1903-13.

Concerning a Mortality in the City of Florence in Which Many People Died.

In the year of the Lord 1348 there was a very great pestilence in the city and district of Florence. It was of such a fury and so tempestuous that in houses in which it took hold previously healthy servants who took care of the ill died of the same illness. Almost none of the ill survived past the fourth day. Neither physicians nor medicines were effective. Whether because these illnesses were previously unknown or because physicians had not previously studied them, there seemed to be no cure. There was such a fear that no one seemed to know what to do. When it took hold in a house it often happened that no one remained who had not died. And it was not just that men and women died, but even sentient animals died. Dogs, cats, chickens, oxen, donkeys sheep showed the same symptoms and died of the same disease. And almost none, or very few, who showed these symptoms, were cured. The symptoms were the following: a **bubo** in the groin, where the thigh meets the trunk; or a small swelling under the armpit; sudden fever; spitting blood and saliva (and no one who spit blood survived it). It was such a frightful thing that when it got into a house, as was said, no one remained. Frightened people abandoned the house and fled to another. Those in town fled to villages. Physicians could not be found because they had died like the others. And those who could be found wanted vast sums in hand before they entered the house. And when they did enter, they checked the pulse with face turned away. They inspected the urine from a distance and with something odoriferous under their nose. Child abandoned the father, husband the wife, wife the husband, one brother the other, one sister the other. In all the city there was nothing to do but to carry the dead to a burial. And those who died had neither confessor nor other sacraments. And many died with no one looking after them. And many died of hunger because when someone took to bed sick, another in the house, terrified, said to him: "I'm going for the doctor." Calmly walking out the door, the other left and did not return again. Abandoned by people, without food, but accompanied by fever, they weakened. There were many who pleaded with their relatives not to abandon them when night fell. But [the relatives] said to the sick person, "So that during the night you did not have to awaken those who serve you and who work hard day and night, take some sweetmeats, wine or water. They are here on the bedstead by your head; here are some blankets." And when the sick person had fallen asleep, they left and did not return. If it happened that he was strengthened by the food during the night he might be alive and strong enough to get to the window. If the street was not a major one, he might stand there a half hour before anyone came by. And if someone did pass by, and if he was strong enough that he could be heard when he called out to them, sometimes there might be a response and sometimes not, but there was no help. No one, or few, wished to enter a house where anyone was sick, nor did they even want to deal with those healthy people who came out of a sick person's house. And they said to them: "He is stupefied, do not speak to him!" saying further: "He has it because there is a bubo in his house." They call the swelling a bubo. Many died unseen. So they remained in their beds until they stank. And the neighbors, if there were any, having smelled the stench, placed them in a shroud and sent them for burial. The house remained open and yet there was no one daring enough to touch anything because it seemed that

---

bubo: swelling of the lymph nodes

things remained poisoned and that whoever used them picked up the illness.

At every church, or at most of them, they dug deep trenches, down to the waterline, wide and deep, depending on how large the parish was. And those who were responsible for the dead carried them on their backs in the night in which they died and threw them into the ditch, or else they paid a high price to those who would do it for them. The next morning, if there were many [bodies] in the trench, they covered them over with dirt. And then more bodies were put on top of them, with a little more dirt over those; they put layer on layer just like one puts layers of cheese in a lasagna.

The **beccamorti** who provided their service, were paid such a high price that many were enriched by it. Many died from [carrying away the dead], some rich, some after earning just a little, but high prices continued. Servants, or those who took care of the ill, charged from one to three florins per day and the cost of things grew. The things that the sick ate, sweetmeats and sugar, seemed priceless. Sugar cost from three to eight florins per pound. And other confections cost similarly. Capons and other poultry were very expensive and eggs cost between twelve and twenty-four pence each; and he was blessed who could find three per day even if he searched the entire city. Finding wax was miraculous. A pound of wax would have gone up more than a florin if there had not been a stop put [by the communal government] to the vain ostentation that the Florentines always make [over funerals]. Thus it was ordered that no more than two large candles could be carried[in any funeral]. Churches had no more than a single bier which usually was not sufficient. Spice dealers and beccamorti sold biers, burial palls, and cushions at very high prices. Dressing in expensive woolen cloth as is customary in [mourning] the dead, that is in a long cloak, with mantle and veil that used to cost women three florins climbed in price to thirty florins and would have climbed to 100 florins had the custom of dressing in expensive cloth not been changed. The rich dressed in modest woolens, those not rich sewed [clothes] in linen. Benches on which the dead were placed cost like the heavens and still the benches were only a hundredth of those needed. Priests were not able to ring bells as they would have liked. Concerning that [the government] issued ordinances discouraging the sounding of bells, sale of burial benches, and limiting expenses. They could not sound bells, sell benches, nor cry out announcements because the sick hated to hear of this and it discouraged the healthy as well. Priests and friars went [to serve] the rich in great multitudes and they were paid such high prices that they all got rich. And therefore [the authorities] ordered that one could not have more than a prescribed number [of clerics] of the local parish church. And the prescribed number of friars was six. All fruits with a nut at the center, like unripe plums and unhusked almonds, fresh broadbeans, figs and every useless and unhealthy fruit, were forbidden entrance into the city. Many processions, including those with relics and the painted tablet of Santa Maria Inpruneta, went through the city crying our "Mercy" and praying and then they came to a stop in the piazza of the Priors. There they made peace concerning important controversies, injuries and deaths. This [pestilence] was a matter of such great discouragement and fear that men gathered together in order to take some comfort in dining together. And each evening one of them provided dinner to ten companions and the next evening they planned to eat with one of the others. And sometimes if they planned to eat with a certain one he had no meal prepared because he was sick. Or if the host had made dinner for the ten, two or three were missing. Some fled to villas, others to villages in order to get a change of air. Where there had been no [pestilence], there they carried it; if it was already there, they caused it to increase. None of the guilds in Florence was working. All the shops were shut, taverns closed; only the apothecaries and the churches remained open. If you went outside, you found almost no one. And many good and rich men were carried from home to church on a pall by four beccamorti and one tonsured clerk who carried the cross. Each of them wanted a florin. This mortality enriched apothecaries, doctors, poultry vendors, beccamorti, and greengrocers who sold

---

beccamorti: grave-diggers

of poultices of mallow, nettles, mercury and other herbs necessary to draw off the infirmity. And it was those who made these poultices who made alot of money. Woolworkers and vendors of remnants of cloth who found themselves in possession of cloths [after the death of the entrepreneur for whom they were working] sold it to whoever asked for it. When the mortality ended, those who found themselves with cloth of any kind or with raw materials for making cloth was enriched. But many found [who actually owned cloths being processed by workers] found it to be moth-eaten, ruined or lost by the weavers. Large quantities of raw and processed wool were lost throughout the city and countryside.

This pestilence began in March, as was said, and ended in September 1348. And people began to return to look after their houses and possessions. And there were so many houses full of goods without a master that it was stupefying. Then those who would inherit these goods began to appear. And such it was that those who had nothing found themselves rich with what did not seem to be theirs and they were unseemly because of it. Women and men began to dress ostentatiously.

How Many Of the Dead Died Because Of the Mortality of the Year of Christ 1348

Now it was ordered by the bishop and the Lords [of the city government]that they should formally inquire as to how many died in Florence. When it was seen at the beginning of October that no more persons were dying of the pestilence, they found that among males, females, children and adults, 96,000 died between March and October.

How They Passed Ordinances Concerning Many Things in Florence

In the said year, when the mortality stopped, women and men in Florence were unmindful of [traditional modesty concerning] their dress. And ordinances were passed concerning this giving authority to the Judge of the Grascia to enforce these ordinances. The tailors made such boundless demands for payment that they could not be satisfied. Authority was granted [to the judge] that he should handle all matters himself. Servants were so unhappy about the very high prices [they paid] that it was necessary to make great efforts to restrain [the price rises]. The workers on the land in the countryside wanted rent contracts such that you could say that all they harvested would be theirs. And they learned to demand oxen from the landlord but at the landlord's risk [and liability for any harm done to the animal]. And then they helped others for pay by the job or by the day. And they also learned to deny [liability for] loans and [rental] payments. Concerning this serious ordinances were instituted; and [hiring] laborers became much more expensive. You could say that the farms were theirs; and they wanted the oxen, seed, loans quickly and on good terms. It was necessary to put a brake on weddings as well because when they gathered for the betrothal each party brought too many people in order to increase the pomp. And thus the wedding was made up of so many trappings. How many days were necessary and how many women took part in a woman's wedding. And they passed many other ordinances concerning [these issues].

Reading and Discussion Questions

1. It is clear from di Stefani's description that some people profited from the Black Death. Who were they and how did they profit?
2. What are the economic repercussions of the Black Death for the city of Florence?
3. According to di Stefani, how did the Catholic Church deal with the plague? What are the long-term results for the Church of how it reacted?
4. In what ways did the plague bring the people of Florence closer together? How did it cause divisions in communities?

11.6   The Medieval World View

Centuries before the heliocentric ideas of Copernicus were gradually accepted, the traditional geocentric, or earth-centered universe was usually depicted by concentric circles. In his *Buch der Natur*, a popular work on natural history, science, and medicine, Konrad von Megenburg (1309-1374) of Germany depicted the medieval cosmos in an unusual but effective manner. The seven known planets are contained within straight horizontal bands which separate the Earth below from Heaven, populated by the saints above.

Reading and Discussion Questions

1. What kind of world view is expressed by this illustration?   What place do humans occupy in the cosmos?
2. Compare this world view with the Jain cosmological map (document 8.5).   How are the two world views different?

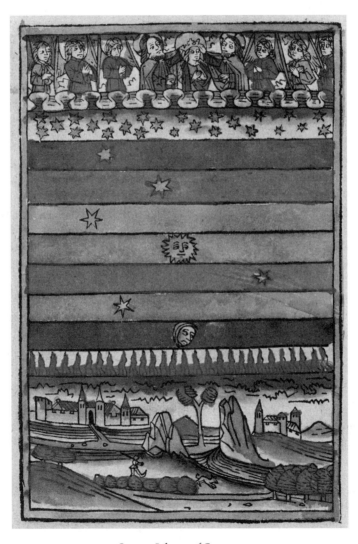

Source: Library of Congress

Contrasting Patterns in India and China

Chapter 12

600 – 1600

The native religions of India, particularly Buddhism and Hinduism, were faced with a significant threat from Islam, beginning in the tenth century. The creation of the Islamic states in India, in the Ghaznavids and the Delhi Sultanate, represented the first major outside incursion since the arrival of the Indo-Europeans over two millennia earlier (see Chapter 3). The imposition of *shari'a*, or Islamic law, did little to weaken the two religious systems, however; if anything, faced with a coherent, systematic faith may have forced the two sprawling religious systems into a bit of coherence as well. The more unfortunate legacy of the Islamic states has been the lasting enmity between Muslims and Hindus that resulted in the partition of India and Pakistan in 1947. There are two texts in this chapter that illustrate the fragile relationship between Muslim rulers and non-Muslims subjects, and which suggested ways for the occupying rulers to govern. The Delhi Sultanate lasted for three centuries, which was usually successful for an Indian state, although the Muslims and non-Muslims (Hindus, Buddhists, and others religions) never moved beyond tense co-existence without any merging of beliefs or traditions.

In contrast, China exhibited a remarkably stable culture that successfully absorbed an outside religious ideology (Buddhism) and moved through several imperial dynasties only to emerge stronger and more centralized than before. One of the most influential of Chinese dynasties was the Tang, which came to power in 618 and lasted for over three centuries. All of Chinese history is in a sense a synthetic process, in which the customs of one dynasty are merged into the customs of the next, to create a new set of customs upon which the next dynasty will be built, and so forth. The Chinese pattern of societal development was one of innovation that becomes tradition. The Tang and Song dynasties contributed many customs to subsequent dynasties, several of which are illustrated by documents in this chapter.

12.1 Al-Biruni on India

Born in Persia in the tenth century, C.E., Abu Raihan Al-Biruni is better known in the West by his westernized name, Al-Biruni. Early in life, Al-Biruni gained a reputation as a scholar, writer, and scientist, and served as an advisor for local princes. Around 1030 C.E., he traveled to India, and wrote with an objective observer's sensibilities about this foreign land. Writing as a Muslim, Al-Biruni does not hesitate to point out things he dislikes about India or its inhabitants; at the same time, however, he is quick to praise things he likes.

Source: *Alberuni's India.* Edited by Edward C. Sachau. (Delhi: S. Chand and Co., 1934)

Before entering on our exposition, we must form an adequate idea of that which renders it so particularly difficult to penetrate to the essential nature of any Indian subject. . . . For the reader must always bear in mind that the Hindus entirely differ from us in every respect, many a subject appearing intricate and obscure which would be perfectly clear if there were more connection between us. The barriers which separate Muslims and Hindus rest on different causes.

First, they differ from us in everything which other nations have in common. And here we first mention the language, although the difference of language also exists between other nations. If you want to conquer this difficulty (i.e. to learn **Sanskrit**), you will not find it easy, because the language is of an enormous range, both in words and inflections, something like the Arabic, calling one and the same thing by various names, . . . and using one and the same word for a variety of subjects, which, in order to be properly understood, must be distinguished from each other by various qualifying epithets. For nobody could distinguish between the various meanings of a word unless he understands the context in which it occurs, and its relation both to the following and the preceding parts of the sentence. The Hindus, like other people, boast of this enormous range of their language, whilst in reality it is a defect.

Further, the language is divided into a neglected vernacular one, only in use among the common people, and a classical one, only in use among the upper and educated classes.

Besides, some of the sounds (consonants) of which the language is composed are neither identical with the sounds of Arabic and Persian, nor resemble them in any way. Our tongue and uvula could scarcely manage to correctly pronounce them, nor our ears in hearing to distinguish them from similar sounds, nor could we trans-literate them with our characters. It is very difficult, therefore, to express an Indian word in our writing.

Add to this that the Indian scribes are careless, and do not take pains to produce correct and well-collated copies. In consequence, the highest results of the author's mental development are lost by their negligence, and his book becomes already in the first or second copy so full of faults, that the text appears as something entirely new, which neither a scholar nor one familiar with the subject, whether Hindu or Muslim, could any longer understand.

Secondly, they totally differ from us in religion, as we believe in nothing in which they believe, and *vice versa*. On the whole, there is very little disputing about theological topics among themselves; at the utmost, they fight with words, but they will never stake their soul or body or their property on religious controversy. On the contrary, all their fanaticism is directed against those who do not belong to them – against all foreigners. They call them **mleecha**, *i.e.* impure, and forbid having any connection with them, be it by intermarriage or any other kind of relationship, or by sitting, eating, and drinking with them, because thereby, they think, they would be polluted. They are not allowed to receive anybody who does not belong to them, even if he wished it, or was inclined to their religion. This,too,renders any connection with them quite impossible, and constitutes the widest gulf between us and them.

In the third place, in all manners and usages they differ from us to such a degree as to frighten their children with us, with our dress, and our ways and customs, and as to declare us to be devil's breed, and our doings as the very opposite of all that is good and proper. By the by, we must confess, in order to be just, that a similar depreciation of foreigners not only prevails among us and the Hindus, but is common to all nations towards each other.

There are other causes, the mentioning of which sounds like a satire – peculiarities of their national character, deeply rooted in them, but manifest to everybody. We can only say, folly is an illness for which there is no medicine, and the Hindus believe that there is no country but theirs, no nation like theirs, no kings like theirs, no religion like theirs, no science like theirs. They are haughty, foolishly vain, self-conceited, and stolid. They are by nature niggardly in communicating that which they know, and they take the greatest possible care to withhold it from men of another caste among their own people, still much more, of course, from any foreigner.

Sanskrit: learned language of Hinduism
mleecha: a member of the "untouchables" caste

Now such is the state of things in India. I have found it very hard to work my way into the subject, although I have a great liking for it, in which respect I stand quite alone in my time, and although I do not spare either trouble or money in collecting Sanskrit books from places where I supposed they were likely to be found, and in procuring for myself, even from very remote places, Hindu scholars who understand them and are able to teach me. What scholar, however, has the same favorable opportunities of studying this subject as I have? That would be only the case with one to whom the grace of God accords, what it did not accord to me, a perfectly free disposal of his own doings and goings; for it has never fallen to my lot in my own doings and goings to be perfectly independent, nor to be invested with sufficient power to dispose and to order as I thought best. However, I thank God for that which He has bestowed upon me, and which must be considered as sufficient for the purpose.

The heathen Greeks, before the rise of Christianity, held much the same opinions as the Hindus; their educated classes thought much the same as those of the Hindus; their common people held the same idolatrous views as those of the Hindus. Therefore I like to confront the theories of the one nation with those of the other simply on account of their close relationship, not in order to correct them. For that which is not the truth (i.e. the true belief or monotheism) does not admit of any correction, and all heathenism, whether Greek or Indian, is in its pith and marrow one and the same belief, because it is only a deviation *from the truth*. The Greeks, however, had philosophers who, living in their country, discovered and worked out for them the elements of science, not of popular superstition, for it is the object of the upper classes to be guided by the results of science, whilst the common crowd will always be inclined to plunge into wrong-headed wrangling, as long as they are not kept down by fear of punishment. Think of Socrates when he opposed the crowd of his nation as to their idolatry and did not want to call the stars gods! At once eleven of the twelve judges of the Athenians agreed on a sentence of death, and Socrates died faithful to the truth.

The Hindus had no men of this stamp both capable and willing to bring sciences to a classical perfection. Therefore you mostly find that even the so-called scientific theorems of the Hindus are in a state of utter confusion, devoid of any logical order, and in the last instance always mixed up with the silly notions of the crowd, e.g. immense numbers, enormous spaces of time, and all kinds of religious dogmas, which the vulgar belief does not admit of being called into question. Therefore it is a prevailing practice among the Hindus ***jurare in verba magistri***; and I can only compare their mathematical and astronomical literature, as far as I know it, to a mixture of pearl shells and sour dates, or of pearls and dung, or of costly crystals and common pebbles. Both kinds of things are equal in their eyes, since they cannot raise themselves to the methods of a strictly scientific deduction.

Reading and Discussion Questions

1. What is the overall attitude of Al-Biruni towards Hindus? How much of his viewpoint is influenced by his Muslim faith?
2. Why does Al-Biruni compare the Hindus to the ancient Greeks? In what ways are the failings of the Hindus comparable to similar defects among the Greeks; in what ways are the ancient Greeks superior to the Hindus?

12.2 Tang Taizong on Effective Government

Tang Taizong (d. 649), a founder of the Tang dynasty, was determined to create an empire that expanded upon the consolidation achieved under the Sui dynasty. The result was a large empire of people diverse in language, religion,

---

jurare in verba magistri: "to swear to a master's words," that is, to accept opinions upon authority

and culture; it was also economically diverse: the south was more productive and more prosperous than the north. Taizong recognized that these were all challenges to his dynasty, and that the Sui had faced similar problems and failed. Determined to be more effective, Taizong identifies what he sees as the weaknesses of the Sui and how he planned to prevent those some weaknesses from hampering his dynasty.

Source: translated by J. Dun Li, 1925

Excerpts from Emperor Taizong on Effective Government

How a Ruler Should Act

A country cannot be a country without people and a ruler cannot be a ruler without a country. When the ruler looks as lofty and firm as a mountain peak and as pure, bright, and illuminating as the sun and the moon, the people will admire and respect him. He must broaden his will so as to be able to embrace both Heaven and earth and must regulate his heart so as to be able to make just decisions. He cannot expand his territory without majesty and virtue; he cannot soothe and protect his people without compassion and kindness. He comforts his relations with benevolence, treats his officials with courtesy, honors his ancestors with filial respect, and receives his subordinates with thoughtfulness. Having disciplined himself, he practices virtue and righteousness diligently. This is how a ruler should act.

Establishing Relatives

The country is huge and responsibility for it is heavy. A huge country cannot be evenly governed by the emperor alone; the responsibility is too great for one man. Thus, the emperor should **enfeoff** relatives to guard the outlying prefectures. Whether the country is at peace or in danger, they cooperate; whether the country is thriving or declining, they work together with one heart. Both distant and close relations are supported and employed; encroachment and rebellion are prevented.

Formerly when the Zhou dynasty was at its height, the empire was divided among the royal clan. Nearby there was Jin and Zheng to help; far off there was Lu and Wei. In this way, the dynasty was able to survive several centuries. Toward the end of the Qin dynasty, however, the emperor rejected Chunyu's scheme [of enfeoffing relatives] and accepted Li Si's plan [to enfeoff nonrelatives]. He thus detached himself from his relatives and valued only the wise. With no relatives to rely on, the dynasty fell after two generations. Isn't this all because of the fact that if a tree has a mass of branches and leaves, it is difficult to root up, but if the limbs are disabled, the trunk has nothing to depend on? Eager to avoid Qin's errors, the Han dynasty, upon stabilizing the land within the passes, enfeoffed the closest relatives generously. Outdoing the ancient system, the largest fiefs were as big as kingdoms, and the smallest had at least several prefectures. But a branch can get so heavy that it breaks the trunk; a tail can get too big to be wagged. Thus, his throne was usurped and his dynasty was overthrown by someone of a different surname. This is a good example of the old saying that a river does not run when its source dries up and branches wither when the root of the tree decays.

Subordinates granted too much power can develop into insurmountable problems for the throne. On the other hand, subordinates granted too little power will not be strong enough to protect the throne. Thus, the best way is to enfeoff many relatives to even up their power and to have them regulate one another and share

---

enfeoff: to invest with an estate or a fee

one another's ups and downs. By doing so, the throne need not suspect its subordinates and the subordinates need not worry about being wronged or injured. These are the precautions one should take in granting fiefs. Neutralizing the power of subordinates so that none of them gets to be too strong or too weak is indeed the key to securing one's throne. …

Evaluating Officials

Differentiation of the ranks and duties of officials is a means of improving customs. A wise emperor, therefore, knows how to choose the right person for the right task. He is like a skillful carpenter who knows to use straight timber to make shafts, curved timber to make wheels, long timber to make beams, and short timber to make posts. Wood of all shapes and lengths is thus fully utilized. The emperor should make use of personnel in the same way, using the wise for their resourcefulness, the ignorant for their strength, the brave for their daring, and the timid for their prudence. As a good carpenter does not discard any timber, so a wise emperor does not discard any gentleman. A mistake should not lead the emperor to ignore a gentleman's virtues, nor should a flaw overshadow his merits.

Government affairs should be departmentalized to make the best use of officials' abilities. A tripod large enough for an ox should not be used to cook a chicken, nor should a raccoon good only at catching rats be ordered to fight against huge beasts. … Those with low intelligence or capability should not be entrusted with heavy tasks or responsibilities. If the right person is given the right task or responsibility, the empire can be governed with ease. This is the proper way of utilizing people. Whether the emperor gets hold of the right person for the right task determines whether his empire will be well governed. …

Welcoming Advice

The emperor, living in the palace, is blocked from direct access to information. For fear that faults might be left untold or defects unattended, he must set up various devices to elicit loyal suggestions and listen attentively to sincere advice. If what is said is right, he must not reject it even though it is offered by a low servant. On the other hand, if what is said is wrong, he must not accept it even though it is given by a high official. He should not find fault with the rhetoric of a comment that makes sense, nor cavil at the wording of a suggestions worth adopting. … If he acts these ways, the loyal will be devoted and the wise will fully employ their resourcefulness. Government officials will not keep any secrets from the emperor and the emperor, through his close ties to them, can thus gain access to the world.

A foolish emperor, in comparison, rebuffs remonstrations and punishes the critics. As a result, high officials do not give any advice lest they lose their salary and low officials do not make any comment lest they lose their lives. Being extremely tyrannical and dissipated, he blocks himself from any access to information. He considers himself more virtuous than the Three Lords and more talented than the Five Emperors. This eventually brings him and his empire to destruction. How sad it is! This is the evil consequence of rejecting remonstrations.

Discouraging Slander

Slanderers and flatterers are as harmful to the country as grubs to seedlings. They devote all their time to getting ahead. At court they compete for power and out of court they compete for profit. They fawn to prevent the loyal and the worthy from outranking them; they cheat out of fear that others will acquire riches and honor before them. Acting in collusion and copying each other, they succeed all too often. They get close to their superiors by using fine words and pleasant manners; they please the emperor by anticipating and attending to his wishes.
…

Advice that grates is difficult to take, but words that fall in with one's wishes are easy for one to follow. This is because while the former is like good medicine that tastes bitter, the latter is like poisoned wine that tastes sweet. A wise emperor accepts bitter criticisms that benefit his conduct; a foolish emperor takes sweet flattery that leads him to destruction. Beware!

Avoiding Extravagance

The ruler cultivates his character through frugality and peacefulness. Restraining himself, he will not tire his people or disturb his subordinates. Thus, his people will not complain and his rule will not go off course. If the emperor indulges himself in curiosities, women, music, hunting, or travel, agriculture will be disturbed and labor service will have to be increased, leading to the exhaustion of the people and the neglect of farming. If the emperor indulges himself in magnificent dwelling, precious jewelry, or fine clothes, taxes will have to be increased, leading the people to flee and the country to be impoverished. A chaotic age is marked by a ruler who is arrogant and extravagant, indulging his desires. While his dwelling and garments are richly ornamented, his people are in need of simple clothes; while his dogs and horses are tired of grain, his people do not have enough husks and chaff. As a result, both the gods and the people become resentful, and the ruler and the ruled become estranged. The dynasty is overthrown before the emperor has satisfied his wishes. Such is the fearsome cost of being arrogant and extravagant.

Maintaining Military Forces

Weapons and armor are a country's tools of violence. A warlike country, however huge and safe it may be, will end up declining and endangering its populace. Military force cannot be entirely eliminated nor used all the time. Teach people military arts when they are free from farming in order to equip them with a sense of military decorum and morale. Remember how Gou Jian, who paid respect to the fighting spirit of frogs, was able to achieve his supremacy, but Xu Yan, who disregarded military forces, lost his state. Why? Because Gou's troops were inspired and Xu was unprepared. Confucius said, "Not teaching people how to fight is the same as discarding them." Hence military might serves to benefit the realm. This is the gist of the art of war.

Esteeming Culture

Music should be played when a victory is gained; ritual should be established when the country is at peace. The ritual and music to be promulgated are rooted in Confucianism. Nothing is better than literature to spread manners and guide customs; nothing is better than schooling to propagate regulations and educate people. The Way is spread through culture; fame is gained through learning. Without visiting a deep ravine, one cannot understand how deep the earth is; without learning the arts, one cannot realize the source of wisdom. Just as the bamboos of the state of Wu cannot be made into arrows without feathers, so a clever man will not achieve any success without accumulating learning. Therefore, study halls and ritual halls should be built, books of various schools of thought should be widely read, and the six arts [propriety, music, archery, charioteering, writing, and mathematics] should be carefully studied. …

Literary arts and military arts should be employed by the state alternately. When the world is in an uproar and a battle will determine the fate of the country, military arts should be highlighted and schools given low priority. Reserve the two when the country is peaceful and prosperous; then slight the military and give weight to the classics. Neither military nor culture can the country do without; which to emphasize depends on circumstances. Neither soldiers nor scholars can be dispensed with.

Reading and Discussion Questions

1. There are hints of the examination system in Taizong's plan for his government; identify these hints and discuss Taizong's intentions.
2. What are the Confucian elements in Taizong's plans for how his government will operate?
3. What are the important elements of an effective bureaucrat according to Taizong? What are the important elements of an effective leader of bureaucrats?

12.3   Two Poems by Li Bo

Tang China is known as the "golden age" of Chinese poetry and Li Bo (701-762) was one of its greatest poets. Li Bo brought an unparalleled grace and eloquence to his treatment of the traditional themes, a flow and grandeur that lift his work far above mere imitation of the past. Playfulness, hyperbole, and outright fantasy infuse Li Bo's poetry and the Daoist reverence for nature runs through his works. A prolific poet, Li Bo strongly influenced succeeding generations of Chinese writers. His poetry has been translated into dozens of languages.

Source: Arthur David Waley, *A Hundred and Seventy Chinese Poems.* (New York: Alfred A. Knopf, 1918)

The Difficulties of the Road to Sichuan

How precipitous and lofty is the road to Sichuan,
Harder to scale than the road to Heaven;
TsanTsung and Yu Fu opened out this kingdom.
How remote that time seems to-day.
After forty-eight thousand years they penetrated the Ch'in barrier and there
was intercourse between the two countries;
Towards the west the Tai-po has paths only birds can climb
Leading across the peak of Omei Shan.
The earth crumpled and the mountains were riven; stout heroes died.
Then afterwards they made a road of ladders and stone bridges like a
connected chain.
Above is the Kao-piao Mountain, where six dragons revolve around the sun;
Below rebellious waves beat and recoil;
Even the yellow cranes find it hard to pass this way,
And gibbons wishing to scale it climb and clutch in great distress.
On the Ching Ni range how the road turns and twists,
In a hundred steps nine bends beneath rock and cliff,
Panting we touch the constellation of Shan and tread the constellation ofChing.
As we gaze up the breath labors under our ribs;
Clasping our hands to our breasts we sit down with a long sigh.
From our western wandering when will we return?
How hazardous are such cliffs and rocks impossible to climb,
Around us naught but sad birds calling from aged trees,
Male pursuing female through the woods.

Or again we hear the nightjar calling sadly under the evening moon among the empty hills.

How hard is the road to Sichuan,

Harder to scale than the road to Heaven.

When one hears only of its dangers cheeks turn pale.

Peak upon peak touch the heavens with scarce a foot between;

Blasted pines topple over to lean out over the uttermost abyss;

Plunging cataracts and hurtling rapids struggle and boil in chorus;

Waves dashing on rocky cliffs roll boulders down ten thousand gullies with a noise like thunder.

These are the dangers all must face who come this way.

Alas! For the wanderers from afar who travel such a road.

Why are they come on such a journey?

The "sword ledge" stands august and dignified on the lofty and rock-crowned heights.

Here a man could close this frontier pass

And ten thousand could not open it.

Ah! If the man who holds it became a traitor

And were to turn fox or wolf!

In the morning we shun tigers,

In the evening we flee from snakes,

Teeth that grind and suck blood,

Mowing down men like hemp.

Chengdu has its pleasures,

But how to be compared with the happiness of an early

Return home.

How hard are the roads of Sichuan,

Harder to scale than the road to heaven.

I turn my body to the west and gaze with a long sad sigh.

Waking from Drunkenness on a Spring Day

Life in the World is but a big dream;

I will not spoil it by any labor or care.

So saying, I was drunk all the day,

Lying helpless at the porch in front of my door.

When I woke up, I blinked at the garden-lawn;

A lonely bird was singing amid the flowers.

I asked myself, had the day been wet or fine?

The Spring wind was telling the mango-bird.

Moved by its song I soon began to sigh,

And as wine was there I filled my own cup.

Wildly singing I waited for the moon to rise;

When my song was over, all my senses had gone.

Reading and Discussion Questions

1. When Li Bo wrote "The Difficulties of the Road to Sichuan," the province of Sichuan, in western China, was a wild, frontier region. What does the road to Sichuan symbolize?
2. What image does Li Bo convey of himself in "Waking from Drunkenness on a Spring Day?" What philosophical traditions does he draw on to create his persona?

12.4 Ibn Wahab, An Arab Merchant visits Tang China

Ibn Wahab was an Arab merchant from Basra (Iraq) who sailed to China via the Indian Ocean around 872 C.E. His travel account includes a description of his interview with the Chinese emperor. Wahab's visit at the height of the Tang dynasty (618-907 C.E.), with its flourishing trade and efficient civil service, provides a first-hand account of China when its influence extended throughout all of Eurasia.

Source: Fitzgerald, C.P. *China: A Short Cultural History* (London: Cresse Press, 1930), pp. 339-340.

"When I was received by the Emperor," Ibn Wahab relates, "he told the interpreter to ask me, 'can you recognize your Master, if you see him?'" The Emperor referred to Mahomet, upon whom be God's Blessing. I replied: 'How can I see him, since he is in Heaven with the Most High God?' 'I am talking of his likeness,' said the Emperor. 'I would know that,' I replied. Then the Emperor called for a box containing rolls which he put in front of him, and passed them to his interpreter, saying: 'Let him see his Master.' I recognized the portraits of the Prophets, and I said a blessing. 'Why are you moving your lips?' asked the Emperor. 'Because I am blessing the Prophets,' I answered. 'How did you know them?' he asked. 'By their attributes; for instance, here is Noah with his Ark, which saved him and his family when at the command of God all the earth was drowned in the Flood.' At these words the Emperor laughed, and said, 'You have certainly recognized Noah. As for the Flood, we do not believe it. The Flood did not submerge the whole world. It did not reach China or India.' 'That is Moses with his staff,' I said. 'Yes,' said the Emperor, 'but he was not important and his people were few.' 'There,' I said, 'is Jesus on his ass, surrounded by his apostles.' 'Yes,' said the Emperor: 'He lived only a short time. His mission lasted only thirty months.' Then I saw the Prophet on a camel, and his companions, also on camels, around him. I wept, being much moved. 'Why do you weep?' asked the Emperor. 'Because I see our Prophet, my ancestor.' 'Yes, it is he,' said the Emperor. 'He and his people founded a glorious empire. He did not see it completed, but his successors have.' Above each picture was an inscription [in Chinese], which I supposed to contain an account of their history. I saw also other pictures, which I did not recognize. The interpreter told me that they were the prophets of China and India."

Reading and Discussion Questions

1. What is the significance of the Chinese emperor being familiar with the Old Testament prophets? With Jesus? With the Prophet Muhammad?
2. What view of the world is revealed when the Chinese emperor says that the Flood did not reach China?

12.5 Marco Polo Describes China under Mongol Rule

Marco Polo was the son of an Italian merchant who traveled the Silk Road to Mongol China in the year 1275. A gifted linguist and master of four languages, Marco Polo was appointed by emperor Kublai Khan as an official in the Privy Council in 1277 and for three years he was a tax inspector in Yanzhou, a city on the Grand Canal near the northeastern coast. He also visited Karakorum, the old capital of the original Mongol empire. Marco Polo stayed in the Khan's court for seventeen years.

Source: *The Travels of Marco Polo* translated by W. Marsden (1818)

It is their custom that the bodies of all deceased grand khans and other great lords from the family of Chinggis Khan are carried for internment to a great mountain called Altai. No matter where they might die, even if it is a hundred days' journey away, they nevertheless are brought here for burial. It is also their custom that, in the process of conveying the bodies of these princes, the escort party sacrifices whatever persons they happen to meet along the route, saying to them: "Depart for the next world and there serve your deceased master." They believe that all whom they kill in this manner will become his servants in the next life. They do the same with horses, killing all the best, so that the dead lord might use them in the next world. When the corpse of **Mongke** Khan was transported to this mountain, the horsemen who accompanied it slew upward of 20,000 people along the way.

Now that I have begun speaking about the **Tartars**, I will tell you more about them. They never remain fixed in one location. As winter approaches they move to the plains of a warmer region in order to find sufficient pasturage for their animals. In summer they inhabit cool regions in the mountains where there is water and grass and their animals are free of the annoyance of gad-flies and other biting insects. They spend two or three months progressively climbing higher and grazing as they ascend, because the grass is not sufficient in any one spot to feed their extensive herds.

Their huts, or tents, are circular and formed by covering a wooden frame with felt. These they transport on four-wheeled carts wherever they travel, since the framework is so well put together that it is light to carry. Whenever they set their huts up, the entrance always faces south. They also have excellent two-wheeled vehicles so well covered with black felt that, no matter how long it rains, rain never penetrates. These are drawn by oxen and camels and serve to carry their wives, children, and all necessary utensils and provisions.

It is the women who tend to their commercial concerns, buying and selling, and who tend to all the needs of their husbands and households. The men devote their time totally to hunting, hawking, and warfare. They have the best falcons in the world, as well as the best dogs. They subsist totally on meat and milk, eating the produce of their hunting, especially a certain small animal, somewhat like a hare, which our people call Pharaoh's rats, which are abundant on the steppes in summer. They likewise eat every manner of animal: horses, camels, even dogs, provided they are fat. They drink mare's milk, which they prepare in such a way that it has the qualities and taste of white wine. In their language they call it *kemurs*.

Their women are unexcelled in the world so far as their chastity and decency of conduct are concerned, and also in regard to their love and devotion toward their husbands. They regard marital infidelity as a vice which is not simply dishonorable but odious by its very nature. Even if there are ten or twenty women in a household, they live in harmony and highly praiseworthy concord, so that no offensive word is ever spoken. They devote full attention to their tasks and domestic duties, such as preparing the family's food, managing the servants, and caring for the children, whom they raise in common. The wives' virtues of modesty and chastity are all the more praiseworthy because the men are allowed to wed as many women as they please. The expense to the husband for his wives is not that great, but the benefit he derives from their trading and from the work in which they are

---

Mongke: the Chinese term for "Mongol"
Tartars: another word for Mongols

constantly employed is considerable. For this reason, when he marries he pays a dowry to his wife's parents. The first wife holds the primary place in the household and is reckoned to be the husband's most legitimate wife, and this status extends to her children. Because of their unlimited number of wives, their offspring is more numerous than that of any other people. When a father dies, his son may take all of his deceased father's wives, with the exception of his own mother. They also cannot marry their sisters, but upon a brother's death they may marry their sisters-in-law. Every marriage is solemnized with great ceremony.

This is what they believe. They believe in an exalted god of heaven, to whom they burn incense and offer up prayers for sound mind and body. They also worship a god called Natigay, whose image, covered with felt or other cloth, is kept in everyone's house. They associate a wife and children with this god, placing the wife on his left side and the children before him. . . . They consider Natigay as the god who presides over their earthly concerns, protecting their children, their cattle, and their grain. They show him great respect. Before eating they always take a fat portion of meat and smear the idol's mouth with it, as well as the mouths of his wife and children. Then they take some of the broth in which the meat has been cooked and pour it outside, as an offering. When this has been done they believe that their god and his family have had their proper share. The Tartars then proceed to eat and drink without further ceremony.

The rich among these people dress in gold cloth and silks and the furs of sable, ermine, and other animals. All their accouterments are expensive.

Their weapons are bows, iron maces, and in some instances, spears. The bow, however, is the weapon at which they are the most expert, being accustomed to use it in their sports from childhood. They wear armor made from the hides of buffalo and other beasts, fire-dried and thus hard and strong.

They are brave warriors, almost to the point of desperation, placing little value on their lives, and exposing themselves without hesitation to every sort of danger. They are cruel by nature. They are capable of undergoing every manner of privation, and when it is necessary, they can live for a month on the milk of their mares and the wild animals they catch. Their horses feed on grass alone and do not require barley or other grain. The men are trained to remain on horseback for two days and two nights without dismounting, sleeping in the saddle while the horse grazes. No people on the earth can surpass them in their ability to endure hardships, and no other people shows greater patience in the face of every sort of deprivation. They are most obedient to their chiefs, and are maintained at small expense. These qualities, which are so essential to a soldier's formation, make them fit to subdue the world, which in fact they have largely done.

When one of the great Tartar chiefs goes to war, he puts himself at the head of an army of 100,000 horsemen and organizes them in the following manner. He appoints an officer to command every ten men and others to command groups of 100, 1,000, and 10,000 men respectively. Thus ten of the officers who command ten men take their orders from an officer who commands 100; ten of these captains of a 100 take their orders from an officer in charge of a 1,000; and ten of these officers take orders from one who commands 10,000. By this arrangement, each officer has to manage only ten men or ten bodies of men. . . . When the army goes into the field, a body of 200 men is sent two days' march in advance, and parties are stationed on each flank and in the rear, to prevent surprise attack.

When they are setting out on a long expedition, they carry little with them. . . . They subsist for the most part on mare's milk, as has been said. . . . Should circumstances require speed, they can ride for ten days without lighting a fire or taking a hot meal. During this time they subsist on the blood drawn from their horses, each man opening a vein and drinking the blood. They also have dried milk. . . . When setting off on an expedition, each man takes about ten pounds. Every morning they put about half a pound of this into a leather flask, with as much water as necessary. As they ride, the motion violently shakes the contents, producing a thin porridge which they take as dinner. . . .

All that I have told you here concerns the original customs of the Tartar lords. Today, however, they are corrupted. Those who live in China have adopted the customs of the idol worshippers, and those who inhabit the western provinces have adopted the ways of the Muslims.

Reading and Discussion Questions

1. What image of the Mongols comes through in Marco Polo's descriptions? How do Mongol practices and beliefs differ from the Chinese customs?
2. Why does Marco Polo write that the Mongols living in China have become "corrupted"?

Religious Civilizations Interacting: Korea, Japan, and Southeast Asia

Chapter 13

100 C.E. – 1400 C.E.

The thirteen centuries covered by this chapter are some of the most formative in the histories of Korea, Japan, and Southeast Asia. They were turbulent years, with many political changes and military undertakings, but also creative years, with many cultural developments from literary works to the creation of new writing systems. The documents were chosen to reflect both the diversity of the cultures and the turbulence of the period.

There are two foundation myths in this chapter. One recounts the founding of the Choson kingdom in Korea by Tangun, the son of Hwanung and grandson to Hwanin. Both Hwanung and Hwanin are heavenly beings; thus the Korean myth of origin is centered on the belief that the first Korean king was a son of heavenly deities. In a similar story, with one important difference, the foundation myth of Japan concerns not the beginning of the first Japanese royal dynasty (although such a myth does exist); rather, the story of Izanaki and Izanami is about the creation of Japan itself, island by island, followed by the creation of various deities. It is a myth rich in details of how the Yamato and Heian era Japanese thought about nature, gender, sex, and the divine. The Izanaki and Izanami myth is taken from the *Kojiki,* or *Records of Ancient Matters,* one of two eighth century histories written in Japan but using Chinese characters.

Japan's textual history is exceptionally diverse, comparable to its neighbor to the west, China. Early Japanese writings include the first novel, the *Tale of Genji,* several early histories (including the *Kojiki*), poetry, scholarly works, political treatises, legal codes, and so forth.

In the background of all three regions loomed China, and this is evidenced in many of the sources. Some of them use China's dynastic history as a way of measuring and registering time; some reference Chinese cultural traditions that had been borrowed or forcibly incorporated during period of Chinese control; while other sources simply refer to China and reveal their awareness of that nation's presence. It is notable that the Korean sources reveal a more explicit awareness of China than the Japanese sources; although Japan will be influenced by China culturally, Korea was at times outright occupied by China. Thus the sources from each of these respective cultures reflect the nuances of influence. The Chinese influence on Japan is revealed not by the content of the sources as much as by the language they are written in; for centuries, both Korea and Japan used Chinese characters to write their languages, until they each developed their own writing systems. In addition to highlighting the influence of China throughout Asia, the documents in this chapter also draw attention to the relationships between Korea and Japan.

13.1 *Nihongi,* or *The Chronicles of Japan*

The *Nihongi,* or *Chronicles of Japan,* were composed in 720 C.E., during the late Yamato era. It is one of two histories written during that time, at the instigation of the emperor. The following excerpt is a version of the Izanaki and Izanami foundation myth, in which two gods come together to create the islands of Japan. Another well-known version is in the *Kojiki,* the other Yamato history.

Source: Aston, W.G. *Nihongi: Chronicles of Japan from Earliest Times to AD 697.* (London: Kegan, Paul, Trench, Trubner & Co., 1896), 19-25.

Their next child was Sosa no wo no Mikoto.
Called in one writing Kami Sosa no Wo no Mikoto or
Haya Sosa no wo no Mikoto.

This God had a fierce temper and was given to cruel acts. Moreover he made a practice of continually weeping and wailing. So he brought many of the people of the land to an untimely end. Again he caused green mountains to become withered. Therefore the two Gods, his parents, addressed Sosa no wo no Mikoto, saying: - "Thou art exceedingly wicked, and it is not meet that thou shouldst reign over the world. Certainly thou must depart far away to the Nether-Land." So they at length expelled him.

In one writing it is said: - "Izanagi no Mikoto said: I wish to procreate the precious child who is to rule the world.' He therefore took in his left hand a White-copper mirror, upon which a Deity was produced from it called Oho-hiru-me no Mikoto. In his right hand he took a white-copper mirror, and forthwith there was produced from it a God who was named Tsukiyumi no Mikoto. Again, while turning his head and looking askance, a God was produced who was named Sosa no Wo no Mikoto. Now Oho-hirume no Mikoto and Tsuki-yumi no Mikoto were both of a bright and beautiful nature, and were therefore made to shine down upon Heaven and Earth. But Sosa no Wo's character was to love destruction, and he was accordingly sent down to rule the Nether Land."

In one writing it is said: - "After the sun and moon, the next, child which was born was the leech-child. When this child had completed his third year, he was nevertheless still unable to stand upright. The reason why the leech-child was born was that in the beginning, when Izanagi no Mikoto and Izanami no Mikoto Went round the pillar, the female Deity was the first to utter an exclamation of pleasure, and the law of male and female was therefore broken. They next procreated Sosa no wo no Mikoto. This God was of a wicked nature, and was always fond of wailing and wrath. Many of the people of the land died, and the green mountains withered. Therefore his parents addressed him, saying: "Supposing that thou wert to rule this country, much destruction of life would surely ensue. Thou must govern the far-distant Nether Land.' Their next child was the bird-rock-camphor-wood boat of Heaven. They forthwith took this boat and, placing the leech-child in it, abandoned it to the current. Their next child was Kagutsuchi."

Now Izanami no Mikoto was burnt by Kagutsuchi so that she died. When she was lying down to die, she gave birth to the Earth-Goddess, Hani-yama-hime, and the Water-Goddess, Midzu-ha-no-me. Upon this Kagutsuchi took to Wife Hani-yama-hime, and they had a child named Waka-musubi. On the crown of this Deity's head were produced the silkworm and the mulberry tree, and in her navel the five kinds of grain.

In one writing it is said: - "When Izanami no Mikoto gave birth to Ho-no-musubi,she was burnt by the child, and died. When she was about to die, she brought forth the Water-Goddess, Midzu-ha-no-me, and the Earth-Goddess, Hani-yama-hime. She also brought forth the gourd of Heaven."

In one writing it is said: - "When about to give birth to the Fire-God, Kagutsuchi, Izanami no Mikoto became feverish and ill. In consequence she vomited, and the vomit became changed into a God, who was called

Kana-yama-hiko.Next her urine became changed into a Goddess, who was called Midzu-ha-no-me. Next her excrement was changed into a Goddess, who was called Hani-yama-hime."

In one writing it is said: - "When Izanami no Mikoto gave birth to the Fire-God, she was burnt, and died. She was, therefore, buried at the village of Arima in Kumano, in the province of Kul. In the time of flowers, the inhabitants worship the spirit of this Goddess by offerings of flowers. They also worship her with drums, flutes, flags, singing and dancing."

In one Writing it is said: - "Izanagi no Mikoto and Izanami no Mikoto, having together procreated the Great-eight-island Land, Izanagi no Mikoto said: "Over the country which we have produced there is naught but morning mists which shed a perfume everywhere!' So he puffed them away with a breath, which became changed into a God, named Shinatohe no Mikoto. He is also called Shinatsuhiko no Mikoto. This is the God of the Wind. Moreover, the child which they procreated when they were hungry was called Uka no mi-tama no Mikoto. Again they produced the Sea-Gods, who were called Watatsu mi no Mikoto, and the Mountain-Gods, Who Were called Yama tsu mi, the Gods of the River-mouths, who were called Hayaaki-tsubi no Mikoto, the Tree-Gods, who were called Ku-ku no chi, and the Earth-Goddess, who Was called Hani-yasuno Kami. Thereafter they produced all manner of things whatsoever. When the time came for the Fire-God Kagutsuchi to be born, his mother Izanami no Mikoto Was burnt, and suffered change and departed. Then Izanagi no Mikoto was wroth, and said: Oh, that I should have given my beloved younger sister in exchange for a single child! So while he crawled at her head, and crawled at her feet, weeping and lamenting, the tears which he shed fell down and became a Deity. It is this Deity who dwells at Unewo no Konomoto, and who is called Naki-saha-me no Mikoto. At length he drew the ten-span sword with which he was girt, and cut Kagutsuchi into three pieces, each of which became changed into a God. Moreover, the blood which dripped from the edge of the sword became the multitudinous rocks which are in the bed of the Easy-River of Heaven. This God was the father of Futsunushi no Kami. Moreover, the blood which dripped from the hilt-ring of the sword spurted out and became deities, whose names Were Mika no Haya-hi no Kami and next Hi no Haya-hi no Kami. This Mika no Haya-hi no Kami was the parent of Take-mika-suchi no Kami."

Another version is: - "Mika no haya-hi no Mikoto, next Hi no haya-hi no Mikoto, and next Take-Mika-tsuchi no Kami."

"Moreover, the blood which dripped from the point of the sword spurted out and became deities, who were called Iha-sakuno Kami, after him Ne-saku no Kami, and next Iha-tsutsu-wo no Mikoto. This Iha-saku no Kami was the father of Futsu-nushi no Kami."

One account says: - "Iha-tsutsu-Wo no Mikoto, and next Iha-tsutsu-me no Mikoto."

"Moreover, the blood which dripped from the head of the sword spurted out and became deities, who were called Kura o Kami no Kami, next Kurayamatsumi no Kami, and next Kura-midzu-ha no Kami."

Thereafter, Izanagi no Mikoto went after Izanami no Mikoto, and entered the land of Yomi. When he reached her they conversed together, and Izanami no Mikotosaid: My lord and husband, why is thy coming so late? I have already eaten of the cooking-furnace of Yomi.

The original has "yellow springs," a Chinese expression. Yomi or Yomo is Hades. It is no doubt connected with yo or yoru, night.

Nevertheless; I am about to lie down to rest. I pray thee, do not thou look on me. Izanami no Mikoto did not give ear to her, but secretly took his many-toothed comb and, breaking off its end tooth, made of it a torch, and looked at her. Putrefying matter had gushed up, and maggots swarmed. This is why people at the present day avoid using a single light at night, and also avoid throwing away a comb at night. Izanagi no Mikoto was greatly shocked, and said: 'Nay! I have come unawares to a hideous and polluted land.' So he speedily ran away back again. Then Izanami no Mikoto was angry, and said: 'Why didn't thou not observe that which I charged thee? Now am I put to shame.' So she sent the eight Ugly Females of Yomi (Shikome, called by some Hisame) to pursue and stay him. Izanagi no Mikoto therefore drew his sword, and, flourishing it behind him, ran away. Then he took his black head-dress and flung it down. It became changed into grapes, which the Ugly Females seeing, took and ate. When they had finished eating them, they again pursued Izanagi no Mikoto. Then he flung down his many-toothed comb, which forthwith became changed into bamboo-shoots. The Ugly Females pulled them up and ate them, and when they had done eating them, again gave chase. Afterwards, Izanami no Mikoto came herself and pursued him. By this time Izanagi no Mikoto had reached the Even Pass of Yomi.

Reading and Discussion Questions

1. The *Nihongi* emphasizes the creation of various gods. What benefit would the Yamato imperial family have derived from the *Nihongi* version?
2. The *Nihongi* is very self-referential to its sources; why does it acknowledge that it is derived from other written texts?
3. Although the story predated the introduction of those two philosophies into Japan, the *Nihongi* was only written down after Japan had officially become Buddhist and Confucian. Are there Buddhist and Confucian elements in this text?

13.2   The "Taika Reform Edicts"

The "Taika Reform Edicts" were issued in 645 to promote Buddhism and to clearly establish that the imperial family supported this relatively new religion. Korean missionaries officially brought Buddhism into Japan in 552. Although it never replaced Shinto, which to this day retains a prominent role in Japanese life, Buddhism was recognized as the official religion of the Yamato in 594. These "Edicts" reinforce that status.

The "Taika Reform Edicts" were much more than just an acknowledgement of the importance of Buddhism in Japan; the name translates to the "Great Reform Edicts" and included a comprehensive program of Sinicization in imperial Japan. Various aspects of Tang government and society were implemented in Japan with this reform, including Tang style bureaucracy, architecture, approaches to history, and Buddhism.

Source: Richard Hooker. intro and ed., W.G. Aston, trans., *Nihongi* (London: Kegan, Paul, Trench, Trubner, 1896), 197-227.

EMPEROR KOTOKU'S VOW

19th day (645 A.D.).

The Emperor, the Empress Dowager, and the Prince Imperial summoned together the Ministers under the great tsuki tree, and made an oath appealing to the Gods of Heaven and Earth, and said,

"Heaven covers us; Earth upbears us; the Imperial way is one and only one way. But in this last degenerate age, the order of Lord and Vassal was destroyed until Supreme Heaven by Our hands put to death the traitors. Now, from this time forward, both parties shedding their heart's blood, the Lord will not tolerate double methods of government, and the Vassal will avoid duplicity in his service of the sovereign! On him who breaks this oath, Heaven will send a curse and earth a plague, demons will slay them, and men will kill them. This is as manifest as the sun and moon."

REGULATION OF THE PROVINCES

8th month, 5th day.

Governors of the Eastern provinces were appointed. Then the Governors were addressed as follows:

"In accordance with the charge entrusted to Us by the Gods of Heaven, We propose at the present for the first time to regulate the myriad provinces.

When you proceed to your posts, prepare registers of all the free subjects of the State and of the people under the control of others, whether great or small. Take account also of the acreage of cultivated land. As to the profits arising from the gardens and ponds, the water and land, deal with them in common with the people.

In addition, it is not right for the provincial Governors, while in their provinces, to decide criminal cases, nor are they permitted by accepting bribes to bring the people to poverty and misery. When they come up to the capital they must not bring large numbers of the people in their train. They are only allowed to bring with them the Kuni no Miyakko and the district officials. But when they travel on public business they may ride the horses of their department and eat the food of their department. From the rank of Suke upwards, those who obey this law will surely be rewarded, while those who disobey it shall be liable to be reduced in rank. From the rank of Hangwan downwards, all those who accept bribes shall be fined double the amount of the bribe, and they shall eventually be criminally punished according to the greater or less severity of the case.

Nine men are allowed as attendants on a Chief Governor, seven on an assistant, and five on a secretary. If this limit is exceeded, and they are accompanied by a greater number, both chief and followers shall be criminally punished...

In addition, on waste pieces of ground let arsenals be erected, and let the swords and armour, with the bows and arrows of the provinces and districts, be deposited together in them. In the case of the frontier provinces which border close on the Yemishi, let all the weapons be gathered together, and let them remain in the hands of their original owners. In regard to the six districts of the province of Yamato, let the officials who are sent there prepare registers of the population, and also take an account of the acreage of cultivated land. This means to examine the acreage of the cultivated ground, and the numbers, houses, and ages of the people.

You Governors of provinces, take careful note of this and withdraw..."

COMPLAINTS AND BIRTH

The Emperor issued an order, saying:

"If there be a complainant, in case the person in question belongs to a Tomo no Miyakko, let the Tomo no Miyakko first make inquiry and then report to Us. In case the person in question has an elder, let the elder first make inquiry and then report to Us. If, however, the Tomo no Miyakko or the elder does not come to a clear decision respecting the complaint, let a document be received and placed in the box, and punishment will be inflicted according to the offence. The person who receives the document should at dawn take it and make report to the Inner Palace, when We will mark on it the year and month, and communicate it to the Ministers. In case there is any neglect to decide it, or if there are malpractices on the part of intriguing persons, let the complainant strike the bell. This is why the bell is hung and box provided in the Court. Let the people of the Empire know and appreciate Our intention.

Moreover, the law of men and women shall be that the children born of a free man and a free woman shall belong to the father: if a free man takes to wife a slave woman, her children shall belong to the mother; if a free woman marries a slave man, the children of the marriage shall belong to the father; if they are slaves of two houses, the children shall belong to the mother. The children of temple serfs shall follow the rule for freemen. But in regard to others who become slaves, they shall be treated according to the rule for slaves. Publish this well to the people as a beginning of regulations."

BUDDHISM

8th day.

A messenger was sent to the Great Temple to summon together the Buddhist priests and nuns, and to address them on the part of the Emperor, saying,

"In the 13th year of the reign of the Emperor who ruled the world in the Palace of Shikishima, King Myong of Pekche reverently transmitted the Law of Buddha to our great Yamato. At this time the Ministers in a body were opposed to its transmission. Only Soga no Iname no Sukune believed in this Law, and the Emperor accordingly instructed him to receive it with reverence. In the reign of the Emperor who ruled the world in the Palace of Wosada, Soga no Mumako no Sukune, influenced by reverence for his deceased father, continued to prize highly the doctrines of Buddha. But the other Ministers had no faith in it, and its institutes had almost perished when the Emperor instructed Mumako no Sukune reverently to receive this Law. In the reign of the Empress who ruled the world in the Palace of Woharida, Mumako no Sukune, on behalf of the Empress, made an embroidered figure of Buddha sixteen feet high and a copper image of Buddha sixteen feet high. He exalted the doctrine of Buddha and showed honour to its priests and nuns. It is our desire to exalt the pure doctrine and brilliantly to promulgate great principles. We therefore appoint as professors the following ten persons: The S'ramana, Poknyang, Hye-un, Syang-an, Nyong-un, and Hye-chi, Taih-shi of Koma, and Subin, Doto, Yerin, Yemyo and Yeon, chief priests of temples. We separately appoint the Hoshi, Yemyo, chief priest of the Temple of Kudara.

Let these ten professors well instruct the priests in general in the practice of the teachings of Shaka. It is needful that they be made to comply with the Law. If there is a difficulty about repairing Temples built by any from the Emperor down to the Tomo no Miyakko, We will in all cases assist in doing so. We shall also cause Temple Commissioners and Chief Priests to be appointed, who shall make a circuit to all the temples, and having ascertained the actual facts respecting the priests and nuns, their male and female slaves, and the acreage of their cultivated lands, report all the particulars clearly to us."

CORRUPTION OF REGIONAL OFFICIALS

19th day

Commissioners were sent to all the provinces to take a record of the total numbers of the people. The Emperor on this occasion made an edict, as follows:

"In the times of all the Emperors, from antiquity downwards, subjects have been set apart for the purpose of making notable their reigns and handing down their names to posterity. Now the Omi and Muraji, the Tomo no Miyakko and the Kuni no Miyakko, have each one set apart their own vassals, whom they compel to labor at their arbitrary pleasure. Moreover, they cut off the hills and seas, the woods and plains, the ponds and rice-fields belonging to the provinces and districts, and appropriate them to themselves. Their contests are never ceasing. Some engross to themselves many tens of thousands of shiro of rice land, while others possess in all patches of ground too small to stick a needle into. When the time comes for the payment of taxes, the Omi, the Muraji, and the Tomo no Miyakko, first collect them for themselves and then hand over a share. In the case of repairs to palaces or the construction of misasagi, they each bring their own vassals, and do the work according to circumstances. The Book of Changes says, "Diminish that which is above: increase that which is below: if measures are framed according to the regulations, the resources of the State suffer no injury, and the people receive no hurt."

"At the present time, the people are still few. And yet the powerful cut off portions of land and water, and converting them into private ground, sell it to the people, demanding the price yearly. From this time forward the sale of land is not allowed. Let no man without due authority make himself a landlord, engrossing to himself that which belongs to the helpless."

The people rejoiced.

REGULATION OF THE CAPITAL; TAXES; WOMEN
A.D. 646. 2nd year, Spring, 1st month, 1st day.
As soon as the ceremonies of the new years congratulations were over, the Emperor promulgated an edict of reforms, as follows:

"I. Let the people established by the ancient Emperors, etc., as representatives of children be abolished, also the Miyake of various places and the people owned as serfs by the Wake, the Omi, the Muraji, the Tomo no Miyakko, the Kuni no Miyakko and the Mura no Obito. Let the farmsteads in various places be abolished."

Consequently fiefs were granted for their sustenance to those of the rank of Daibu and upwards on a descending scale. Presents of cloth and silk stuffs were given to the officials and people, varying in value.

"Further we say, it is the business of the Daibu to govern the people. If they discharge this duty thoroughly, the people have trust in them, and an increase of their revenue is therefore for the good of the people.

II. The capital is for the first time to be regulated, and Governors appointed for the Home provinces and districts. Let barriers, outposts, guards, and post-horses, both special and ordinary, be provided, bell-tokens made, and mountains and rivers regulated.

For each ward in the capital let there be appointed one alderman, and for four wards one chief alderman, who shall be charged with the superintendence of the population, and the examination of criminal matters. For appointment as chief aldermen of wards let men be taken belonging to the wards, of unblemished character, firm and upright, so that they may fitly sustain the duties of the time. For appointments as aldermen, whether of rural townships or of city wards, let ordinary subjects be taken belonging to the township or ward, of good character and solid capacity. If such men are not to be found in the township or ward in question, it is permitted to select and employ men of the adjoining township or ward.

The Home provinces shall include the region from the River Yokogaha at Nabari on the east, from Mount Senoyama in Kii on the south, from Kushibuchi in Akashi on the west, and from Mount Afusakayama in Sasanami in Afumi on the north. Districts of forty townships are constituted Greater Districts, of from thirty to four townships are constituted Middle Districts, and of three or fewer townships are constituted Lesser Districts. For the district authorities, of whatever class, let there be taken Kuni no Miyakko of unblemished character, such as may fitly sustain the duties of the time, and made Tairei and Shorei. Let men of solid capacity and intelligence who are skilled in writing and arithmetic be appointed assistants and clerks.

The number of special or ordinary post-horses given shall in all cases follow the number of marks on the posting bell-tokens. When bell-tokens are given to (officials of) the provinces and barriers, let them be held in both cases by the chief official, or in his absence by the assistant official.

III. Let there now be provided for the first time registers of population, books of account and a system of the receipt and re-granting of distribution-land.

Let every fifty houses be reckoned a township, and in every township let there be one alderman who shall be charged with the superintendence of the registers of population, the direction of the sowing of crops and the cultivation of mulberry trees, the prevention and examination of offences, and the enforcement of the payment of taxes and of forced labor.

For rice-land, thirty paces in length by twelve paces in breadth shall be reckoned a tan. Ten tan make one cho. For each tan the tax is two sheaves and two bundles (such as can be grasped in the hand) of rice; for each cho the tax is twenty-two sheaves of rice. On mountains or in valleys where the land is precipitous, or in remote places where the population is scanty, such arrangements are to be made as may be convenient.

IV. The old taxes and forced labor are abolished, and a system of commuted taxes instituted. These shall consist of fine silks, coarse silks, raw silk, and floss silk, all in accordance with what is produced in the locality. For each cho of rice land the rate is ten feet of fine silk, or for four cho one piece forty feet in length by two and a half feet in width. For coarse silk the rate is twenty feet (per cho), or one piece for every two cho of the same length and width as the fine silk. For cloth the rate is forty feet of the same dimensions as the fine and coarse silk, i.e. one tan for each cho. Let there be levied separately a commuted house tax. All houses shall pay each twelve feet of cloth. The extra articles of this tax, as well as salt and offerings, will depend on what is produced in the locality.

For horses for the public service, let every hundred houses contribute one horse of medium quality. Or if the horse is of superior quality, let one be contributed by every two hundred houses. If the horses have to be purchased, the price shall be made up by a payment from each house of twelve feet of cloth.

As to weapons, each person shall contribute a sword, armour, bow and arrows, a flag, and a drum.

For servants, the old system, by which one servant was provided by every thirty houses, is altered, and one servant is to be furnished from every fifty houses [one is for employment as a menial servant] for allotment to the various functionaries. Fifty houses shall be allotted to provide rations for one servant, and one house shall contribute twenty two feet of cloth and five masu of rice in lieu of service.

For waiting-women in the Palace, let there be furnished the sisters or daughters of district officials of the rank of Shorei or upwards - good-looking women [with one male and two female servants to attend on them], and let 100 houses be allotted to provide rations for one waiting-woman. The cloth and rice supplied in lieu of service shall, in every case, follow the same rule as for servants."

COMPLAINTS AND JUSTICE
2nd month, 1st day.
The Emperor proceeded to the Eastern Gate of the Palace, where, by Soga, Oho-omi of the Right, he decreed as follows:

"The God Incarnate, the Emperor Yamato-neko, who rules the world, gives command to the Ministers assembled in his presence, to the Omi, Muraji, Kuni no Miyakko, Tomo no Miyakko, and subjects of various classes, saying, 'We are informed that wise rulers of the people hung a bell at their gate, and so took cognizance of the complaints of their subjects; they erected buildings in the thoroughfares, where they listened to the censures of the passers-by. Even the opinions of the grass and firewood gatherers they inquired personally and used for their guidance. We therefore, on a former occasion, made an edict, saying: "In ancient times the Empire was ruled by having at the Court flags of honour for the encouragement of good, and a board of censure, the object being to diffuse principles of Government and to invite remonstrances." All this served widely to ascertain the opinions of those below...

The object of hanging up a bell, of providing a box, and of appointing a man to receive petitions, is to make those who have grievances or remonstrances deposit their petitions in the box. The receivers of petitions are commanded to make their report to Us every morning. When We receive this report We shall draw the attention of the Ministers to it, and cause them to consider it, and We trust that this may be done without delay. But if there should be neglect on the part of the Ministers, and a want of diligence or partisan intrigues, and if We, moreover, should refuse to listen to remonstrance, let the complainant strike the bell. There has been already an Imperial command to this effect. But some time afterwards there was a man of intelligence and uprightness who, cherishing in his heart the spirit of a national patriot, addressed Us a memorial of earnest remonstrance, which he placed in the box prepared for the purpose. We therefore now publish it to the black-haired people here assembled. This memorial runs as follows: "Those subjects who come to the capital in connection with the discharge of their duty to the Government of the Country, are detained by the various public functionaries and put to forced labor of various kinds, etc." We are still moved with strong sympathy by this. How could the people expect that things would come to this? Now no long time has elapsed since the capital was removed, so that so far from being at home, we are, as it were, strangers. It is therefore impossible to avoid employing the people, and they have therefore been, against Our will, compelled to labor. As often as Our minds dwell on this We have never been able to sleep in peace. When We saw this memorial we could not refrain from a joyous exclamation. We have accordingly complied with the language of remonstrance, and have put a stop to the forced services at various places.

In a former edict, we said, "Let the man who remonstrates sign his name." Those who disobey this injunction are doubtless actuated by a wish to serve their country, and not by a desire of personal gain. Whether a man signs his name or not, let him not fail to remonstrate with Us on Our neglect or forgetfulness."

CENTRALIZED GOVERNMENT AND SOCIAL RULES
20th day.

The Prince Imperial said,

"In Heaven there are not two suns: in a country there are not two rulers. 1t is therefore the Emperor alone who is supreme over all the Empire, and who has a right to the services of the myriad people.

22nd day.

The Emperor made a decree, as follows,

"We are informed that a Prince of the Western Land admonished his people, saying, 'Those who made interments in ancient times resorted to a high ground which they formed into a tomb. They did not pile up a mound, nor did they plant trees. The inner and outer coffin were merely enough to last till the bones decayed, the shroud was merely sufficient to last till the flesh decayed... Deposit not in them gold or silver or copper or iron, and let earthenware objects alone represent the clay chariots and straw figures of antiquity. Let the interstices of the coffin be varnished. Let the offerings consist of rice presented three times, and let not pearls or jewels be placed in the mouth of the deceased. Bestow not jewel-shirts or jade armour. All these things are practices of the unenlightened vulgar...' Of late, the poverty of our people is absolutely owing to the construction of tombs...

When a man dies, there have been cases of people sacrificing themselves by strangulation, or of strangling others by way of sacrifice, or of compelling the dead man's horse to be sacrificed, or of burying valuables in the grave in honour of the dead, or of cutting off the hair, and stabbing the thighs and pronouncing an eulogy on the dead (while in this condition). Let all such old customs be entirely discontinued.

A certain book says, 'No gold or silver, no silk brocades, and no coloured stuffs are to be buried.' Again it is said, 'From the Ministers of all ranks down to the common people, it is not allowed to use gold or silver...'

Again, there are many cases of persons who, having seen, say that they have not seen, or who, having not seen, say that they have seen, or who, having heard, say that they have not heard, or who, having not heard, say that they have heard, being deliberate liars, and devoid of truth in words and in sight.

Again, there have been many cases in which slaves, both male and female, false to their masters in their poverty, betake themselves of their own accord to influential houses in quest of a livelihood, which influential houses forcibly detain and purchase them, and do not send them to their original owners.

Again, there have been very many cases in which wives or concubines, when dismissed by their husbands, have, after the lapse of years, married other husbands, as ordinary morality allows. Then their former husbands, after three or four years, have made greedy demands on the second husband's property, seeking their own gain.

Again, there have been very many cases in which men, relying on their power, have rudely demanded people's daughters in marriage. In the interval, however, before going to his house, the girl has, of her own accord, married another, and the rude suitor has angrily made demands of the property of both families for his own gain.

Again, there have been numerous cases of this kind. Sometimes a wife who has lost her husband marries another man after the lapse of ten or twenty years and becomes his spouse, or an unmarried girl is married for the first time. Upon this, people, out of envy of the married pair, have made them perform purgation.

Again, there are cases in which women, who have become men's wives and who, being put away owing to their husbands' dislike of them, have, in their mortification at this injury, compelled themselves to become blemished slaves.

Again, there are cases in which the husband, having frequent occasion to be jealous of his wife's illicit intercourse with others, voluntarily appeals to the authorities to decide the matter. Let such persons not lay their information until they have obtained, let us say, three credible witnesses to join with them in making a declaration. Why should they bring forward ill-considered plaints?

Again, there have been cases of men employed on forced labour in border lands who, when the work was over and they were returning to their village, have fallen suddenly ill and lain down to die by the roadside. Upon this the (inmates of the) houses by the roadside say, 'Why should people be allowed to die on our road?' And they have accordingly detained the companions of the deceased and compelled them to do purgation. For this reason it often happens that even if an elder brother lies down and dies on the road, his younger brother will refuse to take up his body (for burial).

Again, there are cases of peasants being drowned in a river. The bystanders say, 'Why should we be made to have anything to do with drowned men?' They accordingly detain the drowned man's companions and compel them to do purgation. For this reason it often happens that even when an elder brother is drowned in a river his younger brother will not render assistance.

Again, there are cases of people who, when employed on forced labor, cook their rice by the roadside. Upon this the (inmates of the) houses by the roadside say, 'Why should people cook rice at their own pleasure on our road?' and have compelled them to do purgation.

Again, there are cases when people have applied to others for the loan of pots in which to boil their rice, and the pots have knocked against something and have been upset. Upon this the owner of the pot compels purgation to be made.

All such practices are habitual among the unenlightened vulgar. Let them now be discontinued without exception, and not permitted again...

THE ROLE OF THE EMPEROR

Autumn, 8th month, 14th day.

An edict was issued, saying,

"Going back to the origin of things, we find that it is Heaven and Earth with the male and female principles of nature, which guard the four seasons from mutual confusion. We find, more over, that it is this Heaven and earth which produces the ten thousand things. Amongst these ten thousand things Man is the most miraculously gifted. Among the most miraculously gifted beings, the sage takes the position of ruler. Therefore the Sage Rulers, that is, the Emperors, take Heaven as their model in ruling the World, and never for a moment dismiss from their breasts the thought of how men shall gain their fit place..."

THE MONARCHY AND THE PEOPLE

Summer, 4th month, 29th day.

An edict was issued as follows,

"The Empire was entrusted (by the Sun-Goddess to her descendants, with the words) 'My children, in their capacity as Deities, shall rule it.' For this reason, this country, since Heaven and Earth began, has been a monarchy. From the time that Our Imperial ancestor first ruled the land, there has been great concord in the Empire, and there has never been any factiousness. In recent times, however, the names, first of the Gods, and then of the Emperors, have in some cases been separated (from their proper application) and converted into the Uji of Omi or Muraji, or they have been separated and made the qualifications of Miyakko, etc. In consequence of this, the minds of the people of the whole country take a strong partisan bias, and conceiving a deep sense of the "me" and "you," hold firmly each to their names. Moreover the feeble and incompetent Omi, Muraji, Tomo no Miyakko and Kuni no Miyakko make of such names their family names; and so the names of Gods and the names of sovereigns are applied to persons and places in an unauthorized manner, in accordance with the bent of their own feelings. Now, by using the names of Gods and the names of sovereigns as bribes, they draw to themselves the slaves of others, and so bring dishonor upon unspotted names.

The consequence is that the minds of the people have become unsettled and the government of the country cannot be carried on. The duty has therefore now devolved on Us in Our capacity as Celestial Divinity, to regulate and settle these things. In order to make them understood, and thereby to order the State and to order the people, we shall issue, one after another, a succession of edicts, one earlier, another later, one to-day and another to-morrow. But the people, who have always trusted in the civilizing influence exercised by the Emperors, and who are used to old customs, will certainly find it hard to wait until these edicts are made. We shall therefore remit to all, from Princes and Ministers down to the common people of all classes, the tax in lieu of service."

Reading and Discussion Questions

1. The "Edicts" begin with a reference to the transmission of Buddhism to Japan from "Pekche," which means the Korean kingdom of Paekche. What do these Edicts, therefore, reveal about the relationship between Japan and Korea?
2. According to the "Edicts," in what ways will the state support Buddhism in Japan?
3. How much authority does the Japanese emperor have over what his subjects can do and believe? How much authority do women have?

13.3   A Korean Foundation Myth

Many foundation myths around the world link a dynasty or nation's founder to the divine or magical. The foundation myth of Korea is no exception. Korean mythology dates Tangun to the year 2333 B.C.E., when it is said he became the first ruler of Korea, known then as Choson. Chronologically, this was before the peninsula was divided into the "Three Kingdoms" and thus refers to a unified Korean kingdom. Records from Zhou China refer to this state, although Chinese records enable us to date it to only 1000 B.C.E. Because there was at that time (c. 1000 B.C.E.) no written Korean language, historians have to rely on either Korean myths such as this one or on records from neighboring states, particularly China. However, the Chinese sources have inherent problems, as the relationship between China and Korea has often been fraught with tension. The version here is from the thirteenth century.

Source: "Tangun: Founder of Choson," from *Anthology of Korean Literature: From Early Times to the Nineteenth Century*, ed. Peter H. Lee. (Honolulu: University Press of Hawaii, 1981), 4

Once upon a time, Heavenly God, Hwan-in, noticed that one of his sons, Hwan-woong, always had his heart set on the world of mortals below. God looked down upon it and found the Samwi-Taebaekmountain the most befitting place for human beings to live.

He gave his son three Cheon Bu-In (God-given seals of king) and let him go down to the earth to rule over the human beings. (Here, we can see the same name of "Cheon Bu-In" and "Cheon Bu Gyeong". So some scholars guess, the Cheon Bu-In of the myth might refer to Cheon Bu Gyeong in real history.)

Hwan-woong, with three thousand subordinates, took leave of his father and came down to the human world and held his ground under the Shindan-soo(sandalwood used to make an alter for God) on top of the Taebaek mountain. He named the place Shin-Si (divine city) and he had himself called Hwan-woong Cheon-wang (Divine king Hwan-woong). He gave people their first lessons in right living and ruled over them, taking care of human affairs of as many as three hundred sixty kinds, such as farming, death, disease, punishment and good and evil, with the three goods of Poong-baek(wind), Woo-sa (rain) and Woon-sa (cloud) under his command.

At this time it so happened that a bear and a tiger were living together in a cave. They always prayed to Divine king Hwan-woong that they be made human beings. Taking notice of their admirable wish, the divine king gave them a bundle of sacred mugworts and twenty cloves of garlic and said, "If you eat these and do not see sunlight for one hundred days you will become human beings."

The bear and the tiger immediately began to practice abstinence, living on the mugworts and garlics in cave. After twenty one days the bear became a woman, but the tiger, unable to endure the abstinence, violated the injunction of the divine king, and failed to become a human being.

Now the woman could not find any man to marry her, so she always prayed under the sandalwood to be given a child of her own. Hwan-woongtok notice of her prayer, transformed himself into a man temporarily and married her. She gave birth to a son, who was to be Tangun-Wanggeum (Kin Wanggeum of Sandalwood).

Wanggeum succeeded Hwan-woong as king. He selected Pyongyang as his capital and named the country to Asadal at the Baekakmountain and reigned over the country for a thousand and five hundred years.

Reading and Discussion Question:

1.   By the time this text was transmitted orally, and then later written down, Korea had been under either the authority or the influence of China. What evidence of that domination by China is there is this source?

2. In Korean tradition, bears represent endurance. Why does Hwanung decide to lie with her to give birth to a son?
3. What is the significance of the plants mentioned by name in the story?
4. What do you think the tiger symbolizes?

13.4 Yi Kyu-bo on Personal Piety (Korea)

Unlike the previous source about Korea, this short essay is much more personal. Influence from Chinese Confucianism and Daoism abound, although they are not mentioned by name in the essay. The author was Yi Kyu-bo (1168 – 1241), a poet, essayist, and critic in the Koryo kingdom. He was also a high-ranking civil servant, who passed the civil-service examination required for government service. The life of Yi Kyu-bo reflects the extent to which Koryo modeled itself on Tang/Song China. Yi Kyu-bo studied and wrote in Chinese, worked in a state organized along Confucian principles, and created literary works that were infused with Confucian and Daoist principles.

Source: Yi Kyu-bo. "On Demolishing the Earthen Chamber," from *Anthology of Korean Literature: From Early Times to the Nineteenth Century*, ed. Peter H. Lee. (Honolulu: University Press of Hawaii, 1981), 61-62.

ON DEMOLISHING THE EARTHEN CHAMBER

On the first day of the tenth month, I came home and saw my sons digging a hole in the earthand building a hut like a grave' I feigned stupidity and asked, "Why are you digging a grave within the pre - mises of the house? "

They replied, "It is not a grave, but an earthen chamber".
"Why have you made it?" I asked.
"It is good to store flowers and melons during the winter," they replied. "Womenfolk may come here and do their spinning and weaving without their hands getting chilled and chapped, even in winter it will be as warm as spring here.

I grew doubly angry and said, "That it is hot in summer and cold in winter is the regular course of the four seasons if the opposite comes about, it will be strange and uncanny. The ancient sages taught man to wear fur garments in winter and hemp in summer. This is sufficient for our needs. Building an earthen chamber to turn cold into heat is to resist the ordinances of heaven. In addition, it is inauspicious for men to dwell in holes in winter like, snakes or toads. As for spinning and weaving, a proper season is set aside for them. Why should they be done in winter? Also, it is natural for flowers to bloom in the spring and fade in winter. If we reverse the process we will surely go astray. To grow unseasonable things for untimely

pleasure is to usurp the prerogative of Heaven. All this is not
what I intend if you don't destroy the earthen chamber at once, you
will not be forgiven and will receive a good flogging from me. "
My sons feared my anger and leveled the earthen chamber and
Made its lumber into firewood. Only then was my mind at peace.

Reading and Discussion Questions

1. Although the sons correct the speaker when he calls the hole they are digging a grave, how is it a meta-phoric grave for him after all?
2. How are the admonitions of the main speaker against the earthen chamber Confucian? Are there any elements that can be identified as Daoist?
3. What does "Heaven" mean to Yi Kyu-bo? What is the extent and the limit of Heaven's power?

———

Patterns of State Formation in Africa

Chapter 14

600 – 1450 C.E.

The sources in this chapter illustrate the diversity of states that developed in sub-Saharan Africa from the seventh century to the fifteenth. These were all kingdoms and states that developed indigenously in Africa, and during this particular period of time (before Europeans arrived) the stories of their development reveal the richness of native African traditions of statehood. However, Africa was not isolated from other regions and cultures during this time period, and the sources in this chapter also explore how native African traditions mix with influences from elsewhere, particularly religious influences.

One of the themes of African history in this period is the expansion of both Islam and Christianity, and at times, competition between the two. In East Africa, there was a long tradition of strong Christian states, beginning with Aksum in the fourth century (see Chapter 6). The Solomonids were successors to Aksum, taking over the region known today as Ethiopia in 1270. Tracing their lineage back to King Solomon of the Israel, the Solomonids not only created a strong state that survived for centuries (until the twentieth century in fact) but also one that created some of the earliest written historical narratives. In Amda Seyon, a fourteenth century Solomonid king, Christian Ethiopians found a strong leader who expanded the boundaries of his state, particularly at the expense of nearby Muslim groups.

Shortly before Amda Seyon came to power, the Solomonids sent an embassy to Italy, to establish relations between themselves and the Christians of the west, by passing the Coptic church of Egypt, which was under the authority of Muslim rulers. In doing so, the Ethiopians revived the European legend of Prester John. A mythic ruler of India converted to Christianity by the apostle Thomas, Prester John's kingdom shifted with expanding European knowledge of the world beyond its borders. The Crusades brought more sub-Saharan Africa to the attention of Europe, who shifted the legend of Prester John, and an enclave of Christianity, to that region.

In reality, of course, one was more likely to find Muslims than Christians in sub-Saharan Africa, although it too remained a minority religion throughout the region during this time period. There were two areas were Islam was the most successful at then; the East African coast, and the West Central African Saharan trade routes. In East Africa, the Swahili city-states along the coast were early converts to Islam, and linked Africa to the Middle East and Asia via the Indian Ocean trade networks. But even here there were limits, and Islam hugged the coast. In the interior native animist practices remained.

In West Central Africa, the Soninke people created the first sub-Saharan kingdom at Ghana in the early 600s. The Soninke used their wealth from dominating the trans-Saharan trade in gold; they controlled various groups on the Inland Delta of the Niger River in the Sahel. Because of their contact with other trade merchants in North Africa, they were introduced to Islam and gradually converted (beginning with the merchant class). But the main source of gold for the trade shifted in the twelfth century to the rainforests west of Ghana, and power shifted to a new people, the Malinke, who founded the state of Mali. The final two sources of this chapter, one from the great 14h century traveler, Ibn Battuta, and the second from the *Sundiata*, the founding epic of the Mandingo, provide a picture of Mali and Ghana during this period.

14.1   *The Glorious Victories of Amda Seyon, King of Ethiopia*

Amda Seyon was a fourteenth century king of the Solomonid Dynasty, which ruled Ethiopia from 1270 until 1974. The name of the dynasty, Solomonid, derives from the Ethiopian belief that the kings of Aksum (whom the Solomonids believed were their ancestors) were descended from King Solomon of Israel and the Queen of Sheba. The kings of Aksum and the later Solomonids were Christian, and their king Amda Seyon, led them into warfare in 1329 against Muslims in the neighboring state of Ifat (in north-east Ethiopia). The Solomonids also fought against other neighboring states, including Christians and animists; however, *the Glorious Victories of Amda Seyon*, portrays the war between the Solomonids and Ifat as a religious war between Christians and Muslims. The following excerpt features the king encouraging his army to fight on, paraphrasing the book of Psalms in the process.

Source: *The Glorious Victories of Amda Seyon, King of Ethiopia,* trans. and ed. G. W. B. Huntingford. (Oxford: Oxford University Press, 1965), 67, 69-71.

….At this time Gemaldin the king of the Moslems came to the king with many gifts and said, 'I pray you, O king, return to your capital, since you have appointed me your (ruler), and I will do your will. For behold, the land of the Moslems is now ruined. Leave what remains (in) the country and do not ravage it again, that they may work for you by trading, because I and all the Moslem peoples are your slaves.' The king answered him angrily, saying,'It is not when I am bitten by hyenas and dogs, sons of vipers and children of evil which trust not in the Son ofGod, that I return to my capital; and if I return before I have ravaged the land of Adal, may I become like her who bore me, my mother; may I not be called a man but may I be called a woman.'

After this the king went to another place (where) he called together his whole army, and on the 28th day of Sane addressed the assembly thus: 'In the east, in the west, in the north, in the south, in Tigre, in Guajam, in Waggard, in Damot, in Hadya, in all (the places) where we have fought, have we not conquered through the power of God, killed (our enemies), and taken prisoner the survivors, great and small, including their rulers? Now be not afraid in face of the rebels; be not divided, for God is fighting for us. And if they come against you with the bow and spear, you (also) have the bow and spear. Have you not heard what these Moslem rebels who not Christ say against the anointed of God: "When the Christians kill us we become martyrs, and when we kill the Christians we gain paradise"? Thus do the rebel Moslems speak, who have no hope of salvation and are (yet) eager to die. Why then do you fear the rebels, you who know the Father, the Son, and the Holy Spirit, who are baptized in His name, and are sanctified by the Blood? For long you have made yourselves ready to fight for me; now be ready to fight for Christ, as it is said in the Book of Canons, "Slay the infidels and renegades with the sword of iron, and draw the sword on behalf of the perfect faith." Gird on then your swords, make ready your hearts, and be not fearful in spirit, but be valiant and put your trust in God, as says the Book of Psalms in Psalm " God have I put mv trust; I shall not fear what living man can do to me. God will help me and I shall see mine enemies."And again it says, "All peoples surround me, but in the name of God I have defeated them."And speaking with indignation the king declared to his army, 'You have left your courage behind you, but (now) put it in front of you, and cast away fear from among you. As for me, I have sworn by the living God, the creator of heaven and earth, that whether there is rain or whether there is drought I will not return to my capital till I have destroyed the rebels through the power of Jesus Christ my Lord, the Son of God. And whether we die or whether we live, we are in (the care of) God. I have strengthened my heart in Christ….

Reading and Discussion Questions

1. What does the quoting of Psalms reveal about the textual history of the Solomonids?
2. What reasons does Amda Seyon give to his army to justify fighting the Muslims? Are his reasons religious, political, or some combination of the two?
3. From this excerpt, what is the role of the king in the Solomonid state? How much power does he have and what is the nature of that power?

14.2 The Swahili Saga of Liyongo Fumo

Liyongo is the trickster-hero of a several East Africa tales, which were transmitted orally and eventually written down in the nineteenth century. They may have been told as early as the tenth century. They represent the intersection between the Islamicized Swahili culture along the East African coast in what is today Kenya and Tanzania, with the native animist cultures closer to the interior. The conversion of East Africans to Islam began quite early, and by the seventh century there were already Swahili trade centers and ports. However, the animists of the interior continue to practice their beliefs until the modern era.

In this excerpt, Liyongo travels to meet the Sultan of Pate, an island off the coast of Kenya. It is literally a meeting of animist traditions, represented by Liyongo, and Islam, represented by the Sultan.

Source: Alice Werner, *The Swahili Saga of Liongo Fumo* (1926)

Liyongo was the son of a king, and extraordinarily talented. His strength was legendary, his skill with the bow was great, and he was a gifted poet. But he did not become king. His mother was a secondary wife, and so his brother Mringwari, born of the principal wife, became the ruler of Shaha instead. The two brothers eventually quarreled, and Liyongo went into exile.

It was most probably before this period of exile that emissaries from the Oromo peoples along the Somali coast came to visit the Sultan of Pate. While they were waiting for their audience they heard people speak of the prowess of Liyongo. They asked the Sultan about Liyongo, and the Sultan sent for him. Liyongo saidhe would come immediately, and he packed a bag with those items he considered necessary. He also hung three great horns about him. Then he set off. The trip that had taken the messengerstwo days he made in half a day, and he arrived at the edge of the town in mid-afternoon. He took one of his three horns and blew such a mighty blast that the horn split in half. In the Sultan's court, the Oromo visitors were startled and asked what the sound had been. The Sultan told them that no doubt Liyongo was on the outskirts of the town. Soon, a second blast from a horn (and again, the horn broke in two) told them thatLiyongo had come to the city gates, and a third announced that he had arrived at the Sultan's palace.

He was quickly admitted and brought before the Sultan and his guests. There, he emptied the bag he had brought from his home: a mortar, a pestle, a large sack of grain to pound, a large iron pot, the three stones upon which to rest the pot, and for good measure a small millstone. The Oromo visitors were amazed at the proof of his strength, and said to themselves that they must form an alliance with such a man, for his strength and his appearance convinced them that he was also a great warrior. So they asked the Sultan to serve as their intermediary, and he negotiated a marriage settlement. When the Oromo returned to their home, Liyongo accompanied them, and there nourished the woman they had chosen for him. She quickly became pregnant, and in due time she gave birth to a son. As the boy grew, everyone agreed that he resembled his father in appearance and in strength.

But Liyongo returned to his home before the boy was grown, and his return caused trouble. His brother Mringwari was very popular as a ruler people admired Liyongo for his skills, but did not trust his judgment - but he found so extraordinary a brother a challenge. Liyongo also may have shown signs of ambition, since he counted the Sultan of Pate and the clans of the Oromo as his allies. At any rate, Liyongo left his home. But he could not go to Pate - he had managed to make an enemy of the Sultan as well, somehow. So he took refuge on the mainland, living with groups of hunters in the bush. Word came to the hunters that there was a price on Liyongo's head, and they were tempted by the thought of wealth. But they did not dare to attack Liyongo openly, because they knew that he would kill them all without a second thought. So they devised a trick. On the pretext of a meal during which each guest took it in turn to climb a palm tree that had an edible nut, they planned to have him climb the tree and to kill him while he was unarmed and relatively helpless at the top of the trunk. But Liyongo avoided the trap. So then it was his turn to bring down the nuts for the meal, he took his bow and arrows and simply shot the nuts down from the tree.

He understood that he was not safe with the hunters any more, and so he returned in hiding to live with his mother on the island of Pate. There the Sultan's men caught him and put him in prison. He was held for a time, and his mother learned where he was jailed. She prepared food and sent it to him with her slave-girl. Little of the food reached him - the guards would take the choice portions and leave him the coarse bread and perhaps some gruel.

The Sultan then announced that Liyongo was to be killed, and asked him if he had a last request. Liyongo asked that they provide the music for a marriage ceremony at the time of his execution, for he had composed several well-known marriage songs.

Then Liyongo taught his mother's slave-girl a new song: the song told his mother to prepare food for him, and to place a metal file into the loaf of coarse bread.

The message reached his mother, and the file reached Liyongo. The night before his execution, the town began the wedding celebration he had requested, with lots of drumming and loud singing. The noise masked the sounds that Liyongo made as he cut through the iron bars of the window with the file. In this way, he escaped.

Other attempts to kill him failed, and the Sultan became convinced that Liyongo had magical protection. He remembered the son Liyongo had fathered among the Oromo, and had the lad brought to Pate. There the Sultan won the boy over with the promise of wealth and a good marriage, if only the boy could help him get rid of his father, who had become an outlaw troubling the kingdom. The boy was convinced. The youth left Pate and went to the town on the mainland where his father was living in exile. He explained who he was, and Liyongo was delighted that his son had come to join him. Over time, the youth won his father's confidence, and discovered that the Sultan had indeed been correct: Liyongo was protected by magic, and ordinary weapons would not harm him. But he was vulnerable. Eventually, Liyongo revealed that a copper spike could pierce his navel and kill him. Even as he revealed this information to his son, Liyongo showed his suspicion: he told the boy that the information would not do him any good, and that if he attempted to betray his father he would have a bitter reward.

The son acquired a copper spike, and one day, summoning all his resolution, approached his father, who was sleeping soundly after the noonday meal. He drove the spike into Liyongo's belly and then fled. Liyongo felt the wound, and rose to his feet. He took his weapons and strode towards the town nearby.

When he reached the well at the edge of town, where the women used to come and fetch the drinking and cooking water, he knelt down on one knee and drew his bow until the arrow's head touched the bow. There he remained, ready to shoot but motionless, for he had died.

Later in the afternoon, the women came from the town to get their water for evening use. They saw Liyongo, his bow drawn, an arrow ready to shoot, and they quickly turned back. They told the townspeople that Liyongo had set himself up by the well, and that he was ready to kill the first person to approach it. For two days no one dared go near the well, and the entire town began to suffer from thirst. Finally, Liyongo's mother determined to approach her son and to learn the reason why he was keeping the people of the town from their water. When she got close to him, she realized he was dead. He is buried in Kipini.

As Liyongo had foretold, his son did not profit from the treason. The Sultan of Pate turned him out, since he had betrayed his father. He returned to his mother's people, but they were disgusted by his deed and refused to welcome him back. He died in misery.

Reading and Discussion Questions

1. What do the items that Liyongo carried in his bag represent? Why are they so important that he wants to display them before the Sultan?
2. What is the function of the Oromo people in the story?
3. Is there any evidence that the final version of this story was preserved by Muslim Swahilis?
4. What does Liyongo's story tell us about the roles of women in this period?

14.3 Ibn Battuta on Mali

One of the great world travelers of all time, Ibn Battuta was an educated Moroccan who journeyed throughout Africa, the Middle East, Persia, and Asia. In 1354, at age fifty, Ibn Battuta dictated an account of his travels, the *Rihla* (*The Journey*), to Ibn Juzayy, a court secretary in Morocco. Both men therefore had a role in shaping the narrative.

Source: Ibn Battuta, "Mali," from *Travels in Asia and Africa, 1325-1354,* trans. and ed. by H. A. R. Gibb. (New York: Robert M. McBride & Company, 1929), 323-327, 329-330.

I set out on the 1st Muharram of the year seven hundred and fifty-three (18 February, 1352 C.E.) with a caravan including amongst others a number of the merchants of Sijilmasa [present day Morocco/Algerian frontier region]. After twenty-five days we reached Taghaza, an unattractive village, with the curious feature that its houses and mosques are built of blocks of salt, roofed with camel skins. There are no trees there, nothing but sand. In the sand is a salt mine; they dig for the salt, and find it in thick slabs, lying one on top of the other, as though they had been tool-squared and laid under the surface of the earth. A camel will carry two of these slabs. No one lives at Taghaza except the slaves of the Masufa tribe, who dig for the salt; they subsist on dates imported from Dara and Sijilmasa [Morocco], camel's flesh, and millet imported from the Negro-lands. The Negroes come up from their country and take away the salt from there. At Walata a load of salt brings eight to ten mithqals; in the town of Mali it sells for twenty to thirty, and sometimes as much as forty. The Negroes use salt as a medium of exchange, just as gold and silver is used elsewhere; they cut it up into pieces and buy and sell with it. The business done at Taghaza, for all its meanness, amounts to an enormous figure in terms of hundredweights of gold dust...

Thus we reached the town of Walata after a journey of two months to a day. Walata is the northernmost province of the Negroes, and the Sultan's representative there was one FarbaHusayn, Farba meaning deputy (in their language)...

... It was an excessively hot place, and boasts a few small date-palms, in the shade of which they sow watermelons. Its water comes from underground water beds at that point, and there is plenty of mutton to be had.

The garments of the inhabitants, most of whom belong to the Masufa tribe, are of fine Egyptian fabrics. Their women are of surpassing beauty, and are shown more respect than the men. The state of affairs amongst these people is indeed extraordinary. Their men show no sign of jealousy whatever; no one claims descent from his father, but on the contrary from his mother's brother. A person's heirs are his sister's sons, not his own sons. This is a thing which I have seen nowhere in the world except among the Indians of Malabar. But those are heathens; these people are Muslims, punctilious in observing the hours of prayer, studying books of law, and memorizing the Koran. Yet their women show no bashfulness before men and do not veil themselves, though they are assiduous in attending prayers. Any man who wishes to marry one of them may do so, they do not travel with their husbands...

The women have their "friends" and "companions" amongst the men outside their own families, and the men in the same way have "companions" amongst the women of other families. A man may go into his house and find his wife entertaining her "companion," but he takes not objection to it. One day at Walata I went into the **qadi's** house, after asking his permission to enter, and found with a young woman of remarkable beauty. When I saw her I was shocked and turned to go out, but she laughed at me, instead of being overcome by shame, and the quadi said to me, "Why are you going out? She is my companion." I was amazed at their conduct, for he was a theologian and a pilgrim to boot. I was told that he had asked the sultan's permission to make the pilgrimage that year with his "companion" (whether this one or not I cannot say) but the sultan would not grant it.

....On feast-days, after Dugha [interpreter] has finished his display, the poets come in. Each of them is inside a figure resembling a thrush, made of feathers, and provided with a wooden head with a red beak, to look like a thrush's head. They stand in front of the sultan in this ridiculous make-up and recite their poems. I was told that their poetry is a kind of sermonizing in which they say to the sultan: "This pempi [throne] which you occupy was that whereon sat this king and that king, and such were this one's noble actions and such and such the other's. So do you too do good deeds whose memory will outlive you." After that the chief of the poets mounts the steps of the pempi and lays hid head on the sultan's lap, then climbs to the top of the pempi and lays his head on first on the sultan's right shoulder and then on his left, speaking all the while in their tongue, and finally he comes down again. I was told that this practice is a very old custom amongst them prior to the introduction of Islam, and they have kept it up.

...The Negroes possess some admirable qualities. They are seldom unjust, and have a greater abhorrence of injustice than any other people. The sultan shows no mercy to anyone who is guilty of the least act of it. There is a complete security in their country. Neither traveler nor inhabitant in it has anything to fear from robbers or men of violence. They do not confiscate the property of any white man [Arab trader] who dies in their country, even if it be accounted wealth. On the contrary, they give it into the charge of some trustworthy person among the whites, until the rightful heir takes possession of it. They are careful to observe the hours of prayer, and assiduous in attending them in congregations, and in bringing up their children to them. On Fridays, if a man does not go early to the mosque, he cannot find a corner to pray in, on account of the crowd. It is a custom of theirs to send each man his boy (to the mosque) with his prayer-mat; the boy spreads it out for his master in a place befitting him and remains on it (until his master comes to the mosque). The pray-mats are made of the leaves of a tree resembling a date-palm, but without fruit.

Another of their good qualities is their habit of wearing clean white garments on Fridays. Even if a man has nothing but an old worn shirt, he washes it and cleans it, and wears it at the Friday service. Yet another is their zeal for learning the Koran by heart. They put their children in chains if they show any backwardness in

---

qadi: a Muslim judge

memorizing it, and they are not set free until they have it by heart. I visited the qadi in his house on the day of the festival. His children were chained up, so I said to him, "Will you not let them loose?" He replied, "I shall not do so until they learn the Koran by heart." Among their bad qualities are the following. The women servants, slave-girls, and young girls go about in front of everyone naked, without a stitch of clothing on them. Women go into the sultan's presence naked and without coverings, and his daughters also go about naked. Then there is the custom of their putting dust and ashes on their heads as a mark of respect, and the grotesque ceremonies we have described when the poets recite their verses.

Reading and Discussion Questions

1. Ibn Battuta describes Mali as the capital of the king of the blacks. Is there anything we would describe as racist about his description of the people of Mali?
2. Why does Ibn Battuta remark so often on the lack of generosity on the part of the sultan of Mali?
3. Ibn Battuta offers many details about the material culture of Mali. What does his description reveal about the interactions between Mali and other cultures? How do they interact?
4. What is idiosyncratically Malian about how the people of Mali practice Islam?

14.4 The *Epic of Sundiata*

The Epic of Sundiata is a foundation myth, handed down orally for centuries by "griots" or stoytellers. The epic tells of the origins of the Mandingo or Malinke peoples, of the kingdom of Mali. Sundiata was a historically real figure, born in c. 1217 and died in 1255, who led the Malinke to overthrow the Soninke kings of Ghana and take over the gold trade that brought gold from the Sahel across the Sahara into North Africa. As with the founding of Ghana, Mali began as a state with Islam at the top, and native animist practices below. Sundiata, as with Dinga of Ghana, claimed to be descended from Bilal, therefore linking the royal family with someone personally close to Muhammad. Mali emphasized its Islamic beliefs more than Ghana had, and the capital of Mali at Timbuktu became a center of Islamic scholarship from the fourteenth century onward.

The excerpts below contain a fascinating description of palace intrigue in the capital city of Niani. Sundiatae-merges as the central hero of the tale through magic, cunning, strength and providence. He becomes a great king noted for his Muslim piety, wisdom, justice and military strength. Sundiata is still regarded by the Mandingo as their national hero.

Source: D.T. Niane ed. and trans. *Sundiata: An Epic of Old Mali* (Harlow: Longman, 1966)

Soumaoro sent a detachment under his son Sosso Balla to block Sundiata's route to Tabon. Sosso Balla was about the same age as Sundiata. He promptly deployed his troops at the entrance to the mountains to oppose Sundiata's advance to Tabon. . . .

Sundiata was immovable, so the orders were given and the war drums began to beat. On his proud horse Sundiata turned to right and left in front of his troops. He entrusted the rearguard, composed of a part of the Wagadou cavalry, to his younger brother Manding Bory. Having drawn his sword, Sundiata led the charge, shouting his war cry.

The Sossos were surprised by this sudden attack for they all thought that the battle would be joined the next day. The lightning that flashes across the sky is slower, the thunderbolts less frightening and floodwaters less surprising than Sundiata swooping down on Sosso Balla and his smiths. In a trice, Sundiata was in the middle of the Sossos like a lion in the sheepfold. The Sossos, trampled under the hooves of his fiery charger, cried out. When he turned to the right the smiths of Soumaoro fell in their tens, and when he turned to the left his sword made heads fall as when someone shakes a tree of ripe fruit. The horsemen of Mema wrought a frightful slaughter and their long lances pierced flesh like a knife sunk into a paw-paw. Charging ever forwards, Sundiata looked for Sosso Balla; he caught sight of him and like a lion bounded towards the son of Soumaoro, his sword held aloft. His arm came sweeping down but at that moment a Sosso warrior came between Djata and Sosso Balla and was sliced like a calabash. Sosso Balla did not wait and disappeared from amidst his smiths. Seeing their chief in flight, the Sossos gave way and fell into a terrible rout. . . .

The news of the battle of Tabon spread like wildfire in the plains of Mali. It was known that Soumaoro was not present at the battle, but the mere fact that his troops had retreated before Sundiata sufficed to give hope to all the peoples of Mali. Soumaoro realized that from now on he would have to reckon with this young man. He got to know of the prophecies of Mali, yet he was still too confident. When Sosso Balla returned with the remnant he had managed to save at Tabon, he said to his father, 'Father, he is worse than a lion; nothing can withstand him.'. . .

The son of Sogolon had already decided on his plan of campaign – to beat Soumaoro, destroy Sosso and return triumphantly to Niani. He now had five army corps at his disposal. . . .

Sundiata caught sight of him and tried to cut a passage through to him. He struck to the right and struck to the left and trampled underfoot. The murderous hooves of his 'Daffeké' dug into the chests of the Sossos. Soumaoro was now within spear range and Sundiata reared up his horse and hurled his weapon. It whistled away and bounced off Soumaoro's chest as off a rock and fell to the ground. Sogolon's son bent his bow but with a motion of the hand Soumaoro caught the arrow in flight and showed it to Sundiata as if to say 'Look, I am invulnerable.'

Furious, Sundiata snatched up his spear and with his head bent charged at Soumaoro, but as he raised his arm to strike his enemy he noticed that Soumaoro had disappeared. Manding Bory riding at his side pointed to the hill and said, 'Look, brother.'

Sundiata saw Soumaoro on the hill, sitting on his black-coated horse. How could he have done it, he who was only two paces from Sundiata? By what power had he spirited himself away on to the hill? The son of Sogolon stopped fighting to watch the king of Sosso. The sun was already very low and Soumaoro's smiths gave way but Sundiata did not give the order to pursue the enemy. Suddenly, Soumaoro disappeared! . . .

The battle of Neguéboria showed Djata, if he needed to be shown, that to beat the king of Sosso other weapons were necessary.

The evening of Neguéboria, Sundiata was master of the field, but he was in a gloomy mood. He went away from the field of battle with its agonized cries of the wounded, and Manding Bory and TabonWana watched him go. He headed for the hill where he had seen Soumaoro after his miraculous disappearance. . . .

But it was time to return to his native Mali. Sundiata assembled his army in the plain and each people provided a contingent to accompany the Mansa to Niani. . . .

Sundiata and his men had to cross the Niger in order to enter old Mali. One might have thought that all the dug-out canoes in the world had arranged to meet at the port of Ka-ba. It was the dry season and there was not much water in the river. The fishing tribe of Somono, to whom Djata had given the monopoly of the water, were bent on expressing their thanks to the son of Sogolon. They put all their dug-outs side by side across the Niger so that Sundiata's sofas could cross without wetting their feet.

When the whole army was on the other side of the river, Sundiata ordered great sacrifices. A hundred oxen and a hundred rams were sacrificed. It was thus that Sundiata thanked God on returning to Mali.

The villages of Mali gave Maghan Sundiata an unprecedented welcome. At normal times a traveller on foot can cover the distance from Ka-ba to Niani with only two halts, but Sogolon's son with his army took three days. The road to Mali from the river was flanked by a double human hedge. Flocking from every corner of Mali, all the inhabitants were resolved to see their savior from close up. The women of Mali tried to create a sensation and they did not fail. At the entrance to each village they had carpeted the road with their multi-coloured cloths so that Sundiata's horse would not so much as dirty its feet on entering their village. . . .

Sundiata was leading the van. He had donned his costume of a hunter king – a plain smock, skin-tight trousers and his bow slung across his back. At his side BallaFasséké was still wearing his festive garments gleaming with gold. Between Djata's general staff and the army Sosso Balla had been placed, amid his father's fetishes. But his hands were no longer tied. As at Ka-ba, abuse was everywhere heaped upon him and the prisoner did not dare look up at the hostile crowd. . . .

The troops were marching along singing the 'Hymn to the Bow', which the crowd took up. New songs flew from mouth to mouth. Young women offered the soldiers cool water and cola nuts. And so the triumphal march across Mali ended outside Niani, Sundiata's city.

It was a ruined town which was beginning to be rebuilt by its inhabitants. A part of the ramparts had been destroyed and the charred walls still bore the marks of the fire. From the top of the hill Djata looked on Niani, which looked like a dead city. He saw the plain of Sounkarani, and he also saw the site of the young baobab tree. The survivors of the catastrophe were standing in rows on the Mali road. The children were waving branches, a few young women were singing, but the adults were mute. . . .

With Sundiata peace and happiness entered Niani. Lovingly Sogolon's son had his native city rebuilt. He restored in the ancient style his father's old enclosure where he had grown up. People came from all the villages of Mali to settle in Niani. The walls had to be destroyed to enlarge the town, and new quarters were built for each kin group in the enormous army. . . .

After a year Sundiata held a new assembly at Niani, but this one was the assembly of dignitaries and kings of the empire. The kings and notables of all the tribes came to Niani. The kings spoke of their administration and the dignitaries talked of their kings. Fakoli, the nephew of Soumaoro, having proved himself too independent, had to flee to evade the Mansa's anger. His lands were confiscated and the taxes of Sosso were payed directly into the granaries of Niani. In this way, every year, Sundiata gathered about him all the kings and notables; so justice prevailed everywhere, for the kings were afraid of being denounced at Niani.

Djata's justice spared nobody. He followed the very word of God. He protected the weak against the strong and people would make journeys lasting several days to come and demand justice of him. Under his sun the upright man was rewarded and the wicked one punished.

In their new-found peace the villages knew prosperity again, for with Sundiata happiness had come into everyone's home. Vast fields of millet, rice, cotton, indigo and **fonio** surrounded the villages. Whoever worked always had something to live on. Each year long caravans carried the taxes in kind to Niani.

You could go from village to village without fearing brigands. A thief would have his right hand chopped off and if he stole again he would be put to the sword.

New villages and new towns sprang up in Mali and elsewhere. 'Dyulas', or traders, became numerous and during the reign of Sundiata the world knew happiness.

There are some kings who are powerful through their military strength. Everybody trembles before them, but when they die nothing but ill is spoken of them. Others do neither good nor ill and when they die they are

---

fonio: a type of cultivated grain commonly found in West Africa

forgotten. Others are feared because they have power, but they know how to use it and they are loved because they love justice. Sundiata belonged to this group. He was feared, but loved as well. He was the father of Mali and gave the world peace. After him the world has not seen a greater conqueror, for he was the seventh and last conqueror. He had made the capital of an empire out of his father's village, and Niani became the navel of the earth. . . .

The griots, fine talkers that they were, used to boast of Niani and Mali saying: 'If you want salt, go to Niani, for Niani is the camping place of the Sahel caravans. If you want gold, go to Niani, for Bouré, Bambougou and Wagadou work for Niani. If you want fine cloth, go to Niani, for the Mecca road passes by Niani. If you want fish, go to Niani, for it is there that the fishermen of Maouti and Djenné come to sell their catches. If you want meat, go to Niani, the country of the great hunters, and the land of the ox and the sheep. If you want to see an army, go to Niani, for it [is] there that the united forces of Mali are to be found. If you want to see a great king, go to Niani, for it is there that the son of Sogolon lives, the man with two names.'. . .

After him many kings and many Mansas reigned over Mali and other towns sprang up and disappeared. Hajji Mansa Moussa, of illustrious memory, beloved of God, built houses at Mecca for pilgrims coming from Mali, but the towns which he founded have all disappeared, Karanina, Bouroun-Kouna – nothing more remains of these towns. Other kings carried Mali far beyond Djata's frontiers, for example Mansa Samanka and Fadi-maMoussa, but none of them came near Djata.

MaghanSundiata was unique. In his own time no one equalled him and after him no one had the ambition to surpass him. He left his mark on Mali for all time and his taboos still guide men in their conduct.

Mali is eternal. To convince yourself of what I have said go to Mali.

Reading and Discussion Questions

1. What are the chief characteristics of Sundiata?   What qualities of kingship does he display?
2. What is the function and importance of the griots in Mali?
3. Is there any evidence of Islamic belief in these excerpts?

The Rise of Empires in the Americas

Chapter 15

600-1550

At their peak from the thirteenth through fifteenth centuries, Native American empires comprised some of the largest political territories in the world. They possessed advanced irrigation technology, vast armies, and enormous cities that rivaled the size of similar empires in Eurasia. They excelled at astronomy, engineering, and perhaps above all, the creation of trading networks that spanned thousands of miles. Their governments also undertook sophisticated planning efforts that directed most aspects of their economy, especially the all-important crop of corn, or *maize*. Because of the hierarchical nature of their states, once an outsider successfully toppled the leadership, organization and control dissipated throughout the empire. Without supervision, irrigation channels dried up, crops died, trade ceased, and the people, weakened by malnutrition, succumbed to foreign disease.

Within the course of a century following European contact, the vast empires of the Americas collapsed. Some civilizations, such as the Mound Builders of North America and the Mayans of Central America, had already disappeared centuries before. Nearly all of the empires revolved around the centralized production of agriculture, notably corn, even though extensive trade of the crop and other goods existed beyond the reaches of a given empire. Religion also played a valuable role in solidifying Native American states, and religious activity often remained inseparable from politics.

All Native American states and empires fluctuated in size and influence, much like pre-modern European states. However, not all Native Americans lived in a large metropolis or engaged in intercontinental trade. A significant number, perhaps even a majority in North America, lived in small tribal units or states that covered only a few hundred square miles. These groups facilitated shifting alliances with other tribes or states, migrated across vast distances, and occasionally shifted the balance of power between competing, larger empires. They seldom developed large, centralized governments, but they did build villages and even cities, especially in parts of North America. In the Caribbean, tribal connections expanded into sophisticated social structures on only the largest islands. The following documents illustrate both the advances of the American empires as well as the strict forms of political organization that held them together.

15.1 The Founding of Tenochtitlán

According to legend, the god Huitzilpochtli led the Aztecs (Mexica) to a location where an eagle sat atop a prickly pear cactus (tenochtli) growing out of a rock and told them to build their capital there. This image now graces the Mexican flag. The first printed record of this scene appeared in 1541 in the Codex Mendoza, a pictorial history of the Aztecs prepared for the first viceroy of New Spain, Antonio Mendoza.

Reading and Discussion Questions
1. Why would the Spanish viceroy have requested a history of the Aztecs?
2. Compare Tenochtitlán's founding myth with ones from other cities around the world. What purpose do founding myths serve?

Photo courtesy of the Library of Congress.

15.2   Human Sacrifice by the Aztecs

To the Christian invaders, no Aztec practice was more deplorable than ritual human sacrifice. However when analyzing the past, it is difficult to screen out contemporary moral perspectives when dealing with multiple cultures over vast time spans. The Aztec believed supernatural forces needed human blood and beating hearts for sustenance. The practice, which always took place at the temple, was a highly ritualized affair. The image shown here is a detail from a mid-sixteenth century Spanish document.

Reading and Discussion Questions

1.   Consider why some societies practiced cannibalism. Consider both social and religious explanations.
2.   Does the fact that this source comes from after the Spanish conquest affect the way you approach it? Why or why not?
3.   How can you tell that the person who created this image likely never set foot in the Americas?

Photo courtesy of the Library of Congress.

15.3 Machu Picchu

The modern day photograph of Machu Picchu, listed as a World Heritage site by the United Nations, shows the ruins of an ancient capital of Inca civilization. Nestled high in the Andes Mountains, Machu Picchu's construction required advanced building techniques, a system of irrigation, and a considerable labor force.

Machu Picchu represents the peak of Inca civilization. Founded in the mid-1400s just before the Spanish arrived, the site was likely either a religious or political center for the Inca Empire. Building a city at such a high altitude and among such rocky terrain required considerable organizational and technological abilities, which often rivaled other contemporary civilizations. Its location also prevented significant outside contact and is why it remained largely unknown to most European explorers, who concentrated most of their efforts in lowland river basins and coastal plains. What happened to those who lived there still remains a mystery, but it is assumed the inhabitants succumbed to European diseases and the city was "lost" to the outside world.

Reading and Discussion Questions

1. What technological achievements were necessary to construct a city in such high and rocky terrain?
2. While it appears geographically isolated today, at its peak Machu Picchu served as a leading Inca city. How does it reflect the ability of the Inca government to supervise such a massive undertaking?
3. With the exception of local peoples living near the ruins, little was known of Machu Picchu until centuries after its collapse, and yet it thrived long after the Spanish destroyed similar Inca cities. How might its isolation have contributed to both its longevity and ultimate demise?

Photo courtesy of H. Micheal Tarver.

15.4 The Inca Census

Hailing from Extremadura, the same region of Spain as fellow conquistadores Hernán Cortès and Francisco Pizarro, Pedro Cieza de Léon (c. 1520-1554) was as much a scholar as a soldier. He recorded the events, places, and characters he encountered in the Andes, and, consequently, he is a major historical source for the time period and region under analysis. The following excerpt comes from *The Second Part of Cieza de Léon's Chronicle*, which was not published until the late nineteenth century. In this chapter, Cieza de Léon describes the annual census taken in each region as well as the storehouse economy practiced by the Inca.

Source: Pedro Cieza de Léon, *The Second Part of the Chronicle of Peru,* translated and edited by Clements R. Markham (London: Hakluyt Society, 1883), 57-59.

CHAPTER XIX.

How the Kings of Cuzco ordered that every year an account should be taken of all persons who died and were born throughout their dominions, also how all men worked, and how none could be poor by reason of the storehouses.

The Orejones who gave me information at Cuzco concurred in saying that formerly, in the time of the Kings, orders were given throughout all the towns and provinces of Peru, that the principal lords and their lieutenants should take note, each year, of the men and women who had died, and also of the births. For as well for the assessment of tribute, as for calculating the number of men that could be called upon to serve as soldiers, and for the defense of the villages, such information was needed. This was easily done, because each province, at the end of the year, was ordered to set down in the **quipus**, by means of the knots, all the men who had died in it during the year, as well as all who were born. In the beginning of the following year, the quipus were taken to Cuzco, where an account was made of the births and deaths throughout the empire. These returns were prepared with great care and accuracy, and without any fraud or deceit. When the returns had been made up, the lord and his officers knew what people were poor, the number of widows, whether they were able to pay tribute, how many men could be taken for soldiers, and many other facts which were considered, among these people, to be of great importance.

As this empire was of such vast extent, a fact which I have frequently pointed out in many parts of this work, and as in each province there were a great number of storehouses for provisions and other necessaries for a campaign, and for the equipment of soldiers, if there was a war these great resources were used where the camps were formed, without touching the supplies of allies, or drawing upon the stores of different villages. If there was no war, all the great store of provisions was divided amongst the poor and the widows. The poor consisted of those who were too old to work, or who were maimed, lame, or infirm; but those who were well and able to work received nothing. Then the storehouses were again filled from the obligatory tributes; and if, by chance, there came a year of great sterility, the storehouses were, in like manner, ordered to be opened, and the necessary provisions were given out to the suffering provinces. But as soon as a year of plenty came, the deficiencies so caused were made up. Although the tributes given to the Incas did not serve for other purposes than the above, yet they were well expended, and the kingdom was well supplied and cared for.

It was not permitted that any should be idle, or should profit by the labor of others, all being commanded to work. Each lord, on certain days, went to his farm, took the plough in his hand and made a furrow, besides

---

quipu: Inca counting device that consisted of bundles of knotted cords. Also spelled, "khipu"

working at other things. Even the Incas themselves did so, to give a good example to others; for they intended it to be understood that there must not be any one so rich that, on account of his riches, he could affront the poor: and by this system, there was no one in the whole land, being in good health, who did not work. The infirm were fed and clothed from the storehouses. No rich man was allowed to wear more ornaments than the poor, nor to make any difference in his dress, except the lords and the *Curacas*. These, as well as the Orejones, to maintain their dignity, could use great freedom in this respect, and they were made much of, among all the nations.

Reading and Discussion Questions

1. In what ways were the Inca's storehouses similar to the modern concept of a social safety net? In what ways do they differ?
2. How did the regional storehouses function as both a political and military institution?
3. For what reason did the Inca leadership require a count of the births and deaths in each providence?
4. Does Cieza de Léon speak favorably of the Inca system? Explain why or why not.

The Ottoman–Habsburg Struggle and European Overseas Expansion

Chapter 16

1450–1600

In 1450, the Habsburgs were nearing the height of their power in Europe at the same time the Ottomans were expanding eastward, capturing Constantinople in 1453. The Ottomans started as mounted nomads, moving out of their steppe homeland in Central Asia around 1300 and within half a century had established themselves across Anatolia into southeastern Europe, conquering much of modern-day Bulgaria and expanding into Greece and the Balkans by 1400. In retrospect, it seems inevitable the Ottoman and Habsburgs would clash as their expansions put each in the direct path of the other.

Spanish monarchs considered Muslims to be enemies of Christianity as well as imperial threats. The Muslim invasions of the eighth century had pushed Iberian aristocrats to the Pyrenees Mountains; their reclamation of the lost lands took the aspect of a crusade, or holy war. In 1492, the conquest of the last Iberian Muslim lands was completed by the armies of Ferdinand II of Aragon and Isabella I of Castile, who took pride in their joint life, *Los Reyes Católicos*, the Catholic Monarchs. Habsburg power increased dramatically when the Habsburg lands merged with Spanish possessions through bedroom politics. Joanna (Joanna the Mad), the daughter of Isabella and Ferdinand, married Philip I of Castile (Philip the Handsome), the son of the Holy Roman Emperor Maximilian I. Joanna and Phillip's son inherited both the Spanish and Habsburg realms, ruling as Charles I of Spain and Charles V of the Holy Roman Empire. The Habsburgs were ambitious, tough, and related to almost every royal family in Europe, despite wars with France, uprisings in Spain, and the pressures of Protestants in Northern Europe who taxed Charles's resources.

16.1 The Tribute of Children

The notion of raising children to be warriors was not limited to the Ottomans, yet the idea of forming slave armies is surprising to modern readers. As the source below details, these children comprised the elite corps, whether as the backbone of the bureaucracy or officers and soldiers charged with defense and keeping order. The possible hazards—such as divided loyalty, loneliness for family and homeland, etc.—spring immediately to mind. Nevertheless, there are also distinct advantages. First, since these soldiers would not have ties to the "great families" of the state, they would be less likely to have mentors or benefactors outside the existing ruling structure to whom they might develop a stronger loyalty than to the existing sovereign. And, of course, one should never underestimate the *esprit de corps* that develops in elite military structures. Elite status is often psychologically addictive.

Source: Anonymous, "The Tribute of Children," in *The World's Story. A History of the World in Story, Song and Art*, edited by Eva March Tappan. Volume VI: *Russia, Austria-Hungary, The Balkan States and Turkey* (Boston: Houghton Mifflin Co, 1914), 491-495.

The advice of the vizier was followed; the edict was proclaimed; many thousands of the European captives were educated in the Mohammedan religion and arms, and the new militia was consecrated and named by a celebrated dervish. Standing in the front of their ranks, he stretched the sleeve of his gown over the head of the foremost soldier, and his blessing was delivered in the following words — "Let them be called Janissaries (*yingi cheri*, or new soldiers); may their countenances be ever bright; their hand victorious; their swords keen; may their spear always hang over the heads of their enemies; and, wheresoever they go, may they return with a white face.""White"and "black"faceare common and proverbial expressions of praise and reproach in the Turkish language. Such was the origin of these haughty troops, the terror of the nations, and sometimes of the sultans themselves. They were kept up by continual additions from the sultan's share of the captives, and by recruits, raised every five years, from the children of the Christian subjects. Small parties of soldiers, each under a leader, and each provided with a particular firearm, went from place to place. Wherever they came, the ***protogeros*** assembled the inhabitants with their sons. The leader of the soldiers had the right to take away all the youth who were distinguished by beauty or strength, activity or talent, above the age of seven. He carried them to the court of the grand seignior, a tithe, as it were, of the subjects. The captives taken in war by the pashas, and presented by them to the sultan, included Poles, Bohemians, Russians, Italians, and Germans.

These recruits were divided into two classes. Those who composed the one, especially in the earlier periods, were sent to Anatolia, where they were trained to agricultural labor, and instructed in the Mussulman faith; or they were retained about the seraglio, where they carried wood and water, and were employed in the gardens, in the boats, or upon the public buildings, always under the direction of an overseer, who with a stick compelled them to work. The others, in whom traces of a higher character were discernible, were placed in one of the four seraglios of Adrianople or Galata, or the old or new one at Constantinople [Istanbul]. Here they were lightly clad in linen or in cloth of Saloniki, with caps of Prusa cloth. Teachers came every morning, who remained with them until evening, and taught them to read and write. Those who had performed hard labor were made Janissaries. Those who were educated in the seraglios became *spahis* or higher officers of state. Both classes were kept under a strict discipline. The former especially were accustomed to privation of food, drink, and comfortable clothing, and to hard labor. They were exercised in shooting with the bow and **arquebus** by day, and spent the night in a long, lighted hall, with an overseer, who walked up and down, and permitted no one to stir. When they were received into the corps of the Janissaries, they were placed in cloister-like barracks, in which the different *odas* or *ortas* lived so entirely in common that the military dignitaries were called from their soups and kitchens. Here not only the younger continued to obey the elders in silence and submission, but all were governed with such strictness that no one was permitted to spend the night abroad, and whoever was punished was compelled to kiss the hand of him who inflicted the punishment.

The younger portion, in the seraglios, were kept not less strictly, every ten being committed to the care of an inexorable attendant. They were employed in similar exercises, but likewise in study. The grand seignior permitted them to leave the seraglio every three years. Those who chose to remain, ascended, according to their age in the immediate service of their master, from chamber to chamber, and to constantly greater pay, till they attained, perhaps, to one of the four great posts of the innermost chamber, from which the way to the dignity of a *beglerbeg*, or a *capitan deiri* (that is, an admiral), or even of a vizier, was open. Those, on the contrary, who took advantage of this permission, entered, each one according to his previous rank, into the four first corps of the paid spahis, who were in the immediate service of the sultan, and in whom he confided more than in his other bodyguards.

---

protogeros: village headman, obliged to offer hospitality to Ottoman officials

arquebus: forerunner of the rifle, an early firearm used in the 15th-17th centuries

Reading and Discussion Questions

1. The image of children being taken from their families seems heart-wrenching, yet the writer does not record resistance or tears when the boys are taken from their families. Why?
2. How is it that these captives are trusted with both the affairs of the state and its defense? Can a slave soldier be really trusted?
3. What is the basis for dividing the boys into two groups? Why does their training differ?
4. The boys are given a chance to leave the seraglio (apartments within a sultan's palace or other official building) every three years. Why would any stay?

16.2   A European Ambassador Reports on the Ottomans

Flemish diplomat Ogier Ghiselin de Busbecq (1522-1592) served as ambassador from Holy Roman Emperors Charles V (r. 1519-1556) and Ferdinand I (r. 1556-1564) to the court of Süleyman I. In the sixteenth-century, one of the Habsburg ambassador's primary duties was to assess the military and economic potential of the states he visited.

Source: Ogier Ghiselin de Busbecq, *The Life and Letters of Ogier Ghiselin de Busbecq*, edited by Charles Thornton Forster and F.H. Blackburne Daniell (London: C. Kegan Paul & Co., 1881), Volume I, 86-88.

At Buda I made my first acquaintance with the Janissaries; this is the name by which the Turks call the infantry of the royal guard. The Turkish state has 12,000 of these troops when the corps is at its full strength. They are scattered through every part of the empire, either to garrison the forts against the enemy, or to protect the Christians and Jews from the violence of the mob. There is no district with any considerable amount of population, no borough or city, which has not a detachment of Janissaries to protect the Christians, Jews, and other helpless people from outrage and wrong.

A garrison of Janissaries is always stationed in the citadel of Buda. The dress of these men consists of a robe reaching down to the ankles, while, to cover their heads, they employ a cowl which, by their account, was originally a cloak sleeve, part of which contains the head, while the remainder hangs down and flaps against the neck. On their forehead is placed a silvergilt cone of considerable height, studded with stones of no great value.

These Janissaries generally came to me in pairs. When they were admitted to my dining room they first made a bow, and then came quickly up to me, all but running, and touched my dress or hand, as if they intended to kiss it. After this they would thrust into my hand a nosegay of the hyacinth or narcissus; then they would run back to the door almost as quickly as they came, taking care not to turn their backs, for this, according to their code, would be a serious breach of etiquette. After reaching the door, they would stand respectfully with their arms crossed, and their eyes bent on the ground, looking more like monks than warriors. On receiving a few small coins (which was what they wanted) they bowed again, thanked me in loud tones, and went off blessing me for my kindness. To tell you the truth, if I had not been told beforehand that they were Janissaries, I should, without hesitation, have taken them for members of some order of Turkish monks, or brethren of some Moslem college. Yet these are the famous Janissaries, whose approach inspires terror everywhere. During my stay at Buda a good many Turks were drawn to my table by the attractions of my wine, a luxury in which they have not many opportunities of indulging. The effect of this enforced abstinence is to make them so eager for drink, that they swill themselves with it whenever they get the chance. I asked them to make a night of it, but at last I got tired of the game, left the table, and retired to my bedroom. On this my Turkish guests made a move to go, and great was their grief as they reflected that they were not yet dead drunk, and could still use their legs. Presently they sent a servant to request that I would allow them access to my stock of wine and lend them some silver cups. 'With my permission,' they said, 'they would like to continue their drinking bout through the night; they were not particular where they sat; any odd corner would do for them.' Well, I ordered them to be furnished with as much wine as they could drink, and also with the cups they asked for. Being thus supplied, the fellows never left off drinking until they were one and all stretched on the floor in the last stage of intoxication.

To drink wine is considered a great sin among the Turks, especially in the case of persons advanced in life: when younger people indulge in it the offence is considered more venial. Inasmuch, however, as they think that they will have to pay the same penalty after death whether they drink much or little, if they taste one drop of wine they must needs indulge in a regular debauch…

Reading and Discussion Questions

1. The ambassador's description of the drinking bouts of the Janissaries' seems rather dismissive. What would have been a purpose for including the episodes?
2. During this period, Western Europeans were concerned about the advance and expansion of the Ottoman Empire. From his descriptions, what do you infer about the ambassador's assessment of the dangers from the Ottomans?
3. In 1555, the first year of the ambassador's visit to the Ottomans, the Holy Roman Emperor, Charles V, relinquished both the crown and his ambition for a global Christian empire. Do you believe the political uncertainty in Europe contributed to the ambassador's assessment of the Janissaries?

16.3 An Ottoman Travel Journal

Travel journals have a long history, serving to record the wonders of strange lands as well as the travelers' adventures. In this passage below, Admiral Sidi Alui Reis (1498-1563) writes of being sent to secure 15 ships from Basra in Iraq, and return them to Egypt, which was then part of the Ottoman Empire. The admiral writes of visiting the holy sites and provides a description of a battle with a Portuguese fleet.

Source: Sidi Alui Reis, "The Mirror of Countries" (1556), printed in Charles F. Horne, ed., *The Sacred Books and Early Literature of the East,* (New York: Parke, Austin, & Lipscomb, 1917), Vol. VI: Medieval Arabia, 332-340.

When Sultan Suleyman had taken up his winter residence in Aleppo, I, the author of these pages, was appointed to the Admiralship of the Egyptian fleet, and received instructions to fetch back to Egypt the ships (15 galleys), which some time ago had been sent to Basra on the Persian Gulf. But, "Man proposes, God disposes." I was unable to carry out my mission, and as I realized the impossibility of returning by water, I resolved to go back to Turkey by the overland route, accompanied by a few tried and faithful Egyptian soldiers. I traveled through Gujarat, Hind, Sind, Balkh, Zabulistan, Bedakhshan, Khotlan, Turan, and Iran, i.e., through Transoxania, Khorassan, Kharezm, and Deshti-Kiptchak; and as I could not proceed any farther in that direction, I went by Meshed and the two Iraqs, Kazwin and Hamadan, on to Bagdad.

Our travels ended, my companions and fellow-adventurers persuaded me to write down our experiences, and the dangers through which we had passed, an accurate account of which it is almost impossible to give; also to tell of the cities and the many wonderful sights we had seen, and of the holy shrines we had visited. And so this little book sees the light; in it I have tried to relate, in simple and plain language, the troubles and difficulties, the suffering and the distress which beset our path, up to the time that we reached Constantinople.

Considering the matter it contains this book ought to have been entitled, "A tale of woe," but with a view to the scene of action I have called it "Mirror of Countries," and as such I commend it to the reader's kind attention.

. . .

I, humble Sidi Ali bin Husein, also known as Kiatibi-Rumi (the writer of the West, i.e., of Turkey), most gladly accepted the post. I had always been very fond of the sea, had taken part in the expedition against Rhodes under the Sultan (Suleiman), and had since had a share in almost all engagements, both by land and by sea. I had fought under Khaireddin Pasha, Sinan Pasha, and other captains, and had cruised about on the Western (Mediterranean) sea, so that I knew every nook and corner of it. I had written several books on astronomy, nautical science, and other matters bearing upon navigation. My father and grandfather, since the conquest of Constantinople, had had charge of the arsenal a at Galata; they had both been eminent in their profession, and their skill had come down to me as an heirloom.

. . .

I had plenty of leisure to visit the mosque of Ali and the graves of Hasan Basri, Talha, Zobeir, Uns-bin-Malik, Abdurrahman-bin-Anf, and several martyrs and companions of the Prophet. One night I dreamed that I lost my sword, and as I remembered that a similar thing had happened to Sheik Muhieddin and had resulted in a defeat, I became greatly alarmed, and, just as I was about to pray to the Almighty for the victory of the Islam arms, I awoke. I kept this dream a secret, but it troubled me for a long time, and when later on Mustafa Pasha sent a detachment of soldiers to take the island of Huweiza (in which expedition I took part with five of my galleys), and the undertaking resulted in our losing about a hundred men all through the fickleness of the Egyptian troops, I fully believed this to be the fulfilment of my dream. But alas! there was more to follow — for:

What is decreed must come to pass,
No matter, whether you are joyful or anxious.

When at last the time of the monsoon came, the Pasha sent a trusty sailor with a frigate to Ormuz, to explore the neighborhood. After cruising about for a month he returned with the news that, except for four boats, there was no sign of any ships of the infidels in those waters. The troops therefore embarked and we started for Egypt.

WHAT TOOK PLACE IN THE SEA OF ORMUZ

On the first of Shawal we left the harhor of Basra, accompanied, as far as Ormuz, by the frigate of Sherifi Pasha. We visited on the way from Mehzari the grave of Khidr, and proceeding along the coast of Duspul (Dizful), and Shushter in Charik, I made pilgrimages to the graves of Imam Mohammed, Hanifi, and other saints.

From the harbor in the province of Shiraz we visited Rishehr (Bushir) and after reconnoitering the coasts and unable to get any clue as to the whereabouts of the enemy by means of the Tshekleva? I proceeded to Katif, situated near Lahsa 2 and Hadjar on the Arabian coast. Unable to learn anything there, I went on to Bahrein, where I interviewed the commander of the place, Reis Murad. But neither could he give me any information about the fleet of the infidels. There is a curious cuetom at Bahrein. The sailors, provided with a leather sack, dive down into the sea and bring the fresh water from the bottom for Reis Murad's use. This water is particularly pleasant and cold in the spring time, and Reis Murad gave me some. God's power is boundless! This custom is the origin of the proverb: "Maradj ul bahreia jaltakian," and hence also the name." Bahrein."

Next we came to Kis, i.e., old Ormuz, and Barhata, and several other small islands in the Green Sea, i.e., the waters of Ormuz, but nowhere could we get any news of the fleet. So we dismissed the vessel, which Mustafa Pasha had sent as an escort, with the message that Ormuz was safely passed. We proceeded by the coasts of Djilgar and Djadi, past the towns of Keimzar or Leime, and forty days after our departure, i.e., on the tenth of Ramazan, in the forenoon, we suddenly saw coming toward us the Christian fleet, consisting of four large ships, three galleons, six Portuguese guard ships, and twelve galleys (Kalita), 25 vessels in all. I immediately ordered the canopy to be taken down, the anchor weighed, the guns put in readiness, and then, trusting to the help of the Almighty, we fastened the filandra to the mainmast, the flags were unfurled, and, full of courage and calling upon Allah, we commenced to fight. The volley from the guns and cannon was tremendous, and with God's help we sank and utterly destroyed one of the enemy's galleons.

Never before within the annals of history has such a battle been fought, and words fail me to describe it.

The battle continued till sunset, and only then the Admiral of the infidel fleet began to show some signs of fear. He ordered the signal-gun to fire a retreat, and the fleet turned in the direction of Ormuz.

With the help of Allah, and under the lucky star of the Padishah, the enemies of Islam had been defeated. Night came at last; we were becalmed for awhile, then the wind rose, the sails were set and as the shore was near . . . until daybreak. The next day we continued our previous course. On the day after we passed Khorfakan, where we took in water, and soon after reached Oman, or rather Sohar. Thus we cruised about for nearly 17 days. When on the sixth of 'Riimazan, i.e., the day of Kadr-Ghedjesi, a night in the month of Ramazan, we arrived in the vicinity of Maskat and Kalhat, we saw in the morning, issuing from the harbor of Maskat, 12 large boats and 22 *gurabs*, 32 vessels in all, commanded by Captain Kuya, the son of the Governor. They carried a large number of troops.

The boats and galleons obscured the horizon with their mizzen sails (*Magistra*) and *Peneta* (small sails) all set; the guard-ships spread their round sails (*Chember-yelken*), and, gay with bunting, they advanced toward us. Full of confidence in God's protection we awaited them. Their boats attacked our galleys; the battle raged, cannon and guns, arrows and swords made terrible slaughter on both sides. The *Badjoalushlca* penetrated the boats and the *Shaikas* and tore large holes in their hulls, while our galleys were riddled through by the javelins (*Darda*) thrown down upon us from the enemy's turrets, which gave them the appearance of bristling porcupines; and they showered down upon us. . . .The stones which they threw at us created quite a whirlpool as they fell into the sea.

One of our galleys was set on fire by a bomb, but strange to say the boat from which it issued shared the like fate. God is merciful! Five of our galleys and as many of the enemy's boats were sunk and utterly wrecked, one of theirs went to the bottom with all sails set. In a word, there was great loss on both sides; our rowers were now insufficient in number to manage the oars, while running against the current, and to fire the cannon. We were compelled to drop anchor (at the stern) and to continue to fight as best we might. The boats had also to be abandoned.

Alemshah Reis, Kara Mustafa, and Kalfat Memi, captains of some of the foundered ships, and Derzi Mustafa Bey, the Serdar of the volunteers, with the remainder of the Egyptian soldiers and 200 carpenters, had landed on the Arabian shore, and as the rowers were Arabs they had been hospitably treated by the Arabs of Nedjd.

The ships (*gurabs*) of the infidel fleet had likewise taken on board the crews of their sunken vessels, and as there were Arabs amongst them, they also had found shelter on the Arabian coast. God is our witness. Even in the war between Khaiveddin Pasha and Andreas Doria no such naval action as this has ever taken place.

When night came, and we were approaching the bay of Ormuz, the wind began to rise. The boats had already cast two *Lenguvurta*, i.e., large anchors, the *Lushtas* were tightly secured, and, towing the conquered *gurabs* along, we neared the shore while the galleys, dragging their anchors, followed. However, we were not allowed to touch the shore, and had to set sail again. During that night we drifted away from the Arabian coast into the open sea, and finally reached the coasts of Djash, in the province of Kerman. This is a long coast, but we could find no harbor, and we roamed about for two days before we came to Kichi Mekran.

As the evening was far advanced we could not land immediately, but had to spend another night at sea. In the morning a dry wind carried off many of the crew, and at last, after unheard-of troubles and difficulties, we approached the harbor of Sheba.

Here we came upon a *Notak*, i.e, a brigantine (pirateship), laden with spoils, and when the watchman sighted us they hailed us. We told them that we were Mussulmans, whereupon their captain came on board our vessel; he kindly supplied us with water, for we had not a drop left, and thus our exhausted soldiers were invigorated. This was on Bairam day, and for us, as we had now got water, a double feast-day. Escorted by the said captain we entered the harbor of Guador. The people there were Beluchistanis and their chief was Malik Djelaleddin, the son of Malik Dinar. The Governor of Guador came on board our ship and assured us of his unalterable devotion to our glorious Padishah. He promised that henceforth, if at any time our fleet should come to Ormuz, he would undertake to send 50 or 60 boats to supply us with provisions, and in every possible way to be of service to us. We wrote a letter to the native Prince Djelaleddin to ask for a pilot, upon which a first-class pilot was sent us, with the assurance that he was thoroughly trustworthy and entirely devoted to the interests of our Padishah.

Reading and Discussion Questions

1. In Admiral Sidi Ali Reis's narrative, in what ways can you discern the growing power of the Portuguese at sea? Support your conclusion with examples.
2. Find and discuss examples of Adiral Reis's piety. Do you think there was a practical impact or did he separate his religious life from his military responsibilities?
3. To what can we attribute the Ottoman victory in the battle of the Sea of Ormuz?

16.4 The *Journal* of Christopher Columbus

Few figures in world history illustrate the clash of civilizations more dramatically than Christopher Columbus (1451-1506), the Italian-born explorer, whose voyage to the Americas ushered in an age of exploration, conquest, trade, and colonization. The story of Columbus's voyages is often portrayed as a catalyst to the expansion of European trade, political might, and the "Columbian Exchange" of biological material that ultimately claimed the life of millions of Native Americans. However, Columbus's first voyage was also characterized by hardened determination, willingness to risk great loss, and an insatiable curiosity. The following except from Columbus' journal is taken from the day his crew first spotted the Caribbean islands. It was not until subsequent voyages that Columbus realized he encountered vast continents and the indigenous populations were not natives of the Indian subcontinent.

Source: E. G. Bourne, ed., *The Northmen, Columbus and Cabot* (New York, 1906).

Wednesday, 10 October. Steered west-southwest and sailed at times ten miles an hour, at others twelve, and at others, seven; day and night made fifty-nine leagues' progress; reckoned to the crew but forty-four. Here the men lost all patience, and complained of the length of the voyage, but the Admiral encouraged them in the best manner he could, representing the profits they were about to acquire, and adding that it was to no purpose to complain, having come so far, they had nothing to do but continue on to the Indies, till with the help of our Lord, they should arrive there.

Thursday, 11 October. Steered west-southwest; and encountered a heavier sea than they had met with before in the whole voyage. Saw pardelas and a green rush near the vessel. The crew of the Pinta saw a cane and a log; they also picked up a stick which appeared to have been carved with an iron tool, a piece of cane, a plant which grows on land, and a board. The crew of the Nina saw other signs of land, and a stalk loaded with rose berries. These signs encouraged them, and they all grew cheerful. Sailed this day till sunset, twenty-seven leagues.

After sunset steered their original course west and sailed twelve miles an hour till two hours after midnight, going ninety miles, which are twenty-two leagues and a half; and as the Pinta was the swiftest sailer, and kept ahead of the Admiral, she discovered land and made the signals which had been ordered. The land was first seen by a sailor called Rodrigo de Triana, although the Admiral at ten o'clock that evening standing on the quarter-deck saw a light, but so small a body that he could not affirm it to be land . . . . At two o'clock in the morning the land was discovered, at two leagues' distance; they took in sail and remained under the square-sail lying to till day, which was Friday, when they found themselves near a small island, one of the Lucayos, called in the Indian language Guanahani. Presently they described people, naked, and the Admiral landed in the boat, which was armed, along with Martin Alonzo Pinzon, and Vincent Yanez his brother, captain of the Nina. The Admiral bore the royal standard, and the two captains each a banner of the Green Cross, which all the ships had carried; this contained the initials of the names of the King and Queen each side of the cross, and a crown over each letter Arrived on shore, they saw trees very green many streams of water, and diverse sorts of fruits. The Admiral called upon the two Captains, and the rest of the crew who landed, as also to Rodrigo de Escovedo notary of the fleet, and Rodrigo Sanchez, of Segovia, to bear witness that he before all others took possession (as in fact he did) of that island for the King and Queen his sovereigns, making the requisite declarations, which are more at large set down here in writing. Numbers of the people of the island straightway collected together. Here follow the precise words of the Admiral: "As I saw that they were very friendly to us, and perceived that they could be much more easily converted to our holy faith by gentle means than by force, I presented them with some red caps, and strings of beads to wear upon the neck, and many other trifles of small value, where-with they were much delighted, and became wonderfully attached to us. Afterwards they came swimming to the boats, bringing parrots, balls of cotton thread, javelins, and many other things which they exchanged for articles we gave them, such as glass beads, and hawk's bells; which trade was carried on with the utmost good will. But they seemed on the whole to me, to be a very poor people. They all go completely naked, even the women, though I saw but one girl.

Reading and Discussion Questions

1. How did Columbus know he was nearing land, and how did his sailors react to the possibility of reaching a destination?
2. What caused Columbus to think the native peoples of the Caribbean were peaceful and good-willed?
3. What in Columbus's journal indicates the key reasons for his voyage across the Atlantic?

Renaissance, Reformation, and the New Science in Europe

Chapter 17

1450–1700

From 1450 to 1700 Europeans experienced significant changes, due in part to developments such as the Renaissance, Reformation, and the progression of science. All aspects of European society changed from politics and religion to the emergence of new forms of economic life. While many aspects of European cultured continued unchanged, others were irrevocably altered due to the rise of capitalism, and the emergence of the modern fiscal-military state.

The Renaissance spanned from the end of the fourteenth century to the end of the sixteenth century and emphasized renewed interest in antiquity. The term "humanism" is often used to describe Renaissance education, which focused on self-fulfillment, philosophy, and the study of previously lost works from antiquity. The Renaissance was both a progenitor and a consequence of new developments in the sciences and the Protestant Reformation.

For centuries, the Catholic Church remained unchallenged in Western Europe, which allowed it to gain a significant amount of power. By the late Middle Ages the use of empirical evidence and reason had replaced faith as an avenue to learning. Men such as Martin Luther (1483-1546) and John Calvin (1509-1564), who disagreed with the theological tenets and practices of the Catholic Church, pressed their challenges and gained a large public following that lead to the Protestant Reformation. Consequently, the Catholic Church lost many of its followers and much of its power and authority over Western Europe.

During the Scientific Revolution, the development of new theories and knowledge of subjects such as physics, medicine, and biology transformed medieval thought and paved the way for future scientists. Knowledge and reason replaced superstitions and speculative theories about the natural world. Early sciences based on description were replaced with sciences based on mathematics. The works of scientists such as Galileo (1564-1642), Newton (1642-1727), and Leeuwenhoek (1632-1723) spurred European intellectuals and political leaders to champion the sciences as a means to further social, political, and economic progress. The Scientific Revolution focused intellectual and popular attention on empirical evidence rather than abstract theories. Techniques such as the scientific method, a system of investigation used to empirically retrieve scientific evidence, promised to scientists a way to question theories without prejudice and bias towards the experiment.

The sources that follow explore the evolving aspects of society during this period. With the Renaissance, Europeans focused on antiquity as well as the revival of subjects and works by previous philosophers and scientists. They reconstructed the old in order to move on to the new. During the Protestant Reformation, western Christianity underwent a schism. Northern Europe mostly embraced Protestantism, while southern Europe mostly remained loyal to Rome. This religious change adjusted the balance of power throughout Europe and the cultural unity formerly provided by Catholicism.

_____

17.1   Marsilio Ficino, "Letter to Paul of Middelburg"

Marsilio Ficino (1433-1499) received a Renaissance education steeped in classical languages and philosophy that fostered a deep appreciation for humanism and antiquity. The first person to translate into Latin all of the works of the ancient Greek philosopher, Plato (423-347 BCE), Ficino also witnessed and wrote about the changes that took place in European art and culture. Ficino wrote a letter to Paul of Middelburg (1436-1534), a Dutch scientist and bishop of Fossombrone, explaining how a "golden age" was upon them. He wrote to Paul not only to demonstrate his knowledge of writing Latin, but also to explain a "breakthrough" in the arts. "Humanism" is a modern term used to describe Renaissance education, whereby the means of achieving self-fulfillment and virtue are stressed through the study of the classical literature, history, and languages. In the source below, Ficino argues that the Renaissance was a rediscovery of antiquity. In addition to mentioning Plato, he also discusses Federigo, Duke of Urbino (1422-1482) also known as Federico da Montefeltro), a condottieri (Italian mercenary) who popularized the importance of Renaissance education.

Source: *The Renaissance,* edited by Alison Brown. (London: Longman, 1999), 69.

Our Plato in *The Republic* transferred the four ages of lead, iron, silver and gold described by poets long ago to types of men, according to their intelligence … So if we are to call any age golden, it must certainly be our age which has produced such a wealth of golden intellects. Evidence of this is provided by the inventions of this age. For this century, like a golden age, has restored to light the liberal arts that were almost extinct: grammar, poetry, oratory, painting, sculpture, architecture, music, the ancient singing of songs to the Orphic lyre, and all this in Florence. The two gifts venerated by the ancients but almost totally forgotten since have been reunited in our age: wisdom with eloquence and prudence with the military art. The most striking example of this is Federigo, Duke of Urbino … and you too, my dear Paul, who seem to have perfected astronomy – and Florence, where Platonic teaching has been recalled from darkness into light. In Germany in our times have been invented the instruments for printing books: and, not to mention the Florentine machine which shows the daily motions of the heavens, tables have been invented which, so to speak, reveal the entire face of the sky for a whole century in one hour.

Reading and Discussion Questions
1.   What does Ficino mean when he states that they were living in a "golden age"?
2.   How might Ficino's depiction of European culture indicate an acceptance of the idea of human progress and beneficial change?
3.   Ficino consistently and positively describes several different subjects that were changing during his life. Judging by his writing, why might he be considered a humanist?

17.2   Laura Cereta to Cardinal Ascanio Maria Sforza

Laura Cereta (1469-1499) was born into a wealthy family and lived in Brescia, Italy, where she received a Renaissance education and became a humanist. Modern scholars identify Cereta as a feminist because her writings stressed the education and training of women beyond what was widely acceptable for her time. She wrote a letter to Cardinal Ascanio Maria Sforza explaining her education, love for reading and writing, and the trials she faced as an aspiring female author, which she published as part of a larger volume in 1488. Cereta sought advice from a respected church official on what to do about the negative treatment she would receive if she were to continue writing. However opinionated her letter may be, it reveals the different educational expectations for men and women during this period.

Source: Cereta, Laura. *Collected Letters of a Renaissance Feminist.* translated and edited by Diana Robin. (Chicago: University of Chicago Press, 1997), pp. 101-2.

To Cardinal Ascanio Maria Sforza

Though I was untrained and scarcely exposed to literature, through my own intelligence and natural talents I was able to acquire the beginnings of an education. While my pleasure in embarking on such a journey of the mind and my love of study were strong at the outset, the weak seeds of my small talent have grown to such a degree that I have written speeches for public occasions, and these I embellished grandly, paintings pictures with words in order to influence people and stimulate their minds. My love of reading caused me to sample different kinds of subjects, and only in study did I feel a sense of inner contentment. And, although I remained ill-equipped for the task despite my passion for learning, I reached a decision that awakened in me a desire for fame and honor, as though my mind were challenging itself to scale new heights….

To get back to my story then, at the end of my childhood, when I was approaching adolescence and was becoming more mature in my understanding of literature, a nobler thought came to me. Accordingly, I devoted myself to other kinds of books, giving myself over to insomniac nights and study, like someone who has a passion for mathematics. If my intellect did not reveal to me things I longed for at that time, at least I had been allowed to cross the fourfold threshold to knowledge….

Now that I have availed myself of the counsel of religious texts, wherein writings about morality combine profundity with unity, I have found satisfaction in literature that would give me not smoke and darkness but something perfect, secure, and lasting. Since men receive an education in literature and other studies, however, so that they may benefit from the example of their forebears, the most elect men of diverse orders have said publicly that education has been wasted on me because it has benefited only me and not others.

I am happy to have the opportunity to express my opinion about something that may exonerate me from criticism. I preferred to please the crowd rather than myself. Stimulated by the desire for fame, I was drawn into a prodigious error in the course of my writing. Namely, the first thing that I wrote was a funeral oration composed to be read over the corpse of a donkey. This one humble oration stirred up the envy of a number of men, who cruelly sharpened the teeth of their spite against me, and as though their mouths had been swords, I was left trembling like a lamb among wolves. Full of their mockery of me, these men did not hesitate to dishonor me with their spittle, while I was hard-pressed by my wounds.

Reading and Discussion Questions

1. Why does Cereta stress the importance of receiving an education? Do you think it was for self-fulfillment or merely because it was socially acceptable?
2. Why might "elect men" have thought that an education was wasted on Cereta?
3. Cereta is writing to a Cardinal of the Catholic Church, seeking his advice. Why does she give him a brief biography of her life? Does it help her gain acceptance and understanding through the eyes of the church?

17.3   John Calvin, Prayer from *Commentary on Hosea*

John Calvin (1509-1564) was the principle leader of the Protestant Reformation in the non-German speaking areas of Western Europe, particularly France, Switzerland, and the Low Countries. While much of his influence depended upon his role as a pastor in Geneva (1541-1564), Calvin also authored several works, in which he translated and provided commentary on several books of the Bible. Among his works is the *Commentary on Hosea,* which is divided into chapters, lectures, and prayers. Below are three of his prayers from *Commentary on Hosea,* each offering summations of his interpretations of key portions of the book. Calvin argues in his *Commentary* that the people of Israel chose to worship other gods and idols, and God chose Hosea to lead the people toward the path of redemption. There were several key doctrinal differences between Calvin and Roman Catholicism, particularly election, faith as a gift from God rather than a human means of meriting grace and salvation, and the continued perseverance of all believers through a process of sanctification. In chapter 1, prayer lecture 3, Calvin mentions the Babylonian exile (586-538 BCE), which was the forced exile of Jews to Babylon (present day Iraq) by King Nebuchadnezzar II (634-562 BCE), the king of Babylon.

Source: Calvin, John. *Commentary on Hosea.* Translated by John Owen (Grand Rapids, Michigan: Christian Classics Ethereal Library, 1816).

Grant, Almighty God, that as we were from our beginning lost, when thou wert pleased to extend to us thy hand, and to restore us to salvation for the sake of thy Son; and that as we continue even daily to run headlong to our own ruin, — O grant that we may not, by sinning so often, so provoke at length thy displeasure as to cause thee to take away from us the mercy which thou hast hitherto exercised towards us, and through which thou hast adopted us: but by thy Spirit destroy the wickedness of our heart, and restore us to a sound mind, that we may ever cleave to thee with a true and sincere heart, that being fortified by thy defence [defense], we may continue safe even amidst all kinds of danger, until at length thou gatherest [gathers] us into that blessed rest, which has been prepared for us in heaven by our Lord Jesus Christ. Amen.

Grant, Almighty God, that as we have not only been redeemed from Babylonian exile, but have also emerged from hell itself; for when we were the children of wrath thou didst freely adopt us, and when we were aliens, thou didst in thine [your] infinite goodness open to us the gate of thy kingdom, that we might be made thy heirs through the Son, O grant that we may walk circumspectly before thee, and submit ourselves wholly to thee and to thy Christ, and not feign to be his members, but really prove ourselves to be his body, and to be so governed by his Spirit, that thou mayest [may] at last gather us together into thy celestial kingdom, to which thou daily invitest [invite] us by the same Christ our Lord. Amen.

Grant, Almighty God, that as thou hast not only of late adopted us as thy children, but before we were born, and as thou hast been pleased to sign us, as soon as we came forth from our mother's womb, with the symbol of that holy redemption, which has been obtained for us by the blood of thy only begotten Son, though we have by our ingratitude renounced so great a benefit, — O grant, that being mindful of our defection and unfaithfulness, of which eve are all guilty, and for which thou hast justly rejected us, we may now with true humility and obedience of faith embrace the grace of thy gospel now again offered to us, by which thou reconciles thyself to us; and grant that we may steadfastly persevere in pure faith, so as never to turn aside from the true obedience of faith, but to advance more and more in the knowledge of thy mercy, that having strong and deep roots, and being firmly grounded in the confidence of sure faith, we may never fall away from the true worship of thee, until thou at length receives us in to that eternal kingdom, which has been procured for us by the blood of thy only Son. Amen.

Reading and Discussion Questions

1. Judging by the prayers, why does Calvin believe it is God's responsibility to purify a person's heart?
2. Why would the Babylonian exile of the ancient Israelites be an important metaphor for Calvin to use in describing the Christian's life on earth?
3. Commentators often describe Calvin's view of humanity as pessimistic. What in the prayers offers Calvin

hope about the ability of human beings to do good?

4. How might the prayers illustrate the doctrinal tensions between Roman Catholicism and Calvin's form of Protestantism?

17.4 Galileo Galilei, *Dialogue Concerning the Two Chief World Systems*

Galileo Galilei (1564-1642) is most well-known for his scientific arguments on the theory of motion, his discoveries in astronomy, and his improvements of the telescope. Due to his influence upon early scientific thought, historians and scientists often refer to him as "the Father of Modern Science." To promote his concerns about the development of the sciences, he wrote *Dialogue Concerning the Two Chief World Systems* in 1632. The book's story occurs over four days in which three philosophers named Salvati, Sagredo, and Simplicio argue about the accuracy of the Ptolemaic theory , the belief that the universe revolves around the earth, and the Copernican theory, the theory that the universe revolves around the sun. The Ptolemaic theory originated in the ancient world and continued to hold sway until the Middle Ages, when new theories surfaced to explain its aberrations and inconsistencies. With advances in astronomy made possible by improvements made to the telescope, the Copernican theory gained increased credibility as it more accurately predicted astronomical occurrences. Salvati, who is supposed to represent Galileo, argues for the diurnal motion of the earth (the daily motion of objects across the sky due to the earth's rotation) and for the Copernican scientific theory. Galileo wrote *Dialogue Concerning the Two Chief World Systems* because he believed that Copernicus's theories had been wrongfully accused as heretical by the Catholic Church, and he wished to contribute his own thoughts on the solar system.

Source: Galilei, Galileo. *Dialogue Concerning the Two Chief World Systems.* translated by Stillman Drake (Berkeley: University of California Press, 1953) 71-2.

SALV. It is obvious, then, that motion which is common to many moving things is idle and inconsequential to the relation of these movables among themselves, nothing being changed among them, and that it is operative only in the relation that they have with other bodies lacking that motion, among which their location is changed. Now, having divided the universe into two parts, one of which in necessarily movable and the other motionless, it is the same thing to make the earth alone move, and to move all the rest of the universe, so far as concerns any result which may depend upon such movement. For the action of such movement is only in the relation between celestial bodies and the earth, which relation alone is changed. Now if precisely the same effect follows whether the earth is made to move and the rest of the universe lay still, or the earth alone remains fixed while the whole universe shares one motion, who is going to believe that nature (which by general agreement does not act by means of many things when it can do so by means of few) has chosen to make an immense number of extremely large bodies move with inconceivable velocities, to achieve what could have been done by a moderate movement of one single body around its own center?

. . .

SALV. Every one of these variations which you recite to me is nothing except in relation to the earth. To see that this is true, remove the earth; nothing remains in the universe of rising and setting of the sun and moon, nor of horizons and meridians, nor day and night, and in a word from this movement there will never originate any changes in the moon or sun or any stars you please, fixed or moving. All these changes are in relation to the earth, all of them meaning nothing except that the sun shows itself now over China, then to Persia, afterward to Egypt, to Greece, to France, to Spain, to America, etc. And the same holds for the moon and the rest of the heavenly bodies, this effect taking place in exactly the same way if, without embroiling the biggest part of the universe, the terrestrial globe is made to revolve upon itself.

And let us redouble the difficulty with another very great one, which is this. If this great motion is attributed to the heavens, it has to be made in the opposite direction from the specific motion of all the planetary orbs, of which each one is incontrovertibly has its own motion from west to east, this being very gentile and moderate, and must then be made to rush the other way; that is, from east to west, with this very rapid diurnal motion. Whereas by making the earth itself move, the contrariety of motions is removed, and the single motion from west east accommodates all the observations and satisfies them all completely.

Reading and Discussion Questions

1. Based on your reading of this source, why did the church condemn Copernicus's and Galileo's works as heretical?
2. How does Galileo defend the Copernican theory?
3. How does he defend the theory of diurnal motion of the Earth?
4. How do his arguments show that descriptive science from earlier times was being replaced by new methods, based on analytical knowledge and mathematics?

17.5   Antony van Leeuwenhoek's "Animalcules"

Antony van Leeuwenhoek (1632-1723) was a Dutch scientist who made improvements to the microscope and was the first person to see living bacteria. Leeuwenhoek made over five hundred microscopic lenses throughout the course his lifetime. In 1683, he wrote a letter to the Royal Society of London for Improving Natural Knowledge (the Royal Society) stating that he had discovered living animalcules (bacteria) in the plaque between his teeth. Leeuwenhoek's discovery led him to find many other types of bacteria and lead modern scientists to refer to him as "The Father of Microbiology."

Source: Leeuwenhoek, Antony van. "Letter 39: 17 September, 1683." In *Antony van Leeuwenhoek and His "Little Animals,"* translated and edited by Clifford Dobell (New York: Dover Publications, Inc., 1960), 241-42.

While I was talking to an old man (who leads a sober life, and never drinks brandy or tobacco, and very seldom any wine), my eye fell upon his teeth, which were all coated over; so I asked him when he had last cleaned his mouth? And I got for answer that he'd never washed his mouth in all his life. So I took some spittle out of his mouth and examined it; but I could find in it nought but what I had found in my own and other people's. I also took some of the matter that was lodged between and against his teeth, and mixing it with his own spit, and also with fair water (in which there was no animalcules), I found an unbelievably great company of living animalcules, a-swimming more nimbly than any I had ever seen up to this time.

. . .

Moreover, the other animalcules were in such enormous numbers, that all the water (notwithstanding only a very little of the matter taken from between the teeth was mingled with it) seemed to be alive. The long particles too, as before described, were also in great plenty.

I have also taken the spittle, and the white matter that was lodged upon and betwixt the teeth, from an old man who makes a practice of drinking brandy every morning, and wine and tobacco in the afternoon; wondering whether the animalcules, with such continual boozing, could even remain alive. I judged that this man, because his teeth were so uncommon foul, never washed his mouth. So I asked him, and got for answer: "Never in my life with water, but it gets a good swill with wine or brandy every day." Yet I couldn't find anything beyond the ordinary in his spittle. I also mixed his spit with the stuff that coated his front teeth, but could make out nothing in it save very few of the least sort of living animalcules hereinbefore described time and again. But in the stuff I had hauled out from between his front teeth (for the old chap hadn't a back tooth in his head), I made out many more little animalcules, comprising two of the littlest sort.

Reading and Discussion Questions

1. What might have prompted Leeuwenhoek to test animalcules in several different solutions, and use samples from multiple people, including himself?
2. Judging from the way Leeuwenhoek tested his samples, how did he follow the scientific method?
3. How has Leeuwenhoek's discovery impacted science today?

17.6   Galileo's Views of the Moon

The first telescopic drawings of the Moon were made by Galileo in 1610. using simple geometry, he showed the Moon to be a solid body, pitted with craters and dissected by mountains. This led him to later argue that the Earth was not unique.

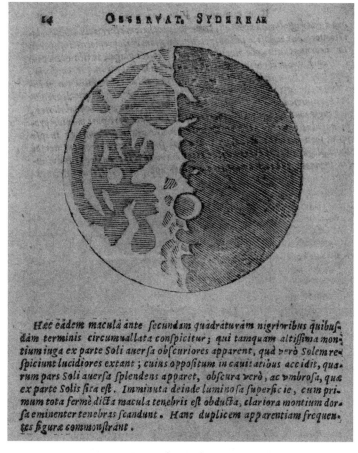

Source: Library of Congress

Reading and Discussion Questions

1. Galileo calculated the height of the lunar mountains by measuring the height cast by their shadows.   How is this evidence of the New Science in action?
2. Why would Galileo's lunar discoveries contribute to his eventual disagreement with Aristotle's theory of an immutable universe?
3. Galileo's lunar discoveries were aided by the the telescope, an innovation in which he played a large part. How is the telescope a prime example of the origins-innovations-adaptations model that forms the core approach of *Patterns of World History*?

17.7   Peter the Great, "Correspondence with Alexis, 1715"

Peter the Great, Czar of Russia (r. 1672-1725) established greater links between his country and Western Europe, and introduced important reforms in the military and government with the goal of making Russia a European power. Borrowing from Western European shipbuilding techniques, Peter oversaw the construction of the first Russian naval fleet. He also made significant changes in the army, for example, putting in place programs to better train and organize the Russian nobles who served as government and military officers. Peter's ambitions for Russian territorial expansion led to numerous wars with Sweden, Poland, and the Ottoman Empire. His son Alexis, born in 1690, was his heir to the throne, but around 1715 Peter changed the terms of this succession so it passed over Alexis to Peter's grandson (Alexis's son). Alexis attempted to flee Russia in 1716, eventually returned, but his father, who believed he was plotting to assassinate him, ordered Alexis's arrest. Alexis died in 1718 as a result of his imprisonment and torture. When Peter died in 1725, a succession crisis and period of instability followed that finally ended with when Catherine the Great (r. 1729-1796), Peter's second wife, came to the throne.

Source: Polnoe sobranie zakonov rossikoi imperii, Vol. VI, No. 11, 1715

October 11, 1715

Declaration to My Son,

You cannot be ignorant of what is known to all the world, to what degree our people groaned under the oppression of the Swedes before the beginning of the present war.

By the usurpation of so many maritime places so necessary to our state. they had cut us off from all commerce with the rest of the world, and we saw with regret that besides they had cast a thick veil before the eyes of the clear-sighted. You know what it has cost us in the beginning of this war (in which God alone has led us, as it were, by the hand. and still guides us) to make ourselves experienced in the art of war, and to put a stop to those advantages which our implacable enemies obtained over us.

We submitted to this with a resignation to the will of God, making no doubt but it was he who put us to that trial, till he might lead us into the right way, and we might render ourselves worthy to experience, that the same enemy who at first made others tremble, now in his turn trembles before us, perhaps in a much greater degree. These are the fruits which, next to the assistance of God, we owe to our own toil and to the labor of our faithful and affectionate children, our Russian subjects.

But at the time that I am viewing the prosperity which God has heaped on our native country, if I cast an eye upon the posterity that is to succeed me, my heart is much more penetrated with grief on account of what is to happen, then I rejoice at those blessings that are past, seeing that you, my son, reject all means of making yourself capable of well-governing after me. I say your incapacity is voluntary, because you cannot excuse yourself with want of natural parts and strength of body, as if God had not given you a sufficient share of either:

and though your constitution is none of the strongest, yet it cannot be said that it is altogether weak.

But you even will not so much as hear warlike exercises mentioned; though it is by them that we broke through that obscurity in which we were involved, and that we made ourselves known to nations, whose esteem we share at present. I do not exhort you to make war without lawful reasons: I only desire you to apply yourself to learn the art of it: for it is impossible well to govern without knowing the rules and discipline of it, was it for no other end than for the defense of the country.

I could place before your eyes many instances of what I am proposing to you. I will only mention to you the Greeks, with whom we are united by the same profession of faith. What occasioned their decay but that they neglected arms? Idleness and repose weakened them, made them submit to tyrants, and brought them to that slavery to which they are now so long since reduced. You mistake, if you think it is enough for a prince to have good generals to act under his order. Everyone looks upon the head; they study his inclinations and conform themselves to them: all the world owns this. My brother during his reign loved magnificence in dress, and great equipages of horses. The nation was not much inclined that way, but the prince's delight soon became that of his subjects. For they are inclined to imitate him in liking a thing as well as disliking it.

If the people so easily break themselves of things which only regard pleasure, will they not forget in time, or will they not more easily give over the practice of arms, the exercise of which is the more painful to them, the less they are kept to it?

You have no inclination to learn war. you do not apply yourself to it, and consequently you will never learn it: And how then can you command others, and judge of the reward which those deserve who do their duty. or punish others who fail of it? You will do nothing, nor judge of anything but by the eyes and help of others. like a young bird that holds up his bill to be fed.

You say that the weak state of your health will not permit you to undergo the fatigues of war: This is an excuse which is no better than the rest. I desire no fatigues, but only inclination, which even sickness itself cannot hinder. Ask those who remember the time of my brother. He was of a constitution weaker by far than yours. He was not able to manage a horse of the least mettle, not could he hardly mount it: Yet he loved horses. hence it came, that there never was, nor perhaps is there actually now in the nation a finer stable than his was.

By this you see that good success does not always depend on pain, but on the will.

If you think there are some, whose affairs do not fail of success, though they do not go to war themselves; it is true: But if they do not go themselves, yet they have an inclination for it, and understand it.

For instance, the late King of France did not always take the field in person; but it is known to what degree he loved war, and what glorious exploits he performed in it, which made his campaigns to be called the theatre and school of the world. His inclinations were not confined solely to military affairs, he also loved mechanics, manufactures and other establishments, which rendered his kingdom more flourishing than any other whatsoever.

After having made to you all those remonstrances, I return to my former subject which regards you.

I am a man and consequently I must die. To whom shall I leave after me to finish what by the grace of God I have begun, and to preserve what I have partly recovered? To a man, who like the slothful servant hides his talent in the earth, that is to say, who neglects making the best of what God has entrusted to him?

Remember your obstinacy and ill-nature, how often I reproached you with it, and even chastised you for it, and for how many years I almost have not spoke to you; but all this has availed nothing, has effected nothing. It was but losing my time: it was striking the air. You do not make the least endeavors. and all your pleasure seems to consist in staying idle and lazy at home: Things of which you ought to be ashamed (forasmuch as they make you miserable) seem to make up your dearest delight, nor do you foresee the dangerous consequences of it for yourself and for the whole state. St. Paul has left us a great truth when he wrote: If a man know not how to rule his own house, how shall he take of the church of God?

After having considered all those great inconveniences and reflected upon them, and seeing I cannot bring you to good by any inducement, I have thought fit to give you in writing this act of my last will, with this resolution however to wait still a little longer before I put it in execution to see if you will mend. If not, I will have you to know that I will deprive you of the succession, as one may cut off a useless member.

Do not fancy, that, because I have no other child but you, I only write this to terrify you. I will certainly put it in execution, if it please God; for whereas I do not spare my own life for my country and the welfare of my people, why should I spare you who do not render yourself worthy of either? I would rather choose to transmit them to a worthy stranger, than to my own unworthy son.

Peter

Reading and Discussion Questions

1.   What were Peter the Great's views on war?   What beliefs or ideas informed his views?
2.   How did Peter the Great hope to increase the power and prestige of Russia?

New Patterns in New Worlds: Colonialism and Indigenous Responses in the Americas

Chapter 18

1500–1800

The economic impetus to gain control of the lucrative trade with Asia spurred Europeans to venture out into the Atlantic. The resulting explorations helped to create networks that spanned the globe. And what would become known as the Colombian Exchange would alter the course of natural evolution.

The Spanish—with a combination of advanced technology, ruthless diplomacy, and luck—conquered the two largest empires in the New World. Their conquest of the Aztecs and the Incas greatly enriched Spain and injected large amounts of silver into the global economy. The Portuguese would also amass an equally large colonial empire by conquering many disparate tribes and establishing sugar plantations and trading posts.

Less successfully, the English, Dutch, and French also sought to establish colonial empires in the sixteenth century. Colonies were often established to escape political persecution at home but also satisfy the demand for more land. After a halting start, trade in furs, tobacco, and other commodities led to rapid expansion and the displacement of the land's original occupants.

By the seventeenth century, most major European powers had colonial claims in the New World. The native peoples who had developed complex agriculture, religion, and societies were decimated by cross currents of the ensuing ecological exchange. The benefits of the ecological exchange that took place are debated to this day. The cataclysms that began as a search for alternate trade routes would eventually lead European kingdoms to establish a permanent presence across the globe.

18.1 Aztecs Recount the Beginning of the War with the Conquistadors

The Aztecs depended heavily upon religious devotion and ritual to maintain control over the diverse tribes of their empire. Aspects of their religious devotion involved considerable violence, which generated fear as much as piety. While Spanish conquistadors disliked much in Aztec culture, Aztec religion was the element they found most repugnant. When the opportunity arose, the conquistadors took action against religious forms they deemed demonic, and often murdered priests and those in authority. For their part, the Aztecs' religious practices often included violence levied against captured enemies and weaker tribes.

Source: From Miguel Leon Portilla, ed., The Broken Spears: *The Aztec Account of the Conquest of Mexico* (Boston: Beacon Press, 1962).

Massacre in the Main Temple

During this time, the people asked Motecuhzoma [Moctezuma or Montezuma] how they should celebrate their god's fiesta. He said: "Dress him in all his finery, in all his sacred ornaments."

During this same time, The Sun commanded that Motecuhzoma and Itzcohuatzin, the military chief of Tlatelolco, be made prisoners. The Spaniards hanged a chief from Acolhuacan named Nezahualquentzin. They also murdered the king of Nauhtla, Cohualpopocatzin, by wounding him with arrows and then burning him alive.

For this reason, our warriors were on guard at the Eagle Gate. The sentries from Tenochtitlán stood at one side of the gate, and the sentries from Tlatelolco at the other. But messengers came to tell them to dress the figure of Huitzilopochtli. They left their posts and went to dress him in his sacred finery: his ornaments and his paper clothing.

When this had been done, the celebrants began to sing their songs. That is how they celebrated the first day of the fiesta. On the second day they began to sing again, but without warning they were all put to death. The dancers and singers were completely unarmed. They brought only their embroidered cloaks, their turquoises, their lip plugs, their necklaces, their clusters of heron feathers, their trinkets made of deer hooves. Those who played the drums, the old men, had brought their gourds of snuff and their timbrels.

The Spaniards attacked the musicians first, slashing at their hands and faces until they had killed all of them. The singers-and even the spectators- were also killed. This slaughter in the Sacred Patio went on for three hours. Then the Spaniards burst into the rooms of the temple to kill the others: those who were carrying water, or bringing fodder for the horses, or grinding meal, or sweeping, or standing watch over this work.

The king Motecuhzoma, who was accompanied by Itzcohuatzin and by those who had brought food for the Spaniards, protested: "Our lords, that is enough! What are you doing? These people are not carrying shields or macanas. Our lords, they are completely unarmed!"

The Sun had treacherously murdered our people on the twentieth day after the captain left for the coast. We allowed the Captain to return to the city in peace. But on the following day we attacked him with all our might, and that was the beginning of the war.

Reading and Discussion Questions
1. According to the Aztecs, why did the Spanish attack their temple?
2. Why would the Spanish launch their attack first upon the unarmed performers in the Aztec religious ritual rather than the political leaders?
3. Why did the Aztec king supposedly not do more to prevent the Spanish from attacking the temple other than placing a few guards to protect it?

18.2 Letter from Hernando de Soto

Hernando de Soto (c. 1497–1542) was a Spanish conquistador from the Spanish region of Extremadura. In 1539 he set out with roughly 600 men, plus horses, chattel, and equipment. The trip would last beyond De Soto's death in 1542. In the course of the three years, the expedition would traverse much of what would become the southeastern United States. De Soto's relationship with the natives was cordial at best and often times fell far short of that. He was not above using torture and violence to achieve his ends.

Source: *Narratives of the Career of Hernando de Soto in the Conquest of Floria, as told by a Knight of Elvas and in a Relation by Luys Hernandez de Biedma, factor of the Expedition.* Edited with an Introduction by Edward Gaylord Bourne (New York: Allerton Book Co, 1904), 159-164.

VERY NOBLE GENTLEMEN:

Being in a new country, not very distant indeed from that where you are, still with some sea between, a thousand years appear to me to have gone by since anything has been heard from you; and although I left some letters written at Havana, to go off in three ways, it is indeed long since I have received one. However, since opportunity offers by which I may send an account of what it is always my duty to give, I will relate what passes, and I believe will be welcome to persons I know favourably, and are earnest for my success.

I took my departure from Havana with all my armament on Sunday, the XVIIIth of May, although I wrote that I should leave on the XXVth of the month. I anticipated the day, not to lose a favourable wind, which changed, nevertheless, for calms, upon our getting into the Gulf; still these were not so continuous as to prevent our casting anchor on this coast, as we did at the end of eight days, which was on Sunday, the festival of Espiritu Santo.

Having fallen four or five leagues below the port, without any one of my pilots being able to tell where we were, it became necessary that I should go in the brigantines and look for it. In doing so, and in entering the mouth of the port, we were detained three days; and likewise because we had no knowledge of the passage a bay that runs up a dozen leagues or more from the sea we were so long delayed that I was obliged to send my Lieutenant-General, Vasco Porcallo de Figueroa, in the brigantines, to take possession of a town at the end of the bay. I ordered all the men and horses to be landed on a beach, whence, with great difficulty, we went on Trinity Sunday to join Vasco Porcallo. The Indians of the coast, because of some fears of us, have abandoned all the country, so that for thirty leagues not a man of them has halted.

At my arrival here I received news of there being a Christian in the possession of a Cacique, and I sent Baltazar de Gallegos, with XL men of the horse, and as many of the foot, to endeavour to get him. He found the man a day's journey from this place, with eight or ten Indians, whom he brought into my power. We rejoiced no little over him, for he speaks the language; and although he had forgotten his own, it directly returned to him. His name is Juan Ortiz, an hidalgo, native of Sevilla.

In consequence of this occurrence, I went myself for the Cacique, and came back with him in peace. I then sent Baltazar de Gallegos, with eighty lancers, and a hundred foot-soldiers, to enter the country. He has found fields of maize, beans, and pumpkins, with other fruits, and provision in such quantity as would suffice to subsist a very large army without its knowing a want. Having been allowed, without interruption, to reach the town of a **cacique** named Urripacoxit, master of the one we are in, also of many other towns, some Indians were sent to him to treat for peace. This, he writes, having been accomplished, the Cacique failed to keep certain promises, whereupon he seized about 18 persons, among whom are some of the principal men; for in this way, it appears to him, he can best secure a performance. Among those he detains are some old men of authority, as great as can be among such people, who have information of the country farther on. They say that three days' journey from where they are, going by some towns and huts, all well inhabited, and having many maize-fields, is a large town called Acuera, where with much convenience we might winter; and that afterwards, farther on, at the distance of two days' journey, there is another town, called Ocale. It is so large, and they so extol it, that I dare not repeat all that is said. There is to be found in it a great plenty of all the things mentioned; and fowls, a multitude of turkeys, kept in pens, and herds of tame deer that are tended. What this means I do not understand, unless it be the cattle, of which we brought the knowledge with us. They say there are many trades among that people, and much intercourse, an abundance of gold and silver, and many pearls. May it please God that this may be

---

cacique: an Indian chief

so; for of what these Indians say I believe nothing but what I see, and must well see; although they know, and have it for a saying, that if they lie to me it will cost them their lives. This interpreter puts a new life into us, in affording the means of our understanding these people, for without him

I know not what would become of us. Glory be to God, who by His goodness has directed all, so that it appears as if He had taken this enterprise in His especial keeping, that it may be for His service, as I have supplicated, and do dedicate it to Him.

I sent eighty soldiers by sea in boats, and my General by land with 40 horsemen, to fall upon a throng of some thousand Indians, or more, whom Juan de Anasco had discovered. The General got back last night, and states that they fled from him; and although he pursued them, they could not be overtaken, for the many obstructions in the way. On our coming together we will march to join Baltazar de Gallegos, that we may go thence to pass the winter at the Ocale, where, if what is said to be true, we shall have nothing to desire. Heaven be pleased that something may come of this that shall be for the service of our Divine Master, and whereby I may be enabled to serve Your Worships, and each of you, as I desire, and is your due.

Notwithstanding my continual occupation here, I am not forgetful of the love I owe to objects at a distance; and since I may not be there in person, I believe that where you, Gentlemen, are, there is little in which my presence can be necessary. This duty weighs upon me more than every other, and for the attentions you will bestow, as befits your goodness, I shall be under great obligations. I enjoin it upon you, to make the utmost exertions to maintain the repose and well-being of the public, with the proper administration of justice, always reposing in the Licentiate, that every thing may be so done in accordance with law, that God and the King may be served, myself gratified, and every one be content and pleased with the performance of his trust, in such a manner as you, Gentlemen, have ever considered for my honor, not less than your own, although I still feel that I have the weight thereof, and bear the responsibility.

As respects the bastion which I left begun, if laboring on it have been neglected, or perhaps discontinued, with the idea that the fabric is not now needed, you, Gentlemen, will favor me by having it finished, since every day brings change ; and although no occasion should arise for its employment, the erection is provident for the well-being and safety of the town: an act that will yield me increased satisfaction, through your very noble personages.

That our Lord may guard and increase your prosperity is my wish and your deserving.

In this town and Port of Espiritu Santo, in the Province of Florida, July the IX., in the year 1539.

The servant of you, Gentlemen,

EL ADELANTADO DON HERNANDO DE SOTO.

Reading and Discussion Questions
1. How does de Soto describe the land? In what does he appear to be most interested?
2. Discuss the significance of the natives leaving the county upon de Soto's arrival.
3. How would you describe de Soto's diplomatic relations with the native peoples he meets? Use specific examples.

18.3 Coronado's Report to Viceroy Mendoza

Within a few years of Christopher Columbus's return to Spain from his first trip to the Americas, the Spanish quickly explored the new lands they had discovered. For three generations, Spanish explorers scoured river valleys, jungles, and mountain ranges from the lower plains of North America to the highlands of South America. They sought treasure, potential trading partners, and natives to proselytize. In many respects, they successfully accomplished all three goals, but not to the extent Spanish leaders and investors hoped. While episodes of intense conflict and battles occurred during the exploration period, contact between Europeans and Native Americans varied between violence and peaceful trade depending upon the tribe and the explorers. Francisco Vasquez de Coronado (1510–1554), who traveled through southwestern North America between 1540 and 1542 searching for the fabled "cities of gold," effectively illustrates the conquistador outlook. His depiction of encounters with local tribes illustrates a common pattern of violence, but also shows how Europeans often remained dependent upon natives for common necessities.

Coronado's description of Native American society and military tactics in southwestern North America shows how Native Americans equaled the might of the Spanish, especially when the Spanish failed to gain the assistance of native allies. Yet, their centralized states and economies could not repel Europeans and their Indian allies, who were anxious to overthrow their imperial masters. Their inability to resist European encroachments caused some Europeans to view Native Americans as backward, or at least primitive. Consequently, some Europeans believed the New World was a wilderness, if not an Edenic paradise filled with vast resources and friendly natives.

Source: Winship, George Parker. *The Journey of Coronado, 1540-1542, from the City of Mexico to the Grand Canyon of the Colorado and the Buffalo Plains of Texas, Kansas and Nebraska, as Told by Himself and His Followers* (Allerton Book Company, 1922), 167-169.

Coronado's Report to Viceroy Mendoza Sent from Cibola, August 3, 1540

. . . Ferrando Alvarado came back to tell me that some Indians had met him peaceably, & that two of them were with the army-master waiting for me. I went to them forthwith and gave them some paternosters and some little cloaks, telling them to return to their city and say to the people there that they could stay quietly in their houses and that they need not fear. After this I ordered the army-master to go and see if there were any bad passages which the Indians might be able to defend, and to seize and hold any such until the next day, when I would come up. He went, and found a very bad place in our way where we might have received much harm. He immediately established himself there with the force which he was conducting. The Indians came that very night to occupy that place so as to defend it, and finding it taken, they assaulted our men. According to what I have been told, they attacked like valiant men, although in the end they had to retreat in flight, because the army-master was on the watch and kept his men in good order. The Indians sounded a little trumpet as a sign of retreat, and did not do any injury to the Spaniards. The army-master sent me notice of this the same night, so that on the next day I started with as good order as I could, for we were in such great need of food that I thought we should all die of hunger if we continued to be without provisions for another day, especially the Indians, since altogether we did not have two bushels of corn, and so I was obliged to hasten forward without delay. The Indians lighted their fires from point to point, and these were answered from a distance with as good understanding as we could have shown. Thus notice was given concerning how we went and where we had arrived.

As soon as I came within sight of this city, I sent the army-master, Don Garcia Lopez, Friar Daniel and Friar Luis, and Ferrando Vermizzo, with some horsemen, a little way ahead, so that they might find the Indians and tell them that we were not coming to do them any harm, but to defend them in the name of our lord the Emperor. The summons, in the form which His Majesty commanded in his instructions, was made intelligible to the people of the country by an interpreter. But they, being a proud people, were little affected, because it seemed to them that we were few in number, and that they would not have any difficulty in conquering us. They pierced the gown of Friar Luis with an arrow, which, blessed be God, did him no harm. Meanwhile I arrived with all the rest of the horse and the footmen, and found a large body of the Indians on the plain, who began to shoot with their arrows. In obedience to the orders of Your Lordship and of the marquis, I did not wish my company, who were begging me for permission, to attack them, telling them that they ought not to offend them, and that what the enemy was doing was nothing, and that so few people ought not to be insulted. On the other hand, when the Indians saw that we did not move, they took greater courage, and grew so bold that they came up almost to the heels of our horses to shoot their arrows. On this account I saw that it was no longer time to hesitate, and as the priests approved the action, I charged them. There was little to do, because they suddenly took to flight, part running toward the city, which was near and well fortified, and others toward the plain, wherever chance led them. Some Indians were killed, and others might have been slain if I could have allowed them to be pursued. But I saw that there would be little advantage in this, because the Indians who were outside were few, and those who had retired to the city were numerous, besides many who had remained there in the first place.

Reading and Discussion Questions

1. On what basis did the Spaniards hope to achieve peaceful relations with the Indians? Why did such attempts prove unsuccessful in the long term?
2. What kinds of characteristics did the Spaniards appreciate about the Indians? What did they admire most?
3. In what ways were the Indians superior to the Spanish explorers? How did the native tribes use this to their advantage?

18.4 Increase Mather on King Philip's Death

When Plymouth, Massachusetts was established in 1620, it became the third permanent colony to be established in North America. As the settlements and populations along the coast grew, conflict between settlers and natives increased in frequency and intensity. These conflicts finally expressed themselves in what became known as King Philip's War. King Philip, sachem, or leader, of the Wampanoag tribe, led the fight against the Puritan settlers. The war raged from the summer of 1675 until King Phillip's death in the summer of 1676. The description of King Phillip's death is from Increase Mather (1639-1723), an influential Puritan preacher.

Source: From Increase Mather, *A Brief History of the War with the Indian of New England (1676): An Online Electronic Text Edition.* Edited by Paul Royster. Lincoln, Nebraska: University of Nebraska-Lincoln Faculty Publications: accessed on November 8, 2011 at: http://digitalcommons.unl.edu/libraryscience/31.

And in that very place where he first contrived and began his mischief, was he taken and destroyed, and there was he (like as Agag was hewed in pieces before the Lord) cut into four quarters, and is now hanged up as a monument of revenging Justice, his head being cut off and carried away to Plymouth, his Hands were brought to *Boston. So let all thine Enemies perish, O Lord!* When Philip thus slain, five of his men were killed with him, one of which was his chief Captains son, being (as the Indians testify) that very Indian, who shot the first gun at the English, when the War began. So that we may hope that the War in those parts will die with Philip.

Reading and Discussion Questions

1. What are the similarities between de Soto's and Mather's attitude toward the native people's? What are the differences if any?
2. What is the significance of Mather's use of Old Testament imagery to describe the King Phillip and the Indians?
3. What seem to be Mather's hopes for the colony? Do these seem to include a co-existence with the native cultures?

18.5 Reasons for Colonizing North America

Richard Hakluyt the Elder (c. 1553–1616) was one of the foremost geographers in early Elizabethan England. A contemporary of Sir Humphrey Gilbert and Sir Walter Raleigh, Hakluyt encouraged Queen Elizabeth I and her courtiers to support colonization efforts in the New World. England came late to the Western hemisphere, long after the French and a full century after the Spanish. Considered the weakest economy in Western Europe, much of England's economy depended upon the continental wool trade. When that was closed to English merchants, they sought support from the English crown for trade initiatives throughout the northern hemisphere, including around the Baltic Sea and Russia. Hakluyt proposed to shift English attention to North America, where he insisted the most lucrative trade would be found. His writings, which portrayed North America as a new Garden of Eden, encouraged hundreds of people to migrate. They soon discovered the New World would not welcome them with the warm climate, friendly natives, and bountiful harvests that Hakluyt promised. Nonetheless, the Edenic and agrarian imagery he used provided a rich tapestry for generations of British North Americans. Below are excerpts from 31 reasons Hakluyt gave for colonizing North America.

Source: Richard Hakluyt, "Inducements to the Liking of the Voyage Intended towards Virginia" (1585).

11. In the voyage we are not to cross the burnt zone, nor to pass through frozen seas encumbered with ice and fogs, but in temperate climate at all times of the year; and it requireth not, as the East Indies voyage doth, the taking in of water in divers places, by reason that it is to be sailed in five or six weeks; and by the shortness the merchant may yearly make two returns (a factory once being erected there), a matter in trade of great moment. . . .

13. By this ordinary trade we may annoy the enemies to Ireland and succour the Queen's Majesty's friends there, and in time we may from Virginia yield them whatsoever commodity, they now receive from the Spaniard; and so the Spaniards shall want the ordinary victual that heretofore they received yearly from thence, and so they shall not continue trade, nor fall so aptly in practice against this government as now by their trade thither they may. . . .

15. The great plenty of' buff hides and of many other sundry kinds of hides their now presently to be had, the tirade of whale and seal fishing and of divers other fishing in the great rivers, great hays, and seas there, shall presently defray the charge in good part or in all of the first enterprise, and so we shall be in better case than our men were in Russia, where many years were spent and great sums of it sums of money consumed before gain was found.

16. The great broad rivers of that main that we are to enter into, so many leagues navigable or portable into the mainland, lying so long a tract with so excellent and so fertile a soil on both sides, do seem to promise all things that the life of man doth require and whatsoever men may wish may wish that are to plant upon the same or to traffic in the same. . . .

20. Where there be many petty kings or lords planted on the rivers' sides, and by all likelihood maintain the frontiers of' their several territories by wars, we may by the aid of this river join with this king here, or with that king there, at our pleasure, and may so with a few men be revenged of any wrong offered by any of them; or may, if we will proceed with extremity, conquer, fortify, and plant in soils most sweet, most fertile, in and in the end bring them all in subjection and to civility.

21. The known abundance of fresh fish in the rivers, and the known plenty of fish on the sea-coast there, may assure us of sufficient victual in spite of the people, if we will use salt and industry. . . .

27. Since great waste woods be there of oak, cedar, pine, walnuts, and sundry other sorts, many of our waste people may be employed in making of ships, hoys, busses [types of ships], and boats, and in making of rosin, pitch, and tar, the trees natural for the same being certainly known to be near Cape Breton and the Bay of Menan, and in many other palaces thereabout. . . .

29. Sugar-canes may be planted as well as they are now in the South of Spain, and besides the employment of our idle people, we may receive the commodity cheaper and not enrich the infidels or our doubtful friends, of whom now we receive that commodity. . . .

31. This land that we propose to direct our course to, lying in part in the 40th degree of latitude, being in like heat as Lisbon in Portugal doth, and in the more southerly part, as the most southerly coast of Spain doth, may by our diligence yield unto us, besides wines and oils and sugars, oranges, lemons, figs, raisins, almonds, pomegranates, rice, raw silks such as come from Granada, and divers commodities for dyers, as **anil** and **cochineal**, and sundry other colors and materials. Moreover, we shall not only receive many precious commodities besides from thence, but also shall in time find ample vent of the labor of our poor people at home, by sale of hats, bonnets, knives, fish-hooks, copper kettles, beads, looking-glasses, bugles, and a thousand kinds of other wrought wares that in short time may be brought in use among the people of that country, to the great relief of the multitude of our poor people and to the wonderful enriching of this realm. And in time, such league and intercourse may arise between our stapling seats there, and other ports of our North America, and of the islands of the same, that incredible things, and by few as yet undreamed of, may speedily follow, tending to the impeachment of our mighty enemies and to the common good of this noble government.

Reading and Discussion Questions

1. In what ways does Hakluyt portray the New World as a new Garden of Eden?
2. What geopolitical and economic conditions shape Hakluyt's reasons for colonization, and how would a presence in North America assist the English with both foreign and domestic issues?
3. Given Hakluyt's sensational account of North America, a place he never visited, how might colonists have reacted when they reached Virginia?

---

anil: blue dye obtained from the indigo plant

cochineal: a scaly insect bred for dye in pre-colonial and colonial times